RSF: The Russell Sage Foundation Journal of the Social Sciences

Wealth Inequality: Economic and Social Dimensions

VOLUME 2 • NUMBER 6 • OCTOBER 2016

RSF: The Russell Sage Foundation Journal of the Social Sciences ISSN 2377-8261

The Russell Sage Foundation

The Russell Sage Foundation, one of the oldest of America's general purpose foundations, was established in 1907 by Mrs. Margaret Olivia Sage for "the improvement of social and living conditions in the United States." The foundation seeks to fulfill this mandate by fostering the development and dissemination of knowledge about the country's political, social, and economic problems. While the foundation endeavors to assure the accuracy and objectivity of each book it publishes, the conclusions and interpretations in Russell Sage Foundation publications are those of the authors and not of the foundation, its trustees, or its staff. Publication by Russell Sage, therefore, does not imply foundation endorsement.

Board of Trustees

Sara S. McLanahan, *Chair*
Larry M. Bartels
Karen S. Cook
W. Bowman Cutter III
Sheldon H. Danziger
Kathryn Edin
Lawrence F. Katz
David Laibson
Nicholas Lemann
Martha Minow
Peter R. Orszag
Claude M. Steele
Shelley E. Taylor
Richard H. Thaler
Hirokazu Yoshikawa

Mission Statement

RSF: The Russell Sage Foundation Journal of the Social Sciences is a peer-reviewed, open-access journal of original empirical research articles by both established and emerging scholars. It is designed to promote cross-disciplinary collaborations on timely issues of interest to academics, policymakers, and the public at large. Each issue is thematic in nature and focuses on a specific research question or area of interest. The introduction to each issue will include an accessible, broad, and synthetic overview of the research question under consideration and the current thinking from the various social sciences.

RSF Journal Editorial Board

Elizabeth O. Ananat, Duke University
Annette Bernhardt, University of California, Berkeley
Karen S. Cook, Stanford University
Sheldon H. Danziger, RSF President
Janet C. Gornick, The CUNY Graduate Center
Jennifer Hochschild, Harvard University
Douglas S. Massey, Princeton University
Mary E. Pattillo, Northwestern University
James Sidanius, Harvard University
Mary C. Waters, Harvard University
Bruce Western, Harvard University

Copyright © 2016 by Russell Sage Foundation. All rights reserved. Printed in the United States of America. No part of this publication may be reproduced, stored in a retrieval system, or transmitted in any form or by any means, electronic, mechanical, photocopying, recording, or otherwise, without the prior written permission of the publisher. Reproduction by the United States Government in whole or in part is permitted for any purpose.

Opinions expressed in this journal are not necessarily those of the editors, editorial board, trustees, or the Russell Sage Foundation.

We invite scholars to submit proposals for potential issues through the *RSF* application portal: https://rsfjournal.onlineapplicationportal.com/. Submissions should be addressed to Suzanne Nichols, Director of Publications.

To view the complete text and additional features online please go to **www.rsfjournal.org**.

Russell Sage Foundation
112 East 64th Street
New York, NY 10065

ISSN (print): 2377-8253
ISSN (electronic): 2377-8261
ISBN: 978-0-87154-680-7

*RSF: The Russell Sage Foundation
Journal of the Social Sciences*
VOLUME 2 NUMBER 6
OCTOBER 2016

Wealth Inequality: Economic and Social Dimensions

ISSUE EDITORS
Fabian T. Pfeffer, University of Michigan
Robert F. Schoeni, University of Michigan

CONTENTS

Part I. Introduction

How Wealth Inequality Shapes Our Future **2**
Fabian T. Pfeffer and Robert F. Schoeni

Part II. Economic Dimensions of Wealth Inequality

Household Wealth Trends in the United States, 1962 to 2013: What Happened over the Great Recession? **24**
Edward N. Wolff

Inequality and Mobility Using Income, Consumption, and Wealth for the Same Individuals **44**
Jonathan Fisher, David Johnson, Jonathan P. Latner, Timothy Smeeding, and Jeffrey Thompson

Is the U.S. Retirement System Contributing to Rising Wealth Inequality? **59**
Sebastian Devlin-Foltz, Alice Henriques, and John Sabelhaus

Turning Citizens into Investors: Promoting Savings with Liberty Bonds During World War I **86**
Eric Hilt and Wendy M. Rahn

Part III. Social Dimensions of Wealth Inequality

Does Your Home Make You Wealthy? **110**
Alexandra Killewald and Brielle Bryan

A Wealth of Inequalities: Mass Incarceration, Employment, and Racial Disparities in U.S. Household Wealth, 1996 to 2011 **129**
Bryan L. Sykes and Michelle Maroto

Health Shocks and Social Drift: Examining the Relationship Between Acute Illness and Family Wealth **153**
Jason Thompson and Dalton Conley

Passing It On: Parent-to-Adult Child Financial Transfers for School and Socioeconomic Attainment **172**
Emily Rauscher

Wealth and Inequality in the Stability of Romantic Relationships **197**
Alicia Eads and Laura Tach

Part IV. Essay

Wealth and Secular Stagnation: The Role of Industrial Organization and Intellectual Property Rights **226**
Herman Mark Schwartz

PART I
Introduction

How Wealth Inequality Shapes Our Future

FABIAN T. PFEFFER AND ROBERT F. SCHOENI

Liz, Mary, and Howard are three teenagers in the 1980s.[1] Although unrelated, their families have much in common: stable two-parent households, at least one parent completed high school (though none of them went to college), and all three are white. They differ in one important aspect: their parents command quite different levels of wealth (here measured as net worth, that is, the total sum of financial and real assets minus debt). Liz's parents own less than $700 (inflation adjusted to 2013 dollars), meaning that Liz grows up at the bottom of the wealth distribution. Still, she is far from living in poverty thanks to her parents' annual income of about $50,000. Mary's parents have a somewhat higher income, about $70,000, but also markedly more wealth than Liz's parents: their net worth of roughly $60,000 puts them at about the national median of the time. Also unlike Liz's parents, they are homeowners. Howard is lucky enough to grow up in affluence. Not in terms of income, given that his parents have a household income of only about $40,000, but they have considerable wealth. With a net worth of nearly a quarter million dollars, Howard's parents are in the top 20 percent of wealth holders. They, too, own their home.

Liz (Low parental wealth), Mary (Middle parental wealth), and Howard (High parental wealth) graduate high school in the late 1980s and establish their own households in the early 1990s. They are off to distinct life paths. Liz marries, gives birth to a son, and does not work outside the home for several years. She takes up a job as a nursing aid in the early 2000s and stays in this occupation for a few more years. She never goes back to school. Liz and her husband manage to accumulate some wealth, but lose it during the two most recent recessions. Because they lost most of their financial resources during the dot-com bubble of 2001, their debt is larger than their assets. They recover to about $20,000 of net worth in

Fabian T. Pfeffer is research assistant professor at the Institute for Social Research and assistant professor of sociology at the University of Michigan. **Robert F. Schoeni** is research professor at the Institute for Social Research and professor of economics and public policy at the University of Michigan.

This research was supported in part by a grant from the Russell Sage Foundation (#99-15-10). We thank Matthew Gross and Kelsey Moran for their valuable research assistance and John Sabelhaus for his close review of the manuscript. Direct correspondence to: Fabian T. Pfeffer at fpfeffer@umich.edu, University of Michigan, Institute for Social Research, 426 Thompson St., Ann Arbor, MI, 48104; and Robert F. Schoeni at bschoeni@umich.edu, University of Michigan, Institute for Social Research, 426 Thompson St., Ann Arbor, MI, 48106.

1. The individuals mentioned here represent clusters of individuals drawn from the Panel Study of Income Dynamics (PSID) and its Child Development Supplement to represent life stories that are consistent with results from quantitative analyses. Although we base our description of these life stories on publicly available data, to avoid data disclosure the stories do not represent specific PSID respondents.

2007 only to lose it again in the aftermath of the Great Recession. By 2013 they are in their mid-forties, their son is beginning to ask them whether he can afford college, and their net worth is negative $5,000. Complicating their lives further, they lost their house and, for the first time as an adult, Liz becomes a renter. In terms of her relative position among American families, she is back to where her parents were three decades earlier: among the bottom 15 percent of families in terms of wealth.

Mary attends a one-year educational program after high school, gets married, and becomes a technician in a laboratory, an occupation she works in for the next two decades. She earns a decent wage—her average annual earnings over the last five years are about $45,000—and thanks to her husband's salary family income is nearly $170,000 in 2013. They have been homeowners ever since they moved in together and their home's value has appreciated continuously over the years, though it has plateaued since the Great Recession at about $200,000. Although they took out a second mortgage on the house in 2009, their accumulated home equity still accounts for more than half of their total net worth in 2013 ($60,000). Like her parents in the 1980s, Mary has arrived at a typical level of family wealth, about the median.

Finally, Howard goes to college straight from high school. He earns a bachelor's degree and begins a career as a teacher. He later earns a master's degree, which gives his earnings a considerable boost; they average $85,000 over the last five years. His family income in 2013 is still below Mary's, however. The house he owns lost some value during the Great Recession and is now valued at about $250,000—not much more than Mary's. However, unlike Mary, Howard has accumulated more home equity (about $80,000). Even more important, he holds several other highly valued assets: about $30,000 in financial assets, about $60,000 in other real assets, and about $100,000 as an individual retirement account (IRA). Given his resulting total net worth of close to $300,000, Howard has surpassed his parents' wealth level in real terms and is just within the top quarter of wealthiest Americans in 2013.

Liz, Mary, and Howard thus all end up about where their parents were when it comes to their rank in the wealth distribution. However, although their relative position in the wealth structure is largely unchanged, the wealth gap between the three has widened compared to that between their parents. Especially the distance between Howard and the other two has increased, reflecting the growing polarization of the wealth distribution. That Howard commands more wealth than his parents but is still lower in the overall wealth structure than his parents were shows that the wealthiest—above Howard's level—have been pulling away. The polarization of the wealth distribution is also visible in comparing the wealth position of Liz with that of her parents. Both end up similarly situated in the wealth distribution, but whereas Liz's parents held a few hundred dollars in assets, she is in net debt.

WEALTH TRANSMISSION AND RACE

Like Liz, Mary, and Howard, Lakesha and Mike are teenagers in the 1980s and come from households with a married mother and father who have high school degrees. But Lakesha and Mike are black.

Lakesha grows up at the bottom of the wealth distribution, her parents owning less than $500, putting them—like Liz's parents—into the bottom 15 percent. Lakesha's family income is lower than that of Liz's—$35,000 versus about $50,000. Still, Lakesha manages to go to college. However, she attends just three years and never receives a bachelor's degree. Her occupational path is less stable than those described so far but marked by a relatively linear progression from clerical work in sales and bookkeeping to jobs with supervisory function. Lakesha marries in her early twenties. Her marriage, which produces two children, lasts only a few years. As a single working mother, she purchases a home in the late 1990s. Her home equity grows continuously—though her home value does not rise over the years. During the Great Recession, Lakesha loses her home. By 2013, her net worth is negative: her net debt is more than $30,000, mostly accounted for by her remaining student debt, which has been growing—not shrinking—in recent years. In the end, despite some postsecondary education, a long-term occupational career, and home ownership without a supporting spouse, Lakesha has fallen further in the wealth distribution, to the bottom 10 percent.

Joining her at the bottom, with about $15,000 in net debt in 2013, is Mike. His wealth position, however, implies considerable intergenerational downward mobility. In the 1980s, his parents had about $80,000 in net worth, which put them just above the national median. What happened? Mike had one year of education after high school. Though he held several occupations, including as a construction worker and a delivery man, Mike was employed continuously—until 2013, when he stopped working. The home Mike owns in 2013 is worth about $150,000, just about two-thirds of its value before the collapse of the housing market in 2007. This sharp decrease in his home value leaves him with negative home equity. Owing $20,000 more in mortgage than the home is worth, Mike is underwater. Whether he will ever emerge seems unlikely: he has no job, he is saddled with additional debt that includes about $10,000 in credit card debt, and his car is his sole notable asset.

THE FAR REACH OF WEALTH INEQUALITY

In the 1980s, Lakesha and Howard grow up at different ends of the wealth distribution—and that is where they also end up in 2013. The intergenerational persistence in family wealth that Lakesha and Howard have, however, extends further: into both the future and the past.

Lakesha has two children. Her first child struggles in school, is held back early on, and has a number of behavioral problems. In contrast, Howard's son shows no behavioral problems and scores at the top of the distribution in a standardized cognitive assessment. Lakesha's daughter scores in the bottom 20 percent of all children nationally.

Remember, Lakesha and Howard come from in many respects similar households: intact families, high school–educated parents, comparable household income. But Howard's family had an order of magnitude more wealth than Lakesha's, more than five hundred times the net worth. Given that Lakesha and Howard were both born in the late 1960s, their parents can very much be counted as part of the civil rights generation. Lakesha's parents may have marched against racial discrimination, for instance, as practiced through residential redlining as one overt mechanism of excluding blacks from asset accumulation. Although the civil rights battle celebrated many victories, that three generations later we observe engrained disadvantage for black children—their grandchildren—should remind us of the long reach of wealth inequality. The effects of discriminatory restrictions to build wealth for Lakesha's parents live on in their granddaughter.

BACKGROUND AND GOALS OF THIS ISSUE

The experiences of Lakesha, Liz, Mike, Mary, and Howard—and the papers in this volume—illustrate that wealth and wealth inequality are intertwined with almost all aspects of social and economic life: child development, education and human capital, success in the labor market, marriage and divorce, health, consumption, retirement decisions and policies, macroeconomic conditions, and historical events. One goal of this volume is to address many of these dimensions together in one publication to underscore the broad set of causes and consequences of wealth inequality. To that end, the authors bring perspectives from a range of academic disciplines, including economics, sociology, political science, history, demography, and health sciences.

The ten manuscripts were identified through an open competition sponsored by the Russell Sage Foundation. Proposals were reviewed and each manuscript went through the normal peer review process. Although all of the ten articles are described here, the goal of this introduction is not to simply summarize the findings of those manuscripts. Instead, it is intended as a broad and hopefully accessible overview of relevant research and provides as well some original analyses to describe why wealth inequality is a central factor influencing the nation's economic, social, and political outcomes and processes and why it therefore deserves the increased attention of scholars, policymakers, and the public.

WEALTH INEQUALITY AS AN ECONOMIC AND SOCIAL CONCERN

Distribution of Opportunity

Equal opportunity is the quintessential American ideal (Reeves 2015). As a principle, it is engrained in our attitudes and expectations but at the same time is squarely at odds with life in America today (Hochschild 1995). Lakesha, Liz, Mike, Mary, and Howard did not choose their parents. But parents' resources are a crucial factor in determining children's success in many spheres of life. Parents' resources heavily influence their children's health, cognitive and academic achievement, and socio-emotional development (Bradley and Corwyn 2004), factors that in turn heavily influence children's well-being throughout their lives. Here we focus on two channels through which the good fortune of being born into affluence determines success in life: human capital accumulation and direct cash or in-kind transfers.

Human Capital

Human capital, and education in particular, translates into more favorable outcomes in the labor market, higher income, greater wealth, and a longer life. One more year of schooling leads to roughly 10 percent higher earnings each year (Card 1999). The wealth of college graduates is three times higher than that of high school graduates (Bricker et al. 2015). Life expectancy is six years higher for college graduates than for high school graduates (Rostron, Boies, and Arias 2010) and this gap is increasing (Montez and Zajacova 2013; Olshansky et al. 2012).

Wealth allows parents to purchase a variety of resources that enhance human capital development: high-quality day care, books and learning tools at home, enrichment activities, and access to better elementary and secondary schools (Duncan and Murnane 2011). The evidence is perhaps most alarming at the postsecondary level. College graduation is strongly related to parental wealth (Conley 2001). The college graduation rates of young adults whose parents are in the top 20 percent of the wealth distribution are more than 40 percentage points higher than among those whose parents are in the bottom 20 percent, and this gap has grown substantially across recent cohorts (Pfeffer 2016).

Elite private colleges are responding to these disparities by increasing need-based grants, providing financial assistance to fully meet the federally determined financial need amount. This is an important development allowing talented youth greater access to the most prestigious educational institutions. However, these elite colleges enroll a very small share of college students in the United States, suggesting that this effort will have negligible effects on disparities at the national level. Many middle-class families who do not qualify for substantial need-based financial assistance may find the price tag too high.

The quantity and quality of formal education is important, but formal education is just one form of human capital. Some individuals are better than others at accumulating assets thanks to better knowledge of and skills in managing their finances (Lusardi, Michaud, and Mitchell 2013). Preferences for risk-taking and saving versus spending may also matter. Parents who have these valuable skills and qualities likely pass them on to their children (Dohmen et al. 2012), although evidence suggests that the intergenerational transmission of risk preferences per se does not account for much of the intergenerational correlation in wealth (Charles and Hurst 2003). Even if it did, an argument could be made that a strong intergenerational transmission of these preferences and skills also goes against common understandings of equality of opportunity: if Liz's failure to accumulate wealth were caused by lack of foresight, why should we consider that an outcome arising from individual shortcoming if foresight is fostered in family lineages with wealth (Roemer 1998; Dworkin 2000; England 2016)?

Direct Economic Assistance

In many families, assistance from parents continues through young adulthood and beyond. Between the ages of eighteen and thirty, the economic transfers received from parents and family—including the value of housing and food, assistance with college, and direct financial transfers—averages $50,000 in 2015 dollars across all young adults, including those who received no such transfers (Schoeni and Ross 2005). Children lucky enough to be born into more affluent families receive substantially more assistance. Young adults whose parents have income that puts them in the top quarter of parents receive $95,000, and those in the bottom quarter receive $31,000. Emily Rauscher (this issue) finds that transfers received from parents for schooling are more than eleven times larger among children whose parents are in the top quarter of the wealth distribution compared to children from the bottom half. She shows that financial transfers from parents for their children's education have the intended positive influence on their attainment outcomes. However, these transfers have not only become more common over time but also increasingly connected to parental wealth, tightening the link between wealth inequality and inequalities in opportunities.

Government transfers and programs offset, to some degree, the large disparity in investment in children across families by providing education and other resources to children whose parents earn lower incomes. However, it is unlikely—especially in the United States, where public support for such investments appears to be relatively low—that public resources will ever come close to making up for the private investments made by families who have the means. For example, Head Start provides an important early investment for disadvantaged children, but children from more affluent families can afford even higher quality developmental opportunities.

Individuals save today so they have the assets to weather periods of unemployment and make ends meet when faced with unfortunate events such as an expensive health procedure or treatment, divorce, or a vehicle or home repair. Such savings are an important buffer to these life events (see Thompson and Conley, this issue). Young adults with wealthy parents may use their parents as a source of insurance when they experience such events, reducing the negative consequences of life's challenges. Parental assets may also enhance children's economic position even if the parents never actually give them a dime. Just knowing that their parents are there for them in case they run into financial challenges may encourage young adults to pursue riskier, high-payoff educational pathways and careers (Shapiro 2004; Destin and Oyserman 2009; Pfeffer 2011; Pfeffer and Hällsten 2012). Furthermore, the psychological stress of making such decisions is reduced if young adults know they will be bailed out if they need to be.

Intergenerational Transmission
Parental wealth heavily influences children's development and success through these and other channels, leading to substantial intergenerational transmission of wealth status (Charles and Hurst 2003; Pfeffer and Killewald, forthcoming). Among adult children in the United States whose parents were in the top 20 percent in terms of wealth holdings, 44 percent ended up in the top 20 percent in their own generation's wealth distribution, and nearly 70 percent ended in the top 40 percent; only 6 percent fell to the bottom 20 percent. At the other end of the economic ladder, among adult children whose parents were in the bottom 20 percent, 35 percent stayed there, and fewer than 6 percent made it to the top 20 percent within their generation (Pfeffer and Killewald, forthcoming). Put differently, the odds of becoming part of the wealthiest 20 percent of Americans are more than 700 percent greater if your parents were in the top 20 percent instead of the bottom. The five individuals described in the beginning of this introduction, who ended up in quite similar places as their parents in the wealth distribution, thus represent quite typical biographies marked by the persistence of wealth positions across generations.

Many Challenges, Not Just for the Next Generation

Unequal Political Representation
Our democratic principle of equal representation is at risk when increased concentration of wealth is combined with laws that allow individuals to make unlimited political contributions. Through February 2016, super-PACs had raised $607 million. 112 donors gave at least $1 million, and their donations accounted for 64 percent of all contributions (Narayanswamy, Williams, and Gold 2016).

Research indicates that U.S. senators' voting

decisions are influenced by the preferences of their constituents, but only their more affluent constituents. Preferences of the least affluent one-third have no influence on their representative's voting (Bartels 2010). The wealthiest Americans—roughly the top 1 percent—are very active in politics and their views of taxation, regulation, and social welfare are much more conservative than the public as a whole (Page, Bartels, and Seawright 2013). Concentrated political power driven by concentrated control of economic resources can lead to policies that protect and enhance the position of those with power, arguably leading to even greater concentration and inefficient policies targeted to benefit a narrow few (Acemoğlu and Robinson 2012; Stiglitz 2012). This type of inequality in turn increases the likelihood of political upheaval and regime change (Boix 2003).

The 2015 Noble Laureate in Economics stated it clearly:

> If democracy becomes plutocracy, those who are not rich are effectively disenfranchised. Justice Louis Brandeis famously argued that the United States could have either democracy or wealth concentrated in the hands of a few, but not both. The political equality that is required by democracy is always under threat from economic inequality, and the more extreme the economic inequality, the greater the threat to democracy. If democracy is compromised, there is a direct loss of well-being because people have good reason to value their ability to participate in political life, and the loss of that ability is instrumental in threatening other harm. The very wealthy have little need for state-provided education or healthcare; they have every reason to support cuts in Medicare and to fight any increase in taxes. They have even less reason to support health insurance for everyone, or to worry about the low quality of public schools that plagues much of the country. They will oppose any regulation of banks that restricts profits, even if it helps those who cannot cover their mortgages or protect the public against predatory lending, deceptive advertising, or even the repetition of the financial crash. To worry about the consequences of extreme inequality has nothing to do with being envious of the rich and everything to do with the fear that rapidly growing top incomes are a threat to the well-being of everyone else. (Deaton 2015, 213)

Economic Growth

The primary argument in favor of inequality is that it leads to innovation, creativity, and productivity because it provides financial reward for such behavior, which in turn leads to greater macroeconomic growth. For many, this argument aligns strongly with their priors and personal experiences. Indeed, labor economists find that financial incentives do change behavior of employees (for recent reviews, see Oyer and Schaefer 2011; Bloom and Van Reenen 2011).

Skeptics question whether monetary rewards are the only or even the most important factor determining productivity and innovation and conclude that the effects of financial incentives depend on the context (Heyman and Ariely 2004) and can have important side effects such as decreased motivation (Festinger and Carlsmith 1959), change in feelings of competence into feelings of being controlled (Deci and Ryan 1985), and various productivity-reducing distortions (Bloom and Van Reenen 2011).

Furthermore, skeptics question just how much inequality is needed to generate innovation. Innovation may in fact be stymied by large inequality if only those at the top of the ladder can afford the ability to be creative. Alex Bell and his colleagues show that likely innovators—namely, those filing for new patents—overwhelmingly come from the upper end of the parental income distribution and that those with similar skills but from less advantaged backgrounds are far less likely to end up being inventors (2016).

At the macro level, empirical support for the claim that large inequalities produce better economic outcomes is lacking.[2] Economic

---

2. Jared Bernstein (2013) provides a thorough, accessible review of the ways in which inequality can affect economic growth.

growth is not higher in more unequal societies (Aghion, Caroli, and García-Peñalosa 1999; Benabou 1996). In fact, the empirical evidence indicates that more unequal societies tend to show lower economic growth than more equal societies (Aghion, Caroli, and Garcia-Peñalosa 1999; Kenworthy 2004; Ostry, Berg, and Tsangarides 2014). Moreover, more redistributive policies have, if anything, beneficial effects on macroeconomic growth (Easterly and Rebelo 1993; Kenworthy 2004) unless redistribution is extreme (Ostry, Berg, and Tsangarides 2014).

Economic growth is driven by strong consumer demand for goods and services (Schwartz, this issue). The fraction of each additional dollar of income used to purchase goods and services is higher for low-income and low-wealth families, particularly families with few liquid assets and living "hand-to-mouth" (Jappelli and Pistaferri 2014; Kaplan, Violante, and Weidner 2014; Johnson, Parker, and Souleles 2004) because any additional income is likely to be spent if families are living on the edge. Families with substantial liquid assets and not living hand to mouth, in contrast, have access to financial resources at relatively low cost, so fluctuations in income are less likely to alter consumption. This pattern explains why tax cuts and increased public spending designed to stimulate aggregate demand would be more efficient if targeted toward less-affluent families and, perhaps, families living hand to mouth even if they have significant nonliquid assets.

It has also been argued that public angst over inequality will lead to inefficient economic policies such as "trade protections, restrictions on immigration, union protections, other anti-competitive measures, and government subsidies" (Posner 2013). In this view, greater redistribution is warranted to avoid these and other "costs" of inequality.

Earlier we argued that the unequal distribution of wealth can inhibit investment in education, which in turn reduces wages and earnings of these workers. But macroeconomic growth also benefits from a highly educated workforce (see, for example, Barro 2000); that my neighbor cannot make optimal investments in education harms not only her, but also me, the entire neighborhood, and beyond (Putnam 2015).

The contrary case for the beneficial effects of inequality on economic outcomes has mostly been made in reference to labor market earnings and wages: inequality serves as a motivator to achieve a higher salary and thus makes everybody work harder. In this perspective, the attainment of wealth may serve as an equally effective motivator. Who does not want the big house and the big savings account? Yet, when considering the attainment of wealth, the main flaw of the functional notion of inequality becomes even more readily apparent (see also Tumin 1953): inequality in wealth has the best chance to serve as an incentive for hard and ingenious work if the only way to attain great wealth was in fact hard and ingenious work. That wealth can also be gained through inheritance or direct transfers from parents and thus ultimately through the lottery of birth should thus be concerning even from this perspective (Beckert 2007; Gates and Collins 2004). The normatively problematic and economically damaging link between inequality in wealth and the opportunity to attain it should thus be met by critique across the political spectrum. Finally, a defense of large inequalities in wealth has to grapple with the question of whether the current distribution indeed reflects the presumed ideal degree of inequality. That seems unlikely given that today's wealth inequality lies far beyond that observed for many decades—as we show in the next section—and that those prior decades with lower wealth inequality were marked by generally greater macroeconomic health and growth.

WEALTH INEQUALITY TODAY AND IN THE PAST

What Is Wealth?

So far, we have defined wealth very briefly as net worth, that is, the sum of all assets less all liabilities. Assets include financial assets, which are typically relatively easy to cash in, and nonfinancial assets. The most commonly held financial asset is a transaction account,

Table 1. Net Worth Distribution

	1989	1992	1995	1998	2001	2004	2007	2010	2013
Median	85.1	80.8	87.7	102.5	113.9	114.8	135.9	82.5	81.4
Mean	342.3	303.9	323.5	405.5	522.1	553.9	625.2	530.4	528.4
% with 0 or less	11.4%	10.3%	9.7%	10.4%	9.5%	8.9%	9.7%	13.1%	12.9%
Share of household wealth owned by									
Top 1%	29.9%	30.1%	34.8%	33.8%	32.1%	33.2%	33.6%	34.1%	35.5%
Top 5%	54.2%	54.4%	56.1%	57.2%	57.4%	57.4%	60.3%	60.9%	62.9%
Top 10%	67.0%	66.9%	67.9%	68.6%	69.6%	69.4%	71.4%	74.4%	75.0%
Top 20%	80.7%	80.1%	80.5%	81.4%	82.5%	82.9%	83.4%	86.7%	87.0%
Bottom 50%	3.0%	3.3%	3.6%	3.0%	2.8%	2.6%	2.5%	1.2%	1.1%
Gini coefficient	0.790	0.786	0.791	0.800	0.805	0.809	0.816	0.846	0.850
Ratio of percentiles									
50/25	8.3	6.8	5.8	7.2	6.8	7.0	8.6	9.3	9.3
75/50	3.1	3.0	2.8	2.9	3.3	3.5	3.1	3.9	3.9
95/75	4.7	4.5	4.3	4.3	4.6	4.3	5.1	6.2	5.9
95/50	14.7	13.4	11.8	12.6	15.2	15.4	15.7	24.2	23.0
No. of observations	3,143	3,906	4,299	4,305	4,442	4,519	4,417	6,482	6,015

Source: Authors' tabulations using the SCF (Survey of Consumer Finances 2013).
Note: All dollar values in thousands of 2013 dollars.

such as a checking or savings account. Other financial assets include certificates of deposit, savings bonds, bonds, stocks, pooled investment funds, cash value of life insurance, and retirement accounts. Retirement savings, which half of households hold (Bricker et al. 2015), include IRAs, Keogh accounts, and many employer-sponsored accounts such as 401(k) and 403(b). Most measures of wealth, including ours, do not include defined-benefit retirement benefits, that is, benefits paid out on a monthly basis with a fixed formula when workers retire (Devlin-Foltz and Sabelhaus 2015; Devlin-Foltz, Henriques, and Sabelhaus, this issue). Nor do they include the present value of the expected stream of Social Security benefits that one would receive when retired. Nonfinancial assets include residential property, nonresidential property, vehicles, business equity, and other assorted assets. Any payment still owed on those assets, such as mortgages and car loans, is subtracted from the market value to obtain the net value. Finally, aggregate net worth also takes into account any other (noncollateralized) debt, such as credit card debt, student loans, medical debt, and other financial obligations.

How Unequal Is the Wealth Distribution?

The gold standard when it comes to the measurement of household wealth is the Survey of Consumer Finances (SCF), a representative household survey typically conducted every three years. The most recent estimates are for 2013, which we report in table 1, along with estimates for every third year since 1989.

Much of the recent focus on wealth inequality has been on the top 1 percent, who owned 35.5 percent of all American household wealth in 2013. Wealth is further concentrated even within the top 1 percent. Estimates vary across data sources, but somewhere between 14 percent and 22 percent of household wealth was held by the 0.1 percent wealthiest households in 2012–2013 (Bricker et al. 2015; Saez and Zucman 2014). Forbes reports 536 billionaires in the United States in 2015. The richest twenty have more wealth than the combined wealth of half of all Americans, some fifty-seven million households (Collins and Hoxie 2015).

Still, a focus solely on the very top of the wealth distribution misses the tremendous and growing disparities throughout the distribution. Median wealth in 2013 was $81,400, and 12.9 percent of households had no wealth or were in debt. Twenty-five percent of households had less than $8,800 and another 25 percent had at least $316,800. Ten percent had at least $942,200 and 5 percent at least $1.87 million. Put a different way, a family at the 95th percentile of the wealth distribution had twenty-three times the wealth of a family at the middle, who in turn had more than nine times that of families at the 25th percentile.

Among families with modest wealth, most is not liquid but instead held as equity in their home. Many families live on the edge, with little savings to accommodate unexpected health expenditures, divorce, or unemployment. Even taking unemployment benefits into account, many families would not be able to maintain their level of consumption for more than a few months if they lost their job (Pew Charitable Trusts 2015a, 2015b) and just about half of all families report that they would be able to cover an unexpected expense of just $400 without selling something or borrowing money (Board of Governors 2015).

Wealth differs substantially across sociodemographic groups. Perhaps most troubling is the gap between racial and ethnic groups (Oliver and Shapiro 2006), differences that Thomas Shapiro and his colleagues at Brandeis University's Institute on Assets and Social Policy have studied extensively. The most recent estimates indicate large and growing gaps between whites and blacks and Hispanics. Average net worth among whites in 2013 was $687,701; the totals for blacks and Hispanics were $95,036 and $112,116, respectively. That is, white families have 7.2 times more wealth than black families and 6.1 times more wealth than Hispanic families. These gaps increased substantially in the wake of the Great Recession, with gaps in 2007 of 5.0 for blacks and 3.6 for Hispanics (Thompson and Suarez 2015; see also Sykes and Maroto in this issue). Given that housing equity is the largest component of wealth among lower and middle-class families,

Alexandra Killewald and Brielle Bryan (this issue) estimate the causal effects of home equity on wealth accumulation with a focus on how this relationship differs by race and ethnicity. They find large racial differences in the wealth returns to home ownership—with the yearly return to wealth for African Americans and Hispanics being just 48 percent and 62 percent of the return for whites, respectively. That one of the main vehicles of asset accumulation in the United States is not only less accessible but also less effective for minority groups is one important explanation for the continued racial disparities in wealth.

Racial gaps in wealth are also tied to racial differences in damaging life events such as incarceration and health shocks. Bryan Sykes and Michelle Maroto (this issue) show that the incarceration of a family member reduces the wealth of the family outside bars. The severe racial inequalities in incarceration therefore suggest possible spillover effects from the justice system to the racial structure of economic well-being, in particular when it comes to the racial wealth gap. Jason Thompson and Dalton Conley (this issue) find that health shocks induce wealth losses for both whites and blacks, but such shocks also widen the black-white wealth gap. Given the lower starting level of wealth among African Americans, health shocks are more likely to cause financial turmoil to these households.

The appreciation for the magnitude and importance of wealth inequality is relatively recent in comparison with income inequality. This delayed interest is certainly not justified by the magnitude of disparities. Wealth inequality dwarfs income inequality (Keister and Moller 2000). The Gini coefficient of wealth—0 representing perfect equality, 1 perfect inequality—is roughly 0.85, versus 0.45 for after-tax income and 0.40 for consumption in 2013 (Fisher et al. this issue). The average income of college graduates is roughly three times that of high school graduates, and mean net worth is five times greater. Annual income of non-Hispanic whites is twice that of other racial-ethnic groups, but their net worth is on average three and a half times that of other racial-ethnic groups (Bricker et al. 2015). Carefully considering the commonalities and differences across

Figure 1. Relative Changes in Net Worth Including Housing Wealth

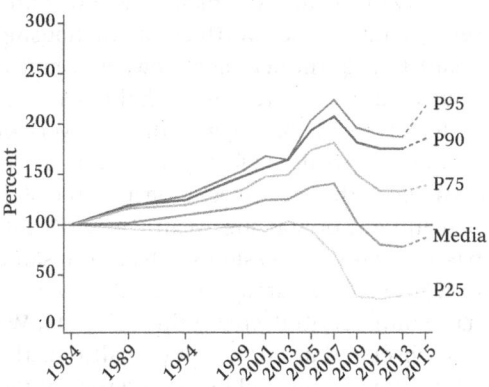

Source: Authors' calculations using the PSID (Panel Study of Income Dynamics 2013).
Note: Adjusted for inflation. 2015 estimates (dotted lines) are based on adjusted early release data (see appendix for details).

Figure 2. Relative Changes in Net Worth Excluding Housing Wealth

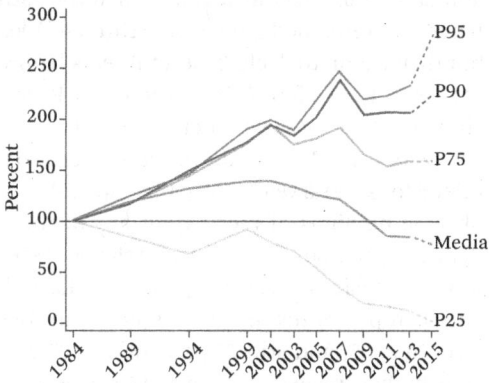

Source: Authors' calculations using the PSID (Panel Study of Income Dynamics 2013).
Note: Adjusted for inflation. 2015 estimates (dotted lines) are based on adjusted early release data (see appendix for details).

wealth, income, and consumption, Jonathan Fisher and his colleagues (this issue) conclude that wealth inequality is the most serious dimension of economic inequality in today's society.

Rising Wealth Inequality

To provide a complete picture of changes in wealth inequality throughout the wealth distribution, we report several different indicators of wealth disparities: the Gini coefficient, shares of wealth held by the top 1 percent, top 5 percent, top 10 percent, top 20 percent, and bottom 50 percent, and ratios of various percentiles of the distribution—50th to 25th, 75th to 50th, 95th to 75th, and 95th to 50th. For each of these ten measures, we report estimates for every available survey year of the SCF since 1989, that is, every third year, in table 1 (for an assessment of trends in wealth inequality in yet earlier years based on predecessors to the SCF, see Wolff, this issue). All measures indicate substantial increases in inequality between the early to mid-2000s and 2013. The share of wealth of the top 1 percent increased from 32.1 percent in 2001 to 35.5 percent in 2013. The share of the bottom 50 percent fell from 2.8 percent to 1.1 percent. The disparities within the bottom half of the distribution increased substantially: in 2001, families at the middle of the distribution had 6.8 times more wealth than families at the 25th percentile, and 9.3 by 2013. Most astounding is the dramatic and rapid increase in the disparity between families at the 95th percentile and those at the middle of the wealth distribution. Between 1989 and the mid-2000s, families at the 95th percentile owned twelve to fifteen times the wealth of families at the middle, but by 2010 this gap had risen to 24.2, and it stayed at a similar level in 2013.

Figures 1 and 2 offer another display of the spreading out of the wealth distribution since the 1980s, this time based on Panel Study of Income Dynamics (PSID) data. They report net worth levels (inflation adjusted) at selected percentiles—the 25th, median, 75th, 90th, and 95th—for each PSID wave with wealth data (every five years between 1984 and 1999 and every other year since then) and expressed relative to 1984 levels (for earlier and additional analyses, see also Pfeffer, Danziger, and Schoeni 2013). In figure 1, which reports estimates for net worth (including housing wealth), we observe a relatively steady increase in the wealth of the typical U.S. family between 1984 and 2007, by about 40 percent in total. Increases further up in the distribution were much larger, net worth at the 90th and 95th percentiles more than doubling between the 1980s and late 2000s. In contrast, wealth at the 25th percentile remained quite stable through 2003 but then began to decline, several years before the Great Recession. During the Great Recession, relative losses in net worth occurred across the wealth distribution and were sustained for several years. Even through 2013, we observe no signs of recovery at any of these distributional points. However, relative losses were less sustained at the top. In 2013, the 90th and 95th percentile are still higher than they were in 2003, and still 75 percent and 87 percent higher, respectively, over 1984 levels. In contrast, the net worth of the typical family in 2013 is about 20 percent below what it was in 1984 and wealth at the 25th percentile fell to just about a quarter of what it was in 1984.

The long-awaited recovery of families' wealth appears to finally materialize in 2015. Based on early release data from the 2015 PSID (for a detailed description of how we use those data to provide the best possible early estimate of trends, see the appendix), it appears that for the first time since the Great Recession, wealth holdings across the distribution are recovering. However, once again, inequality is increasing further as recovery at the 95th percentile outpaces that at lower ranks of the wealth distribution. This striking trend awaits confirmation based on final data release from the PSID and SCF, which is at time of writing still several months away. The early signs of wealth recovery presented here, however, suggest that the celebration of the most recent trend of wealth recovery may be dampened by the fact that it seems to go along with even further wealth concentration at the top.

In addition, for most of the distribution, the recovery of wealth appears to be driven by the recovery of the housing market. Figure 2 presents trends for net worth excluding housing wealth (that is, the net value of owner-occupied housing as well as real estate holdings). The early 2015 estimates suggest that recovery of nonhousing wealth in fact occurred only at the 90th and 95th percentiles. In fact, at the 95th percentile, nonhousing wealth in 2015 surpasses even prerecession levels; at the same time, the typical family's nonhousing wealth has continued to decrease through 2015. We also observe that nonhousing wealth for the typical U.S. family had begun to erode at the turn of the millenium, a trend largely masked by the fast growth and ultimate bubble of the housing market.

For trends in inequality prior to 1989, the article by Edward Wolff in this volume reports an increase between 1962 and 1989 in the Gini (from 0.803 to 0.832) and share of wealth held by the top 1 percent (from 33.4 percent to 37.4 percent), though this rise was not monotonic throughout the twenty-seven years.[3] Emmanuel Saez and Gabriel Zucman provide annual estimates of inequality from 1917 through 2012 (2014). The wealthiest 10 percent of families owned roughly 80 percent of household wealth around 1920; the century's lowest share of 63 percent came in 1986. Since that time, though, the increase has been steady and continuous. In 2012, the share was 77 percent, roughly the inequality of the 1920s.

Given the role of parents' wealth in child and adolescent development described earlier, it is important to also assess changes in wealth and wealth inequality, specifically, among households with children. In 2013, the median wealth

---

3. The estimates provided by Wolff (this issue) diverge from ours (table 1) and those provided by the Federal Reserve (for example, Bricker et al. 2015) for several reasons, including that Wolff relies on a net worth measure that excludes vehicle wealth. Another source may be Wolff's adjustments to SCF estimates geared at matching national balance sheets and at making the earliest SCF waves as comparable as possible to SCF's predecessors from the 1960s (personal communication with John Sabelhaus and Edward Wolff). We consider Wolff's estimates most attractive to allow for a comparison of wealth concentration between the 1960 and 1980s, but focus on our and the Federal Reserve's estimates for later periods. Overall, though, Wolff offers similar interpretations of trends; for example, when he indicates "that mean wealth grew about twice as fast as the median between 1983 and 2007, indicating widening inequality of wealth over these years" (7) and that the growth in wealth inequality was "not limited to the increased gap between the top one percent and everyone else but occurred across the full wealth distribution" (10).

Figure 3. Wealth Inequality and Children in Household

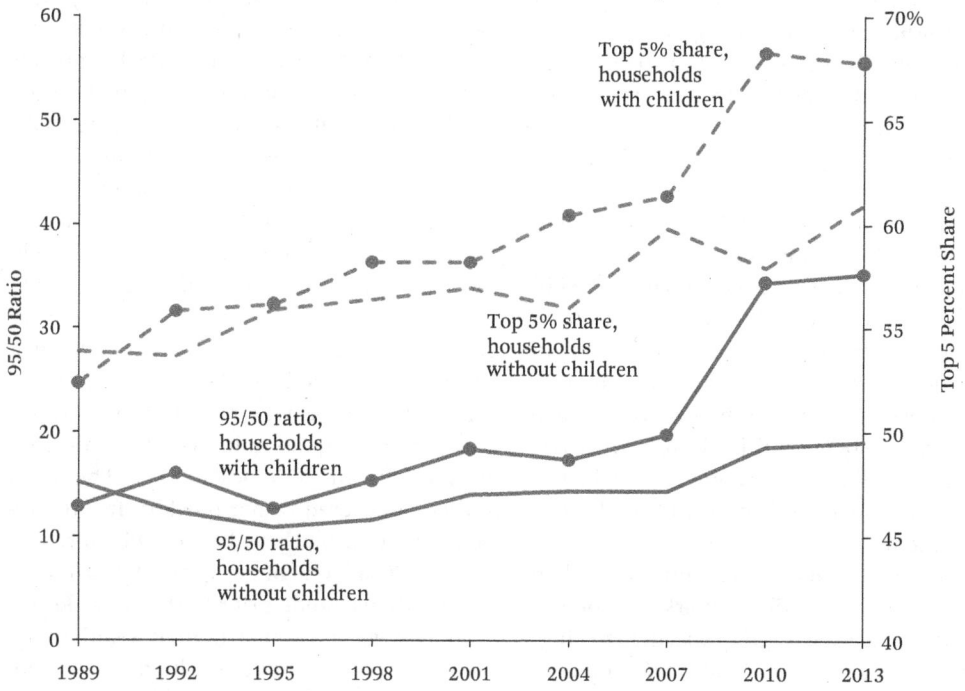

Source: Authors' calculations using the SCF (Survey of Consumer Finances, 2013).

of households with children was $43,200, versus $105,400 for those without children. This gap is not surprising and exists primarily because parents of children are younger and have had less time to accumulate assets. What is surprising and troubling is that wealth inequality is higher and has risen faster among households with children than households without them. Figure 3 displays the 95th to 50th percentile ratio and the share of wealth controlled by the wealthiest 5 percent from 1989 through 2013, separately for households with and without children under eighteen. Inequality was fairly similar across these households at the beginning of this period but substantially higher among households with children by the end. The 95th to 50th ratio more than doubled for households with children, with wealth of families at the 95th percentile thirty-five times larger than middle-wealth families.

Extensive research has demonstrated that socioeconomic factors influencing child development have particularly large effects in the first few years of life (Duncan, Ziol-Guest, and Kalil 2010; Heckman 2006). Young children (up to six years old) are in households with much lower wealth than teenagers (thirteen through seventeen): median wealth of $24,800 versus $82,200 in 2013 (authors' tabulations using the SCF, not shown). This pattern is again not surprising because teenagers tend to have older parents who have had more time to accumulate wealth. However, inequality in household wealth—whether measured by the 95th to 50th ratio, top 5 percent share, or Gini—is higher for households with young children than those with older children (ages seven through sixteen).

The takeoff in wealth inequality among children and especially young children occurred mostly during the latest recession. In this sense, we can expect the effects of the Great Recession to remain with us for a long time, as the children who are being exposed to remarkably high levels of inequality grow up.

Causes of Rising Inequality

Direct evidence on the causes of the rise in wealth inequality is sparse, at least relative to evidence on the causes of the rise in income and earnings inequality since the 1970s. Given that sufficient income allows one to accumulate wealth, the factors driving increases in income inequality are most likely also important drivers of wealth inequality. Research identifies several reasons for increases in income inequality, and inequality in labor market earnings in particular (for a recent and thorough review, see Congressional Budget Office 2011). This list includes increases in the returns to labor market skills and education (that is, skill-biased technological change), reductions in the presence and influence of unions, and globalization of consumer markets, which led to a substantial increase in imports of products manufactured by lower skilled-workers, thereby lowering the demand for domestic production of these products and the workers who produced them.

Research has shown that a substantial share of the rise in inequality in market income in the last few decades is due to particularly high growth among the households in the top 1 percent of income (Congressional Budget Office 2011; Saez and Zucman 2014). These factors may be responsible, at least in part, for increases in the top 1 percent, but additional factors are likely also important. These include reductions in top tax rates (Alvaredo et al. 2013), the superstar effect (Rosen 1981; Kaplan and Rauh 2010, 2013), managerial power (Bebchuk and Fried 2009), increases in market capitalization of large companies (Gabaix and Landier 2008), and the "infectious" takeoff in executive compensation (DiPrete, Eirich, and Pittinsky 2010). This is an important, active area of research, but a consensus has not yet emerged (Congressional Budget Office 2011).

Explanations for growing wealth inequality per se include Thomas Piketty's argument that the rate of return to capital has been greater than the rate of economic growth (2014). This claim has generated a great deal of reaction among social scientists, some of it critical (see Dodd 2014; Moretti 2015).

Recent tax cuts on major assets including inheritances likely also caused some of the increase at the top (Shapiro, Meschede, and Sullivan 2010). Saving rates are substantially higher for wealthier households, and this differential increased substantially in the last few decades. Saving rates in the wealthiest 1 percent of households have stayed at roughly 35 percent for most of the last century. Rates for the bottom 90 percent, which were historically around 5 percent, began to fall in the mid-1980s and were 0 percent in 2012—potentially as an outcome of the stagnation and loss in real earnings and incomes for large parts of the population. This pattern of rising inequality in saving rates is one cause of increases in wealth inequality (see Saez and Zucman 2014).

Several recent analyses of trends in wealth inequality shed light on the specific period just prior to, during, and after the Great Recession (see Wolff, this issue). Before the Great Recession, wealthier households were more likely to have wealth in the stock market. The stock market recovered rather quickly after the recession, allowing these households to return close to 2003 levels of net wealth by 2011. Less wealthy households prior to the Great Recession, however, held most of their wealth in the form of their home and were highly leveraged. To date, the housing market is still recovering, and, as a result, households at the bottom of the distribution remain substantially below their prerecession levels of wealth (Pfeffer, Danziger, and Schoeni 2013).

Because of the tremendous upheaval and slow recovery from the Great Recession, many low- and middle-income and wealth households were forced to draw down their limited financial assets to get by (Wolff, this issue). These families were more likely to cash out their limited stock holdings during the Great Recession and therefore were less likely to benefit from the subsequent recovery of the stock market. At the same time, investors with substantial wealth holdings—who were less likely to lose their jobs or foreclose on their homes—were less likely to cash out, thereby riding out the recession and benefiting from the subsequent recovery (Chen and Stafford 2016; Devlin-Foltz, Henriques, and Sabelhaus, this issue). This pattern widened wealth inequality following the Great Recession. At the same time, families in the middle and upper parts of the income and wealth distribution were not immune. They too experienced substantial turbulence in wealth holdings and consumption (Devlin-Foltz and Sabelhaus 2015).

Assets held in retirement accounts are a large share of household wealth—roughly 30 percent—and have increased in recent decades. The shift has also been substantial toward defined-contribution (DC) plans and away from defined-benefit (DB) plans. Sebastian Devlin-Foltz, Alice Henriques, and John Sabelhaus (this issue) examine the extent to which these developments account for changes in wealth inequality. They conclude that the growth in retirement wealth as a share of total household wealth kept wealth inequality from increasing more than it otherwise would have because retirement wealth is more equally distributed than nonretirement wealth. At the same time, the shift from DB to DC plans is causing a modest increase in wealth inequality because DC wealth is more unequally distributed.

Herman Mark Schwartz (this issue) offers a new argument on the socio-legal determinants of wealth inequality. He discusses and empirically traces the central role of monopolies created by intellectual property rights (IPR) in contributing to rising inequality. Many firms with valuable IPRs are able to outsource physical capital and nonessential labor, leaving the IPR-holding firm with a small and highly paid workforce. Over time, these developments increased inequality among firms in terms of their market capitalization and profitability and among households in income and wealth. In turn, increases in inequality among firms reduced corporate investment, and increases in inequality among households reduced consumer demand, dampening macroeconomic growth.

One way to reduce wealth inequality is to increase savings and asset accumulation among less-affluent families. Eric Hilt and Wendy Rahn's creative and detailed historical study in this issue of the success of one of the largest and most successful public programs to increase personal savings—the Liberty Bond drives of World War I—offers valuable lessons for current efforts to increase savings rates at the lower end of the wealth distribution. Doing so is important since there is an active group of scholars and policymakers with a focus on asset-building among disadvantaged families (for example, Blank and Barr 2009; Shanks Williams 2014; Sherraden 1991) and new federal programs to support it (such as *my*RA savings accounts). However, many of the current programs lack the features Hilt and Rahn consider the key ingredients to the success of the Liberty Bond program, such as coordinated promotional efforts by community groups, businesses, churches, and related organizations.

CONCLUSION

Much of the academic and public debate on wealth inequality has focused on the extreme level of wealth concentration at the very top of the distribution. Although this increasing concentration is concerning for a range of reasons—including the risks it poses to representative democracy—we should not lose sight of the fact that wealth inequality and its effects on society pertain to the full distribution of wealth. Even below the very top, such as the top 1 percent, wealth is distributed highly unequally, much more unequally than (for instance) income. Particularly in the last ten to fifteen years, families who are wealthy but not in the top 1 percent are pulling away from the average family, and the average family is pulling away from less-wealthy families. This development has unique and widespread consequences, such as increasing inequality in opportunity among the next generation, that may in some ways be even more troubling than the rise of the 1 percent. Worries about the long-term consequences of this rise are compounded by the fact that wealth inequality is higher and has risen much more sharply among households with children, particularly young children, as shown here.

Today's extreme levels of wealth inequality stand to shape the future of these children in many ways. Their parents' wealth facilitates their own educational attainment, eases their early labor market transitions, facilitates access to home and business ownership, supports marriage, especially with partners from similar family wealth backgrounds, and sustains the stability of marriage (Eads and Tach, this issue). Before parental wealth is transferred through bequests, it has already exerted much of its beneficial effects on the economic well-being of the next generation. In other words, a great deal of wealth persists across generations even before it is passed on at death (Pfeffer and Killewald, forthcoming).

The association between wealth inequality and inequality in opportunity suggests a moral argument against today's extreme levels of wealth inequality. But an important economic argument also has merit: current levels of wealth inequality are likely impediments to economic growth and fertile ground for social unrest that interferes with economic activity. The redistributive policies of even the earliest Bismarckian welfare state were motivated much less by moral considerations than by those about social conflict that would eventually upend the existing social order and economic structure. The recent surge in wealth inequality appears to add weight to a similar economic argument for the efficiency of wealth redistribution.

One way of reining in wealth inequality is to address its roots. As we have suggested, a number of explanations for the growth in wealth inequality have been proposed, including those offered to explain rising income inequality (skill-bias technological change, union decline, global competition, and others), the historically high returns on capital, changes in industrial organization and corporate practices, and the ways in which differential asset portfolios determined the extent of losses during the Great Recession and the pace of recovery following it. Of course, a more direct way of reducing wealth inequality could be the direct taxation of wealth. Emerging evidence suggests that taxation of wealth or bequests at the level considered by policy analysists may have limited redistributive effects (Wolff 1995; Kopczuk 2013; Elinder, Erixson, and Waldenström 2015; Gale, Kearney, and Orszag 2016; Quiggin 2016). However, any assessment of the potential of changes to wealth taxation needs to take into account several important considerations. First, although their redistributive effects are debatable, the impact of wealth and inheritance taxes on public budgets are large (Wolff 1995). They could, in the end, provide resources to fund the public goods that support child development and human capital acquisition and maintenance the same way private wealth currently does: high-quality early childcare and K–12 public schools, public support for colleges, labor market policies that smooth unemployment trajectories, and many more. Second, some components of the existing tax system increase rather than decrease wealth inequality. A myriad of exemptions in the current tax code tend to favor those who already have accumulated large amounts of wealth (Howard 1999; Faricy 2015). Third, tax evasion—not least by off-shoring large private wealth holdings, in some cases legally, thanks to regulatory loopholes, in other cases illegally—is also more pervasive than formerly believed (Zucman 2015; Harrington 2016; see also the Panama Papers investigation by the International Consortium of Investigative Journalists).

Wealth inequality has only recently become a major focus of the scientific and policy research community. The contributions in this issue make important inroads, assessing the extent and development of wealth inequality, its sources, and its consequences. But more needs to be done. More research is needed on the causes of changes in wealth inequality throughout the wealth distribution, not just the top 1 percent. How have changes in tax policy, monetary policy, industrial organization, savings preferences and decisions, and banking practices and availability altered the distribution of wealth? What are the consequences of increased wealth concentration for disparities in the quality of education, health and longevity, residential segregation, assimilation and integration of immigrants, community cohesion, and political representation and public decision-making at the state and local level?

As is often the case, even as scientific research seeks to provide answers to these questions, political debate and decisions march on. In fact, the run-up to the impending presidential election featured much commentary on wealth by presidential hopefuls. Particular focus was again put on the top of the wealth distribution, a candidate from one side decrying the top 1 percent and a candidate from the other boasting about his own membership in it. The ideological distance between these poles of the waging political debate is large. If our volume can contribute in any way to this debate, it is by encouraging discussion about and providing evidence for the broad importance of wealth for the rest of families below the top 1 percent in terms of their economic well-being, their health, their marriages, their own future, and that of their children.

APPENDIX

The Panel Study of Income Dynamics is an attractive data source for the assessment of wealth inequality and its consequences (see also Pfeffer et al. 2016), perhaps most importantly because it is the only nationally representative survey that provides regular and long-term longitudinal information on families' wealth holdings. Another particularly attractive feature, however, is that the PSID releases a preliminary version of its wealth data within a few weeks of the close of data collection, which occurs every other calendar year. These PSID early release files first became available for the 2009 wave and were devised specifically in response to the Great Recession, which was in full swing during the 2009 data collection. Our report of the most recent trends in wealth inequality through the year 2015 includes data from the early release file for 2015.

The PSID invests substantial resources in the editing of its data, including the reliable determination of family relationships among all household members through individual look-ups, the editing of values based on interviewer notes and data consistency checks, the imputation of missing values, and the construction of generated variables—such as net worth. The early release files contain none of these edits and instead provide raw data as collected in the field.

As one would expect, estimates based on early release (ER) data therefore diverge somewhat from those based on final release (FR) data. However, we know by how much they diverged in the past given that both ER and FR data are now available for a number of waves (2009, 2011, and 2013). We use this information to adjust current ER data. That is, to adjust 2015 ER data, we take into account the divergence between ER and FR data in the prior wave. We scale each estimated percentile by the degree of ER-FR divergence at that percentile in the 2013 wave. For instance, median net worth in the 2013 FR data was 4.8 percent

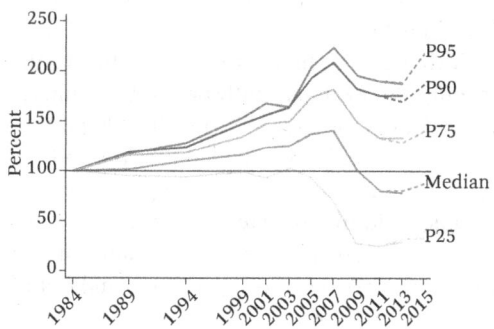

Figure A1. Relative Changes in Net Worth

Source: Authors' calculations using the PSID (Panel Study of Income Dynamics 2013).
Note: Adjusted for inflation. Dotted lines are based on adjusted early release data.

higher than in the 2013 ER data (54,500 versus 52,000), leading us to adjust the 2015 ER net worth median upwards by 4.8 percent (from 59,989 to 60,777 in 2013 dollars).

We have used these kinds of adjustments for ER data for prior analyses (Pfeffer, Danziger, and Schoeni 2014). Figure A1 displays how closely the adjusted 2013 ER data (adjusted by the factor of divergence between 2011 ER and FR data) approximated the FR results for 2013: the estimates for net worth at the median and the 25th percentile based on adjusted 2013 ER data are very close to those based on the eventual 2013 FR data, especially for the purpose of assessing long-term historical trends in the wealth distribution. Adjusted 2013 ER data provided slight underestimates of wealth at the 75th and 90th percentiles for 2013 (though the adjustments still moved the estimates in the right direction: for example, for the 75th percentile, the raw ER data provided an estimate of roughly $250,000, the adjusted ER data of roughly $260,000, and the FR data of roughly $270,000). Finally, our adjustments were most successful at the 95th percentile, providing a near perfect match between the early and final release data. Knowing that the adjustment at that percentile was particularly successful is reassuring because the size of adjustment is also particularly large here, inflating the estimate by a full 14 percent. But the size of this adjustment has remained remarkably stable across the last two waves (divergence of 14.3 percent based on 2011 and of 14.8 percent based on 2013).

Although the final word on wealth trends through 2015 will naturally depend on final release data (in several months after this publication), the analyses provided here thus add to our confidence in describing long-term wealth trends, including the steep recovery of wealth at the 95th percentile in 2015, arguably one of the most striking findings of our analysis of the 2015 ER data.

REFERENCES

Acemoğlu, Daron, and James Robinson. 2012. *Why Nations Fail: The Origins of Power, Prosperity, and Poverty*. New York: Crown Publishing.

Aghion, Philippe, Eve Caroli, and Cecilia García-Peñalosa. 1999. "Inequality and Economic Growth: The Perspective of the New Growth Theories." *Journal of Economic Literature* 37(4): 1615-60.

Alvaredo, Facundo, Anthony B Atkinson, Thomas Piketty, and Emmanuel Saez. 2013. "The Top 1 Percent in International and Historical Perspective." *Journal of Economic Perspectives* 27(3): 3-20.

Barro, Robert J. 2000. "Education and Economic Growth." *Annals of Economics and Finance* 14(2): 301-28.

Bartels, Larry. 2010. *Unequal Democracy: The Political Economy of the New Gilded Age*. Princeton, N.J.: Princeton University Press.

Bebchuk, Lucian A., and Jesse Fried. 2009. *Pay Without Performance: The Unfulfilled Promise of Executive Compensation*. Cambridge, Mass.: Harvard University Press.

Beckert, Jens. 2007. *Inherited Wealth*. Princeton, N.J.: Princeton University Press.

Bell, Alex, Raj Chetty, Xavier Jaravel, Neviana Petkova, and John Van Reenen. 2016. "The Lifecycle of Inventors." Unpublished manuscript, Harvard University.

Benabou, Roland. 1996. "Inequality and Growth." In *NBER Macroeconomics Annual 1996*, vol. 11, edited by Ben S. Bernanke and Julio J. Rotemberg. Cambridge, Mass.: MIT Press. Accessed May 10, 2016. http://www.nber.org/chapters/c11027.pdf.

Bernstein, Jared. 2013. "The Impact of Inequality on Growth." Center for American Progress. Accessed June 6, 2016. https://www.americanprogress.org/wp-content/uploads/2013/12/BerensteinInequality.pdf.

Blank, Rebecca, and Michael Barr. 2009. *Insufficient Funds: Savings, Assets, Credit, and Banking Among Low-Income Households*. New York: Russell Sage Foundation.

Bloom, Nicholas, and John Van Reenen. 2011. "Human Resource Management and Productivity." In *Handbook of Labor Economics*, vol. 4(B), edited by David Card and Orley Ashenfelter. Amsterdam: Elsevier.

Board of Governors of the Federal Reserve System (Board of Governors). 2015. "Report on the Economic Well-Being of U.S. Households in 2014." Washington: Federal Reserve System.

Boix, Carles. 2003. *Democracy and Redistribution*. Cambridge: Cambridge University Press.

Bradley, Robert, and Robert Corwyn. 2004. *Socioeconomic Status and Child Development*. Weinheim: Wiley-VCH.

Bricker, Jesse, Alice Henriques, Jake Krimmel, and John Sabelhaus. 2015. "Measuring Income and Wealth at the Top Using Administrative and Survey Data." *Finance and Economics Discussion Series* 2015(30): 1-63.

Card, David E. 1999. "The Causal Effect of Education on Earnings." In *Handbook of Labor Economics*, vol. 3, edited by David Card and Orley Ashenfelter. Amsterdam: Elsevier.

Charles, Kerwin Kofi, and Erik Hurst. 2003. "The Correlation of Wealth Across Generations." *Journal of Political Economy* 111(6): 1155-82.

Chen, Bing, and Frank P. Stafford. 2016. "Stock Market Participation. Family Responses to Housing Consumption Commitments." *Journal of Money, Credit, and Banking* 48(4): 635-59.

Collins, Chuck, and Josh Hoxie. 2015. "Billionaire Bonanza: The Forbes 400 and the Rest of Us—IPS." Washington, D.C.: Institute for Policy Studies. Accessed May 10, 2016. http://www.ips-dc.org/billionaire-bonanza/.

Congressional Budget Office. 2011. "Trends in the Distribution of Household Income Between 1979 and 2007." Washington: Government Printing Office. Accessed May 10, 2016. https://www.cbo.gov/sites/default/files/112th-congress-2011-2012/reports/10-25-HouseholdIncome_0.pdf.

Conley, Dalton. 2001. "Capital for College. Parental Assets and Postsecondary Schooling." *Sociology of Education* 74(1): 59-72.

Deaton, Angus. 2015. *The Great Escape: Health,*

Wealth, and the Origins of Inequality*. Reprint edition. Princeton, N.J.: Princeton University Press.

Deci, Edward L., and Richard M. Ryan. 1985. "The General Causality Orientations Scale: Self-Determination in Personality." *Journal of Research in Personality* 19(2): 109–34

Destin, Mesmin, and Daphna Oyserman. 2009. "From Assets to School Outcomes: How Finances Shape Children's Perceived Possibilities and Intentions." *Psychological Science* 20(4): 414–18.

Devlin-Foltz, Sebastian, Alice Henriques, and John Sabelhaus. 2016. "Is the U.S. Retirement System Contributing to Rising Wealth Inequality." *RSF: The Russell Sage Foundation Journal of the Social Sciences* 2(6). doi: 10.7758/RSF.2016.2.6.04.

Devlin-Foltz, Sebastian, and John Sabelhaus. 2015. "Heterogeneity in Economic Shocks and Household Spending." *Finance and Economics Discussion Series* 2015(49): 1–43. doi: 10.17016/FEDS.2015.049.

DiPrete, Thomas A., Gregory M. Eirich, and Matthew Pittinsky. 2010. "Compensation Benchmarking, Leapfrogs, and the Surge in Executive Pay." *American Journal of Sociology* 115(6): 1671–712.

Dodd, Nigel, ed. 2014. "Special Issue: Piketty Symposium." *British Journal of Sociology* 65(4): 589–747.

Dohmen, Thomas J, Armin Falk, David Huffman, and Uwe Sunde. 2012. "The Intergenerational Transmission of Risk and Trust Attitudes." *Review of Economic Studies* 79(2): 645–77.

Duncan, Greg J., and Richard J. Murnane, eds. 2011. *Whither Opportunity? Rising Inequality, Schools, and Children's Life Chances*. New York: Russell Sage Foundation.

Duncan, Greg J., Kathleen M. Ziol-Guest, and Ariel Kalil. 2010. "Early-Childhood Poverty and Adult Attainment, Behavior, and Health." *Child Development* 81(1): 306–25.

Dworkin, Ronald. 2000. *Sovereign Virtue: The Theory and Practice of Equality*. Cambridge, Mass.: Harvard University Press.

Eads, Alicia, and Laura Tach. 2016. "Wealth and Inequality in the Stability of Romantic Relationships." *RSF: The Russell Sage Foundation Journal of the Social Sciences* 2(6). doi: 10.7758/RSF.2016.2.6.10.

Easterly, William, and Sergio Rebelo. 1993. "Fiscal Policy and Economic Growth: An Empirical Investigation." *Journal of Monetary Economics* 32(3): 417–58.

Elinder, Mikael, Oscar Erixson, and Daniel Waldenström. 2015. "Inheritance and Wealth Inequality: Evidence from Population Registers." *Uppsala Center for Fiscal Studies* working paper no. 3. Uppsala, Sweden: Uppsala University.

England, Paula. 2016. "Sometimes the Social Becomes Personal Gender, Class, and Sexualities." *American Sociological Review* 81(1): 4–28.

Faricy, Christopher G. 2015. *Welfare for the Wealthy: Parties, Social Spending, and Inequality in the United States*. New York: Cambridge University Press.

Festinger, Leon, and James M. Carlsmith 1959. "Cognitive Consequences of Forced Compliance." *Journal of Abnormal and Social Psychology* 58(2): 203–10.

Fisher, Jonathan, David Johnson, Jonathan P. Latner, Timothy Smeeding, and Jeffrey Thompson. 2016. "Inequality and Mobility Using Income, Consumption, and Wealth for the Same Individuals." *RSF: The Russell Sage Foundation Journal of the Social Sciences* 2(6). doi: 10.7758/RSF.2016.2.6.03.

Gabaix, Xavier, and Augustin Landier. 2008. "Why Has CEO Pay Increased So Much." *NBER* working paper no. 12365. Cambridge, Mass.: National Bureau of Economic Research. Accessed May 10, 2016. http://www.nber.org/papers/w12365.

Gale, William G., Melissa S. Kearney, and Peter R. Orszag. 2015. "Would a Significant Increase in the Top Income Tax Rate Substantially Alter Income Inequality?" Washington, D.C.: Brookings Institution. Accessed May 10, 2016. http://www.brookings.edu/~/media/research/files/papers/2015/09/28-taxes-inequality/would-top-income-tax-alter-income-inequality.pdf.

Gates, William H., and Chuck Collins. 2004. *Wealth and Our Commonwealth: Why America Should Tax Accumulated Fortunes*. Boston, Mass.: Beacon Press.

Harrington, Brooke. 2016. *Capital Without Borders. Wealth Managers and the One Percent*. Cambridge, Mass.: Harvard University Press.

Heckman, James J. 2006. "Skill Formation and the Economics of Investing in Disadvantaged Children." *Science* 312(5782): 1900–2. doi: 10.1126/science.1128898.

Heyman, James, and Dan Ariely. 2004. "Effort for Payment: A Tale of Two Markets." *Psychological Science* 15(11): 787–93.

Hilt, Eric, and Wendy M. Rahn. 2016. "Turning Citizens into Investors: Promoting Savings with Liberty Bonds During World War I." *RSF: The Russell Sage Foundation Journal of the Social Sciences* 2(6). doi: 10.7758/RSF.2016.2.6.05.

Hochschild, Jennifer L. 1995. *Facing Up to the American Dream. Race, Class, and the Soul of a Nation*. Princeton, N.J.: Princeton University Press.

Howard, Christopher. 1999. *The Hidden Welfare State*. Princeton, N.J.: Princeton University Press.

Jappelli, Tullio, and Luigi Pistaferri. 2014. "Fiscal Policy and MPC Heterogeneity." *American Economic Journal: Macroeconomics* 6(4): 107–36.

Johnson, David S., Jonathan A. Parker, and Nicholas S. Souleles. 2004. "Household Expenditure and the Income Tax Rebates of 2001." *NBER* working paper no. 10784. Cambridge, Mass.: National Bureau of Economic Research.

Kaplan, Greg, Giovanni Violante, and Justin Weidner. 2014. "The Wealthy Hand-to-Mouth." *NBER* working paper no. 20073. Cambridge, Mass.: National Bureau of Economic Research.

Kaplan, Steven N., and Joshua Rauh. 2010. "Wall Street and Main Street: What Contributes to the Rise in the Highest Incomes?" *Review of Financial Studies* 23(3): 1004–50.

———. 2013. "It's the Market: The Broad-Based Rise in the Return to Top Talent." *Journal of Economic Perspectives* 27(3): 35–55.

Keister, Lisa A., and Stephanie Moller. 2000. "Wealth Inequality in the United States." *Annual Review of Sociology* 26: 63–81.

Kenworthy, Lane. 2004. *Egalitarian Capitalism: Jobs, Incomes, and Growth in Affluent Countries*. Rose Series in Sociology. New York: Russell Sage Foundation.

Killewald, Alexandra, and Brielle Bryan. 2016. "Does Your Home Make You Wealthy?" *RSF: The Russell Sage Foundation Journal of the Social Sciences* 2(6). doi: 10.7758/RSF.2016.2.6.06.

Kopczuk, Wojciech. 2013. "Taxation of Intergenerational Transfers and Wealth." In *Handbook of Public Economics*, vol. 5, edited by Alan J. Auerbach, Raj Chetty, Martin Feldstein, and Emmanuel Saez. Amsterdam: Elsevier.

Lusardi, Annamaria, Pierre-Carl Michaud, and Olivia S. Mitchell. 2013. "Optimal Financial Knowledge and Wealth Inequality." *NBER* working paper no. 18669. Cambridge, Mass.: National Bureau of Economic Research.

Montez, Jennifer Karas, and Anna Zajacova. 2013. "Trends in Mortality Risk by Education Level and Cause of Death among US White Women from 1986 to 2006." *American Journal of Public Health* 103(3): 473–79.

Moretti, Enrico, ed. 2015. "Symposium on Wealth and Inequality." *Journal of Economic Perspectives* 29(1): 3–88.

Narayanswamy, Anu, Aaron Williams, and Matea Gold. 2016. "Meet the Wealthy Donors Who Are Funneling Millions into the 2016 Elections." *Washington Post*, April 15, 2016. Accessed May 10, 2016. https://www.washingtonpost.com/graphics/politics/superpac-donors-2016.

Oliver, Melvin, and Thomas Shapiro. 2006. *Black Wealth / White Wealth: A New Perspective on Racial Inequality*, 2nd ed. New York: Routledge.

Olshansky, S. Jay, Toni Antonucci, Lisa Berkman, Robert H. Binstock, Axel Boersch-Supan, John T. Cacioppo, Bruce A. Carnes, Laura L. Carstensen, Linda P. Fried, Dana P. Goldman, James Jackson, Martin Kohli, John Rother, Yuhui Zheng, and John Rowe. 2012. "Differences in Life Expectancy Due to Race and Educational Differences Are Widening, and Many May Not Catch Up." *Health Affairs* 31(8): 1803–13.

Ostry, Jonathan David, Andrew Berg, and Charalambos G. Tsangarides. 2014. *Redistribution, Inequality, and Growth*. International Monetary Fund.

Oyer, Paul, and Scott Schaefer. 2011. "Personnel Economics: Hiring and Incentives." In *Handbook of Labor Economics*, vol. 4(B), edited by David Card and Orley Ashenfelter. Amsterdam: Elsevier.

Page, Benjamin I., Larry M. Bartels, and Jason Seawright. 2013. "Democracy and the Policy Preferences of Wealthy Americans." *Perspectives on Politics* 11(1): 51–73.

Panel Study of Income Dynamics. 2013. Public use dataset produced and distributed by the Survey Research Center, Institute for Social Research, University of Michigan, Ann Arbor, Mich. (downloaded 2015).

Pew Charitable Trust. 2015a. "The Precarious State of Family Balance Sheets." Washington, D.C.: Pew Charitable Trust.

———. 2015b. "The Role of Emergency Savings in Family Financial Security." Washington, D.C.: Pew Charitable Trust.

Pfeffer, Fabian T. 2011. "Status Attainment and Wealth in the United States and Germany." In *Persistence, Privilege, and Parenting*, edited by Timothy M. Smeeding, Robert Erikson, and

Markus Jäntti. New York: Russell Sage Foundation.

———. 2016. "Growing Wealth Gaps in Education." *National Poverty Center* working paper no. 16-06.

Pfeffer, Fabian T., Sheldon H. Danziger, and Robert F. Schoeni. 2013. "Wealth Disparities Before and After the Great Recession." *Annals of the American Academy of Political and Social Science* 650(1): 98–123.

———. 2014. "Wealth Levels, Wealth Inequality, and the Great Recession." Recession Brief. New York: Russell Sage Foundation. Accessed May 10, 2016. http://www.russellsage.org/blog/wealth-levels-wealth-inequality-and-great-recession.

Pfeffer, Fabian T., and Martin Hällsten. 2012. "Mobility Regimes and Parental Wealth: The United States, Germany, and Sweden in Comparison." *Population Studies Center* research report no. 12-766. Ann Arbor: University of Michigan.

Pfeffer, Fabian T., and Alexandra Killewald. Forthcoming. "Intergenerational Correlations in Wealth." *Economic Mobility: Research and Ideas on Strengthening Families, Communities, and the Economy*. St. Louis. Mo.: Federal Reserve Bank of St. Louis.

Pfeffer, Fabian T., Robert F. Schoeni, Arthur Kennickell, and Patricia Andreski. 2016. "Measuring Wealth and Wealth Inequality: Comparing Two U.S. Surveys." *Journal of Economic and Social Measurement* 41(2): 103–20.

Piketty, Thomas. 2014. *Capital in the Twenty-First Century*. Cambridge, Mass.: Belknap Press of Harvard University Press.

Posner, Richard. 2013. "Does Redistributing Income from Rich to Poor Increase or Reduce Economic Growth or Welfare?" *The Becker-Posner Blog*, December 29, 2013. Accessed May 10, 2016. http://www.becker-posner-blog.com/2013/12/does-redistributing-income-from-rich-to-poor-increase-or-reduce-economic-growth-or-welfare-posner.html.

Putnam, Robert D. 2015. *Our Kids: The American Dream in Crisis*. New York: Simon & Schuster.

Quiggin, John. 2016. "Would a Significant Increase in the Top Income Tax Rate Substantially Alter Income Inequality?" *Crooked Timber*, October 5, 2015. Accessed May 10, 2016. http://crookedtimber.org/2015/10/05/would-a-significant-increase-in-the-top-income-tax-rate-substantially-alter-income-inequality/.

Rauscher, Emily. 2016. "Passing It On: Parent-to-Adult Child Financial Transfers for School and Socioeconomic Attainment." *RSF: The Russell Sage Foundation Journal of the Social Sciences* 2(6). doi: 10.7758/RSF.2016.2.6.09.

Reeves, Richard. 2015. "The Measure of a Nation." *The Annals of the American Academy of Political and Social Science* 657(1): 22–26.

Roemer, John. 1998. *Equality of Opportunity*. Cambridge, Mass.: Harvard University Press.

Rosen, Sherwin. 1981. "The Economics of Superstars." *American Economic Review* 71(5): 845–58.

Rostron, Brian L., John L. Boies, and Elizabeth Arias. 2010. "Education Reporting and Classification on Death Certificates in the United States." *Vital and Health Statistics* 2(151): 1–14.

Saez, Emmanuel, and Gabriel Zucman. 2014. "Wealth Inequality in the United States Since 1913. Evidence from Capitalized Income Tax Data." *NBER* working paper no. 20625. Cambridge, Mass.: National Bureau of Economic Research.

Schoeni, Robert F., and Karen E. Ross. 2005. "Material Assistance from Families During the Transition to Adulthood." In *On the Frontier of Adulthood*, edited by Richard A. Settersten and Frank F. Furstenberg. Chicago: University of Chicago Press.

Schwartz, Herman Mark. 2016. "Wealth and Stagnation: The Role of Industrial Organization and Intellectual Property Rights." *RSF: The Russell Sage Foundation Journal of the Social Sciences* 2(6). doi: 10.7758/RSF.2016.2.6.11.

Shanks Williams, Trina 2014. "The Promise of Child Development Accounts: Current Evidence and Future Directions." *Community Investments* 26(2): 12–15.

Shapiro, Thomas M. 2004. *The Hidden Cost of Being African American: How Wealth Perpetuates Inequality*. Oxford: Oxford University Press.

Shapiro, Thomas M., Tatjana Meschede, and Laura Sullivan. 2010. "The Racial Wealth Gap Increases Fourfold." *IASP* Research and Policy Brief. Waltham, Mass.: Brandeis University.

Sherraden, Michael W. 1991. *Assets and the Poor: A New American Welfare Policy*. Armonk, N.Y.: M. E. Sharpe.

Stiglitz, Joseph E. 2012. *The Price of Inequality: How Today's Divided Society Endangers Our Future*. New York: W. W. Norton.

Survey of Consumer Finances. 2013. Public use dataset distributed by the Board of Governors of the Federal Research System (downloaded 2015).

Sykes, Bryan L., and Michelle Maroto. 2016. "A Wealth of Inequalities: Mass Incarceration, Employment, and Racial Disparities in U.S. Household Wealth, 1996 to 2011." *RSF: The Russell Sage Foundation Journal of the Social Sciences* 2(6). doi: 10.7758/RSF.2016.2.6.07.

Thompson, Jason, and Dalton Conley. 2016. "Health Shocks and Social Drift: Examining the Relationship Between Acute Illness and Family Wealth." *RSF: The Russell Sage Foundation Journal of the Social Sciences* 2(6). doi: 10.7758/RSF.2016.2.6.08.

Thompson, Jeffrey P., and Gustavo A. Suarez. 2015. "Exploring the Racial Wealth Gap Using the Survey of Consumer Finances." *Finance and Economics Discussion Series* no. 2015-76. Washington: Board of Governors of the Federal Reserve System.

Tumin, Melvin M. 1953. "Some Principles of Stratification: A Critical Analysis." *American Sociological Review* 18(4): 387–94.

Wolff, Edward N. 1995. *Top Heavy: A Study of the Increasing Inequality of Wealth in America*. New York: Twentieth Century Fund Press.

———. 2016. "Household Wealth Trends in the United States, 1962 to 2013: What Happened over the Great Recession?" *RSF: The Russell Sage Foundation Journal of the Social Sciences* 2(6). doi: 10.7758/RSF.2016.2.6.02.

Zucman, Gabriel. 2015. *The Hidden Wealth of Nations*. Chicago: University of Chicago Press.

PART II
Economic Dimensions of Wealth Inequality

Household Wealth Trends in the United States, 1962 to 2013: What Happened over the Great Recession?

EDWARD N. WOLFF

I look at wealth trends from 1962 to 2013, particularly for the middle class. Asset prices plunged between 2007 and 2010 but then rebounded from 2010 to 2013. The most telling finding is that median wealth plummeted by 44 percent between 2007 and 2010, almost double the drop in housing prices. Wealth inequality, after almost two decades of little movement, was up sharply from 2007 to 2010. This sharp fall in median net worth and rise in overall wealth inequality are traceable primarily to the high leverage of middle-class families, the high share of homes in their portfolio, and the plunge in house prices. Rather remarkably, median (and mean) wealth did not essentially change from 2010 to 2013 despite the rebound in asset prices. The proximate cause was the high dissavings of the middle class. Wealth inequality also remained largely unchanged.

Keywords: household wealth, inequality, portfolio composition

The paper considers household wealth trends over a half century, from 1962 to 2013. Particular attention is given to the years of the Great Recession, from 2007 to 2013, and to how the middle class fared in terms of wealth over these six years. The first three saw one of the sharpest contractions in stock and real estate prices, and the second three saw a recovery in asset prices. The debt of the middle class exploded from 1983 to 2007, making it quite fragile. Did its position deteriorate even more over years 2007 to 2013?

This paper addresses four issues: What happened to median household wealth over time, particularly from 2007 to 2013? Did the inequality of household wealth rise over time, particularly over the Great Recession? Did the debt of the middle class increase over time? What are the trends in home ownership and home equity and what happened, in particular, from 2007 to 2013? The full period covered is from 1962 to 2013. By 2013, we will be able to see the fallout from the financial crisis and associated recession.

A key focus of the paper is to highlight the role of leverage (the ratio of debt to net worth) in explaining movements in household wealth over the Great Recession. It will be seen that the collapse in median wealth between 2007 and 2010 was largely due to the high leverage of the middle class (as well as the steep drop in house prices). Moreover, the sharp jump in

---

Edward N. Wolff is professor of economics at New York University, research associate at the National Bureau of Economic Research, and editorial board member of the *Journal of Economic Inequality* and the *Review of Income and Wealth*.

I would like to express my appreciation to the Institute of New Economic Thinking (INET) for financial support. Direct correspondence to: Edward N. Wolff at ew1@nyu.edu, Department of Economics, New York University, 19 West 4th Street, New York, NY 10012.

wealth inequality over these years can be traced to differential leverage between the rich and the middle class.

Previous work, using the Survey of Consumer Finances (SCF), presented evidence of sharply increasing household wealth inequality between 1983 and 1989 followed by little change between 1989 and 2007 (see Wolff 1994, 1998, 2002, 2011). Both mean and median wealth holdings climbed briskly from 1983 to 2007. However, most of the wealth gains from 1983 to 2007 were concentrated among the richest 20 percent of households. Moreover, despite the buoyant economy over the 1990s and 2000s, overall indebtedness rose among American families, particularly those in the middle class.

In this study, I look at wealth trends from 1962 to 2013. Asset prices plunged between 2007 and 2010 but then rebounded from 2010 to 2013. The most telling finding is that median wealth plummeted by 44 percent between 2007 and 2010, almost double the drop in housing prices, and by 2010 was at its lowest since 1969. The inequality of net worth, after almost two decades of little movement, was up sharply from 2007 to 2010. Relative indebtedness expanded from 2007 to 2010, particularly for the middle class, though the proximate causes were declining net worth and income. In fact, the average debt of the middle class fell by 25 percent in real terms. The sharp fall in median net worth and the rise in overall wealth inequality from 2007 to 2010 are traceable primarily to the high leverage of middle-class families and the high share of homes in their portfolio. Rather remarkably, median wealth essentially did not change from 2010 to 2013 despite the rebound in asset prices. The proximate cause was the high dissavings of the middle class. Relative indebtedness fell for the middle class as outstanding debt continued to drop.

HISTORICAL BACKGROUND

The last two decades witnessed some remarkable events. Perhaps most notable is the housing value cycle, which first led to an explosion in home prices and then to a collapse, affecting net worth and helping to precipitate the Great Recession, followed by a modest recovery. The median house price was virtually the same in 2001 as in 1989 in real terms (U.S. Census Bureau 2008, table 935; National Association of Realtors 2012).[1] However, according to SCF data, the home ownership rate shot up from 62.8 to 67.7 percent. Then, 2001 saw a recession, albeit a short one. Despite this, house prices took off, the median sales price of existing single-family homes spurting by 17 percent. From 2004 to 2007, housing prices slowed, the median price advancing only 1.7 percent. Between 2001 and 2007, housing prices gained 19 percent. The home ownership rate continued to expand, though at a somewhat abbreviated rate, to 68.6 percent.

Then came the Great Recession and the associated financial crisis. The recession officially began in December 2007 and officially ended in June 2009 (NBER 2010). Over this period, real gross national product (GDP) fell by 4.3 percent. Between the second quarter of 2009 and the second quarter of 2013, it gained 9.2 percent. The unemployment rate shot up from 4.4 percent in May of 2007 to a peak of 10.0 percent in October 2009 but by February 2014 was down to 6.7 percent (BLS 2016).

One consequence was that asset prices plummeted. From 2007 to 2010, in particular, the median home price nosedived by 24 percent, and the share of households owning their own home fell off, from 68.6 to 67.2 percent. This was followed by a partial recovery, median house prices rising 7.8 percent through September 2013, though still considerably below their 2007 value. However, the homeownership rate continued to contract, falling to 65.1 percent.

In contrast to the housing market, the stock market boomed during the 1990s. On the basis of the Standard & Poor (S&P) 500 index, stock prices surged 159 percent between 1989 and 2001 (Council of Economic Advisers 2013, table B-96; Dow Jones 2013). Stock ownership spread

---

1. Figures are based on median prices of existing houses for metropolitan areas only. All figures are in constant dollars unless otherwise indicated.

and by 2001 more than half of U.S. households owned stock either directly or indirectly. However, between 2001 and 2007, the S&P 500 was up 6 percent, and the share of households who owned stock, whether directly or indirectly, fell to 49 percent. Then stock prices crashed by 26 percent from 2007 to 2010, and the stock ownership rate declined to 47 percent. The stock market rose after 2010, and by 2013 the S&P 500 index was up 39 percent over 2010 and above its previous high in 2007. However, the stock ownership rate continued to drop, to 46 percent.

What have all these major changes in asset prices wrought in terms of household wealth, particularly over the Great Recession? This is the subject of the remainder of the paper.

DATA SOURCES AND METHODS

My primary data source is the SCF, conducted by the Federal Reserve Board. Each survey consists of a core representative sample combined with a high-income supplement. The wealth (net worth) concept used here is marketable wealth, defined as the current value of all marketable or fungible assets less current debt. Assets are the sum of eight items: housing; other real estate; bank deposits, certificates of deposit, money market accounts, and the cash surrender value of life insurance plans (collectively, *liquid assets*); financial securities; defined contribution pension plans, including individual retirement accounts (IRAs), Keogh, and 401(k) plans; corporate stock and mutual funds; unincorporated businesses equity; and trust fund equity. Liabilities are the sum of three: mortgage debt, consumer debt (such as auto loans), and other debt (such as student loans).

This measure reflects wealth as a store of value and therefore a source of potential consumption. I believe that this is the concept that best reflects the level of well-being associated with a family's holdings. Thus, only assets that can be readily converted to cash (that is, fungible ones) are included. As a result, consumer durables such as automobiles are excluded here because such items are not easily marketed. Another justification for their exclusion is that this treatment is consistent with the national accounts, in which purchase of vehicles is counted as expenditures, not savings. Also excluded is the value of future Social Security benefits the family may receive on retirement (Social Security wealth), as well as the value of retirement benefits from defined benefit private pension plans (defined benefit pension wealth). Even though these funds are a source of future income to families, they are not in their direct control and cannot be marketed (for a discussion of retirement wealth, see Devlin-Foltz, this volume).

Two other data sources are used in the study. The first of these is the 1962 Survey of Financial Characteristics of Consumers (SFCC). This survey was also conducted by the Federal Reserve Board of Washington and is a precursor to the SCF. The second is the so-called 1969 MESP database, a synthetic dataset constructed from income tax returns and information provided in the 1970 Census. A statistical matching technique was employed to assign income tax returns for 1969 to households in the 1970 Census. Property income flows (such as dividends) in the tax data were then capitalized into corresponding asset values (such as stocks) to obtain estimates of household wealth (for detail, see Wolff 1980).[2]

MEDIAN WEALTH PLUMMETS OVER THE GREAT RECESSION

Table 1 documents a robust growth in wealth from 1983 to 2007, even back to 1962 (see also

---

2. The 1962 SFCC, the 1969 MESP, and the 1983 and 1989 SCF files are aligned to national balance sheet totals to provide consistency in the household wealth estimates for these years, because they each use somewhat different sampling frames and methodologies. (The methodology for the 1983 SCF differs to some extent from that for the 1989 SCF, while the same methodology is used for SCF files for 1989 and onward). My baseline estimates also exclude vehicles. Moreover, my calculations are based on the public-use samples provided by the Federal Reserve Board, which are to some degree different from the internal files it maintains. As a result, my figures on mean and median net worth, as well as on wealth inequality, will in general vary from the standard estimates provided by the Federal Reserve Board, which include the value of vehicles (see, for example, Kennickell and Woodburn 1999), and from those of Fabian Pfeffer and Robert Schoeni (this volume).

Table 1. Mean and Median Wealth and Income

	1962	1969	1983	1989	2001	2007	2010	2013
Variable								
Net worth								
1. Median	55.5	68.0	78.0	83.5	96.7	115.1	64.6	63.8
2. Mean	207.4	248.4	303.8	348.1	500.0	602.3	505.7	508.7
3. Percent with zero or negative net worth	18.2	15.6	15.5	17.9	17.6	18.6	21.8	21.8
Income (CPS)[a]								
1. Median	40.9	53.3	46.4	52.4	55.6	56.4	52.6	51.9
2. Mean	46.4	60.6	56.5	66.2	76.6	76.0	72.0	72.6
Addendum: net worth standardized by the 2001 age distribution								
1. Median	—	—	89.5	91.7	96.7	106.3	54.5	52.5
2. Mean	—	—	322.5	361.5	500.0	573.3	462.6	462.0

	Annual Growth Rates (Percent)							Percentage Change	
	1962–1983	1983–1989	1989–2001	2001–2007	2007–2010	2010–2013	1962–2013	2007–2010	2010–2013
Annual growth rates (percent)									
Net worth									
1. Median	1.63	1.13	1.22	2.91	-19.27	-0.39	0.28	-43.9	-1.2
2. Mean	1.82	2.27	3.02	3.10	-5.83	0.20	1.76	-16.0	0.6
Income (CPS)[a]									
1. Median	0.61	2.03	0.48	0.26	-2.32	-0.45	0.47	-6.7	-1.3
2. Mean	0.93	2.66	1.21	-0.14	-1.78	0.29	0.88	-5.2	0.9
Addendum: net worth standardized by the 2001 age distribution									
1. Median	—	0.41	0.44	1.59	-22.26	-1.30	—	-48.7	-3.8
2. Mean	—	1.91	2.70	2.28	-7.16	-0.04	—	-19.3	-0.1

Source: Authors' computations from the 1983, 1989, 2001, 2007, 2010, and 2013 SCF.
Note: Figures in thousands of 2013 dollars. Additional sources are the 1962 Survey of Financial Characteristics of Consumers (SFCC) and the 1969 MESP file (Wolff 1980). Wealth figures are deflated using the Consumer Price Index (CPI-U). The 1962 figures are based on family income and the rate of change of family income between 1962 and 1969.
[a]Source for household income data: U.S. Census of the Bureau, Current Populations Surveys, available at: http://www.census.gov/hhes/www/income/data/historical/household/.

figure 1). Median wealth increased at an annual rate of 1.6 percent from 1962 to 1983, then slower at 1.1 percent from 1983 to 1989, about the same at 1.2 percent from 1989 to 2001, and then much faster at 2.9 percent from 2001 to 2007.[3] Then, between 2007 and 2010, median wealth plunged by a staggering 44 percent. Indeed, median wealth was actually lower in 2010 than in 1969 (in real terms). The primary reasons, as we shall see, were the collapse in the

---

3. Unless otherwise indicated, all dollar figures are in 2013 dollars.

Figure 1. Mean and Median Net Worth (in Thousands, 2013 Dollars)

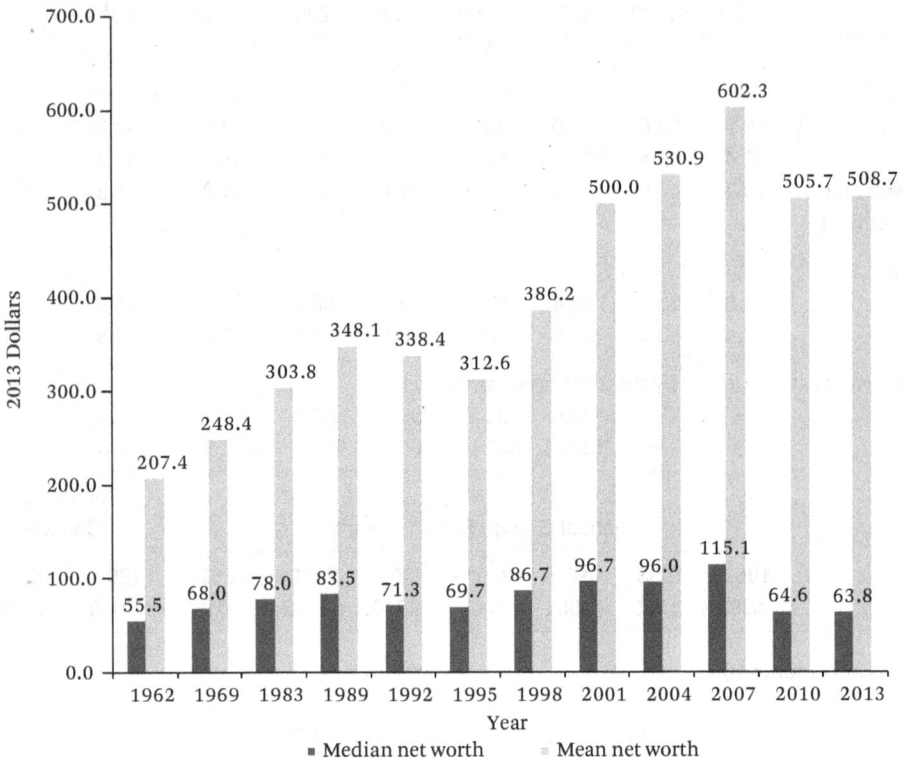

Source: Author's calculations based on the 1962 SFCC, the 1968 MESP (Wolff 1980), and the 1983, 1989, 1992, 1995, 1998, 2001, 2004, 2007, 2010, and 2013 SCF.

housing market and the high leverage of middle class families. There was virtually no change from 2010 to 2013.[4] The share of households with zero or negative net worth, after falling from 18.2 percent in 1962 to 15.5 percent in 1983, increased to 18.6 percent in 2007 and then even more sharply to 21.8 percent in 2010, where it remained in 2013 (see table 1, top panel).

Mean net worth also grew vigorously from 1962 to 1983, at an annual rate of 1.82 percent, a little higher than that of median wealth. Its growth accelerated to 2.27 percent per year from 1983 to 1989, about double the growth rate of median wealth. From 1989 to 2001, the growth rate of mean wealth was 3.02 percent per year, even higher than in the preceding periods. Its annual growth rate accelerated even more, reaching 3.10 percent between 2001 and 2007. This acceleration was due largely to the rapid (19 percent) increase in housing prices over the six years, counterbalanced by a reduced growth in stock prices in comparison with the 1989 to 2001 span, and to the fact that housing made up 28 percent and (total) stocks 25 percent of total assets in 2001. Overall, its 2007 value was almost double its value in 1983 and about three-quarters larger than in 1989. Mean wealth also grew about twice as fast as the median between 1983 and 2007, indicating widening inequality of wealth over these years.

The Great Recession saw an absolute decline in mean household wealth. However, whereas median wealth plunged by 44 percent between 2007 and 2010, mean wealth fell by

---

4. The percentage decline in median net worth from 2007 to 2010 is lower when vehicles are included in the measure of wealth—"only" 39 percent. The reason is that automobiles are a substantial share of middle-class assets. However, median net worth with vehicles remained virtually unchanged from 2010 to 2013.

Figure 2. Mean and Median Household Income (in Thousands, 2013 Dollars)

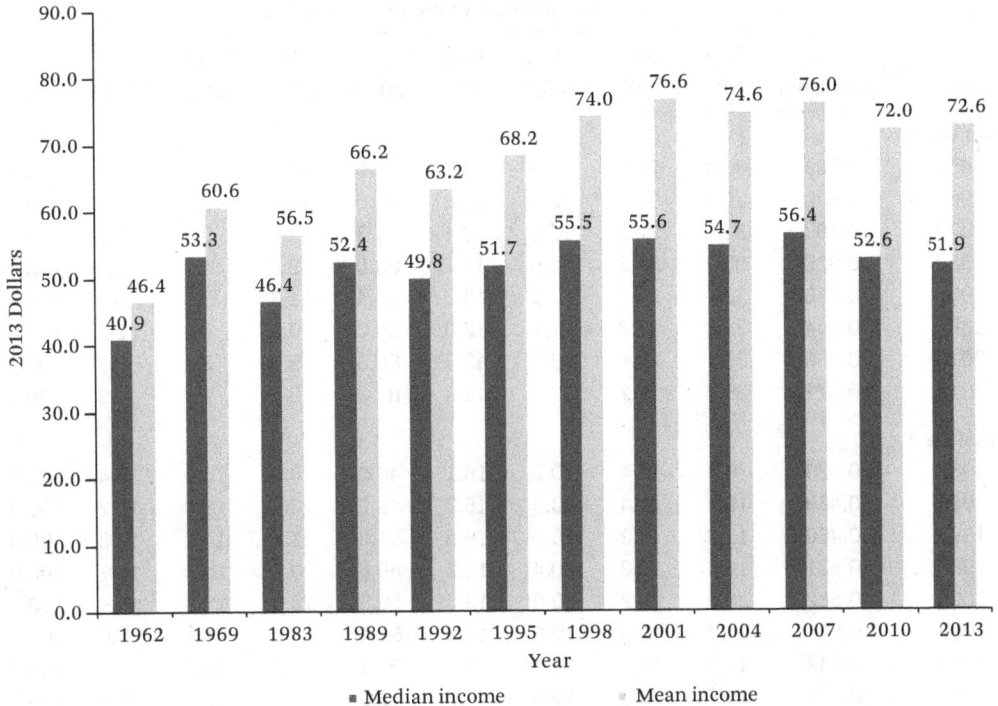

■ Median income   • Mean income

Source: Author's calculations based on the 1962 SFCC, the 1968 MESP (Wolff 1980), and the 1983, 1989, 1992, 1995, 1998, 2001, 2004, 2007, 2010, and 2013 SCF.

(only) 16 percent.[5] In this case, the main cause was both falling housing and stock prices. However, here, too, the relatively faster growth in mean wealth than median wealth (that is, the latter's more moderate decline) was coincident with rising wealth inequality. Again, mean wealth essentially did not change from 2010 to 2013.

Median household income (based on Current Population Survey data) advanced at a fairly solid pace from 1962 to 1983, at 0.61 percent per year (also see figure 2). Then, after gaining 2.03 percent per annum between 1983 and 1989, its annual growth dipped to only 0.48 percent from 1989 to 2001 and then to 0.26 percent from 2001 to 2007, for a net change of 22 percent (overall) from 1983 to 2007. However, from 2007 to 2010, it fell off in absolute terms by 6.7 percent. Although this change is not insignificant, the reduction was not nearly as great as that in median wealth. From 2010 to 2013, median income slipped by another 1.3 percent (overall). Mean income also dropped in real terms from 2007 to 2010, by 5.2 percent, slightly less than that of median income, but gained 0.9 percent from 2010 to 2013.

What role does the shift in age distribution play in accounting for trends in household wealth? One method to answer this question is to standardize the age distribution for a selected year—say, 2001, because it is near the midpoint of the period. I use five-year age intervals and reweight net worth in each year by the corresponding 2001 share of households in each age interval. Results are shown in the addenda to table 1. Not surprisingly, given that the population is aging between 1983 and 2013, reweighting will increase median and mean net worth before 2001 and decrease them after 2001 because older households have greater wealth. However, because the age distribution shifts only slowly over time, the effects should

---

5. The decline in mean net worth is 16 percent when vehicles are included in net worth.

Table 2. Distribution of Wealth and Income

		Percentage Share of Wealth or Income								
Year	Gini Coefficient	Top 1.0%	Next 4.0%	Next 5.0%	Next 10.0%	Top 20.0%	4th 20.0%	3rd 20.0%	Bottom 40.0%	All
Net worth										
1962	0.803	33.4	21.2	12.4	14.0	81.0	13.4	5.4	0.2	100.0
1969	0.828	35.6	20.7	12.5	13.8	82.5	12.2	5.0	0.3	100.0
1983	0.799	33.8	22.3	12.1	13.1	81.3	12.6	5.2	0.9	100.0
1989	0.828	35.2	22.8	11.9	13.2	83.0	12.0	4.7	0.2	100.0
2001	0.826	33.4	25.8	12.3	12.9	84.4	11.3	3.9	0.3	100.0
2007	0.834	34.6	27.3	11.2	12.0	85.0	10.9	4.0	0.2	100.0
2010	0.866	35.1	27.4	13.8	12.3	88.6	9.5	2.7	-0.8	100.0
2013	0.871	36.7	28.2	12.2	11.8	88.9	9.3	2.7	-0.9	100.0
Income										
1962	0.428	8.4	11.4	10.2	16.1	46.0	24.0	16.6	13.4	100.0
1969	0.469	10.4	12.4	10.3	15.9	48.9	23.4	16.4	11.2	100.0
1982	0.480	12.8	13.3	10.3	15.5	51.9	21.6	14.2	12.3	100.0
1988	0.521	16.6	13.3	10.4	15.2	55.6	20.6	13.2	10.7	100.0
2000	0.562	20.0	15.2	10.0	13.5	58.6	19.0	12.3	10.1	100.0
2006	0.574	21.3	15.9	9.9	14.3	61.4	17.8	11.1	9.6	100.0
2009	0.549	17.2	16.5	10.7	14.7	59.1	18.7	14.9	7.3	100.0
2013	0.574	19.8	16.5	10.8	14.7	61.8	17.8	11.1	9.4	100.0

Addendum: Gini coefficients for net worth standardized by the 2001 age distribution

	1983	1989	2001	2007	2010	2013
Gini	0.789	0.824	0.826	0.837	0.874	0.879

Source: Author's computations from the 1983, 1989, 2001, 2007, 2010, and 2013 SCF.
Note: Additional sources are the 1962 SFCC and the 1969 MESP (Wolff 1980) file. Income data are from these files. For the computation of percentile shares of net worth, households are ranked according to their net worth; and for percentile shares of income, households are ranked according to their income.

be relatively small. The results show precisely this. The reweighted results still indicate fairly robust growth in wealth from 1983 to 2007, a substantial collapse from 2007 to 2010, and little change from 2010 to 2013.

In sum, although household income virtually stagnated for the average American household from 1989 to 2007, median net worth grew strongly. The Great Recession, on the other hand, saw a massive reduction in median net worth but more modest declines in mean wealth and both median and mean income.

WEALTH INEQUALITY JUMPS IN THE LATE 2000S

Wealth is highly concentrated, the richest 1 percent owning 37 percent of total household wealth in 2013 and the top 20 percent owning 89 percent (see table 2). The figures in table 2 also show that wealth inequality in 1983 was quite close to its level in 1962 (also see figure 3).[6] It then climbed sharply between 1983 and 1989, the share of wealth held by the top 1 percent rising by 3.6 percentage points and the Gini coefficient increasing from 0.80 to 0.83.

6. This is not to say that wealth inequality did not change over these years. Indeed, on the basis of estate tax data, wealth inequality dropped sharply from about 1969 to 1976 and then rose just as sharply from 1976 to 1983 (Wolff 2002). Emmanuel Saez and Gabriel Zucman (2015) find a similar trajectory from 1963 to 1983 on the basis of their income capitalization method. They report that the wealth share of the top percentile declined

Figure 3. Wealth and Income Inequality (Gini Coefficients)

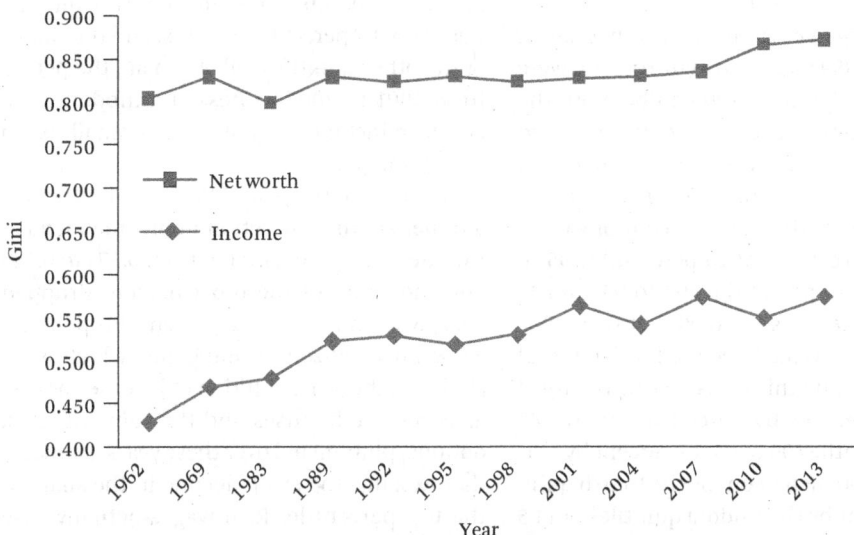

Source: Author's calculations based on the 1962 SFCC, the 1968 MESP (Wolff 1980), and the 1983, 1989, 1992, 1995, 1998, 2001, 2004, 2007, 2010, and 2013 SCP.

Between 1989 and 2007, the share of the top percentile actually declined, from 37.4 to 34.6 percent, though this was more than compensated by an increase in the share of the next four percentiles. As a result, the share of the top 5 percent increased from 58.9 percent in 1989 to 61.8 percent in 2007, and the share of the top quintile from 83.5 to 85.0 percent. The share of the fourth and middle quintiles each declined by about a percentage point from 1989 to 2007, while that of the bottom 40 percent increased by almost one percentage point. Overall, the Gini coefficient was virtually unchanged—0.832 in 1989 and 0.834 in 2007.

In contrast, the period from 2007 to 2010 saw a sharp elevation in wealth inequality, the Gini coefficient rising from 0.834 to 0.866. Interestingly, the share of the top percentile showed a smaller relative gain—less than 1 percentage point. Most of the rise in wealth share took place in the remainder of the top quintile, and overall the share of wealth held by the top quintile climbed by almost 4 percentage points. The shares of the other quintiles correspondingly dropped, that of the bottom 40 percent falling from 0.2 to −0.9 percent.

The period between 2010 and 2013 saw a very small rise in the Gini coefficient, from 0.866 to 0.871. The share of the top 1 percent did increase by 1.6 percentage points, but that of the top quintile did not. In constant dollar terms, the net worth of the top 1 percent grew by 5.9 percent over those years but that of the next 19 percent dropped by 1.8 percent. The wealth of the fourth quintile also lost 1.7 percent, that of the middle quintile lost 0.7 percent, and that of the bottom two quintiles 5.7 percent.

Standardizing the population weights on the basis of the 2001 age distribution makes only a minor difference in estimated Gini coefficients—one Gini point or less. Standardization does lower estimated Gini coefficients before 2001 because it gives lower weights to younger, poorer households and, conversely,

---

from 29 percent in 1983 to 23 percent in 1976 and then rebounded somewhat to 25 percent in 1983. However, although the Saez and Zucman data do show a net decline in wealth concentration from 1963 to 1983, my data show a similar level in the two years. It is likely that the discrepancy in results is attributable to a different trend in the concentration of capital income than in the concentration of nonfinancial assets, like business equity, over these years. However, the two series show similar time trends from 1983 onward.

raises them after 2001 because it gives greater weights to the younger households.

The two large spurts in wealth inequality, from 1983 to 1989 and from 2007 to 2010, were not limited to the increased gap between the top 1 percent and everyone else but occurred across the full wealth distribution. Between 1983 and 1989, 43 percent of the gain in mean wealth accrued to the top 1 percent of wealth holders, 25 percent went to percentiles 95 to 99, 10 percent to percentiles 90 to 95, and 13 percent to percentiles 80 to 90. Between 2007 and 2010, mean wealth declined. Of the total loss in wealth, one-third was lost by the top 1 percent, 26 percent by percentiles 95 to 99, none by percentiles 90 to 95, 10 percent by percentiles 80 to 90, 18 percent by the fourth quintiles, 10 percent by the middle quintiles, and 5 percent by the bottom two quintiles.

The top 1 percent of families (as ranked by income on the basis of SCF data) earned 20 percent of total household income in 2012 and the top 20 percent accounted for 62 percent—large figures but lower than the corresponding wealth shares.[7] The time trend for income inequality also contrasts with that for net worth (see also figure 3). Income inequality showed a sharp rise from 1961 to 1982, the Gini coefficient expanding from 0.43 to 0.48 and the share of the top 1 percent from 8.4 to 12.8 percent. Income inequality increased sharply again between 1982 and 1988, the Gini coefficient rising to 0.52 and the share of the top 1 percent to 16.6 percent. In both periods, capital gains played an important role in explaining the gains of the top 1 percent.

Inequality again surged from 1988 to 2000: the share of the top percentile rising by 3.4 percentage points, of the top quintile up by 3.0 percentage points, of the other quintiles falling again, and the Gini index advancing from 0.52 to 0.56. Once again, strong capital gains resulting from rising stock prices played a key role. As a result, the years from 1989 to 2001 saw almost the same increase in income inequality as the 1983 to 1989 period. Inequality once again rose from 2001 to 2007, though the pace slackened, as the stock market softened. The Gini coefficient increased from 0.562 to 0.574,

the share of the top 1 percent was up by 1.3 percentage points, the share of the top quintile was up by 1.7 percentage points, and the shares of the other quintiles fell. All in all, the period from 2001 to 2007 witnessed a moderate increase in income inequality and a small rise in wealth inequality.

In contrast, the years 2007 to 2010 witnessed a rather sharp contraction in income inequality. The Gini coefficient fell from 0.574 to 0.549 and the share of the top 1 percent dropped sharply from 21.3 to 17.2 percent. Property income and realized capital gains (which is included in the SCF definition of income), as well as corporate bonuses and the value of stock options, plummeted over these years, a process that explains the steep decline in the share of the top percentile. Real wages actually rose over these years, though the unemployment rate also increased. As a result, the income of the middle class was down but not nearly as much in percentage terms as that of the high-income groups. In contrast, transfer income such as unemployment insurance rose, so that the bottom also did better in relative terms than the top. As a result, overall income inequality fell between 2006 and 2009.

The second half of the Great Recession saw a reversal in this trend, income inequality once again increasing sharply. The Gini coefficient increased by 0.025 points to 0.574, the same level as in 2007. The share of the top percentile rose to 19.8 percent, slightly below its level in 2007; the share of the top quintile was up to 61.8 percent, slightly above its 2007 level. The same set of factors, though in reverse, help explain this turnaround in income inequality. Property income, realized capital gains, and associated income rose sharply over these years as the stock market recovered, accounting for the sharp rise in the share of the top percentile. The unemployment rate fell over these years but, according to BLS figures, real wages were down. As a result, the income of the middle class rose but not as much in percentage terms as that of the high-income groups. Transfer income such as unemployment insurance fell, as the extensions of benefits enacted in the early days of the recession ended.

---

7. The income in each survey year (say, 2013) is for the preceding year (2012, in this case).

Table 3. Composition of Total Household Wealth

Wealth component	1983	1989	2001	2007	2010	2013
Principal residence	30.1	30.2	28.2	32.8	30.7	28.5
Other real estate	14.9	14.0	9.8	11.3	11.6	10.2
Unincorporated business equity	18.8	17.2	17.2	20.1	17.7	18.3
Liquid assets[a]	17.4	17.5	8.8	6.6	7.7	7.6
Pension accounts[b]	1.5	2.9	12.3	12.1	15.1	16.5
Financial securities[c]	4.2	3.4	2.3	1.5	1.8	1.5
Corporate stock and mutual funds	9.0	6.9	14.8	11.8	11.2	12.7
Net equity in personal trusts	2.6	3.1	4.8	2.3	2.4	3.2
Miscellaneous assets[d]	1.3	4.9	1.8	1.7	1.7	1.5
Total	100.0	100.0	100.0	100.0	100.0	100.0
Debt on principal residence	6.3	8.6	9.4	11.4	12.7	11.2
All other debt[e]	6.8	6.4	3.1	3.9	4.4	4.0
Total debt	13.1	15.0	12.5	15.3	17.1	15.2
Selected ratios in percent						
Debt to equity ratio	15.1	17.6	14.3	18.1	20.6	17.9
Debt to income ratio	68.4	87.6	81.1	118.7	127.0	107.1
Net home equity to total assets	23.8	21.6	18.8	21.4	18.1	17.3
Principal residence debt as ratio to house value	20.9	28.6	33.4	34.9	41.2	39.3
Stocks, directly or indirectly owned as a ratio to total assets[f]	11.3	10.2	24.5	16.8	17.5	20.7

Source: Author's computations from the 1983, 1989, 2001, 2007, 2010, and 2013 SCF.
Note: Percentage of gross assets.
[a]Checking accounts, savings accounts, time deposits, money market funds, certificates of deposits, and the cash surrender value of life insurance.
[b]IRAs, Keogh plans, 401(k) plans, the accumulated value of defined contribution pension plans, and other retirement accounts.
[c]Corporate bonds, government bonds (including savings bonds), open-market paper, and notes.
[d]Gold and other precious metals, royalties, jewelry, antiques, furs, loans to friends and relatives, future contracts, and miscellaneous assets.
[e]Mortgage debt on all real property except principal residence; credit card, installment, and other debt.
[f]Includes direct ownership of stock shares and indirect ownership through mutual funds, trusts, and IRAs, Keogh plans, 401(k) plans, and other retirement accounts.

All in all, income inequality increased much more than either net worth or nonhome wealth inequality between 1983 and 2013. On the basis of the Gini coefficient, net worth inequality was up by 9 percent and income inequality by 20 percent.

As a result, one of the issues we have to contend with is that net worth inequality rose sharply from 2007 to 2010 and income inequality fell, at least according to the SCF. A second is the reverse, namely, that wealth inequality remained virtually unchanged from 2010 to 2013 and income inequality increased. I return to these questions in the following section.

HOUSEHOLD DEBT FINALLY RECEDES

In 2013, owner-occupied housing was the most important household asset in the average portfolio breakdown for all households shown in table 3, accounting for 29 percent of total assets. However, net home equity—the value of the house minus outstanding mortgages—amounted to only 17 percent of total assets. Real estate, other than owner-occupied housing, made up 10 percent, and business equity another 18 percent. Liquid assets made up 8 percent and pension accounts 17 percent. Bonds and other financial securities made up 2 percent; corporate stock, including mutual funds, 13 percent; and trust fund equity 3 percent. Debt as a proportion of gross assets was 15 percent, and the ratio of total household debt to net worth was 0.18.

Some changes in the composition of household wealth over time were notable. First, the share of housing wealth in total assets, after fluctuating between 28 and 30 percent from 1983 to 2001, jumped to 34 percent in 2004 and then declined to 29 percent in 2013. Two factors explain this movement. The first is that the homeownership rate rose from 63 percent in 1983 to 69 percent in 2004 and then fell off to 65 percent in 2013. The second is that the median price of existing single-family homes climbed 18 percent between 2001 and 2004 but plunged 17 percent from 2004 to 2013.[8] A second and related trend is that net home equity fell from 24 percent in 1983 to 17 percent in 2013. The difference between the two series (gross versus net home values) is attributable to the changing magnitude of mortgage debt on homeowner's property, which increased from 21 percent in 1983 to 39 percent in 2013.

Third, relative indebtedness first increased, the debt to net worth ratio climbing from 15 percent in 1983 to 21 percent in 2010, and falling off to 18 percent in 2013. Likewise, the debt to income ratio surged from 68 percent in 1983 to 127 percent in 2010 but then dropped to 107 percent in 2013. If mortgage debt on principal residence is excluded, then the ratio of other debt to total assets actually fell off over time from 6.8 percent in 1983 to 4.0 percent in 2013.

The large rise in relative indebtedness among all households between 2007 and 2010 could be due to a rise in the absolute level of debt or a fall off in net worth and income, or both. As shown in table 1, both mean net worth and mean income fell over the three years. Debt also contracted slightly in constant dollars by 4.4 percent. The steep rise in relative indebtedness over the three years was almost entirely due to reductions in wealth and income. In contrast, from 2010 to 2013, relative indebtedness declined. In this case, both net worth and incomes were relatively unchanged, so that the proximate cause was a sizable reduction in household debt by 13 percent.

A fourth change is that pension accounts rose from 1.5 to 16.5 percent of total assets from 1983 to 2013. This increase largely offset the decline in the share of liquid assets in total assets, from 17.4 to 7.6 percent, so that it is reasonable to infer that households to a large extent substituted tax-deferred pension accounts for taxable savings deposits. Fifth, if we include the value of stocks indirectly owned through mutual funds, trusts, IRAs, 401(k) plans, and other retirement accounts, then the value of total stocks owned as a share of total assets more than doubled from 11.3 percent in 1983 to 24.5 percent in 2001 but then fell to 20.7 percent in 2013. The rise during the 1990s reflected the robust stock market as well as increased stock ownership, and the decline in the 2000s was due to a sluggish stock market as well as a drop in stock ownership.

Portfolio Composition by Wealth Class

The tabulation in table 3 provides a picture of the average holdings of all families in the economy, but class differences in how middle-class families and the rich invest their wealth are marked. As shown in table 4, the richest percentile invested almost three-quarters of their savings in investment real estate, businesses, corporate stock, and financial securities in 2013. Corporate stocks directly or indirectly owned made up 25 percent. Housing, liquid assets, and pension accounts together made up 24 percent. Their ratio of debt to net worth was only 3 percent and their ratio of debt to income was 38 percent.

Among the next richest 19 percent, housing was 28 percent of total assets, liquid assets 8 percent, and pension assets another 22 percent. Investment assets—real estate, business equity, stocks, and bonds—made up 41 percent; 23 percent was in the form of stocks directly or indirectly owned. Debt amounted to

---

8. It may seem surprising that the share of housing in gross assets declined very little between 2007 and 2010, given the steep drop in housing prices, but the prices of other assets also fell, particularly those of stocks and business equity.

Table 4. Composition of Household Wealth by Wealth Class, 2013

Asset	All Households	Top 1 Percent	Next 19 Percent	Middle 3 Quintiles
Principal residence	28.5	8.7	28.0	62.5
Liquid assets (bank deposits, money market funds, and cash surrender value of life insurance)	7.6	6.1	8.4	8.1
Pension accounts	16.5	9.2	21.7	16.1
Corporate stock, financial securities, mutual funds, and personal trusts	17.4	27.3	16.3	3.4
Unincorporated business equity and other real estate	28.5	46.9	24.2	8.6
Miscellaneous assets	1.5	1.9	1.4	1.2
Total assets	100.0	100.0	100.0	100.0
Memo (selected ratios in percent)				
Debt to equity ratio	17.9	2.6	11.8	64.0
Debt to income ratio	107.1	38.2	96.6	125.0
Net home equity to total assets[a]	17.3	7.3	19.7	31.4
Principal residence debt to house value	39.3	16.5	29.5	49.8
All stocks to total assets[b]	20.7	24.6	22.7	9.5
Ownership rates (percent)				
Principal residence	65.1	96.9	95.1	66.7
Other real estate	17.4	75.5	44.0	12.4
Pension assets	49.2	88.7	84.0	44.4
Unincorporated business	10.4	76.6	25.6	6.6
Corporate stock, financial securities, mutual funds, and personal trusts	21.5	84.4	59.5	14.2
Stocks, directly or indirectly owned[b]	46.1	94.0	84.6	41.0
(1) $5,000 or more	36.4	92.9	81.7	30.3
(2) $10,000 or more	32.4	92.8	79.7	25.3

Source: Author's computations from the 2013 SCF.
Note: Percentage of gross assets. Households are classified into wealth class according to their net worth. Brackets for 2013 are as follows. Top 1 percent: Net worth of $7,766,500 or more. Next 19 percent: Net worth between $401,000 and $7,766,500. Quintiles 2 through 4: Net worth between $0 and $401,000. See also notes to table 3.
[a]Ratio of gross value of principal residence less mortgage debt on principal residence to total assets.
[b]Includes direct ownership of stock shares and indirect ownership through mutual funds, trusts, and IRAs, Keogh plans, 401(k) plans, and other retirement accounts.

12 percent of net worth and 97 percent of income.

In contrast, more than three-fifths of the assets of the middle three quintiles of households was invested in their own home in 2013. However, home equity amounted to only 31 percent of total assets, a reflection of their large mortgage debt. Another quarter went into monetary savings of one form or another and pension accounts. Together housing, liquid assets, and pension assets accounted for 87 percent of the total assets of the middle class. The remainder was about evenly split among non-home real estate, business equity, and various financial securities and corporate stock. Stocks directly or indirectly owned amounted to only

10 percent of their total assets. The ratio of debt to net worth was 64 percent, substantially higher than for the richest 20 percent, and the ratio of debt to income was 125 percent, also much higher than that of the top quintile. Finally, their mortgage debt amounted to about half the value of their principal residences.

Almost all households among the top 20 percent of wealth holders owned their own home, but only 67 percent of households in the middle three quintiles did. Three-quarters of very rich households (in the top percentile) owned some other form of real estate, versus 44 percent of rich households (those in the next 19 percent of the distribution) and only 12 percent of households in the middle 60 percent. Eighty-nine percent of the very rich owned some form of pension asset, versus 84 percent of the rich and 44 percent of the middle. A somewhat startling 77 percent of the very rich reported owning their own business. The comparable figures are 26 percent among the rich and 7 percent of the middle class.

Among the very rich, 84 percent held corporate stock, mutual funds, financial securities or a trust fund, in contrast to 60 percent of the rich and only 14 percent of the middle class. Ninety-four percent of the very rich reported owning stock either directly or indirectly, versus 85 percent of the rich and 41 percent of the middle. If we exclude small holdings of stock, then the ownership rates drop off sharply among the middle three quintiles, from 41 percent to 30 percent for stocks worth $5,000 or more and to 25 percent for stocks worth $10,000 or more.

Table 5 presents trends in the wealth composition of the middle three wealth quintiles as well as asset ownership rates. Perhaps the most striking development is in the homeownership rate, which, after rising almost continuously from 72 percent in 1983 to 78 percent in 2004, dropped to 67 percent in 2013. This trend was more pronounced than that among all households, for which it dropped from 69 percent in 2004 to 65 percent in 2013. A similar trend is evident for the share of homes in total assets. It remained virtually unchanged from 1983 to 2001 but rose sharply in 2004. This increase was largely a result of rising house prices and secondarily a consequence of continued gains in homeownership. The share then declined from 2004 through 2013 as housing prices fell and homeownership plummeted.

It might once again seem surprising that despite the steep drop in home prices from 2007 to 2010, housing as a share of total assets actually fell only slightly. The reason is that the other components of wealth fell even more than housing. Although the mean value of housing among households in the middle three quintiles fell by 31 percent in real terms, the mean value of other real estate was down by 39 percent and that of stocks and mutual funds by 47 percent.

Likewise, despite the modest recovery in housing prices from 2010 to 2013, the share of housing in total assets dropped by 2.3 percentage points. The mean value of housing fell by 7.3 percent. Of this, the decline in the homeownership rate accounted for only 19 percent of the overall decline; the main culprit was the drop in house prices, which explained 81 percent. This result seems contrary to the finding that the median value of existing homes rose by 8 percent, according to data from the National Association of Realtors (2012). The most likely reason for the difference in results is that the 8 percent figure is based on data for existing homes only, whereas the SCF data includes the value of homes that were owned by the household prior to the current year as well as newly bought homes. Another difference is that the former include all families, whereas my figure is based on households in the middle three wealth quintiles. In fact, according to the SCF data, the median value of homes among middle-class households was down by 14 percent in real terms from 2010 to 2013. This result, in turn, may reflect the possibility that new homes bought by families in the SCF sample were cheaper than existing ones.

The share of pension accounts in total assets rose by 15 percentage points from 1983 to 2013, and that of liquid assets declined by 13 percentage points. These trends were more or less continuous over time. This set of changes paralleled that of all households. In contrast, the share of middle-class households holding a pension account, after surging from 12 percent in 1983 to 53 percent in 2007, collapsed to

Table 5. Household Wealth of the Middle Three Wealth Quintiles

Asset	1983	1989	1998	2001	2004	2007	2010	2013
Principal residence	61.6	61.7	59.8	59.2	66.1	65.1	64.8	62.5
Liquid assets (bank deposits, money market funds, and cash surrender value of life insurance)	21.4	18.6	11.8	12.1	8.5	7.8	8.0	8.1
Pension accounts	1.2	3.8	12.3	12.7	12.0	12.9	13.9	16.1
Corporate stock, financial securities, mutual funds, and personal trusts	3.1	3.5	5.5	6.2	4.2	3.6	3.1	3.4
Unincorporated business equity and other real estate	11.4	9.4	8.8	8.5	7.9	9.3	8.9	8.6
Miscellaneous assets	1.3	2.9	1.8	1.2	1.4	1.3	1.3	1.2
Total assets	100.0	100.0	100.0	100.0	100.0	100.0	100.0	100.0
Memo (selected ratios in percent)								
Debt to equity ratio	37.4	41.7	51.3	46.4	61.6	61.1	69.2	64.0
Debt to income ratio	66.9	83.0	101.6	100.3	141.2	156.7	134.3	125.0
Net home equity to total assets[a]	43.8	39.2	33.3	33.8	34.7	34.8	31.4	31.4
Principal residence debt to house value	28.8	36.5	44.4	42.9	47.6	46.6	51.5	49.8
All stocks to total assets[b]	2.4	3.3	11.2	12.6	7.5	7.0	8.1	9.5
Ownership rates (percent)								
Principal residence	71.6	71.5	73.3	75.9	78.2	76.9	68.0	66.7
Other real estate	15.4	15.5	13.7	13.2	13.6	14.7	12.4	12.4
Pension assets	12.2	27.3	48.5	52.9	51.4	53.4	45.8	44.4
Unincorporated business	8.5	8.4	8.5	7.9	8.1	8.8	8.2	6.6
Corporate stock, financial securities, mutual funds, and personal trusts	21.6	24.2	26.7	27.5	27.1	23.1	15.3	14.2
All stocks[b]	16.5	29.4	46.6	51.1	49.7	47.8	41.4	41.0
Mean debt (thousands, 2013$)								
Debt on principal residence	23.5	34.2	33.2	49.7	71.4	76.1	58.5	52.4
All other debt	12.5	10.5	9.2	12.2	15.1	19.2	13.1	13.3
Total debt	36.0	44.7	42.4	61.9	86.5	95.2	71.6	65.7

Source: Author's computations from the 1983, 1989, 1998, 2001, 2004, 2007, 2010, and 2013 SCF.
Note: Percentage of gross assets. Households are classified into wealth class according to their net worth. See also notes to table 3.
[a] Ratio of gross value of principal residence less mortgage debt on principal residence to total assets.
[b] Includes direct ownership of stock shares and indirect ownership through mutual funds, trusts, and IRAs, Keogh plans, 401(k) plans, and other retirement accounts.

44 percent in 2013. From 2007 to 2010, the mean value of pension accounts fell quite sharply, by 25 percent, though this was less than that of average overall assets, so that the share of pension accounts in total assets rose. From 2010 to 2013, in contrast, mean pension accounts were up by 12 percent, despite the slight decline in the ownership rate, so that the share of pension accounts in total assets strengthened considerably (by 2.2 percentage points).

The stock ownership rate among the middle

class shot up from 17 percent in 1983 to 51 percent in 2001, when it peaked, and then dropped to 41 percent in 2013. The share of all stocks in total assets mushroomed from 2.4 percent in 1983 to 12.6 percent in 2001 and then fell off to 9.5 percent in 2013, reflecting trends in stock prices and the stock ownership rate. Likewise, the proportion of these households owning corporate stock, financial securities, mutual funds, or personal trusts rose from 22 percent in 1983 to 28 percent in 2001 and then collapsed almost by half to 14 percent in 2013. Much of the decline took place between 2007 and 2010 as middle-class households were scared off by the stock market collapse in that period.

Middle-Class Debt
The rather staggering debt level of the middle class in 2013 raises the question of whether this phenomenon is recent or has been going on for some time. The debt to income ratio peaked in 2010 and then receded in 2013; meanwhile, the debt to net worth ratio peaked in 2007 and then contracted substantially in 2010 and a bit more in 2013.

The debt to net worth ratio of the middle class rose sharply from 37 percent in 1983 to 61 percent in 2007. The debt to income ratio skyrocketed as well, more than doubling. In constant dollar terms, the mean debt of the middle class shot up by a factor of 2.6 between 1983 and 2007, the mean mortgage debt by a factor of 3.2, and the average value of other debt by a factor of 1.5. The rise in the debt to net worth ratio and the debt to income ratio was much steeper than those for all households. In 1983, for example, the debt to income ratio was about the same for the middle class as for all households but by 2007 was much larger.

Then the Great Recession hit. The debt to net worth ratio continued to rise, reaching 72 percent in 2010, but the debt to income ratio fell to 134 percent in 2010. The reason is that from 2007 to 2010, the mean debt of the middle class actually contracted by 25 percent in constant dollars. Average mortgage debt declined by 23 percent as families paid down their outstanding balances, and the mean value of other debt plummeted by 32 percent as families paid off credit card balances and other consumer debt. The significant rise in the debt to net worth ratio of the middle class between 2007 and 2010 was due to the steeper drop off in net worth than in debt, and the decline in the debt to income ratio almost exclusively to the sharp contraction of overall debt.

Both the debt to net worth and the debt to income ratios fell from 2010 to 2013. The proximate cause was a decline in overall mean debt, which fell by 8.2 percent in real terms over these years. This, in turn, was due to a decline in average mortgage debt, which dropped by 10.4 percent. The average balance on other debt actually increased slightly, by 1.6 percent.

As for all households, net home equity as a percentage of total assets fell for the middle class from 1983 to 2013 and mortgage debt as a proportion of house value rose. The decline in the former between 2007 and 2010 was relatively small despite the steep decrease in home prices, a reflection of the sharp reduction in mortgage debt. There was virtually no change from 2010 to 2013. On the other hand, the rise in the ratio of mortgage debt to house values was relatively large from 2007 to 2010 because of the falloff in home prices. This ratio actually contracted somewhat from 2010 to 2013 as outstanding mortgage debt fell.

THE ROLE OF LEVERAGE IN EXPLAINING WEALTH TRENDS
In 2002, regression analysis indicated that wealth inequality was positively and significantly related to income inequality and to the ratio of stock prices to housing prices, given that stocks are heavily concentrated among the rich and homes are the chief asset of the middle class (Wolff 2002). This presents six puzzles, two of which have been addressed. The first is why median wealth surged from 2001 to 2007 and median income was sluggish. The second is why wealth inequality was flat over these years when income inequality grew. The third is why median wealth plunged steeply, by 44 percent, between 2007 and 2010, despite a moderate drop in median income and smaller declines in housing and stock prices, of 24 and 26 percent in real terms, respectively.

The fourth is why wealth inequality increased so steeply, by 0.035 Gini points, from 2010 to 2013, given that income inequality actually fell and the ratio of stocks to housing

Table 6. Average Annual Real Rates of Return by Period and Wealth Class

	1983–1989	1989–2001	2001–2007	2007–2010	2010–2013	1983–2013
Gross assets (percentage)						
1. All households	2.33	3.33	3.10	−6.38	4.83	2.27
2. Top 1 percent	3.07	3.92	3.75	−6.37	5.91	2.88
3. Next 19 percent	2.33	3.44	2.88	−6.07	4.78	2.29
4. Middle three quintiles	1.35	2.32	2.71	−7.07	3.28	1.36
Net worth (percentage)						
1. All households	3.32	4.35	4.04	−7.28	6.20	3.10
2. Top 1 percent	3.45	4.19	3.92	−6.52	6.16	3.11
3. Next 19 percent	3.00	4.09	3.46	−6.63	5.66	2.83
4. Middle three quintiles	3.35	4.67	5.58	−10.55	6.94	3.30
Memo: difference between top 1% and middle quintiles						
	−0.10	0.48	1.67	−4.04	0.79	0.18

Source: Author's computations from the 1983, 1989, 2001, 2007, 2010, and 2013 SCF.
Note: Households are classified into wealth class according to their net worth. Calculations are based on household portfolios averaged over the period. Miscellaneous assets are excluded from the calculation.

prices remained virtually unchanged. The fifth and perhaps most perplexing question is why median (and mean) wealth failed to recover between 2010 and 2013, when asset prices surged. The sixth is why wealth inequality increased so moderately from 2010 to 2013 when income inequality shot up and the ratio of stock to house prices climbed by 29 percent.

Most of these puzzles can be largely explained by the high leverage (that is, debt to net worth ratio) of the middle class. This is particularly the case for the strong gains in median net worth from 2001 to 2007 and its steep fall from 2007 to 2010. Trends in wealth inequality are largely accountable by differential leverage between the rich and the middle class. This factor helps explain the constancy of wealth inequality over the 2001 to 2007 and the 2010 to 2013 periods and its spike between 2007 and 2010. In regard to median net worth's showing no improvement between 2010 and 2013, a different explanation is called for. It appears that substantial dissavings over this period accounts for the failure of wealth to grow.

Table 6 presents the average annual real rates of return for both gross assets and net worth from 1983 to 2013. Results are based on the average portfolio composition over the period and assume that all households receive the same rate of return by asset type. The average annual rate of return on gross assets among all households rose from 2.33 percent between 1983 and 1989 to 3.33 percent between 1989 and 2001 and then fell slightly to 3.10 percent between 2001 and 2007 before plummeting to −6.38 percent during the Great Recession. This was followed by a substantial recovery to 4.83 percent from 2010 to 2013.

The average annual return on net worth among all households also increased from 3.32 percent in the first period to 4.35 percent in the second, declined somewhat to 4.04 percent in the third, and then fell off sharply to −7.28 percent between 2007 and 2010. Once again, recovery was strong, to 6.20 percent, between 2010 and 2013. Annual rates of return on net worth are uniformly higher—by about 1 percentage point—than those on gross assets over the first three periods and the last period, when asset prices were generally rising. However, between 2007 and 2010, the annual return on net worth was about 1 percentage point lower than that on gross assets. These results illustrate the effect of leverage, raising the return when asset prices rise and lowering the return when asset prices fall. Over the full 1983 to 2013 period, the annual return on net worth was 0.83 percentage points higher than that on gross assets.

Rates of return by wealth class reveal some striking differences. The highest rates of return on gross assets were generally registered by the top 1 percent of wealth holders, followed by the next 19 percent and then the middle three wealth quintiles. Differences are substantial. Over the full period, the average return on gross assets for the top 1 percent was 0.59 percentage points greater than that of the next 19 percent and 1.52 percentage points greater than that of the middle quintiles. The differences reflect the greater share of high-yield investments, such as stocks, in the portfolios of the rich and the greater share of housing in the portfolio of the middle class (see table 4). Indeed, between 2010 and 2013, the difference in returns between the top 1 percent and the middle group was huge, 2.63 percentage points, reflecting the much higher gains on stocks and investment assets than on housing in those years.

This pattern is almost exactly reversed when we look at rates of return for net worth. In this case, in the first three periods and the last when asset prices were generally rising, the highest return was recorded by the middle three wealth quintiles. Meanwhile, between 2007 and 2010, when asset prices were declining, the middle three quintiles registered the lowest (that is, most negative) rate of return. The exception was the first period, when the top 1 percent had a slightly higher return than the middle class. The reason was the substantial spread in returns on gross assets between the top 1 percent and the middle group—1.72 percentage points.

Differences in returns between the top 1 percent and the middle three quintiles were substantial in some years. From 2001 to 2007, the average annual rate of return on net worth was 5.58 percent for the latter and 3.92 percent for the former—a difference of 1.67 percentage points. The spread was less from 2010 to 2013, only 0.79 points. The smaller difference was due to the much higher returns on gross assets held by the top percentile than by the middle group. On the other hand, from 2007 to 2010, when asset prices declined, the rate of return on net worth was −6.52 percent for the top 1 percent and −10.55 percent for the middle three quintiles—a differential of 4.04 percentage points in favor of the top 1 percent.

The spread in rates of return between the top 1 percent and the middle three quintiles reflects the much higher leverage of the middle class. In 2013, for example, the debt to net worth ratio of the middle three quintiles was 0.64 and that of the top 1 percent was 0.026.

The huge negative return on net worth of the middle group was largely responsible for the precipitous drop in median net worth between 2007 and 2010. This factor, in turn, was due to the steep drop in housing prices and their very high leverage. The very high return on net worth of the middle group between 2001 and 2007 played a significant role in explaining the robust advance of median net worth despite sluggish gains in median income. This in turn was a result of their high leverage coupled with the boom in housing prices. However, that the rate of return on net worth of the middle group was very high between 2010 and 2013—in fact, the highest of any period—and yet median wealth stagnated is puzzling. We return to this issue later.

The substantial differential in rates of return on net worth between the middle three wealth quintiles and the top helps explain why wealth inequality rose sharply between 2007 and 2010 despite the decline in income inequality. Likewise, this differential between 2001 and 2007 (a spread of 1.67 percentage points in favor of the middle quintiles) helps account for the stasis in wealth inequality despite the increase in income inequality. The higher rate of return of the middle than the top group from 2010 to 2013 also helps account for the relative constancy in wealth inequality despite the rise in income inequality

CONCLUDING REMARKS

The paper highlights the role of leverage in explaining trends in household wealth over the Great Recession. In particular, it shows that the collapse in median wealth between 2007 and 2010 was largely due to the high leverage of the middle class, as well as the steep drop in housing prices. Moreover, the sharp jump in wealth inequality over these years was traced to differential leverage between the rich and the middle class.

After a period of robust growth, median wealth continued to climb by 19 percent from 2001 to 2007, even faster than during the 1990s and 1980s. Then the Great Recession hit, and from 2007 to 2010 house prices fell by 24 percent in real terms, stock prices by 26 percent, and median wealth by a staggering 44 percent. From 2010 to 2013, asset prices recovered, stock prices up by 39 percent and house prices by 8 percent. Despite this, median wealth stagnated.

Wealth inequality, after remaining relatively stable from 1989 to 2007, showed a steep advance between 2007 and 2010, the Gini coefficient climbing from 0.834 to 0.866 and the share of the top 20 percent from 85 to 89 percent, even though house prices and stock prices collapsed at about the same rate. The Gini coefficient for net worth, on the other hand, remained relatively unchanged between 2010 and 2013 despite the fact that stock prices recovered much more than real estate.

Another notable development was the sharply rising debt to income ratio during the early and middle 2000s, reaching its highest level in almost twenty-five years—119 percent among all households in 2007. The debt to net worth ratio was also way up, from 14.3 percent in 2001 to 18.1 percent in 2007. Most of the rising debt was from increased mortgages on homes: From 2007 to 2010, both ratios continued to rise, the former moderately, from 119 to 127 percent, and the latter more steeply, from 18.1 to 20.6 percent. This was true despite a moderate retrenchment of overall average debt of 4.4 percent and reflected the drop in both mean wealth and income. Both ratios fell off sharply by 2013, to 107 percent and 17.9 percent, respectively, as outstanding debt continued to shrink, by 13 percent. Home values as a share of total assets among all households remained relatively unchanged from 1983 to 2013 (around 30 percent). However, net home equity fell from 24 to 17 percent of total assets, reflecting rising mortgage debt, which grew from 21 to 39 percent.

Among the middle three wealth quintiles, the increase in the debt to income ratio was huge, from 100 to 157 percent from 2001 to 2007, as was that in the debt to net worth ratio, from 46 to 61 percent. The debt to net worth ratio was also much higher among the middle group in 2007, at 0.61, than among the top 1 percent, at 0.028. From 2007 to 2010, although the debt to net worth ratio continued to advance, to 69 percent, the debt to income ratio actually fell off, to 134 percent. The reason is the substantial retrenchment of average debt among the middle class over these years: overall debt fell by 25 percent in real terms. That the debt to net worth ratio rose over these years reflected the steep drop in median net worth. Both ratios dropped from 2010 to 2013 as outstanding debt fell by 8 percent.

The key to understanding the plight of the middle class during the Great Recession was their high degree of leverage, the high concentration of assets in their home, and the plunge in housing prices. The steep decline in median net worth between 2007 and 2010 was primarily due to the very high negative rate of return on net worth of the middle three wealth quintiles (−10.6 percent per year). This, in turn, was tied to the precipitous fall in home prices and their very high degree of leverage. High leverage, moreover, helps explain why median wealth fell more than house (and stock) prices over these years and declined much more than median income.

This, however, is not the full story. On the basis of the rates of return computed for the middle three wealth quintiles, median wealth should have fallen by only 27 percent, instead of the actual 44 percent. If we ignore net flows of inheritances and gifts over the period, the discrepancy must be due to dissavings.[9] Indeed, the results imply a substantial dissaving rate over this period, of 5.6 percent per year relative to initial wealth.

That median net worth showed no improvement between 2010 and 2013 calls for a different explanation—namely, dissavings. Asset prices more than recovered from 2010 to 2013, except for housing, which was still up by 8 percent (in real terms). On the basis of rates of

---

9. Net inheritance flows for middle-class households are quite small on an annual basis (Wolff 2015).

return computed for the middle group, median net worth should have gained 36 percent. It appears that substantial dissavings over this period accounts for wealth stagnation. In particular, the middle class must have had an annual dissavings rate of 8.1 percent relative to initial wealth.

The stagnation of median wealth from 2010 to 2013 can be traced to the depletion of assets. This shows up, in particular, in reduced asset ownership rates—from 68.0 percent to 66.7 percent for homes, from 45.8 percent to 44.4 percent for pension accounts, from 8.2 percent to 6.6 percent for businesses, and from 15.3 percent to 14.2 percent for stocks and financial securities.

The likely reason for the high rate of dissavings of the middle class from both 2007 to 2010 and 2010 to 2013 is income stagnation (actually, a reduction in median income) over these years. It appears that the middle class was depleting its assets to maintain its previous level of consumption. The evidence, moreover, suggests that middle-class households, experiencing stagnating incomes, expanded their debt (at least until 2007) mainly to finance normal consumption expenditures rather than to increase their investment portfolio.

The large spread in rates of return on net worth between the middle and the top (more than 4 percentage points) also largely explains why wealth inequality advanced steeply from 2007 to 2010 despite the decline in income inequality and constancy in the ratio of stock to housing prices. (Both declined at about the same rate over these years.) Thus the middle class took a bigger relative hit on their net worth from the decline in home prices than the top 20 percent did from the stock market plunge. This factor is also reflected in the larger percentage drop in median wealth than in mean income. In contrast, change in wealth inequality from 2010 to 2013 was relatively scant. This is true despite a large increase in income inequality and a sharp rise of 29 percent in the ratio of stock to housing prices. The offsetting factor in this case was the higher rate of return on net worth of the middle class than the top 1 percent, a 0.79 percentage point difference.

REFERENCES

Bureau of Labor Statistics (BLS). 2016. "Labor Force Statistics from the Current Population Survey." Washington: U.S. Department of Labor. Accessed May 13, 2016. http://data.bls.gov/timeseries/LNS14000000.

Council of Economic Advisers. 2013. *2013 Economic Report of the President*. Washington: Government Printing Office. Accessed May 13, 2016. https://www.whitehouse.gov/sites/default/files/docs/erp2013/full_2013_economic_report_of_the_president.pdf.

Devlin-Foltz, Sebastian, Alice Henriques, and John Sabelhaus. 2016. "Is the U.S. Retirement System Contributing to Rising Wealth Inequality." *RSF: The Russell Sage Foundation Journal of the Social Sciences* 2(6). doi: 10.7758/RSF.2016.2.6.04.

Dow Jones. 2013. "S&P Composite 1500." Accessed May 13, 2016. http://us.spindices.com/indices/equity/sp-composite-1500.

Kennickell, Arthur B., and R. Louise Woodburn. 1999. "Consistent Weight Design for the 1989, 1992, and 1995 SCFs, and the Distribution of Wealth." *Review of Income and Wealth* Series 45(2)(June): 193–216.

National Association of Realtors. 2012. "Median Sales Price of Existing Single-Family Homes for Metropolitan Areas." Accessed May 13, 2016. http://www.realtor.org/sites/default/files/reports/2012/embargoes/2012-q1-metro-home-prices-49bc10b1efdc1b8cc3eb66dbcdad55f7/metro-home-prices-q1-single-family-2012-05-09.pdf.

National Bureau of Economic Research (NBER). 2010. "U.S. Business Cycle Expansions and Contractions." Cambridge, Mass.: NBER. Accessed May 13, 2016. http://www.nber.org/cycles/cyclesmain.html.

Pfeffer, Fabian T., and Robert F. Schoeni. 2016. "How Wealth Inequality Shapes Our Future." *RSF: The Russell Sage Foundation Journal of the Social Sciences* 2(6). doi: 10.7758/RSF.2016.2.6.01.

Saez, Emmanuel, and Gabriel Zucman. 2015. "Wealth Inequality in the United States since 1913: Evidence from Capitalized Income Tax Data," *Quarterly Journal of Economics* 128(4)(October): 1687–724.

Survey of Consumer Finances. Various years. Public use dataset distributed by the Board of Governors of the Federal Research System (downloaded 2015).

Survey of Financial Characteristics of Consumers. Various years. Public use dataset distributed by the Board of Governors of the Federal Research System (downloaded 2015).

U.S. Census Bureau. 2008. *Statistical Abstract of the United States: 2009*, 128th ed. Washington: Government Printing Office. Accessed May 13, 2016. https://www.census.gov/library/publications/2008/compendia/statab/128ed.html.

Wolff, Edward N. 1980. "Estimates of the 1969 Size Distribution of Household Wealth in the U.S from a Synthetic Data Base." In *Modeling the Distribution and Intergenerational Transmission of Wealth*, edited by James D. Smith. Chicago: Chicago University Press.

———. 1994. "Trends in Household Wealth in the United States, 1962-1983 and 1983-1989." *Review of Income and Wealth* 40(2)(June): 143-74.

———. 1998. "Recent Trends in the Size Distribution of Household Wealth." *Journal of Economic Perspectives* 12(3)(Summer): 131-50.

———. 2002. *Top Heavy: A Study of Increasing Inequality of Wealth in America*, updated and expanded edition. New York: The New Press.

———. 2011. "Recent Trends in Household Wealth in the U.S.: Rising Debt and the Middle Class Squeeze." In *Economics of Wealth in the 21st Century*, edited by Jason M. Gonzales. Hauppauge, N.Y.: Nova Science Publishers.

———. 2015. *Inheriting Wealth in America: Future Boom or Bust?* New York: Oxford University Press.

Inequality and Mobility Using Income, Consumption, and Wealth for the Same Individuals

JONATHAN FISHER, DAVID JOHNSON, JONATHAN P. LATNER, TIMOTHY SMEEDING, AND JEFFREY THOMPSON

Recent studies of economic inequality almost always separately examine income inequality, consumption inequality, and wealth inequality, and hence, these studies miss the important synergy between the three measures explicit in the life-cycle budget constraint. Using the Panel Study of Income Dynamics (PSID), we study inequality in three dimensions, focusing on the conjoint distributions of income, consumption, and wealth for the same individuals. We find that the trends in inequality in income, consumption, and wealth similarly increase between 1999 and 2013. We examine the pairwise distributions of our measures using the average propensity to consume and the wealth-income ratios. Using the longitudinal nature of the PSID, we follow people over this period and find mobility is similar using income, consumption, and wealth. We conclude that while all three types of inequality are rising, wealth increasingly acts as a buffer to cushion income changes, which could reduce mobility—both intra- and inter-generational mobility.

Keywords: inequality, mobility, income, consumption, wealth

Growing interest in economic inequality and mobility continues to dominate the headlines. In 2013, President Obama spoke about inequality and mobility, reiterating a theme from earlier speeches: "This increasing inequality is most pronounced in our country, and it challenges the very essence of who we are as a people." Similarly, the chair of the Federal Reserve System, Janet Yellen (2014), in a speech to the Boston Federal Reserve Bank, observed that both income and wealth inequality were rising in the United States and that such increases called into question American beliefs in equality of opportunity.[1] As for consumption, an-

Jonathan Fisher is research scholar at the Stanford Center on Poverty and Inequality at Stanford University. **David Johnson** is deputy director of PSID and research professor at the University of Michigan. **Jonathan P. Latner** is postdoctoral fellow at Bremen International Graduate School of Social Sciences. **Timothy Smeeding** is Lee Rainwater Distinguished Professor of Public Affairs and Economics at the University of Wisconsin. **Jeffrey Thompson** is principal economist at the Federal Reserve Board of Governors.

The views expressed in this research, including those related to statistical, methodological, technical, or operational issues, are solely those of the authors and do not necessarily reflect the official positions or policies of the Federal Reserve Board of Governors, Bremen International Graduate School of Social Sciences (BIGSSS), Stanford University, University of Michigan or the University of Wisconsin-Madison. The authors thank the Russell Sage Foundation and the Washington Center for Economic Growth for their support. All errors of commission and omission are the responsibility of the authors alone. Direct correspondence to: David Johnson at johnsods@umich.edu, 426 Thompson St., Room 3234, Ann Arbor, MI 48106; Jonathan Fisher at jdfisher@stanford.edu; Jonathan P. Latner at jonlatner@gmail.com; Timothy Smeeding at smeeding@lafollette.wisc.edu; and Jeffrey Thompson at Jeffrey.p.thompson@frb.gov.

1. Yellen remarked, "It is no secret that the past few decades of widening inequality can be summed up as significant income and wealth gains for those at the very top and stagnant living standards for the majority. I think

other measure of well-being and the preferred welfare measure for most economists, Bill Gates suggested that "It's not that we should ignore the wealth and income data. But consumption data may be even more important for understanding human welfare" (Gates 2014; Piketty 2015). Hence income, wealth, and consumption are all three important gauges of inequality in economic status and their effects on social and economic mobility.

Most research shows, and Yellen (2014) stresses, the increase in income and wealth inequality has been large. Emmanuel Saez and Gabriel Zucman (2014) and Edward Wolff (2014) find that income and wealth inequality are highly related. Thomas Piketty (2015) makes this point more dramatic by arguing that the increase in income inequality yields more wealth inequality, which in turn increases income inequality. Jonathan Fisher, David Johnson, and Timothy Smeeding (2015) find that consumption inequality is about 80 percent as large as disposable income inequality and that the rise in consumption inequality was two-thirds that of income inequality in the United States from 1984 to 2011.

Income, consumption, and wealth distributions inform our perceptions of inequality. Yet most research on inequality limit analysis to just one of these variables. Even the studies using more than one almost invariably do so one at a time.[2] The most influential studies on income inequality examine income alone (Piketty and Saez 2003; Congressional Budget Office 2011). Those studying consumption inequality compare the trends in consumption inequality and income inequality, but the focus is on the univariate distributions and not the conjoint distribution (Fisher, Johnson, and Smeeding 2015; Attanasio and Pistaferri 2014; Aguiar and Bils 2015). Similarly, wealth inequality is studied by itself or with income inequality, but the focus is on the univariate distributions (Saez and Zucman 2014; Wolff, this volume; Pfeffer and Schoeni, this issue). In contrast, the *Report by the Commission on the Measurement of Economic Performance and Social Progress* states that "the most pertinent measures of the distribution of material living standards are probably based on *jointly* considering the income, consumption, and wealth position of households or individuals.... Give more prominence to the distribution of income, consumption and wealth" (Stiglitz, Sen, and Fitoussi 2009, 33).[3]

Studying these measures separately misses the important synergy between the three measures explicit in the life-cycle budget constraint. An increase in income held by the top of the distribution means that consumption or wealth of the top also increases. The joint distribution between any two, and more importantly the conjoint distribution among all three, provides more information than any of the univariate distributions. The concern is whether the increases over time in all three are similar, or whether the rankings across countries are similar. Recent evidence shows that the levels of income, consumption, and wealth inequality are different, wealth inequality being greater than income, which is greater than consumption (see figure 1). One must also ask how inequality of income translates to consumption or wealth. Alternatively, if one increases and another remains constant—what does that mean about well-being or the effects of inequality on social mobility? Piketty suggests that increases in wealth inequality translate to increases in income inequality: "many shocks to the wealth trajectories of families can contribute to making the wealth distribution highly unequal (indeed, in every country

---

it is appropriate to ask whether this trend is compatible with values rooted in our nation's history, among them the high value Americans have traditionally placed on equality of opportunity" (2014).

2. One exception is the work of Markus Jäntti, Eva Sierminska, and Timothy Smeeding (2008), who model the joint distribution of income and wealth in a cross-national context.

3. Richard Blundell, in an address to the Royal Statistical Society, states the importance of all three measures: "One thing is for sure, the results of the research presented here provide a strong motivation for collecting consumption data, along with asset and earnings data, in new longitudinal household surveys and linked administrative register data" (2014, 316).

and time period for which we have data, wealth distribution *within each age group* is substantially more unequal than income distribution)" (2015, 50). Alternatively, Dirk Krueger and Fabrizio Perri (2006) show that the increased availability of financial markets could suggest that increases in income inequality do not lead to increases in consumption inequality.

Following Jonathan Fisher and his colleagues in their study of inequality in three dimensions (2015b), we focus here on the conjoint distributions of income, consumption, and wealth for the same individuals. We examine all three measures of inequality using the 1999–2013 Panel Study of Income Dynamics (PSID). The PSID allows for longitudinal analysis and intra- and inter-generational mobility issues not feasible with any other dataset.[4]

We compare the level and trend in inequality in income, consumption, and wealth (or net worth) in the Panel Study of Income Dynamics from 1999 to 2013, and find that, similar to other research, all three measures similarly increase during this period. We also examine the pairwise distributions of our measures using the average propensity to consume (APC) and the wealth-to-income ratios and evaluate how these have changed over time. We use the longitudinal aspect of the PSID to follow people over time and find that mobility is similar using income, consumption, and wealth. Future work will examine how the changes in income and consumption are affected by changes in wealth and calculate the marginal propensities to consume for various levels of wealth.

The results improve our understanding of inequality in the United States since 1999 by exploring the joint relationship between various measures of economic inequality. The results indicate that the correlation between the three measures is high, but not perfect. Therefore, the individuals at the top in any one measure are not necessarily at the top in another measure. Further, individuals at the top in one year do not necessarily stay in the top over many years. Despite stickiness at both the top and the bottom of individual measures, fluidity also exists, especially given that the ranking of one measure relates to the ranking of another. Therefore, the picture of inequality proposed here not only aligns with previous research, in that it is rising, but also improves the clarity by incorporating the relationship between various measures of economic well-being that constitute inequality.

DIFFERENCES IN THE MEASURES

The differences in income, consumption, and wealth across the income distribution provide insight into why it is necessary to look at income, consumption, and wealth together rather than individually. Previous research (see Fisher et al. 2015a) shows that the APC falls with income and is extremely high for the low-income households. Alternatively, wealth increases with income and yields extremely high wealth-to-income ratios at the highest percentiles. As a result, consumption inequality is less than income inequality, and income inequality is less than wealth inequality. This suggests that households at the bottom of the income distribution appear relatively better off using consumption as a measure of inequality at any point in time, because consumption exceeds income (and wealth) in the lower ends of the conjoint distributions.[5] High-income households are better off using wealth to measure relative well-being than either income or consumption because amassed wealth can be used for future consumption and for transfers across generations. Hence, our perception of relative well-being changes depending on whether we use consumption, income, or wealth.

Some have estimated the flow value of wealth

---

4. In other ongoing comparable work, we combine income and wealth in the SCF with consumption in the Consumer Expenditure (CE) Survey databases to pursue similar aims. Although the SCF does not follow individuals longitudinally, it does include a special sample of the top one percent of the income and wealth distributions, something missing from the PSID and all other household income or consumption databases. The SCF aggregates compare well with National income and Product Accounts, suggesting an important confluence of both macro and microeconomic accounts (Dettling et al. 2015).

5. Consumption is a better measure of permanent income (see Fisher et al. 2015); however, another method to obtain a measure of permanent income would be to use a five- to ten-year average income measure.

Figure 1. Gini Index for Income, Consumption, and Wealth

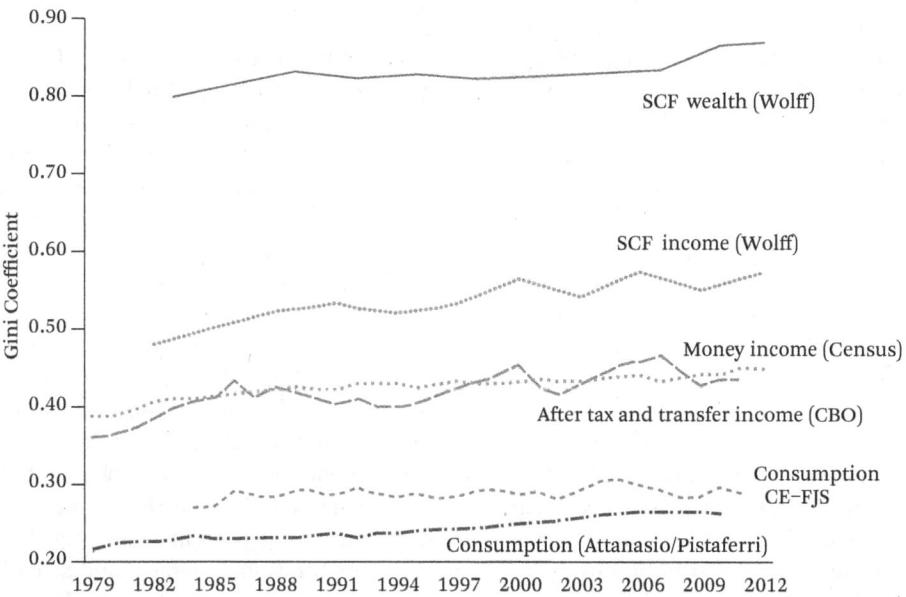

Source: Wolff (2014); Hardy et al. (2015); CBO (2011); Fisher, Johnson, and Smeeding (2015); and Attanasio and Pistaferri (2014).

to add to income in order to incorporate wealth into a measure of economic well-being (Burkhauser et al. 2009; Smeeding and Thompson 2011). But regardless of the flow values, the build-up of stocks of wealth presents opportunities and advantages (or in the case of debt, disadvantages) that may in the end be more important than any flows, as Piketty (2015) argues. In our data, wealth clearly accumulates over time and financial wealth is especially prevalent in the top strata of the wealth distribution. Wealth buildup takes place when large shares of national income go to top income families (top 3 to 5 percent) who have APCs of around 0.5 to 0.6. In these cases, high wealth and high income does not translate into consumption that is relatively as high. And so the question is what happens to unconsumed income, how does it accumulate and for what purposes, and how is economic well-being affected for such high-income and high-wealth households? None of the current analyses of inequality have fully captured the full effect of wealth on consumption and income by considering all three measures of well-being simultaneously for the same households. We know, however, that each gives a differing and important perspective on the distribution of economic well-being when considering the effects of inequality on say educational attainment of off-spring, intergenerational mobility, or even health.[6]

Figure 1 shows a variety of measures of inequality from 1979 through the most recent data available for each series—one measure of wealth inequality, three measures of income inequality and two measures of consumption inequality. As shown, all measures have increased in the past two or three decades. The money income measure is produced by the U.S. Census Bureau, and includes cash incomes received on a regular basis (exclusive of certain money receipts such as capital gains) and before payments for personal income taxes, but gross of cash income transfers such as social security. This is the most commonly referenced income measure, dating back to 1967 for households, with adjustments for household size. This measure suggests the income inequality Gini for the United States increased

---

6. Elsewhere in this volume, Thompson and Conley show how wealth inequality affects consumption and health.

from 0.39 in 1979 to 0.44 in 2007 and 0.46 in 2012.[7]

A second income measure shown in figure 1 is from the U.S. Congressional Budget Office, or CBO (2011). The CBO merges CPS household survey data with tax records and thus provides a more accurate picture of incomes at the very top of the distribution. According to this measure, the Gini for household income increased from 0.37 in 1979 to 0.49 in 2007. The CBO series with the more comprehensive income and an accurate top end suggests a steeper rise in inequality than does the census series. Because this CBO series suggests the importance of capital income and capital gains, it also makes the case for why changes in wealth are an important cause of growing inequality. The final income measure uses SCF income, which includes capital gains and oversamples the high end of the income distribution using an IRS list sample (see Wolff 2014). Given its more complete and more accurate coverage of the wealthy and high income (Dettling et al. 2015), the SCF income inequality measure is higher than the other measures, yet shows a similar rise in inequality. All three income Ginis increase over this period. If the purpose is to argue that inequality in the United States is or is not rising, all income measures regardless of source yield the same conclusion. If the question is by how much it is rising, that depends on the series used.

Figure 1 also shows two measures of consumption inequality using both the CE (Fisher, Johnson, and Smeeding 2015) and PSID (Attanasio and Pistaferri 2014). Both show an increase between 1985 and 2006, but consumption inequality fell (or remained flat) during the Great Recession, and has only started to increase again in the last few years. As with income and consumption, various researchers have examined inequality in wealth. Elsewhere in this issue, Wolff reports Gini coefficients for wealth using the SCF, which also increase during this period. Showing the changes in wealth held by the top 5 percent, Yellen also shows rising wealth inequality across the SCF years (2014).

In summary, all three measures of well-being matter, wealth inequality being higher than income inequality, which is higher than consumption inequality. Consumption and income inequality have diverged since 2007 (Fisher, Johnson, and Smeeding 2015), mainly because of the fall in house prices. Consumption from assets, especially housing, rose in the early 2000s and then fell sharply after the financial crisis (Cooper and Dynan 2013). The role of assets, debts, and changes in net worth are the key missing elements that connect income and consumption to produce a complete picture of economic inequality. The rise, fall, and change in wealth (net worth) over the past twenty-five years has been instrumental in financing consumption generally, and schooling, health care, entrepreneurship, and retirement especially.

DATA AND DEFINITIONS

Using a consistent theoretical framework to define these measures is critical. The most comprehensive concept of income and consumption is drawn from the suggestions of Robert Haig (1921) and Henry Simons (1938), where income represents the capacity to consume without drawing down net worth. Economists have used the equation that income (Y) equals consumption (C) plus the change in net worth (Δ) as the working definition of Haig-Simons income. No studies use this definition to the fullest extent because no household survey has the necessary variables to create a full measure of Haig-Simons income.[8] Our research goal is to have measures of disposable income, consumption, and net worth that are accurate and as closely linked as possible given the data limitations. Our measures of income and consumption do not completely characterize the Haig-Simons income measure. One particular item missing from both income and consump-

---

7. This series is adjusted to remove the break in series between 1992 and 1993 that is attributable to survey changes (see Atkinson, Piketty, and Saez 2011; Hardy et al. 2015).

8. Timothy Smeeding and Jeffrey Thompson (2011) discuss the Haig-Simons income measure and construct a "More Complete Income" measure that attempts to account for the realized and unrealized returns on asset income.

tion is government-provided in-kind health benefits, which would lead to lower levels of inequality (see Hardy et al. 2015).

To evaluate all three measures it is important to have one data set with all three measures. Most evaluations use different data sets to examine income inequality or wealth inequality, or consumption vs income inequality. As Jonathan Heathcote, Fabrizio Perri, and Giovani Violante write, "The conclusion we draw is that one should be very cautious when combining data on inequality in wages and earnings from the CPS or PSID, and data on inequality in net worth from the SCF" (2010, 41). Building on earlier results that use the SCF and impute consumption (Fisher et al. 2015b), we use the PSID that includes all three measures.

Since 1968, the PSID has collected a broad range of socioeconomic and other information on families on an annual basis and since 1997 on a biannual basis. The PSID first introduced an extensive wealth module in 1984, which was repeated every five years until 1999 and on a biannual basis since then. The PSID first introduced something approaching a full measure of consumption in 1999. Before 1999, the PSID only had spending on food and housing. Thus our analysis starts in 1999 because it is the first year with all three measures in every wave.

Data are collected in the year of the survey; income is reported for the previous taxable year, wealth is reported for the time of interview (the survey year), and consumption is a mixture of time periods. In our analysis, we use the survey year to represent the year for the resource means and convert measures to constant 2013 dollars, we adjust by family size using an equivalence scale given by the square root of family size, and we use the family level file and longitudinal weights.[9]

Total family income is the sum total of taxable, transfer, and social security income of the head, wife, and other family units. We use after-tax income, by imputing taxes using a model that Sara Kimberlin, Jiyoun Kim, and Luke Shaefer constructed using NBER TAXSIM (2014).

Total household wealth is the sum total of eight asset variables minus debt. Asset variables are farm and business, checking and savings, other real estate (such as second home, land, rental real estate, or money owed on a land contract), stocks, vehicles, other assets (such as life insurance policy), annuity or individual retirement account (IRA), and home equity. Until 2007, debt was total debt. Beginning in 2009, debt is the sum total of debt from farm or business, real estate, credit card, student loan, medical, legal, family loan, or other. The PSID wealth module also covers all major wealth components—namely, housing wealth, a range of financial and real assets, retirement wealth, and various types of liabilities—but it draws on fewer survey items than the SCF does. Total wealth estimates produced from the PSID are comparable to those from the SCF. The primary exception is for the wealthiest 1 to 3 percent of households, which the SCF reaches through its IRS oversample and the PSID does not (Juster, Smith, and Stafford 1999; Pfeffer et al. 2016).[10]

The definition of consumption changes in the PSID. Until 2003, consumption is the sum of food, housing, transportation, education, and child care.[11] Beginning, in 2005, consumption also includes spending on travel, clothing, other recreation, home repair, home furnishings, and home phones. Hence, we use a consistent measure of consumption over the entire period and include a rental value of home ownership given by 6 percent of the house value.[12]

9. Results are similar if we exclude the supplemental low-income (SEO) sample, and restrict the analysis to the Survey Research Center (SRC) sample. We also compare the cross-section results using the family weights; results are qualitatively similar.

10. Wealth does not include defined-benefit retirement or Social Security holdings (see Wolff, this issue). Future work will attempt to include this pension wealth following Sebastian Devlin-Foltz and his colleagues (this issue).

11. Following Fisher and David Johnson (2006) and Orazio Attanasio and Luigi Pistaferri (2014), we include the amount of food stamps (SNAP) in the total food consumption.

12. We also compare the cross-section results using the family weights, and results are qualitatively similar.

Figure 2. Gini Coefficients for Income, Consumption, and Wealth

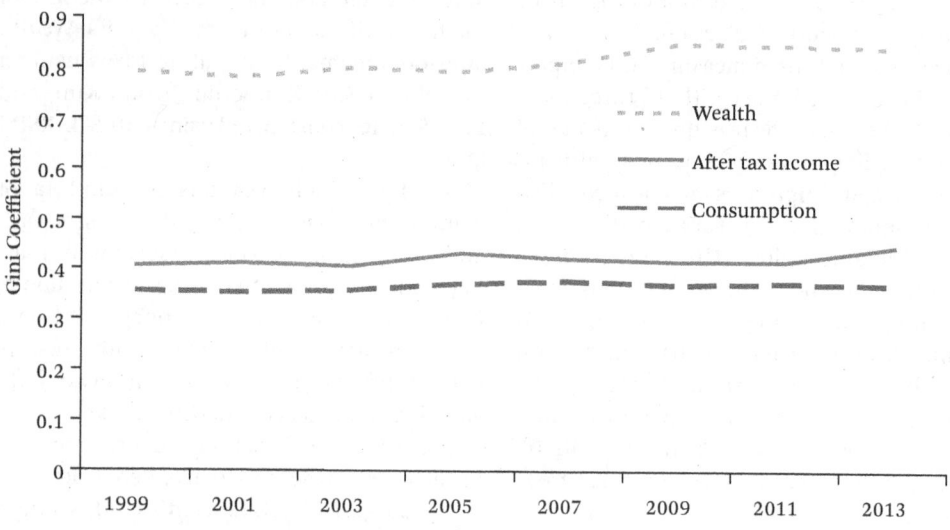

Source: Authors' calculations based on PSID.

As Patricia Andreski and her colleagues show (2014), the consumption measure from PSID is similar to that in the CE. Other research also shows the consistency between the PSID and SCF wealth measures: Dirk Krueger, Kurt Mitman, and Fabrizio Perri (2015) confirm that the trends in income and consumption from the PSID are similar to the trends shown in the national accounts from the Bureau of Economic Analysis (BEA).[13] Fisher and Johnson demonstrate that the PSID captures more income than the CE (2006). Andreski and her colleagues compare the income levels in the PSID to the CPS (2014). However, Bruce Meyer, Wallace Mok, and James Sullivan demonstrate that all of the income and consumption surveys do not fully capture the level of government transfers in their income measure (2015).

RESULTS

Between 1999 and 2013, inequality has increased. As shown in figure 1, using the equivalized money income from the Census Bureau yields an increase in the Gini of 4.6 percent between 1999 and 2012; all of the other measures also increase. Our measures for income, consumption, and wealth are shown in figure 2 and display increases in all three measures (comparable to other measures shown in figure 1)—consumption Gini increases 6 percent, income increases 9 percent, and wealth increases 6 percent. Wealth inequality increases substantially during the Great Recession (see also Wolff, this issue). These results are similar to those obtained using the SCF (Fisher et al. 2015b). In fact, the level and trend in wealth inequality using the PSID and SCF are almost identical, even though the SCF captures more wealth than the PSID (see also Pfeffer, Danziger, and Schoeni 2014), whereas income and consumption inequality differ because of the slightly different definitions used.

Top Shares

Inequality can also be examined using the share of the resource measure held by the top percentages of each resource (as in Piketty and Saez 2003; Saez and Zucman 2014). Table 1 shows the shares for the top 5, 10 and 20 percent for each measure. The increases are more apparent in the changes in the top 20 percent, the wealth share increasing the most. The shares for the top 5 percent for income and wealth are lower than those found using the SCF (from Fisher et al. 2015b); this is mainly because the SCF captures more wealth and in-

---

13. Dettling and her colleagues, however, suggest that only the SCF has levels of wealth accumulation that correspond well to the national aggregates in the Financial Accounts from the Federal Reserve (2014).

Table 1. Shares for Income, Consumption, and Wealth

	Top 5 Percent			Top 10 Percent			Top 20 Percent		
	W	I	C	W	I	C	W	I	C
1999	51.2	18.9	16.4	64.9	29.3	26.2	79.9	45.4	41.5
2001	48.8	20.7	16.1	62.8	30.9	26.1	78.8	46.4	41.5
2003	51.9	19.6	16.0	65.2	29.9	26.1	80.7	45.7	41.6
2005	49.6	22.1	16.9	64.1	32.4	27.2	80.4	47.9	42.9
2007	52.3	20.4	17.7	66.2	31.1	28.0	82.1	46.9	43.8
2009	57.0	20.1	17.1	70.7	30.7	27.1	85.6	46.6	42.5
2011	53.1	19.5	17.8	69.0	30.0	27.9	85.8	46.1	43.1
2013	52.7	21.2	16.5	68.6	32.0	26.8	85.6	48.2	42.4

Source: Authors' calculations based on PSID.
Note: I = income; C = consumption; W = wealth.

come at the top of the distribution than the PSID.[14] Thus the rest of the results using the PSID focus on the top 20 percent.

For the top 20 percent of the consumption distribution, we again see an increase in the share of consumption held by the top between 1999 and 2007 and then a fall during the Great Recession (similar to Fisher, Johnson, and Smeeding 2015). The income and wealth shares tend to show a consistent rise over the period, with the income share showing a slight dip after the recession. Wolff (this issue), Killewald and Bryan (this issue), and Fisher, Johnson, and Smeeding (2015) show that changes in home values substantially affected the change in inequality during the Great Recession.

These separate (or marginal) changes are similar to previous measures of inequality. But as Krueger, Mitman, and Perri explain, "Although the marginal distributions of earnings, income and wealth are interesting in their own right, the more relevant object for our purposes is the joint distribution of wealth, earnings, disposable income and consumption expenditures" (2015, 7). The PSID allows us to examine the conjoint distribution of all of these measures.

One method to evaluate the joint distribution is to examine the shares of income and consumption held by the top 20 percent of wealth holders. Table 2 shows the separate shares of the other resources held by the top 20 percent of wealth, income, and consumption. For example, in 2013 the top 20 percent of wealth holders (86 percent of wealth) also have about 37 percent of income and 34 percent of consumption. The proportion of consumption held by the top 20 percent of wealth holders increases between 1999 and 2007, and decreases during the Great Recession, similar to the patterns for consumption inequality found in Fisher, Johnson, and Smeeding (2015). Although the share of wealth held by the top 20 percent of wealth-holding households increases after 2007, the share of consumption falls slightly and the share of income remains fairly constant. This suggests that the wealthy decreased consumption by a greater percentage than lower wealth households did over the course of the Great Recession. Another way to consider these relationships is that only 34 percent of consumption can be attributed to the top 20 percent of wealth holders. This is consistent with Krueger, Mitman, and Perri (2015) and suggests that a significant amount of consumption occurs outside the wealthy.

Because wealth is so skewed toward the top end, those in the top 20 percent of wealth holders are likely better off than those in the top 20 percent of the consumption or income distributions. However, households in the top 20 percent of the consumption distribution ap-

---

14. These are also comparable to Krueger, Mitman, and Perri (2015), who find the top 10 percent of wealth holds 67.4 percent, income holds 31.6 percent, and consumption holds 29.8 percent.

Table 2. Shares of Resources Within Top 20 Percent

	Top 20% Wealth			Top 20% Income			Top 20% Consumption		
	W	I	C	I	C	W	C	I	W
1999	79.9	33.1	32.4	45.4	31.9	52.3	41.5	35.3	58.2
2001	78.8	34.4	32.2	46.4	32.7	56.3	41.4	36.6	58.0
2003	80.7	33.3	33.4	45.7	33.6	57.1	41.6	36.7	60.7
2005	80.4	36.4	35.9	47.9	35.4	53.3	42.9	40.2	57.3
2007	82.1	36.9	35.8	46.9	36.1	59.9	43.8	38.7	65.3
2009	85.6	34.9	34.9	46.6	33.5	50.9	42.5	36.2	55.9
2011	85.8	35.1	35.2	46.1	35.4	55.6	43.1	37.5	63.5
2013	85.6	36.9	34.4	48.2	35.4	61.3	42.4	40.2	63.5

Source: Authors' calculations based on PSID.
Note: I = income; C = consumption; W = wealth.

pear to be well off by all three measures. A consistent pattern for the entire period is that households in the top 20 percent of consumption own slightly more of the wealth than those in the top 20 percent of income, and households in the top 20 percent of consumption earned slightly more income than the top 20 percent of wealth holders.[15] Regardless, looking at the top 20 percent of income is less informative than looking at the top 20 percent of wealth or consumption when using all three measures, despite the fact that most of the research attention in the general inequality literature as well as the top shares literature has focused heavily on the top 5 or top 1 percent's shares of income alone (see Fisher et al. 2015a).

Average Propensity to Consume

Another measure of the joint distribution unfolds when considering the APC and wealth-to-income ratios. Figures 3 and 4 show the APCs and wealth-to-income ratios for each income vingtile (each 5 percentile point) using the PSID for 1999 to 2007 and 2013.[16] These APCs are slightly lower than those found using the CE because the PSID consumption measure captures about 80 percent of CE consumption on average.

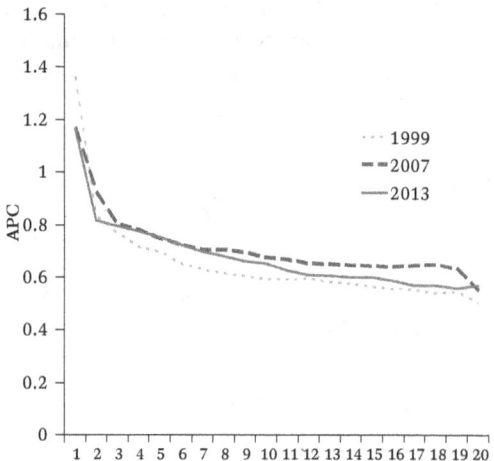

Figure 3. APC and Wealth-to-Income Ratio, APC

Source: Authors' calculations based on PSID.

Figures 3 and 4 confirm that the APC falls and wealth-to-income increases with income. However, the numbers change over the years. The APC uniformly increases between 1999 and 2007, except for the bottom vingtile, and then falls in 2013. The wealth-to-income ratio displays a similar pattern for much of the income distribution, except that the highest income

---

15. This may be because many higher wealth households are living on retirement incomes, which are below their preretirement income levels. The elderly are more likely to be in the top of the wealth and consumption distribution and thus the impacts of the shares may be sensitive to the age distribution of the population.

16. The figures use the ratios of median income, consumption, and wealth for each vingtile.

Figure 4. APC and Wealth-to-Income Ratio, Wealth to Income

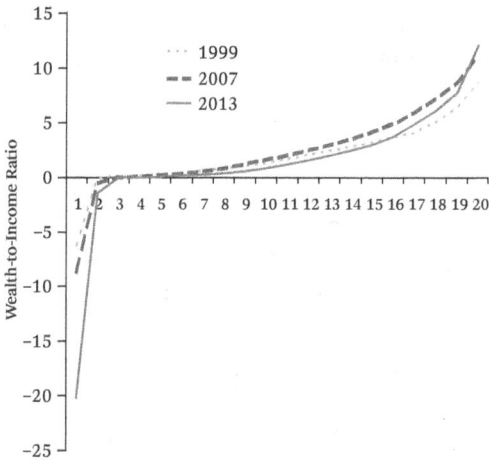

Source: Authors' calculations based on PSID.

households experience an increase in the wealth-to-income ratio between 2007 and 2013. This confirms other research that the top 5 percent are experiencing much of the gains in wealth as well as income during this latter period (Yellen 2014).

A third measure of the joint distribution would be the transition matrices for each pair of measures (as in Fisher et al. 2015b). Income and consumption are more highly correlated than income and wealth or wealth and consumption (see also Fisher et al. 2015b).[17] The distribution of each of the measures by age differs (see Fisher et al. 2015a). Specifically, elderly are more likely to be in the top wealth and consumption quintiles. This suggests that the high APCs for higher wealth households at the bottom of the income distribution are in large part due to retirees, and that the joint distributions will be affected by the age distributions.

Intragenerational Mobility
Finally, we can exploit this longitudinal availability of all three measures in the PSID to examine the mobility of people across the various distributions. To examine intragenerational mobility, we restrict the sample to those adults who are between twenty-five and fifty in 1999, and construct transition matrices between 1999 and 2013 for these adults (we also examined mobility between 1999 and 2007, and 2007 and 2013). Fisher and Johnson use the PSID to show that income mobility and consumption mobility were similar between 1984 and 1999 using an imputed measure of consumption (2006). Table 3 shows the transition mobility matrices for income, consumption, and wealth. All three show the standard twin peaks phenomenon seen in the relative mobility literature—larger percentages remaining in the top and bottom quintiles (see Fisher and Johnson 2006). These tables suggest that mobility for all three measures is similar. The main difference is that the stickiness at the top is more apparent in wealth than in income and consumption. Table 3 shows that 64 percent of people in the top wealth quintile in 1999 remain there in 2013, and only 53 percent for income and 50 percent for consumption remain in the top quintile. The respective percentages remaining in the bottom quintiles are much more evenly split, 51 percent for both income and consumption and 46 percent for wealth.

The PSID is viewed as the cornerstone survey to examine mobility (see Haskins, Isaacs, and Sawhill 2008; Pew Charitable Trusts 2012). Fabian Pfeffer and Alexandra Killewald (2015) examine intergenerational wealth mobility and also find that the top is more immobile, 44 percent of children being in the top wealth quintile at the same age as when their parents were in the top quintile, and 34 percent having both in the bottom wealth quintile at the same age. Given that this is a longer period than fourteen years, it could be that extending our results to twenty-five years (or a generation) may yield similar levels of individual mobility as compared to intergenerational mobility (and this extension is part of future research).

One method to summarize the levels of mobility is to use the Shorrocks mobility index (as in Fisher and Johnson 2006).[18] These summary measures, shown in table 4, confirm that mo-

17. Results from the PSID are not shown but are available on request.

18. The Shorrocks measure for a quintile transition matrix is (5−sum of main diagonal)/4. A higher Shorrocks number indicates higher mobility. Another measure Fisher and Johnson use is the Gini index of mobility (2006).

Table 3. Mobility Transition Matrices Between 1999 and 2013

	Q1	Q2	Q3	Q4	Q5
Income					
Q1	51	28	14	4	3
Q2	27	29	25	14	5
Q3	10	21	27	30	12
Q4	7	15	21	30	27
Q5	3	8	14	22	53
Consumption					
Q1	51	25	15	7	2
Q2	27	28	21	17	7
Q3	11	24	24	24	17
Q4	6	16	24	29	25
Q5	4	7	16	24	50
Wealth					
Q1	46	32	14	5	3
Q2	27	33	25	13	4
Q3	16	22	33	22	6
Q4	7	9	19	39	25
Q5	3	4	8	21	64

Source: Authors' calculations based on PSID.
Note: Figures are percentages; rows add to 100.

Table 4. Shorrocks Mobility Coefficient

	Income	Consumption	Wealth
1999–2013	0.775	0.794	0.713
2001–2007	0.677	0.741	0.668
2007–2013	0.664	0.731	0.674
1984–1999 (Fisher/Johnson)	0.815	0.819	
1984–1990 (Fisher/Johnson)	0.701	0.676	
1990–1999 (Fisher/Johnson)	0.745	0.702	

Source: Authors' calculations based on PSID.

bility for all three measures is similar over the 1999 to 2013 period. This is also similar to the results of Fisher and Johnson (2006) shown in the bottom part of table 4.[19] The Shorrocks index can be interpreted as the proportion of individuals moving across the distribution. Hence, between 1999 and 2013, 77.5 percent of individuals move across the income distribution and 79.4 percent move across the consumption distribution and fewer, 71.3 percent, move across the wealth distribution. As usual, shorter periods yield less mobility. Although consumption mobility is slightly smaller than income mobility in Fisher and Johnson (2006), we find it to be slightly larger in the more recent time periods.

Finally, we can examine the mobility for income and consumption by the level of wealth by creating separate mobility matrices for each wealth quintile. Results show less income mo-

---

19. Because Fisher and Johnson (2006) use a different sample, one cannot make the claim that mobility has fallen between decades even though both sets of results use the PSID.

Table 5. Percentage Who Remain in Same Quintile

	1999–2007	2007–2013	1999–2013
Q1 income	35.0	45.5	23.4
Q1 consumption	31.5	38.2	20.3
Q1 wealth	32.8	28.8	16.4
Q5 income	37.5	47.2	27.1
Q5 consumption	35.1	40.1	25.1
Q5 wealth	47.0	55.7	39.0
Q1 for all three	8.7	5.6	3.8
Q5 for all three	12.1	15.7	8.0

Source: Authors' calculations based on PSID.

bility at lower wealth quintiles. Although half of those in the bottom income quintile in 1999 remain in the bottom in 2013, 60 percent of those in the bottom wealth quintile remain in the bottom income quintile in 2013, but only 20 percent of those in the top wealth quintile do. Wealth creates more stickiness at the top, suggesting that intragenerational income mobility decreases with wealth.

These measures show the stickiness at the bottom and top of the distributions, but they also show a fair amount of intertemporal mobility. One manifestation of overall economic inequality comes from the number of people who continuously remain in the top or bottom of the distributions. We can examine the permanency of the lack of mobility by finding the percent of people who are always in the top and bottom quintiles for each period between 1999 and 2013. Table 5 shows the percentage of people who were in the top or bottom quintiles in 1999 and remained there for each period until 2013. As expected, because the period before the recession began (in 2007) is longer, fewer people are stagnant for all years. But for the entire period, 23 percent of people in the bottom income quintile are stuck there for all periods, and 4 percent of those in the bottom wealth quintile in 1999 remain there for all three measures in 2013. Similarly, 8 percent of those in the top quintile in 1999 remain in the top for all three measures for all years.

As before, the top is stickier; 7.5 percent of people in the top quintile remain in the top quintile of all three measures from 1999 to 2013, compared with 4 percent in the bottom quintile of all three measures over the same span of years. In fact, 40.7 percent of all people in the top wealth quintile in 1999 remained there for all eight periods (2001, 2003, 2005, 2007, 2009, 2011, and 2013). Additionally, 8 percent of people in the top quintile (for one measure) in 1999 remain in the top quintiles for all three measures for all years.

CONCLUDING REMARKS

Our work on the conjoint distributions of income, consumption, and wealth is just beginning. Inequality in all three measures is rising, but the changes are not perfectly correlated. Many households have relatively high consumption but low income, suggesting spending out of wealth (or increases in wealth not recorded in standard income definitions). Many high-wealth households consume modestly and have lower incomes, suggesting that retirees play a role in what we see here. However, when the elders are removed from the sample in our SCF work, the patterns observed are not much changed (see Fisher et al. 2015b). Still, we find a high correlation where 20 percent of all people in the top quintile and 10 percent of those in the bottom quintile for all three measures in 1999 remain there for all three measures in every year between 1999 and 2013.

By presenting results using income, consumption, and wealth for the same households, we have improved our understanding of inequality in the United States. The three measures are not perfectly correlated, but correlation in the tails of the distribution is much higher, suggesting that unidimensional inequality understates the true level of overall economic inequality. Most research on inequality focuses on income alone, but that may well not be the best single measure of inequality. Economists prefer consumption as a measure of permanent income, and wealth incorporates both the ability to increase income and the ability to consume directly. Although this paper focuses on the overall population without a complete examination of the differences by age, race, or other demographics, future work will follow the methods of Fisher and his colleagues (2015a) to evaluate the demographics of mobility.

Wealth is a stock that can be used to stabilize consumption in times of misfortune, or to increase realized income flows. Because wealth is so highly skewed and becoming more skewed over time, it also allows the wealthy to ensure the economic success of their children. That is, personal and business wealth provides an ever-increasing cushion against economic misfortune and a dynastic advantage to maintaining social position over time. Alicia Eads and Laura Tach demonstrate elsewhere in this issue that wealth increases family stability, which affects the well-being of children, and hence could affect the level of intergenerational mobility. This advantage can also extend across generations, providing the ability to save, purchase durables, finance education, and borrow at less cost. This can also increase the ability to provide more inter-vivos transfers, which affects intergenerational mobility (see Rauscher, this issue). Accumulated wealth clearly leads to benefits for the children of high-wealth households over other children, and thus may compromise equality of opportunity and diminish intergenerational mobility (Fisher et al. 2015a).

Increasing wealth inequality also provides the wealthy with increased ability to use their wealth and power to shape public policy and receive favorable legal treatment and tax treatment (Stiglitz 2012). One method to shift more benefits to lower and middle-income families could be to modify the personal and child tax exemptions, which are of equal value to all (Smeeding 2016). This increase in inequality and concentration of power may also lead to lower rates of human capital accumulation, and hence slow economic growth (OECD 2014). The accumulations of wealth suggest that policy is needed to limit the influence of the wealthy without diminishing overall savings behavior.

We document the rise in income, consumption, and wealth inequality in the United States and identify some of the ways in which these three are correlated. We also argue that the most serious inequality is that of wealth as it influences consumption, income, and tax policy. Because this increase in inequality reduces equality of opportunity and mobility, policy could focus on methods to reduce the concentration of wealth as it passes from generation to generation and to lessen its impact on mobility and political life.

REFERENCES

Andreski, Patricia, Greg Li, Mehmet Samancioglu, and Robert Schoeni. 2014. "Estimates of Annual Consumption Expenditures and Its Major Components in the PSID in Comparison to the CE." *American Economic Review* 104(5): 132–35.

Aguiar, Mark, and Mark Bils. 2015. "Has Consumption Inequality Mirrored Income Inequality?" *American Economic Review* 105(9): 2725–56.

Atkinson, Anthony, Thomas Piketty, and Emmanuel Saez. 2011. "Top Incomes in the Long Run of History." *Journal of Economic Literature* 49(1): 3–71.

Attanasio, Orazio, and Luigi Pistaferri. 2014. "Consumption Inequality over the Last Half Century: Some Evidence Using the New PSID Consumption Measure." *American Economic Review* 104(5): 122–26.

Blundell, Richard. 2014. "Income Dynamics and Life-Cycle Inequality: Mechanisms and Controversies." *Economic Journal* 124(576): 289–318.

Burkhauser, Richard V., Shuaizhang Feng, Stephen P. Jenkins, and Jeff Larrimore. 2009. "Recent Trends in Top Income Shares in the USA: Reconciling Estimates from March CPS and IRS Tax Return Data." *NBER* working paper no. 15320. Cambridge, Mass.: National Bureau of Economic Research. Accessed May 6 2016. http://www.nber.org/papers/w15320.

Congressional Budget Office. 2011. "Trends in the Distribution of Household Income Between 1979 and 2007." *CBO* report no 4031. Washington: U.S. Government Printing Office.

Cooper, Daniel, and Karen Dynan. 2016. "Wealth Effects and Macroeconomic Dynamics." *Journal of Economic Surveys* 30(1): 34–55. doi: 10.1111/joes.12090.

Dettling, Lisa J., Sebastian Devlin-Foltz, Jacob Krimmel, Sarah Pack, and Jeffrey Thompson. 2015. "Comparing Micro and Macro Sources for Household Accounts in the United States: Evidence from the Survey of Consumer Finances." *Finance and Economics* Discussion Series no. 2015-086. Washington: Board of Governors of the Federal Reserve System.

Devlin-Foltz, Sebastian, Alice Henriques, and John Sabelhaus. 2016. "Is the U.S. Retirement System Contributing to Rising Wealth Inequality." *RSF: The Russell Sage Foundation Journal of the Social Sciences* 2(6). doi: 10.7758/RSF.2016.2.6.04.

Eads, Alicia, and Laura Tach. 2016. "Wealth and Inequality in the Stability of Romantic Relationships." *RSF: The Russell Sage Foundation Journal of the Social Sciences* 2(6). doi: 10.7758/RSF.2016.2.6.10.

Fisher, Jonathan, and David Johnson. 2006. "Consumption Mobility in the U.S.: Evidence from Two Panel Data Sets." *Topics in Economic Analysis and Policy* 6(1)(September): 1–38.

Fisher, Jonathan, David Johnson, and Timothy M. Smeeding. 2015. "Inequality of Income and Consumption: Measuring the Trends in Inequality from 1984–2011 for the Same Individuals." *Review of Income and Wealth* 61(4): 630–50.

Fisher, Jonathan, David Johnson, Timothy M. Smeeding, and Jeffrey Thompson. 2015a. "The Demography of Inequality: Income, Wealth, and Consumption 1989–2010." Paper presented at Population Association of America annual meeting. Washington, D.C. (May 2, 2015).

———. 2015b. "Inequality in 3-D: Income, Consumption and Wealth." Paper presented at the Association for Public Policy Analysis and Management's 37th Annual Fall Research Conference. Miami, Fl. (November 12, 2015).

Gates, Bill. 2014. "Why Inequality Matters." *GatesNotes*, October 13 2014. Accessed May 6 2016. https://www.gatesnotes.com/Books/Why-Inequality-Matters-Capital-in-21st-Century-Review.

Haig, Robert M. 1921. "The Concept of Income: Economic and Legal Aspects." In *The Federal Income Tax*, edited by Robert Murray Haig. New York: Columbia University Press.

Hardy, Bradley, Marina Gindelsky, Dennis Fixler, and David Johnson. 2015. "Inequality in America: The Role of National Income, Household Income, and Transfers." Unpublished working paper, Bureau of Economic Analysis, Washington, D.C.

Haskins, Ron, Julia B. Isaacs, and Isabel V. Sawhill. 2008. *Getting Ahead or Losing Ground: Economic Mobility in America*. Washington, D.C.: Brookings Institution. Accessed May 6, 2016. http://www.brookings.edu/~/media/research/files/reports/2008/2/economic-mobility-sawhill/02_economic_mobility_sawhill.pdf.

Heathcote, Jonathan, Fabrizio Perri, and Giovanni Violante. 2010. "Unequal We Stand: An Empirical Analysis of Economic Inequality in the US 1967–2006." *Review of Economic Dynamics* 13(1): 15–51.

Jäntti, Markus, Eva Sierminska, and Timothy M. Smeeding. 2008. "How Is Household Wealth Distributed? Evidence from the Luxembourg Wealth Study." In *Growing Unequal: Income Distribution and Poverty in OECD Countries*. Paris: OECD Publishing.

Juster, F. Thomas, James P. Smith, and Frank Stafford. 1999. "The Measurement and Structure of Household Wealth." *Labour Economics* 6(2): 253–75.

Killewald, Alexandra, and Brielle Bryan. 2016. "Does Your Home Make You Wealthy?" *RSF: The Russell Sage Foundation Journal of the Social Sciences* 2(6). doi: 10.7758/RSF.2016.2.6.06.

Kimberlin, Sara, Jiyoun Kim, and Luke Shaefer. 2014. "An updated method for calculating income and payroll taxes from PSID data using the NBER's TAXSIM, for PSID survey years 1999 through 2011." Unpublished manuscript, University of Michigan. Accessed May 6, 2016. http://ebp-projects.isr.umich.edu/NCRN/papers/PSID-TAXSIM.pdf.

Krueger, Dirk, Kurt Mitman, and Fabrizio Perri. 2015. "Macroeconomics and Household Heterogeneity." *Handbook of Macroeconomics*. Accessed May 6, 2016. http://economics.sas.upenn.edu/~dkrueger/research/Handbook.pdf.

Krueger, Dirk, and Fabrizio Perri. 2006. "Does Income Inequality Lead to Consumption Inequality? Evidence and Theory." *Review of Economic Studies* 73: 163–93.

Meyer, Bruce, Wallace Mok, and James Sullivan. 2015. "Household Surveys in Crisis. *NBER* working paper no. 21399. Cambridge, Mass.: National Bureau of Economic Research.

OECD. 2014. "Focus on Inequality and Growth." Paris: Organisation for Economic Co-operation and Development. Accessed May 6, 2016. https://www.oecd.org/social/Focus-Inequality-and-Growth-2014.pdf.

Pew Charitable Trusts. 2012. "Pursuing the American Dream: Economic Mobility Across Generations." Washington, D.C.: The Pew Charitable Trusts. Accessed May 6, 2016. http://www.pewtrusts.org/~/media/legacy/uploadedfiles/pcs_assets/2012/pursuingamericandreampdf.pdf.

Pfeffer, Fabian T., Sheldon Danzinger, and Robert D. Schoeni. 2014. *Wealth Levels, Wealth Inequality, and the Great Recession*. New York: Russell Sage Foundation.

Pfeffer, Fabian T., and Alexandra Killewald. 2015. "How Rigid Is the Wealth Structure and Why? Inter- and Multigenerational Associations in Family Wealth." *Population Studies Center* research report no. 15-845. Ann Arbor: University of Michigan. Accessed May 6, 2016. http://www.psc.isr.umich.edu/pubs/pdf/rr15-845.pdf.

Pfeffer, Fabian T., and Robert F. Schoeni. 2016. "How Wealth Inequality Shapes Our Future." *RSF: The Russell Sage Foundation Journal of the Social Sciences* 2(6). doi: 10.7758/RSF.2016.2.6.01.

Pfeffer, Fabian T., Robert F. Schoeni, Arthur Kennickell, and Patricia Andreski. 2016. "Measuring Wealth and Wealth Inequality: Comparing Two U.S. Surveys." *Journal of Economic and Social Measurement* 41(2): 103–20.

Piketty, Thomas. 2015. "About *Capital in the Twenty-First Century*." *American Economic Review: Papers and Proceedings* 105(5): 48–53.

Piketty, Thomas, and Emmanuel Saez. 2003. "Income Inequality in the United States 1913–1998," *Quarterly Journal of Economics* 118(1): 1–39.

Rauscher, Emily. 2016. "Passing It On: Parent-to-Adult Child Financial Transfers for School and Socioeconomic Attainment." *RSF: The Russell Sage Foundation Journal of the Social Sciences* 2(6). doi: 10.7758/RSF.2016.2.6.09.

Saez, Emmanuel, and Gabriel Zucman. 2014. "Wealth Inequality in the United States Since 1913: Evidence from Capitalized Income Tax Data." *NBER* working paper no. 20625. Cambridge, Mass.: National Bureau of Economic Research.

Simons, Henry. 1938. Personal Income Taxation: *The Definition of Income as a Problem of Fiscal Policy*. Chicago: University of Chicago Press.

Smeeding, Timothy M. 2016. "The Case for Reducing Child Poverty in America." *Pathways*. Stanford Center on Poverty & Inequality, Stanford University, in press.

Smeeding, Timothy M., and Jeffrey P. Thompson. 2010. "Recent Trends in the Distribution of Income: Labor, Wealth and More Complete Measures of Well Being." *Research in Labor Economics* working paper no. 225. Amherst: University of Massachusetts.

Stiglitz, Joseph E. 2012. *The Price of Inequality: How Today's Divided Society Endangers Our Society*. New York: W. W. Norton.

Stiglitz, Joseph E., Amartya Sen, and Jean-Paul Fitoussi. 2009. *Report by the Commission on the Measurement of Economic Performance and Social Progress*. New York: United Nations Press.

Thompson, Jason, and Dalton Conley. 2016. "Health Shocks and Social Drift: Examining the Relationship Between Acute Illness and Family Wealth." *RSF: The Russell Sage Foundation Journal of the Social Sciences* 2(6). doi: 10.7758/RSF.2016.2.6.08.

Wolff, Edward. 2014. "Household Wealth Trends in the United States 1962–2013: What Happened over the Great Recession?" *NBER* working paper no. 20733. Cambridge, Mass.: National Bureau of Economic Research.

———. 2016. "Household Wealth Trends in the United States, 1962 to 2013: What Happened over the Great Recession?" *RSF: The Russell Sage Foundation Journal of the Social Sciences* 2(6). doi: 10.7758/RSF.2016.2.6.02.

Yellen, Janet. 2014. "Perspectives on Inequality and Opportunity from the Survey of Consumer Finances." Remarks at the Conference on Economic Opportunity and Inequality, Federal Reserve Bank of Boston. Boston, Mass. (October 17, 2014).

Is the U.S. Retirement System Contributing to Rising Wealth Inequality?

SEBASTIAN DEVLIN-FOLTZ, ALICE HENRIQUES, AND JOHN SABELHAUS

Data from the Survey of Consumer Finances for 1989 through 2013 reveal five broad findings. First, overall retirement plan participation was stable or rising through 2007, though overall participation fell noticeably in the wake of the Great Recession and has remained lower. Second, cohort-based analysis of life-cycle trajectories shows that participation in retirement plans is strongly correlated with income, and that the recent decline in participation is concentrated among younger and low- to middle-income families. Third, the shift in the type of pension coverage from defined benefit (DB) to defined contribution (DC) occurred within—not just across—income groups. Fourth, retirement wealth is less concentrated than nonretirement wealth, so the growth of retirement wealth relative to nonretirement wealth helped offset the increasing concentration in nonretirement wealth. Fifth, the shift from DB to DC had only a modest effect in the other direction because DC wealth is more concentrated than DB wealth.

Keywords: retirement, wealth, life cycle, synthetic panel

The share of wealth owned by top wealth holders in the United States has risen over the past few decades, despite some debate about exactly how concentrated wealth is and how fast those top shares are rising (Saez and Zucman 2016; Bricker et al., forthcoming). One reason for varying estimates is that different types of wealth dominate at various points in the wealth distribution. For example, changes in house values and mortgage borrowing play a key role in determining wealth changes in the middle of the wealth distribution, and corporate equities and directly held businesses disproportionately affect the very top.[1] Retirement wealth lies somewhere between those other types of assets, being less concentrated than directly held

---

Sebastian Devlin-Foltz is senior research assistant, **Alice Henriques** is senior economist, and **John Sabelhaus** is assistant director in the Division of Research and Statistics at the Board of Governors of the Federal Reserve System.

The analysis and conclusions are those of the authors and do not indicate concurrence by other members of the research staff or the Board of Governors. This paper was prepared for the Russell Sage Foundation conference, "Wealth Inequality: Sources, Consequences, and Responses," October 30, 2015. We thank our colleagues at the Federal Reserve Board, Wojciech Kopczuk, Russell Sage, NTA, and SOLE conference participants, and the volume editors for many helpful comments. Direct correspondence to: Sebastian Devlin-Foltz at sebastian.j.devlin-foltz@frb.gov; Alice Henriques at alice.m.henriques@frb.gov; and John Sabelhaus at john.sabelhaus@frb.gov; Mail Stop 143, 20th and C Streets NW, Washington, D.C., 20551.

1. Elsewhere in this issue, Alexandra Killewald and Brielle Bryan show that homeownership is a positive contributor to wealth accumulation in the middle of the wealth distribution, even after controlling for selection effects, though there is some heterogeneity in the effects of homeownership by race, with the returns to homeowning for white families more than double that for African American families.

businesses and corporate equities but more concentrated than widely held balance sheet components such as housing and durable goods.

Understanding the role that retirement wealth plays in rising wealth inequality requires comprehensively measuring and then distributing retirement assets. Retirement wealth in the United States today is increasingly made up of account-type defined contribution (DC) assets, most of which are accumulated in 401(k) or similar employer-sponsored plans, and often rolled over into individual retirement accounts (IRAs) when employees leave their jobs. Retirement wealth also includes the claims to future defined benefit (DB) retirement income streams for both current and future DB beneficiaries. The need to comprehensively account for both types of retirement assets is underscored by the shift from DB to DC that has occurred during the past several decades.

The triennial Survey of Consumer Finances (SCF) is well suited for measuring and distributing retirement wealth and evaluating the impact on overall wealth inequality.[2] The SCF covers a long period, includes households headed by all age groups, and combines careful measurement of work-related pensions, personal retirement accounts, and earnings histories with other relevant demographic, income, and balance sheet information. DC and IRA assets are measured directly in the survey. DB payments received by current beneficiaries are also captured; the asset value of those claims is estimated by discounting survival-weighted income streams. The expected value of DB payments (for families holding claims to but not yet receiving DB payments) can be estimated using employment history and other relevant SCF data elements.

Given the baby boom and rapid aging of the U.S. population, any analysis of whether and how retirement wealth is reinforcing or offsetting overall trends in wealth inequality should begin with a life-cycle perspective. In particular, stable aggregate retirement wealth (in levels or relative to income) gives a misleading picture when the population is aging, and the appropriate benchmark is one in which total retirement wealth should be rising. Thus, most of the analysis here is based on constructing synthetic-panel life-cycle trajectories for the outcomes of interest. SCF data for 1989 through 2013 show that retirement plan participation was stable or even increasing through the early 2000s when viewed from a life-cycle perspective. Specifically, younger generations were achieving systematically higher rates of participation than their predecessor cohorts, at any given age. That upward trend stalled after 2000 and ended with the onset of the Great Recession. The 2010 SCF showed a decrease in retirement plan participation that, as of the 2013 survey, has yet to be reversed. The declines after 2007 in participation trajectories, relative to previous cohorts, are widespread, but most pronounced for the youngest families and those in bottom half of income distribution.

The SCF also makes it possible to break down these cohort-level trends and look within birth cohorts to investigate how retirement plan participation is evolving across income groups, which is the first step in thinking about the implications for wealth inequality. It is not surprising, given labor market fundamentals and the structure of Social Security, that participation in employment-related retirement plans is always and everywhere very positively correlated with income. The life-cycle peak for participation in (any form of past, current, or future) retirement plans is now just over 60 percent for the cohort approaching retirement in the bottom half of the income distribution, but over 90 percent for families in the 50th through 95th percentiles, and near 100 percent for those in the top 5 percent.

The conditional distributions of DB versus DC coverage within income groups provide an important input to the discussion about whether the shift from DB to DC might be affecting wealth inequality. Even though overall retirement plan participation is greater for the highest income groups in every year, the mix of coverage by type in any given year does not vary substantially by income. Higher-income

---

2. Studies by Edward Wolff (this issue) and Jesse Bricker and colleagues (2014) use the SCF to describe the levels and trends in the distribution of total wealth across the population.

families are more likely to have a combination of DB and DC coverage, but the overall rate for DB inclusion (conditional on having any retirement plan coverage) is roughly the same across income groups. Thus, the data confirm that all income groups saw the same dramatic compositional shift from DB to DC.

At the same time, the life-cycle perspective applied to the SCF across income groups shows that the historical differences in retirement plan coverage by income have widened in recent years, and especially since the Great Recession. The relative declines in participation in recent years are widespread but most pronounced for younger cohorts and, within any given cohort, most pronounced for lower-income families, suggesting that the retirement system might be contributing to rising wealth inequality. The divergence in coverage has not (at least not yet) had a substantial impact on the key life-cycle outcome measure—retirement wealth relative to income—but that is in large part because of differential slowdown in income growth across income groups. In that sense, the evidence suggests that systematic retirement saving was sacrificed by many families with diminishing economic resources, especially in the wake of the Great Recession.

The bottom line estimates on how retirement wealth is affecting overall trends in wealth inequality require some perspective. The share of total wealth (including DB wealth) held by the top 1 percent of families (sorted by total wealth) rose 6 percentage points between 1989 and 2013, from 26 percent in 1989 to 32 percent by 2013. The share owned by the top 25 percent of families rose 5 percentage points, from 83 percent in 1989 to 88 percent in 2013. At the same time, the shares of nonretirement wealth held by these same groups were much higher and increased much more, suggesting that the overall effect of retirement wealth was toward reducing overall concentration, both in the levels and growth of wealth shares at the top of the distribution.

On the other hand, the greater concentration of DC assets relative to DB assets for wealth holders at the very top combined with the shift from DB to DC suggests some modest contribution to rising wealth inequality from that dimension, offsetting some of the overall mitigating trend. In particular, the differential in shares of DB versus DC wealth held by the top 1 percent (who own about 5 percent of DB wealth versus about 15 percent of DC wealth) interacted with the shift in retirement asset composition from DB to DC (DB fell from about 70 percent of total retirement assets in 1989 to about 50 percent of the total in 2013) yields a 0.4 to 0.6 percentage point increase in the share of wealth owned by the top 1 percent.

MEASURING RETIREMENT PLAN PARTICIPATION AND RETIREMENT WEALTH

The data used here to study retirement plan participation and wealth accumulation is the series of cross-sections from the triennial Survey of Consumer Finances conducted between 1989 and 2013. The SCF is well suited for analyzing retirement savings from a life-cycle perspective because the survey covers a long period, includes households headed by all age groups, and combines careful measurement of work-related pensions, personal retirement accounts, and earnings with other relevant demographic, income, and balance sheet information. Tracking of tax-preferred retirement resources in the SCF is intended to be comprehensive and includes all forms of past, current, and future claims in both defined benefit and defined contribution pensions, as well as IRAs.

The analysis here begins with the observation that data on aggregate household retirement wealth tells us very little about trends in retirement preparedness and any possible contribution to wealth inequality over time.[3] The ratio of aggregate (non–Social Security) retirement claims to aggregate personal income has risen since 1989, with most of that growth oc-

---

3. The focus of this paper is on overall retirement plan participation and the distribution of non–Social Security retirement assets across income and cohort groups. Other questions in the SCF about earnings histories can be used to estimate Social Security (for examples of more comprehensive estimates of retirement wealth using the SCF, see Poterba 2014; Wolff 2015).

Figure 1. Aggregate Retirement Assets to Aggregate Personal Income

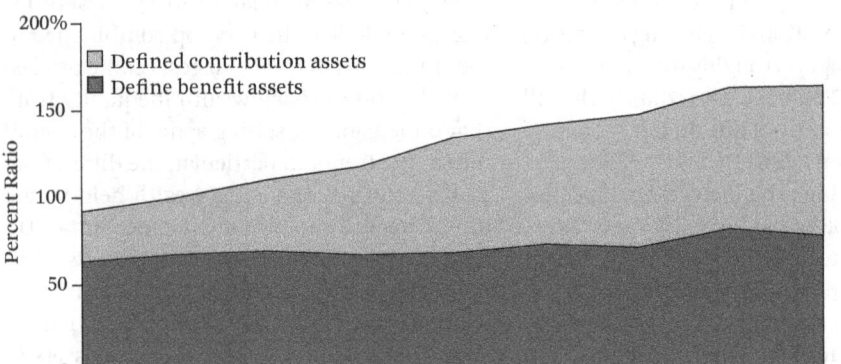

Source: Authors' calculations based on Federal Reserve Board 2014, 2016 and Bureau of Economic Analysis 2016.
Note: Aggregate DC assets are from the Federal Reserve Board, Survey of Consumer Finances. Aggregate DB assets are from the Federal Reserve Board, Financial Accounts of the United States. Aggregate personal income is from the Bureau of Economic Analysis, National Income and Product Accounts.

curring in DC assets (figure 1). Whether retirement wealth relative to income should have increased more rapidly because of population aging or decreasing Social Security replacement rates requires developing appropriate counterfactuals, that is, how much should retirement wealth for a given individual have changed given lifetime earnings, retirement age, and life expectancy.[4] Potentially relevant for wealth inequality is the observation that the share of retirement assets accounted for by defined benefit plans has fallen slightly on net, and DC has risen substantially, leading to a net increase in the share of retirement wealth in total household sector net worth since 1989 (figure 2). The implications for wealth inequality begin with whether differences in the distribution of DB and DC assets across household types are first order, which in turn begins with employer-sponsored retirement plan participation.

The concept of retirement plan participation used here is based on observing any evidence of claim to retirement resources through a current account balance or current income stream, or as an expected income stream to commence in some future year. The financial asset section of the SCF questionnaire captures IRAs; the employment section captures information about DB and DC pensions associated with current employment; and the future pensions section captures claims to future DB pension benefits or DC accounts associated with past jobs and not rolled over (as most are) to an IRA.

Based on this comprehensive measure, overall retirement plan participation has not evolved much in the past quarter century even though the retirement landscape has gone through substantial changes. The proportion of all families with any retirement plan participation has hovered between 60 and 70 per-

---

4. The analysis here is closely related to retirement preparedness across and within generations in the United States. James Poterba provides an excellent overview of the literature (2014). John Scholz, Ananth Seshadri, and Surachai Khitatrakun argue that most households have retirement resources that are largely consistent with the predictions of a life-cycle planning model (2006). Both Alicia Munnell, Anthony Webb, and Francesca Golub-Sass (2012) and Wolff (2015) argue that retirement preparedness is deteriorating for many. Douglas Bernheim, Jonathan Skinner, and Steven Weinberg argue that standard life-cycle determinants of retirement preparedness do not explain substantial differences between households nearing retirement (2001).

Figure 2. Aggregate Retirement Assets to Aggregate Household Sector Net Worth

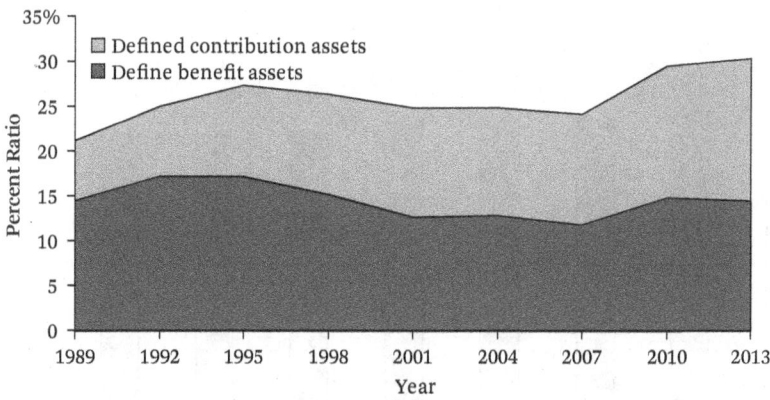

Source: Authors' calculations based on Federal Reserve Board 2014, 2016.
Note: Aggregate DC assets and aggregate household sector net worth are from the Federal Reserve Board, Survey of Consumer Finances. Aggregate DB assets are from the Federal Reserve Board, Financial Accounts of the United States.

Figure 3. Aggregate Retirement Plan Participation, All Households

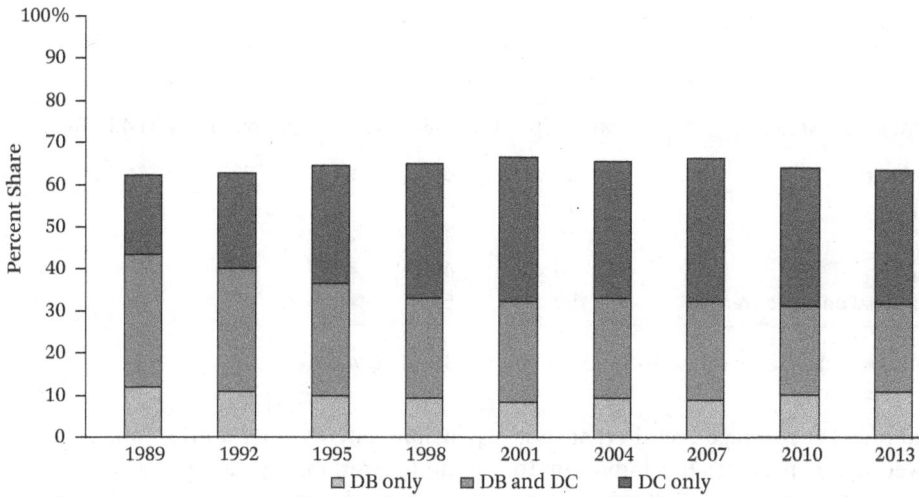

Source: Authors' calculations based on Federal Reserve Board 2014.
Note: DB coverage includes any traditional pension benefits through a current or past job. DC coverage includes IRA and DC pension coverage from a current or former employer in the PEU or observed holdings of such accounts.

cent (figure 3) and that of working-age families (ages twenty-five to fifty-nine) with coverage between 70 and 80 percent (figure 4). Overall coverage trends for all and working-age families indicate recent overall declines in participation.

The more noteworthy change in retirement plan participation is in the type of pension coverage (see table 1). The shift in employer-sponsored plans from DB to DC was well under way before the 1989 SCF was conducted, and few families (and even fewer working-age fam-

Figure 4. Aggregate Retirement Plan Participation, Working-Age Households

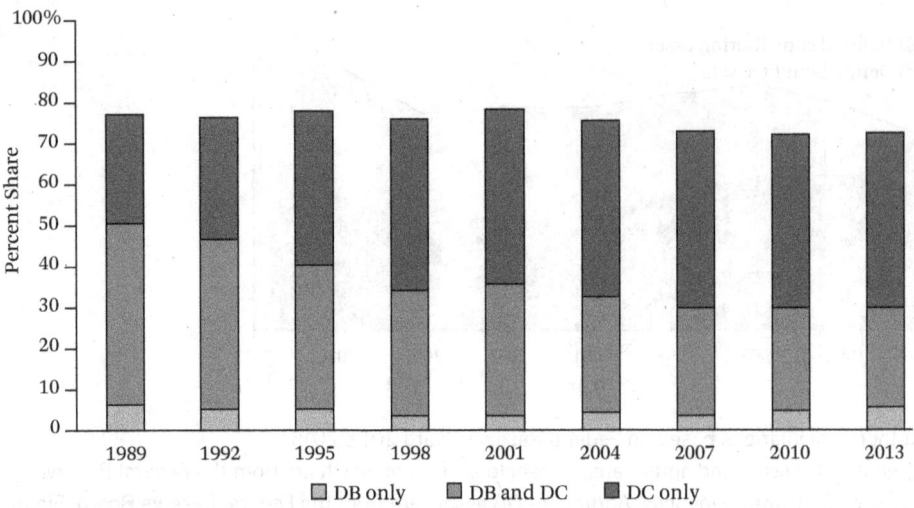

Source: Authors' calculations based on Federal Reserve Board 2014.
Note: DB coverage includes any traditional pension benefits through a current or past job. DC coverage includes IRA and DC pension coverage from a current or former employer in the PEU or observed holdings of such accounts.

Table 1. Pension Coverage by Income

	1995			2013		
Retirement plan coverage	Bottom 50	Next 45	Top 5	Bottom 50	Next 45	Top 5
Any coverage	49	86	94	38	84	94
DB only	10	4	1	9	5	1
DB and DC	19	40	45	8	31	23
DC only	20	42	48	21	48	70
DB, conditional on any coverage	59	51	49	45	43	25

Source: Authors' calculations based on Federal Reserve Board 2014.

ilies) had only DB coverage even in that base year (fewer than 15 percent). It is important to remember that a family with a DB plan in their current job and any form of DC balance, including the (generally small) IRAs opened during the IRA heyday of the early 1980s or a rolled-over distribution from a previous job DB plan, will show up as having both DB and DC coverage in these tabulations.

The trend away from DB plus DC coverage has been toward only DC. The top part of the stacked bars in figures 3 and 4 shows that the fraction of all families with only DC coverage nearly doubled since 1989. The trend for all families includes retirees who are receiving DB pension benefits from a prior job. Thus, the trend for working-age families is a clearer indicator of the trajectory for retirement resources going forward. About 50 percent of working-age families had some form of DB coverage in 1989, and that fell to about 30 percent by 2013.

Sample representativeness and respondent reporting bias are sources of concern when using household surveys, and it is useful to benchmark the survey values before looking at trends in retirement wealth from a distributional perspective. Benchmarking to available evidence suggests the SCF does a good job identifying participation in tax-advantaged re-

Figure 5. Aggregate Assets in DC Accounts and IRAs

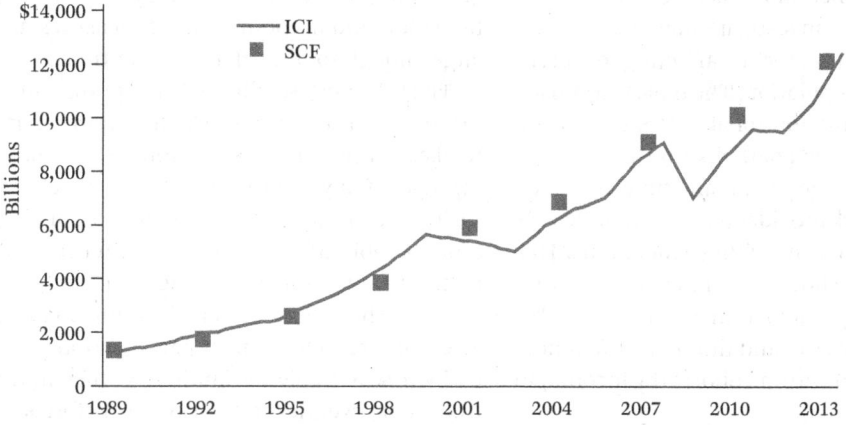

Source: Authors' calculations based on Investment Company Institute 2016 and Federal Reserve Board 2014.

tirement accounts (for a comparison of SCF retirement plan participation with information from tax returns, see Argento, Bryant, and Sabelhaus 2015).[5] The SCF is also unique among U.S. household surveys in terms of capturing wealthy families and thus provides a comprehensive view of the retirement wealth distribution (for an overview of the SCF sampling strategy, see Bricker et al. 2014, appendix).

Direct comparison of the SCF with published aggregates confirms that the survey has indeed done a good job capturing the entirety of DC balances over the sample period (figure 5). Some evidence indicates that respondent-reported values for retirement account balances diverge from the estimates based on financial institution and government sources following dramatic swings in asset values, such as in 2001 and 2010. Those deviations seem temporary, however, perhaps due to respondent lags in updating account balances. Even those deviations are never more than a few percentage points, and overall aggregate DC holdings are well captured by the SCF from 1989 to 2013.

The SCF does not attempt to collect the asset value of current and future DB claims from households, though the survey does have comprehensive information on DB benefits currently being received, DB coverage on current jobs, and some details on expected future DB benefits from past jobs. The approach in this paper to distributing DB assets is described in detail in the appendix. The overall idea is to begin with aggregate household sector DB assets from the Financial Accounts of the United States (FA) and to distribute those assets across and between current and future beneficiaries using fixed real discount rates, life tables, benefits currently received for those receiving, wages and years in the plan for those not yet receiving benefits, and the assumption that current beneficiaries have first claim to DB plan assets.[6]

RETIREMENT PLAN PARTICIPATION ACROSS AND WITHIN BIRTH COHORTS

Overall trends in retirement plan participation are a good starting point for understanding the contribution of retirement-saving behavior on

---

5. Evidence of participation using tax returns is based on the same principles, because form W2 indicates current job coverage, and forms 5498 and 1099-R indicate account balances or flows for accounts.

6. One piece of information not used here is the respondent-reported value for future DB benefits, if those benefit payments have not yet begun. Some evidence indicates substantial respondent errors in these estimates (see, for example, Starr-McCluer and Sunden 1999) as well as indications that (especially in the early SCFs) expected payouts from (say) stock options are intermingled with DB benefits.

wealth inequality, and the SCF makes it possible to go further and look across and within birth cohorts to investigate how the evolving retirement landscape is affecting different groups in the population. The typical approach in this sort of distributional analysis is to measure retirement plan participation and account balances across age groups and time, but a life-cycle framework provides a more dynamic view of changes across and within generations. This life-cycle view shows dramatic swings in retirement plan participation across cohorts between 1989 and 2013 and dramatic differences in participation within cohorts (by income) in every period.

The SCF lacks a long panel component that would make it possible to directly observe changes in retirement plan participation and account balances for a sample of families, but the synthetic-panel approach used here is well suited to studying typical outcomes across types of families at various points in the life cycle.[7] Synthetic-panel analysis makes it possible to study outcomes across the population using different cross-sections at different points in time, such as in the SCF. The identifying assumption is that any given cohort is well represented in each of the cross-sections, and the summary statistics observed from one cross-section to another provide useful information about the changes for that group over time. The SCF is an excellent data source for the analysis here across broad birth cohorts and income groups because the sample sizes for generating the summary retirement plan participation and account balance measures are large enough to infer changes over time.[8]

The SCF cross-sections used here span 1989 to 2013, and thus any given birth cohort can be tracked for (at most) twenty-four years. Looking across ten-year birth cohorts born between 1920 and 1990, and using all of the SCF surveys, a predictable life-cycle pattern in retirement plan participation by age (figure 6) is quite evident. The overall pattern is hump shaped, given that retirement plan participation (generally) rises steeply for families as they move from their twenties to their fifties, before stabilizing and then declining (though perhaps only slightly) for families that have crossed over into retirement.[9]

Comparing the life-cycle trajectories across birth cohorts at similar ages tells a more interesting story about evolving retirement coverage, however. The height difference (at a given age) for any two overlapping cohort lines indicates the difference in participation (at that age) between the two cohorts. Figure 6 thus shows two clearly different stories about trends in retirement plan participation between 1989 and 2013. In the early part of the period, before the early 2000s, more recent cohorts showed generally higher rates of plan participation at younger ages. That trend reversed around 2007.

The 1961–1970 birth cohort provides the

---

7. The Health and Retirement Study (HRS) is a good resource for studying retirement wealth trajectories for U.S. families approaching or in retirement, and the HRS has a panel structure (see, in particular, Gustman, Steinmeier, and Tabatabai 2010, 2011, 2014; Poterba et al. 2007; Poterba, Venti, and Wise 2012, 2013). Unfortunately, the HRS does not include the younger families and the very wealthy families who are included in the SCF, and those missing groups are the focus of much of the analysis in this paper.

8. This is not meant to imply that the synthetic cohort approach used here is necessarily inferior to panel data for this type of long-run distributional analysis across groups and time. True micro panels suffer from nonrandom attrition bias on top of any selection bias associated with participation in a cross-section survey, and reporting or measurement variability in panel surveys is such that analyzing the distribution of individual changes in retirement wealth can be highly problematic. Indeed, most analysis of data sets such as the HRS involve comparing summary statistics for a given cohort at different times, just like those produced here. The more salient difference is in how families are grouped—for example, by current versus permanent income—when estimating those summary statistics at each time.

9. The tendency of retirees to not draw down tax-preferred accounts has been analyzed extensively (Love, Palumbo, and Smith 2009; Poterba, Venti, and Wise 2013). Whether these trajectories are consistent with optimizing behavior depends on the underlying model, and even the concept of consumption versus spending one has in mind (see, for example, Aguiar and Hurst 2005; Hurd and Rohwedder 2013).

Figure 6. Retirement Plan Participation, 1989 to 2013

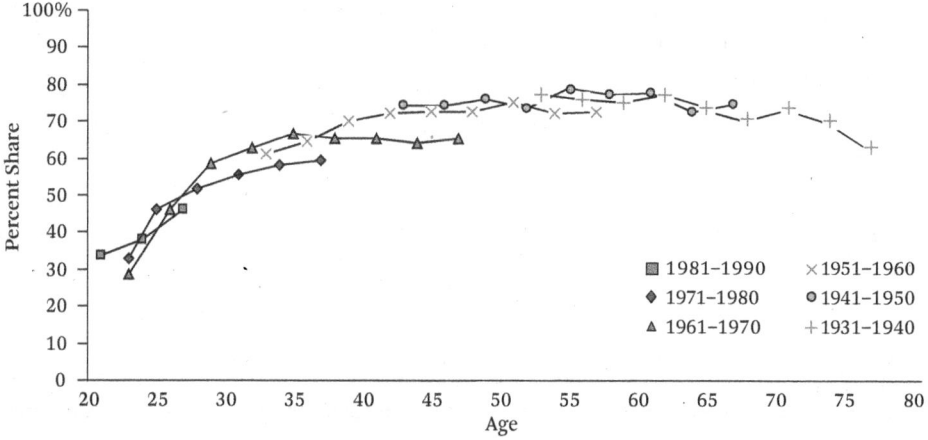

Source: Authors' calculations based on Federal Reserve Board 2014.
Note: Retirement plan participation includes holding of an individual retirement account (IRA) or participation in defined benefit or defined contribution plan through a current or former employer.

clearest example of this sharp break in trend. When that cohort was first observed in their early twenties in the 1989 survey, just under 30 percent were participating in retirement plans. A decade later, when they were in their early thirties, some 70 percent of families had coverage, nearly 10 percentage points above the rate for the 1951–1960 cohort when they were in their early thirties (as observed around 1990). However, not only did the 1961–1970 cohort seem to peak in terms of coverage in their early thirties, their participation has now fallen: the last time they were observed, in 2013, when they were approaching age fifty, their participation rate was nearly 10 percentage points below the 1951–1960 cohort's (as observed in the early 2000s) and even the 1941–1950 cohort's (as observed in the early 1990s). Although the 1961–1970 cohort is the most extreme example, every cohort shows the pattern of first exceeding and then falling below earlier cohorts at the same age in terms of overall retirement plan participation.

This dramatic takeaway from the life-cycle perspective on cohort-level retirement plan participation provides a sharp contrast with the conclusions arising from the aggregate participation charts (figures 3 and 4). The key to reconciling the two is demographic trends. As baby boomers approached middle age, if life-cycle trajectories had not changed, the overall retirement plan participation would have risen substantially because the baby boom generation has a greater population weight and is at its life-cycle peak in retirement plan participation. The only reason aggregate participation stabilized and then fell slightly was that within-cohort changes dominated the demographic effect.

Acknowledging that participation in retirement plans is down substantially from a life-cycle perspective, especially for younger cohorts, is an important starting point for thinking about the effect of retirement plans on wealth inequality. The more pressing question, though, is who within those birth cohorts is experiencing those changes. The obvious dimension on which to cut the cohort data is income, given that differences in retirement plan offerings and participation across income groups are well known. The SCF makes it possible to look—from the same life-cycle perspective—within birth cohorts across income groups to study both levels and changes in participation over time.

One potential problem in synthetic-panel analysis is the possibility that families in a specific group in a given year are not the same ones (probabilistically) as in that group in a different year. This is obviously not a problem with something mechanical like birth cohorts, but sorting families on income could be prob-

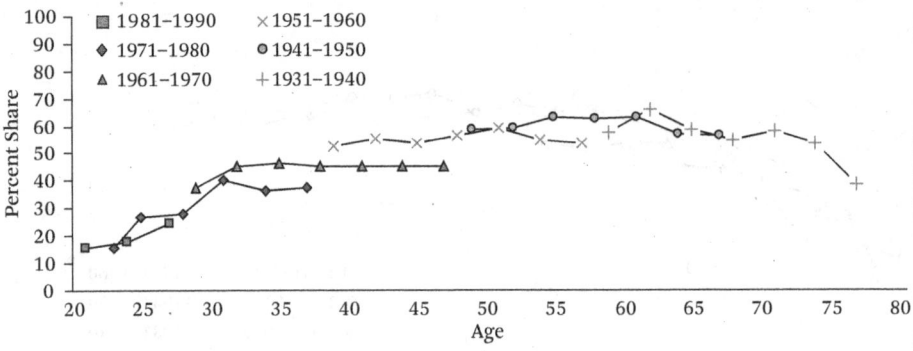

Figure 7. Retirement Plan Participation, 1995 to 2013, Bottom 50 Percent

Source: Authors' calculations based on Federal Reserve Board 2014.
Note: Ranking determined by normal income distribution within each cohort. For definitions, see notes to figure 6.

lematic, especially if transitory shocks to incomes in a given year are large. When that is the case, for example, (usually) higher-income families who experience large negative shocks will be grouped with (usually) lower-income families, and their accumulated retirement wealth will be averaged with that of (usually) lower-income families.

Since 1995, the SCF has included a set of income questions that make it possible to eliminate most of this sorting bias in the synthetic-panel analysis. The measure used in this paper is derived from the survey questions about the gap between actual and usual income in the SCF. Toward the end of the SCF interview, after detailed income components have been summed, respondents are asked whether that total income is higher than, lower than, or about the same as their income in a usual year. Most respondents say that it is in fact about normal—the median gap between actual and usual income is zero in every survey year. However, sizable minorities of respondents indicate that their income is either unusually high or unusually low, and those proportions vary predictably and systematically with business cycle conditions. Those who say they experienced a shock are then asked what their income would be in a usual year, and that (along with actual income for the majority who say their income is equal to the usual value) is the classifier used here.[10]

Differences in life-cycle patterns for retirement plan participation across usual income groups are not surprising (figures 7 through 9).[11] Retirement plan participation is always and everywhere strongly and positively associated with usual income, and there are very different life-cycle trajectories and peaks across the three usual income groups represented here: the bottom 50 percent of families, the next 45 percent (percentiles 50 through 95), and the top 5 percent.[12] Indeed, it really does not make sense to think of retirement plan participation among the top 5 percent as having an age component per se, because participa-

10. Bricker and his colleagues show how the usual income classifier affects conclusions about changes in family finances over time (2014, box 2).

11. Relative to figure 6, which plotted participation across birth cohorts from 1989 to 2013, the sorting by usual income eliminates the first two points (representing six years) for the cohorts who could have been observed prior to the 1995 survey.

12. Families are sorted by usual income within their respective birth cohorts. The specific usual income groups are motivated in part by analysis of income inequality that suggests a clear trend separation near the top few percentiles of families by income, the top 5 percent chosen specifically to provide a large enough sample size for the synthetic cohort tabulations. The oversampling of the SCF at the very top plays an important role here, because that top 5 percent is represented by a disproportionate number of families.

Figure 8. Retirement Plan Participation, 1995 to 2013, Next 45 Percent

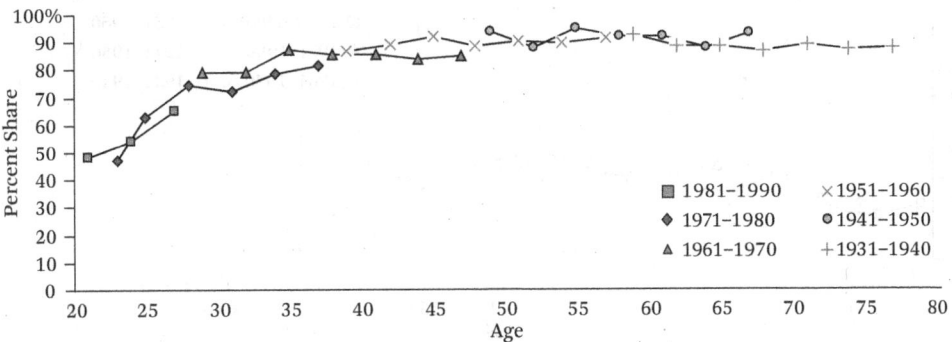

Source: Authors' calculations based on Federal Reserve Board 2014.
Note: Ranking determined by normal income distribution within each cohort. For definitions, see notes to figure 6.

Figure 9. Retirement Plan Participation, 1995 to 2013, Top 5 Percent

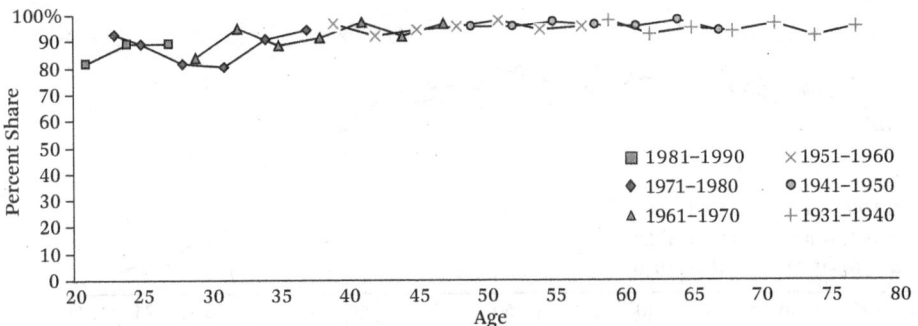

Source: Authors' calculations based on Federal Reserve Board 2014.
Note: Ranking determined by normal income distribution within each cohort. For definitions, see notes to figure 6.

tion is nearly universal for that income group at every point in the life cycle.

The possible (and perhaps competing) explanations for these differences in retirement plan participation rates by income are well known. Families in the bottom 50 percent of the usual income distribution have not just lower overall compensation, of which retirement plan offerings are a component, but also much more employment volatility, which also affects retirement plan offerings and participation. On the positive side, those lower-income families also receive a much higher replacement rate from Social Security (as shown later in the paper) such that their need to save is greatly diminished relative to higher-income families, for whom Social Security is much less adequate in terms of replacing earned income.[13]

Although comprehensively explaining the levels of participation by income and age is beyond the scope of this paper, the life-cycle trajectories do make it possible to address the distributional question about changes in participation. The largest decreases in retirement plan participation, relative to the life-cycle trajectories of previous cohorts in the same in-

---

13. This assertion is based on the highly progressive formula for determining Social Security benefits—specifically, the primary insurance amount (PIA)—relative to lifetime earnings—specifically, average indexed monthly earnings (AIME). Olivia Mitchell and John Phillips discuss conceptual issues involved with measuring Social Security replacement rates (2006).

Figure 10. Retirement Plan Offers, 1995 to 2013, Bottom 50 Percent

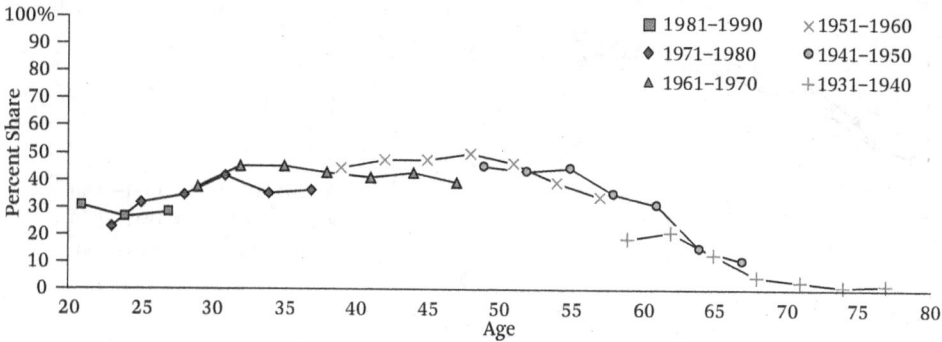

Source: Authors' calculations based on Federal Reserve Board 2014.
Note: Ranking determined by usual income distribution within each cohort. For definitions, see notes to figure 6.

Figure 11. Retirement Plan Offers, 1995 to 2013, Next 45 Percent

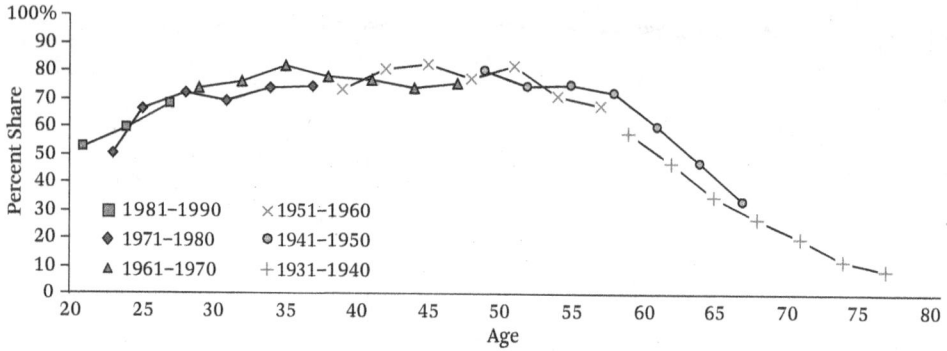

Source: Authors' calculations based on Federal Reserve Board 2014.
Note: Ranking determined by usual income distribution within each cohort. For definitions, see notes to figure 6.

come groups, have occurred for preretirement families in the bottom 50 percent by usual income, and to some extent for the younger cohorts in the next 45 percent. The only groups that have not seen large changes in retirement coverage are older families across all income groups, and all age groups at the top of the usual income distribution. Again, the 1961–1970 cohort is a useful benchmark: families in the bottom half have only a 50 percent participation rate as they approach age fifty, in 2013, well below the life-cycle peak for lower-income families in the three previous cohorts.

Why did retirement plan participation change, especially after 2007? The life-cycle decline in retirement plan participation across and within cohorts is attributable to either a decline in opportunities to participate or the choice to not participate, given the opportunity. Most tax-preferred retirement participation comes through the workplace. (Although everyone is eligible to participate in IRA saving, if they do not have employer-sponsored coverage, they generally choose not to). Thus participation generally begins with employment itself and then whether employers offer retirement plans and how they set eligibility criteria for those plans. The SCF has questions about whether (nonparticipating) respondents' employers offered plans, and whether the respondent was eligible (but declined to) participate. Based on that information, declines in offers for the lower half of the income distribution seem to be responsible for most of the divergence in participation across and within cohorts (figures 10 through 12). Participation,

Figure 12. Retirement Plan Offers, 1995 to 2013, Top 5 Percent

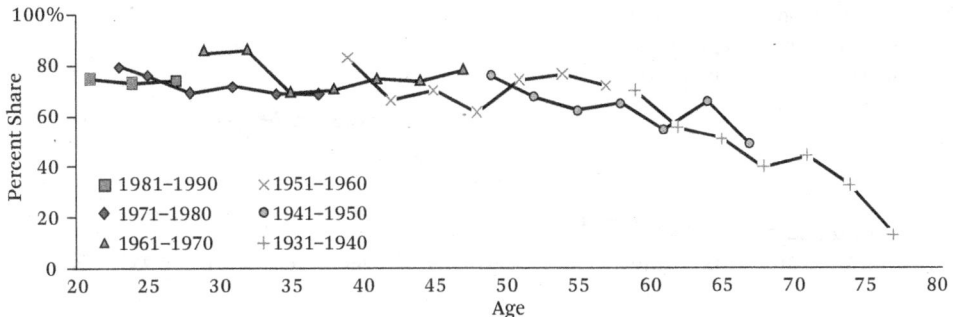

Source: Authors' calculations based on Federal Reserve Board 2014.
Note: Ranking determined by usual income distribution within each cohort. For definitions, see notes to figure 6.

conditional on having a pension offer, is fairly constant across and within cohorts.[14]

RETIREMENT WEALTH-TO-INCOME RATIOS

The life-cycle perspective on participation in retirement saving plans shows a somewhat dramatic recent decline for many younger and lower-income families, but participation is only the first margin of behavior. It is possible, for example, that the decrease in participation was concentrated among those for whom (conditional) retirement wealth accumulations or entitlements are relatively small, at least relative to their incomes or other resources, leading to little impact on retirement preparedness or overall wealth inequality.[15] The same life-cycle framework used earlier for tracking retirement plan participation is used in this section to look at accumulated DB and DC retirement claims by cohort, income, and age. The primary statistics of interest are retirement claims relative to income, first for all retirement wealth, and then for DB and DC plans separately.

There are several ways to (statistically) look across and within cohort groups to evaluate the importance of accumulated retirement wealth at any point in time. The unconditional mean of retirement balances captures both the participation and accumulation dimensions in one statistic, the conditional median gives an

---

14. There is also an important corollary that ties together the shift in type of pension coverage (figures 3 and 4) with changes in the *distribution* of retirement plan participation by usual income and cohort (figures 7 through 9). Overall participation is positively correlated with income, but the type of coverage, conditional on any participation, is roughly proportional across income groups at every point in time. Among working-age families (headed by individuals twenty-five to fifty-nine years old) the overall retirement plan participation rates in 1995 were 54 percent for the bottom half by usual income, and 96 percent for the top 5 percent of families by usual income. By 2013 the overall participation rates had fallen to 44 percent for the bottom half and 94 percent for the top 5. However, conditional on having coverage, the types of coverage were about the same across income groups. In 1995, 53 percent of those with coverage in the bottom half by usual income had a DB or mixed DB+DC, versus 48 percent of those in the top 5 percent. By 2013, the conditional DB+DC coverage rates had fallen to 38 percent among the bottom half, and 25 percent in the top 5 percent. Barbara Butrica and her colleagues (2009) and Wolff (2015) also explore the distributional implications of the decline in DB coverage for future retirement outcomes.

15. As noted, an overall assessment of retirement wealth requires comprehensive measures of accumulated balances and claims to all future income streams, including Social Security. Measuring retirement adequacy comprehensively also requires assumptions about retirement ages, and increasing lifespans suggests that measuring retirement wealth using fixed retirement or Social Security claim ages across cohorts may be misguided (for a discussion of trends and determinants of claiming and retirement ages, see Henriques 2012; Behaghel and Blau 2012).

Figure 13. Retirement Assets to Income, 1995 to 2013, Bottom 50 Percent

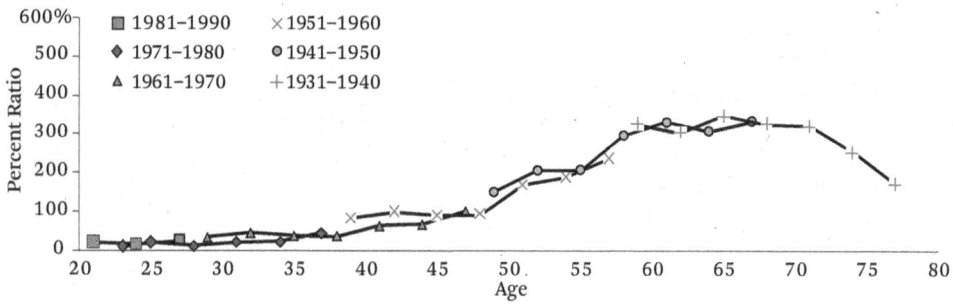

Source: Authors' calculations based on Federal Reserve Board 2014.
Note: Ranking determined by usual income distribution within each cohort. For definitions, see notes to figure 6. For details on how DB assets are distributed in the SCF, see appendix.

Figure 14. Retirement Assets to Income, 1995 to 2013, Next 45 Percent

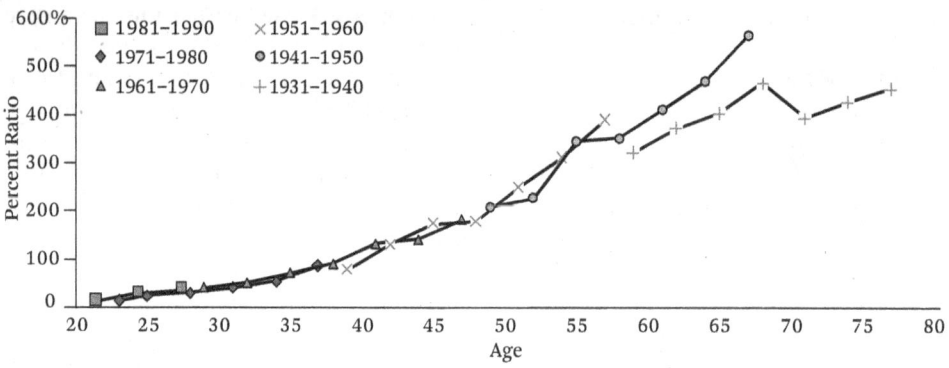

Source: Authors' calculations based on Federal Reserve Board 2014.
Note: Ranking determined by usual income distribution within each cohort. For definitions, see notes to figure 6. For details on how DB assets are distributed in the SCF, see appendix.

indication of importance of accumulated balances for the typical family in the group with any retirement balances, and the conditional mean further shows how skewed balances are (relative to the conditional median) among families in the group who have balances. Although the three measures diverge somewhat in terms of levels, the patterns across and within birth cohorts are generally similar.

The 1961–1970 birth cohort is once again a good example. As of 2013, members of this group were on average forty-eight years old, and their retirement plan participation around 70 percent (figure 6). Differences in participation (figures 7 through 9) and retirement assets across the three usual income groups are large, however. The unconditional mean retirement balances for this group in 2013 (not shown) differ dramatically (though not unexpectedly) from about $38,000 for the bottom half by usual income, to $219,000 for the next 45 percent, and to $769,000 for the top 5 percent.

The across- and within-cohort differences in unconditional mean retirement assets at a particular time are not direct evidence about retirement planning and adequacy of resources; normalizing by income is thus an important step in that direction. The static measures also do not indicate anything about changes over time, which (as with participation) is best conveyed using the life-cycle framework that shows within- and across-cohort movements. Thus, the following analysis focuses on the ratio of (unconditional) average retirement assets to average usual income across and within cohorts, 1995 through 2013 (figures 13 through 15).

Figure 15. Retirement Assets to Income, 1995 to 2013, Top 5 Percent

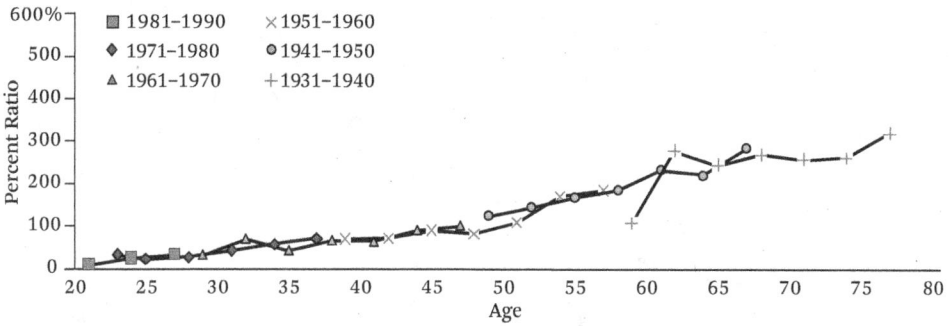

Source: Authors' calculations based on Federal Reserve Board 2014.
Note: Ranking determined by usual income distribution within each cohort. For definitions, see notes to figure 6. For details on how DB assets are distributed in the SCF, see the appendix.

Figure 16. DB Assets to Income, 1995 to 2013, Bottom 50 Percent

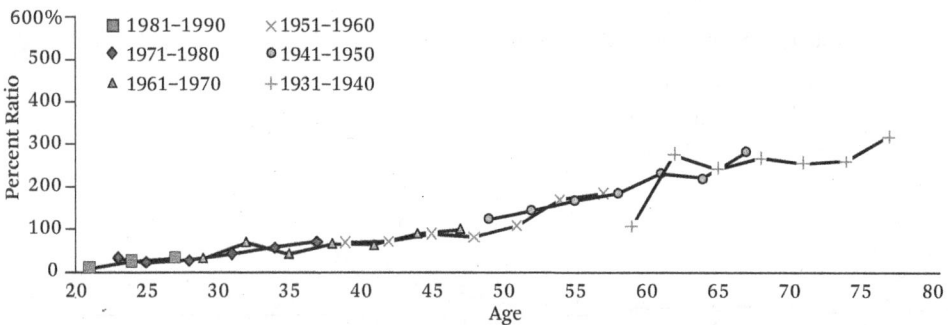

Source: Authors' calculations based on Federal Reserve Board 2014.
Note: Ranking determined by usual income distribution within each cohort. For definitions, see notes to figure 6. For details on how DB assets are distributed in the SCF, see the appendix.

These differences in retirement wealth to income ratios by usual income are much less stark than those in retirement plan participation (figures 7 through 9), because the much higher average incomes at the top offset higher participation and (conditional) retirement balances for those higher-income families. Indeed, average retirement balances for those about sixty years old in 2007 (that is, the 1941–1950 cohort) were all roughly 300 percent of average usual income across all three usual income groups.[16] However, especially when viewed from the life-cycle perspective, the patterns by age and the contributions of DC and DB assets to overall retirement wealth accumulation varied widely across the income distribution (see figures 16 through 21).

Retirement wealth accumulation is much slower early in the life cycle for lower-income families than it is for middle- and higher-income families. To some extent, this reflects the participation patterns described earlier, because fewer lower-income families participate in retirement saving at all ages, but especially

16. These similarities across usual income groups helps to explain why Robert Clark and John Sabelhaus find that relatively modest changes in retirement ages, extending working lives by just a few months for many people, would be needed to completely offset the drop in asset values associated with the Great Recession (2009). Similarly, Gopi Goda, John Shoven, and Sita Slavov find though stock market fluctuations do affect expected retirement ages for workers close to retirement, the increase in respondent-reported expected time until retirement that occurred during the Great Recession cannot be explained by losses on financial assets alone (2011).

Figure 17. DB Assets to Income, 1995 to 2013, Next 45 Percent

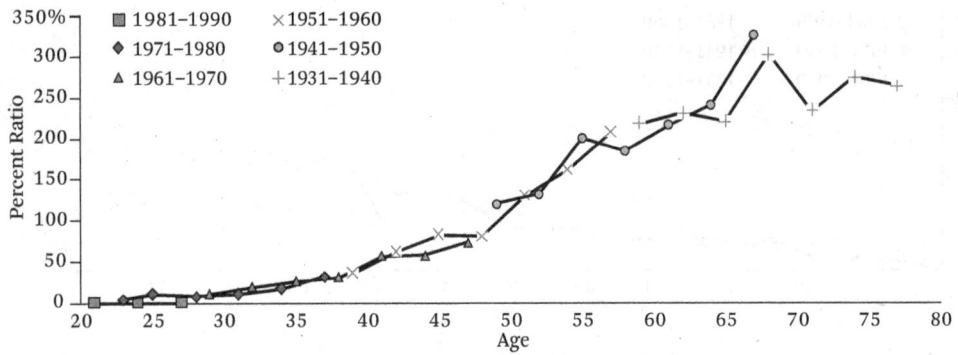

Source: Authors' calculations based on Federal Reserve Board 2014.
Note: Ranking determined by usual income distribution within each cohort. For definitions, see notes to figure 6. For details about how DB assets are distributed in the SCF, see the appendix.

Figure 18. DB Assets to Income, 1995 to 2013, Top 5 Percent

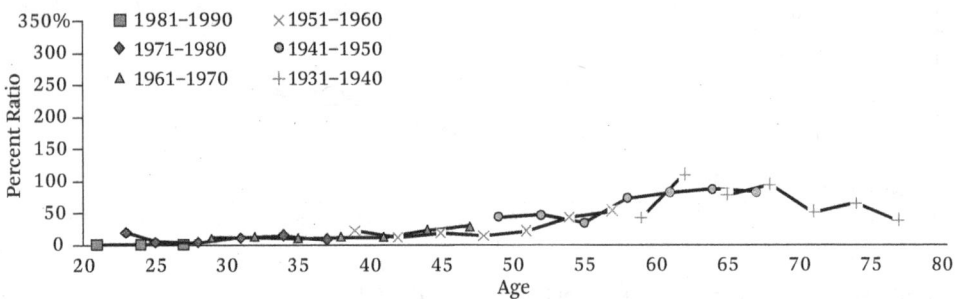

Source: Authors' calculations based on Federal Reserve Board 2014.
Note: Ranking determined by usual income distribution within each cohort. For definitions, see notes to figure 6. For details on how DB assets are distributed in the SCF, see the appendix.

Figure 19. DC Assets to Income, 1995 to 2013, Bottom 50 Percent

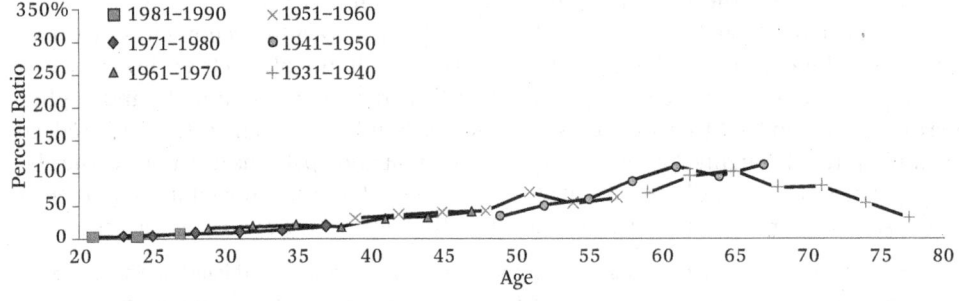

Source: Authors' calculations based on Federal Reserve Board 2014.
Note: Ranking determined by usual income distribution within each cohort. For definitions, see notes to figure 6.

Figure 20. DC Assets to Income, 1995 to 2013, Next 45 Percent

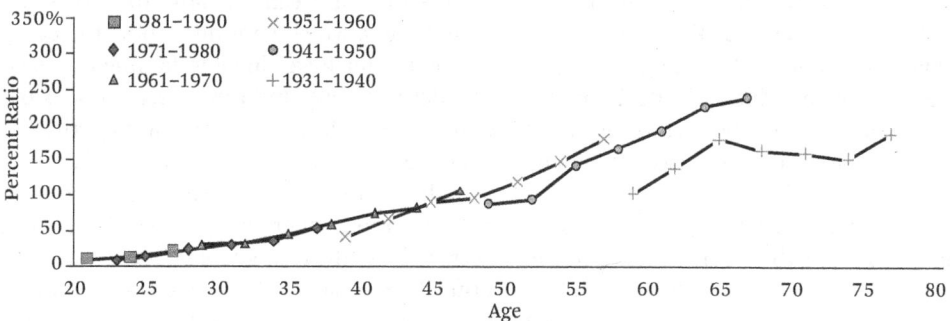

Source: Authors' calculations based on Federal Reserve Board 2014.
Note: Ranking determined by usual income distribution within each cohort. For definitions, see notes to figure 6.

Figure 21. DC Assets to Income, 1995 to 2013, Top 5 Percent

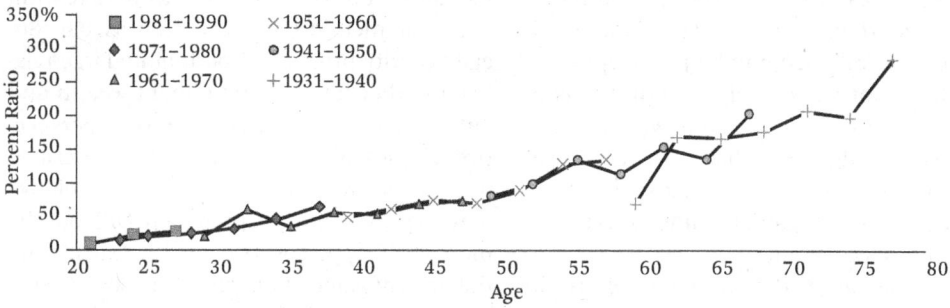

Source: Authors' calculations based on Federal Reserve Board 2014.
Note: Ranking determined by usual income distribution within each cohort. For definitions, see notes to figure 6.

when young (see figures 7 through 9). However, that pattern is compounded by the differential reliance on DB versus DC wealth accumulation. Young families who do participate in DB plans receive relatively small DB asset allocations based on our algorithm, because of the actuarial discounting principles used to distribute the aggregate DB plan assets across families.[17] That same phenomenon causes DB wealth accumulation to accelerate sharply (relative to income) as these families approach retirement (see figures 16 through 18).

The trajectories after retirement age also diverge, and again in a way consistent with changes in retirement plan participation at older ages. The suggestion is, of course, that lower-income families are more likely than others to spend down their DC accounts after

---

17. The estimated DB portion of the life-cycle retirement wealth-to-income ratios depends to some extent on the specific algorithm for distributing aggregate DB assets (described in the appendix), but the results are fairly robust to changes in that algorithm. For example, raising or lowering the real discount factor by 1 percentage point shifts about 5 percent of retirement wealth between retirees and workers, which does not substantially change the life-cycle patterns. Another concern is differential mortality, which implies that the value of a given DB income stream for a lower-income family with (statistically) lower life expectancy is diminished relative to those at the top of the income distribution. In the DB allocation, differential mortality is less likely to be a problem because the income-mortality gradient is dominated by differences between the very bottom and every other income group. As shown later, most DB assets are concentrated at the top of the distribution, so differential mortality is not a determining factor.

retirement (figures 19 through 21) given that DB assets set aside for all individuals decline systematically but slowly as they age (figures 16 through 18). Some of the change in trajectory after retirement is due to the denominator (usual income) because the various usual income groups exhibit different (usual) income trajectories after retirement.

As with participation rates, a key message that emerges from the within-cohort retirement wealth-to-income trajectories involves those for whom retirement balances are failing to grow with income. In a world with declining DB coverage and less generous Social Security (at any given claim age) for all income groups, one would suspect the DC balance to income trajectories would lie always and everywhere above predecessor cohorts (if expected retirement ages are unchanged). That middle-age families generally seem to be just keeping up with the cohorts ahead of them (in terms of DC balances) is therefore somewhat surprising. It is also suggestive that retirement accumulation may indeed (in a relative sense) be slipping for many (again, holding expected retirement ages constant).

The observation that younger cohorts in both the bottom half of the distribution and the next 45 percent are not even keeping up with the cohorts ahead of them in terms of DC balances is even more worrisome. In addition, middle-age families in the bottom half of the income distribution (notably the 1951–1960 cohort) do not seem to be going through the substantial run-up in wealth-to-income ratios as they get close to retirement, as was true for lower-income families in previous cohorts. This takeaway on recent divergence in the trajectories of DC balance to income ratios closely mirrors the findings on participation described.

Still, it is hard to find any evidence (at least not yet) based on the life-cycle analysis of substantial changes in retirement wealth accumulation across usual income groups. That statement is supported by the lack of across-cohort differences in retirement wealth-to-income ratios. In an important sense, this is explained by lower-income families' having had relatively little retirement wealth (relative to income) in earlier years, which continues to be the case. DB claims for lower-income families in past decades were low, and three decades later remain small. That usual income growth has slowed differentially for lower-income families as well is also a factor contributing to wealth concentration generally. It is not clear, however, whether the retirement system is contributing differentially (relative to business ownership, housing and other real estate, the stock market, or other forms of wealth) to the dynamic relationship between income and wealth.

ROLE OF SOCIAL SECURITY WEALTH

Any analysis of retirement wealth claims across income groups is necessarily incomplete without some mention of Social Security. The Social Security program is both quite large relative to other forms of retirement wealth and quite different from a distributional perspective. The size of the program is often described using measures such as benefit flows relative to total gross domestic product (GDP), but the more striking perspective involves calculating the present value of benefits. The Social Security actuaries estimate that the present value of Old-Age, Survivors, and Disability Insurance (OASDI) benefits for people age fifteen and older in 2013 was about $52 trillion, roughly double in real terms relative to the comparable estimates from two decades prior, due to population aging, increases in lifetime earnings, and increased life expectancy.[18] The present value of future Social Security benefits is also now roughly double the size of all DB and DC claims combined. From a distributional perspective, that income is capped for collecting taxes and paying benefits, and the benefit formula itself is progressive, means that claims to Social Security benefits are much more evenly distributed than other forms of retirement wealth.

The SCF does not collect all of the inputs needed to project Social Security benefits for respondent families and, thus, estimates for

---

18. Based on unpublished numbers from the Office of the Chief Actuary of the Social Security Administration. The estimate for recent years can be found in the annual "Trustees Report" (http://www.ssa.gov/oact/tr/2015/VI_F_infinite.html#, accessed May 3, 2016).

Table 2. Retirement Balances by Income, 2013

	Median Usual Income	Median Private (DB + DC) Retirement Wealth	Median Social Security Wealth	Median Total Retirement Wealth	Private Retirement Wealth to Usual Income	All Retirement Wealth to Usual Income
Bottom 50	$38,552	$6,500	$171,966	$204,465	17%	530%
Next 45	103,669	288,371	343,373	636,085	278	614
Top 5	487,524	716,000	478,707	1,123,748	147	231

Source: Authors' calculations based on Federal Reserve Board 2014.
Note: Numbers are for households in which the respondent was born between 1951 and 1960 and is currently employed.

the entire population would involve strong assumptions about earnings growth and retirement ages. However, it is possible to get a sense of the distributional impact of Social Security (relative to DB and DC wealth) by focusing on one cohort at one point in time, just before retirement. In what follows, the focus is on the 1951 to 1960 birth cohort, as observed in the year 2013. This group ranged from fifty-three to sixty-two years old when the 2013 SCF was conducted. This cohort was close enough to retirement that their current earnings are a reasonable proxy for their lifetime earnings. Benefits are then computed under the (conservative) assumption that everyone retires at age sixty-two.[19]

The importance of Social Security wealth relative to other forms of retirement wealth is illustrated clearly by this simple calculation using current earnings to proxy lifetime earnings, which is the key input to the Social Security benefit calculation (see table 2).[20] The statistics in this table are all medians, in order to focus on representative individuals within each income group, rather than the overall or average retirement wealth for the entire income group. Thus, the very high incomes at the top of the income distribution do not pull down retirement wealth-to-income ratios for that group, and the relatively high DB+DC assets for some families in the bottom half of the income distribution do not distort (upwards) the retirement wealth of the many families in the bottom half with little or no retirement wealth.

The main takeaway from table 2 is that Social Security goes a long way to explaining why differences in DB+DC retirement wealth do not translate into dramatic shocks to living standards as a given cohort crosses over into retirement. Median total retirement wealth (including Social Security) is much lower for the bottom half of the usual income distribution, but relative to median income is roughly the same as for the next 45 percent income group, and more than double that for the top 5 percent. Of course the median family in the top 5 percent owns much more in absolute terms for both DB+DC and Social Security wealth, but, relative to usual income just before retirement, their retirement claims are actually smaller.

EFFECT ON OVERALL WEALTH CONCENTRATION

The synthetic-panel approach to using the SCF to study retirement wealth accumulation in a life-cycle framework provides mixed evidence about the role that pensions and other tax-preferred savings may be playing in rising over-

---

19. Details about the Social Security estimates are provided in the appendix. A substantial proportion of people still claim at age sixty-two, despite increases in the full retirement age. Setting the retirement age low decreases the present value of benefits directly if the reductions for early retirement are not actuarially fair, and indirectly if the individual were to keep working at a high enough income to increase their average indexed monthly earnings. That is the sense in which this calculation is conservative.

20. The calculations are based only on those household heads with reported wages and salaries or self-employment income during the survey year.

Figure 22. Share of Wealth, Top 1 Percent

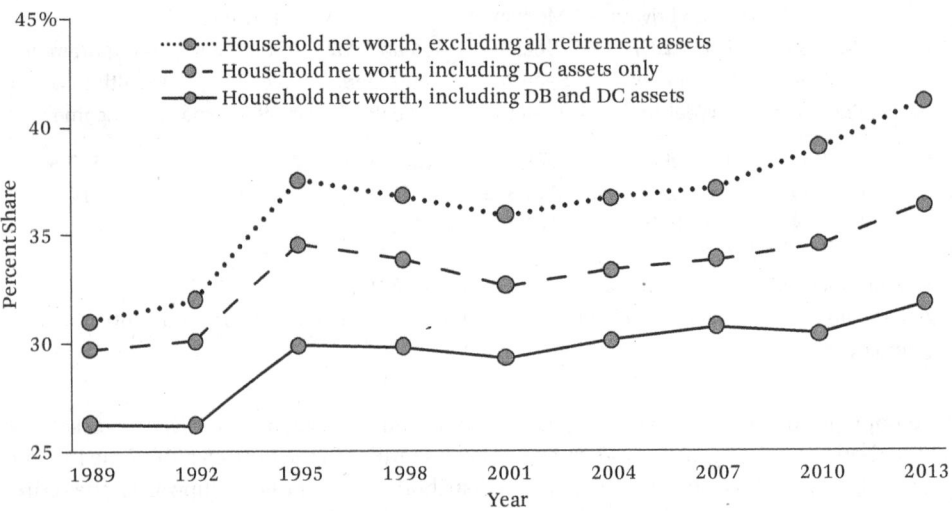

Source: Authors' calculations based on Federal Reserve Board 2014.
Note: Household sector net worth, including DC assets, is from the Survey of Consumer Finances. For a description of the net worth concept used here, see Bricker et al., forthcoming. DB assets are from the Financial Accounts of the United States. For details on how DB assets are distributed in the SCF, see the appendix. Families are resorted by net worth as the measure of net worth varies.

all wealth concentration. The earlier analysis shows that retirement plan participation has fallen, and that decrease is concentrated among low- to middle-income families. At the same time, however, average retirement wealth relative to average (usual) income has not shifted across income groups in ways that suggest pensions and tax-preferred savings are a primary factor driving rising wealth inequality.

Analyzing the net effect of retirement wealth on overall trends in wealth inequality requires some perspective on the concentration of retirement and nonretirement wealth.[21] The share of total wealth (including the distributed DB wealth) held by the top 1 percent of families (sorted by total wealth) rose 6 percentage points between 1989 and 2013, from 26 percent to 32 percent (figure 22, solid line). The share held by the top 25 percent rose 5 percentage points, from 83 percent in 1989 to 88 percent in 2013 (figure 23, solid line). Retirement wealth might affect overall wealth concentration in various ways, but the data suggest the effect has been generally in the direction of mitigating wealth concentration at the very top, with a partial offset because of the shift from DB to DC.

Retirement wealth is much less concentrated than other forms of wealth.[22] The share of total nonretirement wealth held by the top 1 percent of families (sorted by total nonretirement wealth) rose 10 percentage points between 1989 and 2013, from 31 percent to 41 percent (figure 22, dotted line), and the share held

---

21. In addition to thinking about the concentration of retirement and nonretirement wealth, it is also important to note that structural changes in retirement plans themselves may impact the levels of wealth inside and outside accounts. For example, the shift from DB to DC may have led some to shift liquid assets from after-tax holdings to retirement accounts. Household leverage increased in recent decades, and for some we may observe increased debt (such as mortgages) in the nonretirement accounts even though the financial assets (implicitly) funding that debt are in retirement accounts (Wolff, this issue).

22. This is at least in part mechanical, because of binding caps on tax-preferred savings (both DB and DC) in the top wealth groups.

Figure 23. Share of Wealth, Top 25 Percent

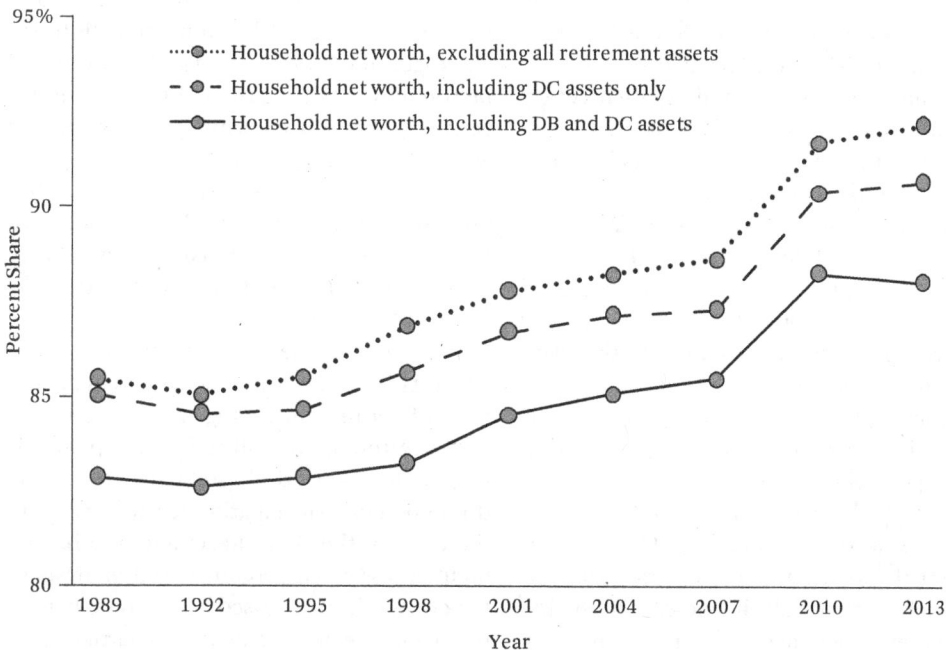

Source: Authors' calculations based on Federal Reserve Board 2014.
Note: Household sector net worth, including DC assets, is from the Survey of Consumer Finances. For a description of the net worth concept used here, see Bricker et al., forthcoming. DB assets are from the Financial Accounts of the United States. For details on how DB assets are distributed in the SCF, see the appendix. Families are resorted by net worth as the measure of net worth varies.

by the top 25 percent rose 7 percentage points, from 85 percent in 1989 to 92 percent in 2013 (figure 23, dotted line). Thus, retirement wealth is less concentrated than nonretirement wealth at the very top, but the concentrations are more similar for the top 25 percent.

Retirement wealth is rising as a share of total wealth (figure 2), from about 20 percent in 1989 to about 30 percent as of 2013. Between this rise and the lower concentration, the first takeaway is that the tax-preferred retirement system helped offset rising wealth concentration at the very top. The top 1 percent of wealth holders own something like 7 to 8 percent of retirement wealth in all years, about 31 percent of nonretirement wealth in 1989, and 41 percent by 2013. Whether one weights by the starting or ending shares of wealth owned by the top 1 percent, the effect of changing wealth composition is certainly noticeable, offsetting 2 to 3 percentage points of the 10 point increase in nonretirement wealth and pushing the overall increase in the top wealth shares down to the actual observed 6 point increase in the top wealth share.

Retirement wealth also mitigated rising wealth concentration for the top 25 percent of wealth holders, though the effect is much more modest, because retirement and nonretirement wealth shares are similar. The top 25 percent of wealth holders (sorted by total wealth) own roughly 82 percent of all DC wealth and about 80 percent of DB wealth. These values are below the nonretirement wealth shares for the top 25 percent, but much less dramatically so than for the top 1 percent. Thus, the increase in retirement wealth on the household balance sheet did less to offset the increasing wealth share of the top 25 percent.

In the other direction, DC wealth is more concentrated than DB wealth, and thus the shift from DB to DC increased wealth concentration (again, the shares of DB and DC assets held by the top 1 percent and top 25 percent of wealth holders have remained relatively stable over time). Measures of concentration using only DC assets and nonretirement wealth (basically the published SCF wealth estimates, the dashed lines in figures 22 and 23) are between the total wealth and nonretirement wealth concentration lines, given that DC assets are more concentrated than DB assets.

The different concentrations of DB and DC wealth lead to the following counterfactual calculations meant to address the question of whether the shift from DB to DC is contributing to rising overall wealth concentration. The top 1 percent owns about 5 percent of DB wealth and about 15 percent of DC wealth, and though the trends over time in those shares may be slightly positive, they are second order. Holding the share of wealth accounted for by retirement wealth constant at the 1989 value (20 percent), the differences in DC versus DB concentration suggest that the increase in the DC share of retirement assets (from 30 percent in 1989 to 50 percent in 2013, figure 2) raised wealth concentration at the top by about 0.4 percentage points (the 10 percentage point differential in DB versus DC concentration * 20 percentage point shift in composition from DB to DC * 20 percent retirement asset share in 1989). Weighting by the 2013 retirement wealth share (30 percent) would raise that to 0.6 percentage points, but either way the effect is modest relative to the overall 6 percentage point increase in the overall top 1 percent wealth share, or the 10 percentage point increase in the nonretirement wealth share. The results are qualitatively similar for the top 25 percent wealth group, the shift from DB to DC accounting for as much as 1 percentage point of the 5 percentage point increase in the top 25 percent total wealth share.

CONCLUSIONS

Retirement wealth is less concentrated than nonretirement wealth in the United States, and that total wealth concentration is rising more slowly than nonretirement is consistent with the growth of retirement wealth relative to overall household sector net worth in recent decades. Put differently, on net, employer-sponsored pensions and other tax-preferred savings have offset some of the rapidly rising wealth inequality in other parts of the household balance sheet. The shift from DB to DC coverage, and the associated shift in the distribution of wealth because of differences in DB versus DC wealth concentration among top wealth holders, has partially offset the equalizing effect of rising retirement wealth. It has done so because top wealth holders now own a substantial share of DC assets, though they have always owned (and continue to own) a big share of DB assets.

At the same time, the life-cycle perspective suggests that even the modest equalizing effects of retirement saving may wane in the future. Although overall retirement plan participation was relatively stable or even rising through 2007, participation fell noticeably in the wake of the Great Recession and has remained lower. The cohort-based analysis of life-cycle trajectories used here shows that the recent decline in retirement plan participation is concentrated among younger families and low- to middle-income families. In previous cohorts, those groups experienced large increases in retirement wealth (relative to income) in middle age, because of realized (actuarial) increases in the value of DB claims. Given that DC accumulation has not been strong enough to replace the lost DB wealth for low- and middle-income families, retirement wealth (relative to income) will not automatically increase in middle age, as it did for previous cohorts, when their pension fund managers increased saving on their behalf.

Retirement plans are evolving in the United States and many other countries as aging populations pressure public systems and changes in labor market conditions pressure employer-sponsored systems. The SCF data show that the decrease (or lack of expected increase) in retirement wealth has been concentrated among those already disadvantaged by rising earnings inequality and rising nonretirement wealth inequality. At the same time, however, the decrease in the value of DB and DC retirement claims for lower-income families has been fairly modest, especially relative to their (stable or falling) incomes. That, though, is just another way of saying that those families had relatively little in the way of non–Social Security claims in the past and now have even less.

One direction for policy emerging from this analysis might be to strengthen and broaden access to voluntary retirement savings plans, though history shows (barring some fundamental design innovation) that such an approach implemented independently of changes to Social Security is unlikely to achieve the goal for many families. One can imagine mandated employer retirement plan coverage or stricter opt-outs, such as in other countries. However, in a philosophical sense, employer mandates are just a particular extension or reform of Social Security, at best giving employers and workers a bit more flexibility in terms of actual implementation. Any serious reform to the private retirement system should take as a starting point that a sound Social Security system is the key to retirement preparedness for most low- and moderate-income families, and that considering the role of both public and private systems in providing retirement security across the entire population is critical.

APPENDIX

Distributing Aggregate DB Pension Assets and Allocating Social Security Wealth to Birth Year Cohort, 1951 to 1960

The Survey of Consumer Finances does not ask respondents about the present value of expected future defined benefit pensions but does collect information about current DB payments of retirees and the expected future claims of workers currently enrolled in DB pension plans. Various papers have used the SCF to estimate household-level DB wealth for distributional and other purposes, and a number of methodological issues need to be addressed to generate these distributional estimates using the data elements available in the survey.

The first decision involves micro-aggregation versus using control totals for aggregate DB pension assets. In this paper, the aggregate value of DB assets by year is taken from the Federal Reserve Board's Financial Accounts (FA) of the United States.[23] DB pension wealth is the portion of Total Pension Entitlements (B.101 line 28) not found in defined contribution pension assets (table L.116, line 26) and annuities held in IRAs at life insurance companies (table L.115, line 24). In the first quarter of 2013, this amounted to $10.9 trillion, or roughly one-sixth of total FA household sector net worth.[24]

In this paper, aggregate DB wealth is distributed across households in a series of steps. We build on the approach of Jesse Bricker and his colleagues (forthcoming), which in turn is largely based on an approach by Emmanuel Saez and Gabriel Zucman (2016). The algorithm we use is still quite rough and does not make use of all of the available information in the SCF. However, that simplicity is also useful because it minimizes the number of behavioral assumptions one needs in order to implement the micro-level allocations.

The first phase of the micro-allocation involves splitting aggregate pension wealth between SCF respondents already receiving benefits, and those who are or were covered by DB plans but not yet receiving benefits. We effectively assume that current beneficiaries have a first claim to plan assets, solve for the present value of promised benefits for those currently receiving benefits, and subtract that amount from total plan assets to solve for the share to be distributed to those not yet receiving benefits. The present value of benefits for those already receiving is based on the respondent-reported values for those benefits, life tables

---

23. FA data is available on the Federal Reserve Board's website, in the quarterly Z1 release. The data can be accessed at https://www.federalreserve.gov/releases/z1/current/ (accessed June 7, 2016).

24. Lisa Dettling and her colleagues (2015) show how total SCF net worth compares with the conceptually equivalent FA measures, but do not discuss DB assets because no direct measure is available in the SCF. One of the SCF values that lines up quite well with FA estimates is the total value of DC balances (including IRAs and other individually held tax-preferred assets). That DC balances track FA assets very well means that we are not introducing any calibration distortion by using FA assets as the control total for DB while using aggregated survey values for DC.

from the Social Security Administration, and an assumed 3 percent real discount factor.

The number of SCF households currently receiving DB benefits increases between 1989 and 2013 (table A1, column 2) and the number of households with promised future benefits decreases (table A1, column 3). The first trend is clearly a function of demographics, in that the aging of the baby boom and increase in life expectancy has led to systematically more DB recipients. The second trend reflects the shift from DB to DC, because fewer current workers are in the queue to receive DB benefits after they retire.

The top-level allocation of assets between current and future beneficiaries is not as obvious, however, because the level of DB assets (table A1, column 1) has grown fast enough that the share of aggregate plan assets we assign to current beneficiaries is actually slightly lower now than at the beginning of the sample period (table A1, column 4). That is, if we assume current beneficiaries have first claim to plan assets, and measure those claims using observed benefits, life tables, and an assumed 3 percent real return, a rising level of plan assets is still left over to be distributed among those who have not yet begun to receive benefits.

Some of the increase in aggregate DB plan assets may be attributable to changes in DB funding principles, but again a key demographic component is also in play, and that underlies how we allocate the remaining DB assets among those not yet receiving benefits. The algorithm we use assigns each future recipient a share of the residual DB plan assets (the amount left over after current beneficiaries claim their share) based on their earnings and the number of years they have been in the plan (to reflect how DB plans generally work) and then discounts those claims relative to a typical benefit commencement age (we use age sixty). The approach is meant to roughly capture how pension actuaries would compute the present value of the obligation. For example, given two observationally equivalent people (in terms of salary and number of years in plan) the actuaries would hold much more in assets for (say) a sixty-year-old than they would for a forty-year-old. Indeed, using the same 3 percent discount rate, those differences in asset holdings are quite large. In acknowledging that the age distribution of those who are expecting but not yet receiving benefits has shifted toward retirement as baby boomers have aged and new labor force entrants are less likely to be covered by DB plans, it becomes clear why (even without a change in funding principles) DB plans are holding much more in assets per future recipient than they did in the past.

The algorithm we use for distributing DB assets among those not yet receiving benefits is not based on SCF respondent-reported expected DB benefits. More elaborate approaches to estimating the asset value of future DB promises have been proposed and implemented by James Poterba (2014), Edward Wolff (2015), and Arthur Kennickell and Annika Sunden (1997). Those papers all discuss the sequence of assumptions about workers' continued participation in their current plans, retirement or claim ages, and life expectancy that one needs to make to bring to bear all of the relevant information in the SCF. In addition to the behavioral assumptions, one also needs to assume that workers have a good understanding of their plan parameters. Based on a match of SCF survey data to participants' actual pension plan details, Martha Starr-McCluer and Sunden (1999) show that assumption is often violated. In addition, there appears to be substantial confusion about certain types of expected payouts, especially in the early years of the SCF (through the late 1990s) before question wording was improved. For example, it may be the case that some of the expected DB benefits are actually payouts of stock options or other compensation that are likely to be of short duration. Including those limited expected payouts in expected DB wealth would greatly distort the time series. Future work should focus on sorting this out, and ideally, one would construct micro-level expected DB benefits that (appropriately discounted) track well with aggregate plan assets in the FA.

The SCF asks several questions about Social Security payments currently being received, and extensive questions about the employment history of both the respondent and spouse or partner. We compute current and future benefits separately and for this paper fo-

Table A1. DB Wealth

Year	DB Wealth ($Billions)	Households Currently Receiving DB Benefits (Thousands)	Households with DB Claims (Thousands)	DB Wealth Allocated to Current DB Recipients	DB Wealth Allocated to Future DB Claims
1989	2,733	15,366	24,873	67%	33%
1992	3,419	14,772	23,126	61	39
1995	4,174	15,978	19,034	64	36
1998	4,895	15,561	18,221	56	44
2001	5,841	15,390	18,283	50	50
2004	6,931	17,342	18,419	58	42
2007	8,317	17,727	16,214	50	50
2010	9,529	18,412	17,518	53	47
2013	10,981	21,047	16,657	59	41

Source: Authors' calculations based on Federal Reserve Board 2014, 2016.

cus specifically on those households interviewed in 2013 and born between 1951 and 1960. Because of differences in mortality between respondents and their spouses, most of these calculations are first done on the individual level before we create a household total.

Starting with current beneficiaries, we take reported Social Security annual benefits for both the respondent and the spouse and then calculate a survival adjusted net present value for each future benefit stream. We use the same life tables and 3 percent discount rate as described in the DB pension process. We then sum these amounts to produce a household-level value for Social Security wealth for those currently receiving benefits.

The calculation for those not currently receiving benefits is more complicated and motivates our approach in this paper of only presenting values for a particular birth year cohort. Household heads in the 1951 to 1960 cohort are between fifty-three and sixty-two, meaning that we have to make a minimum number of assumptions about their work history and current earnings. To simplify the allocation process, we restrict our sample to those households for which the respondent is currently employed. Next, we create a monthly total for all wages and salaries earned by both the respondent and the spouse or partner. We use this monthly wage-salary earnings number as a simplified version of the average indexed monthly earnings (AIME) that we can then input into a "bend point" formula similar to the one the Social Security Administration (SSA) uses to determine monthly benefits. According to SSA data, the monthly bend points in 2013 were $791 and $4,768 and the taxable maximum (at the monthly level) was $9,475. We use these thresholds to compute something similar to the primary insurance amount (PIA) by assigning 90 percent of wages up to the first bend point, 32 percent of earnings between the first and second bend points, and 15 percent of earnings between the second bend point and the taxable maximum. Next, we apply benefit rules associated with each individual's birth year as set by Social Security. Finally, we apply a survival-adjusted discount factor determined by the probability of survival from age sixty-two forward and the number of years before the individual turns sixty-two. This allows us to compute overall retirement wealth for this group of the population.

REFERENCES

Aguiar, Mark, and Erik Hurst. 2005. "Consumption Versus Expenditure." *Journal of Political Economy* 113(5): 919–48.

Argento, Robert, Victoria L. Bryant, and John Sabelhaus. 2015. "Early Withdrawals from Retirement Accounts During the Great Recession." *Contemporary Economic Policy* 33(1)(January): 1–16.

Behaghel, Luc, and David M. Blau. 2012. "Framing

Social Security Reform: Behavioral Responses to Changes in the Full Retirement Age." *American Economic Journal: Economic Policy* 4(4)(November): 41–67.

Bernheim, B. Douglas, Jonathan Skinner, and Steven Weinberg. 2001. "What Accounts for the Variation in Retirement Wealth Among U.S. Households?" *American Economic Review* 91(4): 832–57.

Bricker, Jesse, Lisa J. Dettling, Alice Henriques, Joanne W. Hsu, Kevin B. Moore, John Sabelhaus, Jeffrey Thompson, and Richard A. Windle. 2014. "Changes in U.S. Family Finances from 2010 to 2013: Evidence from the Survey of Consumer Finances." *Federal Reserve Bulletin* 100(4)(September): 1–40.

Bricker, Jesse, Alice Henriques, Jacob Krimmel, and John Sabelhaus. Forthcoming. "Measuring Top Income and Wealth Shares Using Administrative and Survey Data." *Brookings Papers on Economic Activity*.

Bureau of Economic Analysis. 2016. "National Economic Accounts, National Income and Product Accounts." Last modified June 1, 2016. Accessed June 8, 2016. http://www.bea.gov/national/Index.htm.

Butrica, Barbara A., Howard M. Iams, Karen E. Smith, and Eric J. Toder. 2009. "The Disappearing Defined Benefit Pension and Its Potential Impact on the Retirement Incomes of Baby Boomers." *Social Security Bulletin* 69(3): 1–27.

Clark, Robert L., and John Sabelhaus. 2009. "How Will the Stock Market Crash Affect the Choice of Pension Plans?" *National Tax Journal* 62(3)(September): 1–20.

Dettling, Lisa J., Sebastian Devlin-Foltz, Jacob Krimmel, Sarah Pack, and Jeff Thompson. 2015. "Comparing Micro and Macro Sources for Household Accounts in the United States: Evidence from the Survey of Consumer Finances." FEDS working paper no. 2015-86. Washington: Federal Reserve Board.

Federal Reserve Board. 2014. "Survey of Consumer Finances." Last modified October 20, 2014. Accessed January 1, 2016. http://www.federalreserve.gov/econresdata/scf/scfindex.htm.

———. 2016. "Financial Accounts of the United States." Last modified March 10, 2016. Accessed June 1, 2016. https://www.federalreserve.gov/releases/z1/current/.

Goda, Gopi Shah, John B. Shoven, and Sita Nataraj Slavov. 2011. "What Explains Changes in Retirement Plans During the Great Recession," *American Economic Review* 101(3)(May): 29–34.

Gustman, Alan L., Thomas L. Steinmeier, and Nahid Tabatabai. 2010. "What the Stock Market Decline Means for the Financial Security and Retirement Choices of the Near-Retirement Population," *Journal of Economic Perspectives* 24(1): 161–82.

———. 2011. "How Did the Recession of 2007–2009 Affect the Wealth and Retirement of the Near Retirement Age Population in the Health and Retirement Study?" NBER working paper no. 17547. Cambridge, Mass.: National Bureau of Economic Research.

———. 2014. "The Great Recession, Decline and Rebound in Household Wealth for the Near Retirement Population." NBER working paper no. 20584. Cambridge, Mass.: National Bureau of Economic Research.

Henriques, Alice M. 2012. "How Does Social Security Claiming Respond to Incentives? Considering Husbands' and Wives' Benefits Separately." *Finance and Economics Discussion Series* no. 2012-19. Washington: Federal Reserve Board. Accessed May 2, 2016. http://www.federalreserve.gov/pubs/feds/2012/201219/201219abs.html.

Hurd, Michael D., and Susann Rohwedder, 2013. "Heterogeneity in Spending Change at Retirement." *Journal of the Economics of Ageing* 1(2): 60–71.

Investment Company Institute. 2016. "Quarterly Retirement Market Data." Last modified March 24, 2016. Accessed June 1, 2016. http://www.ici.org/research/stats/retirement.

Kennickell, Arthur, and Annika Sunden. 1997. "Pensions, Social Security, and the Distribution of Wealth." *Finance and Economics Discussion Series* no. 1997-55. Washington: Federal Reserve Board. Accessed May 2, 2016. http://www.federalreserve.gov/econresdata/scf/files/pensionk_s.pdf.

Killewald, Alexandra, and Brielle Bryan. 2016. "Does Your Home Make You Wealthy?" *RSF: The Russell Sage Foundation Journal of the Social Sciences* 2(6). doi: 10.7758/RSF.2016.2.6.06.

Love, David A., Michael G. Palumbo, and Paul A. Smith. 2009. "The Trajectory of Wealth in Retirement." *Journal of Public Economics* 93(1-2): 191–208.

Mitchell, Olivia S., and John W. R. Phillips. 2006. "Social Security Replacement Rates for Alternative Earnings Benchmarks." *MRRC working paper* no. 2006-116. Ann Arbor: University of Michigan Retirement Research Center.

Munnell, Alicia H., Anthony Webb, and Francesca Golub-Sass. 2012. "The National Retirement Risk Index: An Update." *Issue in Brief* no. 12-20. Boston, Mass.: Boston College Center for Retirement Research. Accessed May 2, 2016. http://crr.bc.edu/wp-content/uploads/2012/11/IB_12-20-508.pdf.

Poterba, James M. 2014. "Retirement Security in an Aging Society." *NBER* working paper no. 19930. Cambridge, Mass.: National Bureau of Economic Research.

Poterba, James M., Joshua Rauh, Steven Venti, and David Wise. 2007. "Defined Contribution Plans, Defined Benefit Plans, and the Accumulation of Retirement Wealth." *Journal of Public Economics* 91(10): 2062-86.

Poterba, James M., Steven Venti, and David Wise. 2012. "Were They Prepared for Retirement? Financial Status at Advanced Ages in the HRS and Ahead Cohorts." *NBER* working paper no. 17824. Cambridge, Mass.: National Bureau of Economic Research.

———. 2013. "Health, Education, and the Post-Retirement Evolution of Household Assets." *NBER* working paper no. 18695. Cambridge, Mass.: National Bureau of Economic Research.

Saez, Emmanuel, and Gabriel Zucman. 2016. "Wealth Inequality in the United States Since 1913: Evidence from Capitalized Income Tax Data." *Quarterly Journal of Economics* 131(2): 519-78.

Scholz, John Karl, Ananth Seshadri, and Surachai Khitatrakun. 2006. "Are Americans Saving Optimally for Retirement?" *Journal of Political Economy* 114(4): 607-43.

Starr-McCluer, Martha, and Annika Sunden. 1999. "Workers' Knowledge of Their Pension Coverage: A Reevaluation." *Survey of Consumer Finances* working paper. Washington: Federal Reserve Board. Accessed May 2, 2016. https://www.federalreserve.gov/econresdata/scf/files/penknow.pdf.

Wolff, Edward N. 2015. "U.S. Pensions in the 2000s: The Lost Decade?" *Review of Income and Wealth* 61(4): 599-629.

———. 2016. "Household Wealth Trends in the United States, 1962 to 2013: What Happened over the Great Recession?" *RSF: The Russell Sage Foundation Journal of the Social Sciences* 2(6). doi: 10.7758/RSF.2016.2.6.02.

Turning Citizens into Investors: Promoting Savings with Liberty Bonds During World War I

ERIC HILT AND WENDY M. RAHN

Increasing savings rates among households of modest incomes would strengthen their balance sheets and reduce wealth inequality. This paper analyzes one of the largest and most successful efforts to increase the savings of ordinary households in American history. The Liberty Bond drives of World War I persuaded tens of millions of Americans to buy government bonds, which were sold in denominations as low as $50, and could be purchased in installment plans. Using newly collected data on the sales of Liberty Bonds at the county level, we analyze the factors that influenced the degree to which the bond drives were successful. The results highlight the importance of the participation of civil society organizations and local banks in marketing the bonds. We discuss the implications of these findings for the design of modern programs to increase savings.

Keywords: saving, Liberty Bonds, savings bonds, wealth inequality, civil society, financial institutions

Approximately 40 percent of the American population resides in households whose net worth is zero or negative. Among the reasons for the precarious state of the finances of so many American families is their low savings rates (Garon 2012; Wilcox 2008). Fewer than half of all households of median income or below save any money at all in a typical year.[1] In addition, according to Emmanuel Saez and Gabriel Zucman, inequality in savings rates has increased over recent decades, which has contributed to the growth of wealth inequality (2016). Since the early 1980s, the savings rates of households near the top of the wealth distribution have remained fairly steady, but those of middle-class households have declined dramatically. Reversing this trend would strengthen the balance sheets of many American families and reduce the concentration of wealth. In recognition of these facts, in recent years scholars and policymakers have proposed a number of experimental programs and initiatives intended to induce households of modest incomes to save more.

The financial history of the United States offers valuable insights for the design of such initiatives. Especially in wartime, the federal government has sought to encourage ordinary households to save more and purchase government debt securities, with varying degrees of

---

Eric Hilt is associate professor of economics at Wellesley College and research associate at the National Bureau of Economic Research. **Wendy M. Rahn** is professor of political science at the University of Minnesota.

We would like to thank Price Fishback and Paul Rhode for sharing their data on early taxpayers, and Richard Sutch and two anonymous referees for helpful comments. Christina Ferlauto, Polina Soshnin, Ryan Halen, and Lauren Carr provided research assistance. Direct correspondence to: Eric Hilt at ehilt@wellesley.edu, Department of Economics, Wellesley College, Wellesley MA 02481; and Wendy M. Rahn at rahnx003@umn.edu, University of Minnesota, 1414 Social Sciences Building, 267 19th Ave S., Minneapolis MN 55455.

1. Authors' calculations from 2013 Survey of Consumer Finances (Board of Governors 2016).

success. In this paper, we analyze one of the largest and most successful efforts to induce ordinary people to purchase financial assets in American history. The Liberty Bond drives of World War I persuaded tens of millions of American households to buy government bonds, which were sold in denominations as low as $50, and could be purchased in installment plans. The publicity divisions of the Federal Reserve's Liberty Loan committees blanketed the country with materials promoting bond purchases, appealing to a variety of motives to induce the widest possible participation (see figure 1).[2] State and local Liberty Loan committees organized a voluntary sales force that numbered in the hundreds of thousands, enlisting every manner of civic and economic organization in "patriotic partnerships" (Skocpol et al. 2002) as a way to exhort their fellow citizens to do their share. Surveys conducted by the Bureau of Labor Statistics in 1918 and 1919 indicate that around 67 percent of urban, working-class households purchased Liberty Bonds in those years.[3]

Using newly collected data on the sales of Liberty Bonds at the county level, we analyze the factors that influenced the degree to which the bond drives were successful. Our results highlight the importance of the participation of civil society organizations in the bond drives. Conditional on measures of local incomes and wealth, counties with stronger civil society institutions had higher subscription rates. Our analysis also highlights the role of local banks in the promotion of Liberty Bonds and the potential importance of face-to-face contacts in their marketing. Although American society has evolved considerably since World War I, we believe these findings have important implications for to the design of modern programs to increase savings, and we discuss the implications of our findings in the conclusion.

We also discuss subsequent efforts by the federal government to market debt securities to ordinary households. During World War II, a special savings bond, the Series E Defense Bond, was introduced. The promotion of these bonds was guided by the same principles as the promotion of Liberty Bonds, and the sales of Series E bonds were quite successful. In a Gallup Poll conducted in the fall of 1943, fully 80 percent of those surveyed indicated they owned war bonds. In contrast, in December 2001, two months following the terrorist attacks of September 11 of that year, the Treasury Department renamed its Series EE savings bond (the modern successor to the Series E bond) Patriot Bonds. However, no significant campaign was undertaken to promote these bonds, and in particular, no civil society institutions or local banks were enlisted to market the bonds, and no appeals were made (beyond the name change) to individuals' patriotism. The Patriot Bond did not have much success or change household savings rates.

Historians have written extensively about the sales of Liberty Bonds (Kang and Rockoff 2015; Sutch 2015), and have speculated that they contributed to the rapid growth of households' participation in financial markets over subsequent decades (Means 1930; Mitchell 2007; O'Sullivan 2007; Ott 2011; Warshow 1924). This paper presents the first documentation of the rates at which American households purchased Liberty Bonds across a large number of counties. Using new data from archival sources, we present a quantitative analysis of the determinants of Liberty Bond participation across U.S. counties and discuss the results in light of modern initiatives to increase savings.

Before proceeding with our analysis of Liberty Bond sales, we briefly discuss barriers to saving among modern households, which illustrates some of the factors that any program to increase saving would need to overcome.

BARRIERS TO SAVING

For families with very low incomes, saving is difficult. But even households around the median level of income or just above that save at relatively low rates. Many Americans choose to save little or nothing and, as a result, build net worth and accumulate assets very slowly if at all. Only 45 percent of American households have set aside an emergency fund to cover

---

2. Liberty Bond posters are public domain. Digital copies are available at the Library of Congress.

3. Authors' calculations from BLS survey data published in Olney 1995.

Figure 1. Liberty Bond Posters

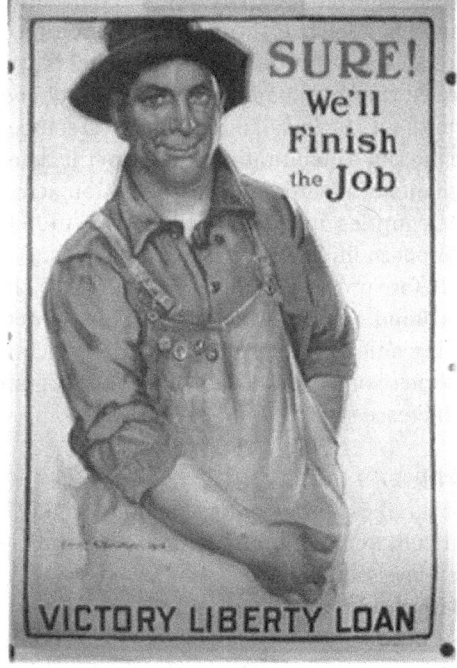

Source: Library of Congress.

three months of expenses in case of a loss of income, and nearly one-third could not deal with such a disruption even through borrowing from family or selling assets. Equally as alarming, one-quarter of nonretired households headed by someone age forty-five or older have no retirement savings and no pension (Board of Governors 2015).

It is possible that this is optimal behavior: people weigh the trade-offs associated with saving and rationally choose not to do much of it. However, evaluating the costs and benefits saving, and choosing how to allocate savings among different financial assets, can be quite difficult. Research by economists shows that behavioral factors may interfere with an individual's ability to make those choices well. Economists argue that people often display time-inconsistent behavior, in that they apply too much weight to current consumption when posed with intertemporal choices (Laibson 1997; O'Donoghue and Rabin 1991). Essentially, savings requires self-control, which many may lack even though they desire to save. More than 80 percent of respondents in a recent national survey reported worrying about not having enough in savings (Pew Charitable Trusts 2015). Even those with savings in retirement accounts reveal that they regard their own savings rates as too low (Choi et al. 2004).

Additional economic explanations for why some people save more than others emphasize other sources of individual-level heterogeneity such as cognitive skills or financially relevant beliefs (for reviews, see Guiso and Sodini 2013; Karlan, Ratan, and Zinman 2014; De Nardi 2015). These individual differences are correlated with underlying demographic traits such as income, race, education, and age, thereby contributing to group-level stratification in wealth. For example, among the poor, the exigencies of everyday living deplete cognitive capacity, making it more difficult to plan for the future (Mani, Mullainathan, Shafir, and Zhao 2013). Minorities, women, and young people score lower on tests of financial literacy, a type of cognitive resource that is linked to savings behavior and other financial decision making, such as investing in stocks (Lusardi and Mitchell 2014).

Regardless of levels of financial sophistication, people may choose to forgo savings in banking institutions because they lack trust in such financial intermediaries (Karlan, Ratan, and Zinman 2014) or because they harbor doubts about the trustworthiness of people whom they do not know (Guiso, Sapienza, and Zingales 2004). According to a Pew Research Center poll in 2015, Americans who believe that banks have a negative influence on the country outnumber those who think the opposite. And in the most recent General Social Survey, only 15 percent of the public reported having a lot of confidence in banks, but more than 40 percent had hardly any. Furthermore, in the same survey, almost two-thirds of the respondents told the interviewers they do not trust most people. The latter belief is demographically patterned in ways that reinforce group-based stratification (Brehm and Rahn 1997), and social mistrust has been linked to lower levels of participation in financial markets, particularly stock ownership (Guiso, Sapienza, and Zingales 2008).

Other explanations for America's low saving rate focus on transaction costs or other supply-side factors that limit people's access to finance. For low- and moderate-income (LMI) individuals, the costs associated with having a checking or savings account can be significant barriers to using mainstream financial services (Tufano and Schneider 2005; Barr and Blank 2011). Bank accounts often come with fees, require minimum balances, and in other ways discourage people of limited means from using them. As a consequence, many simply "don't do banks" (O'Brien 2012, 3). According to the FDIC's 2013 Survey of Unbanked and Underbanked Households, around 30 percent of Americans do not have a savings account, and about 7 percent own neither a checking nor a savings account and are considered unbanked. Roughly 20 percent of U.S. households have a conventional banking account but also rely on alternative financial services (AFS), such as payday lenders, pawn shops, and check cashing services. The FDIC considers such households to be "underbanked" (Burhouse et al. 2014). According to the 2013 FDIC survey, lack of trust in banks is one of the most important reasons unbanked households offer for avoiding mainstream financial institutions.[4]

According to a 2011 FDIC survey of 567 banks, profitability is a major obstacle to developing affordable products for the financially underserved (Rhine and Robbins 2012). Thus banks themselves are reluctant to pursue LMI customers, despite the competition of the rapidly growing AFS sector, by one estimate now a $100 billion business (Wolkoitz and Schmall 2015).

This discussion has a number of important implications. First, many households may be making choices likely contrary to their long-term interests, suggesting a role for intervention by the government or nongovernmental organizations. Second, the banking and financial systems of the United States, as sophisticated as they are, are not meeting the needs of ordinary households very well, and have relatively little incentive to encourage households of modest income levels to save more by offering them attractive savings vehicles. Third, the banking and financial systems are not trusted by ordinary Americans, meaning that an intervention to increase savings may be made more effective by distancing itself from those institutions.

We next turn to the Liberty Bond campaigns of World War I, which we believe offer valuable insights into the design of such an intervention.

LIBERTY BONDS

The scale of the expenditures resulting from the American participation in World War I was unprecedented. For each of the years 1913 through 1916, total expenditures of the federal government were less than $750 million. By 1919, expenditures grew to $18.5 billion, a nearly twenty-five-fold increase (Carter et al. 2006, table Ea584-87).

In the months leading up to America's involvement in the war, vigorous debates raged outside and inside Congress about whether, and how much, to rely on increased taxation rather than debt to finance the war effort. Higher taxes, the alternative favored by most economists of the day, organized labor, and Progressive politicians such as Senator Bob LaFollette, were resisted by banks, businesses, and the wealthy. Initially, Secretary of the Treasury William Gibbs McAdoo called for half of war financing to be provided by increased taxes of various kinds, and the other half to be raised by issuing debt. Persuaded by those who argued that high taxes would reduce support for the war by the wealthy, alarmed by revised estimates of the cost of the war, and equipped with contemporary British and German examples of government efforts to market their war debt to ordinary citizens, McAdoo eventually settled on a one-third to two-thirds split between taxes and borrowing. In the end, taxes financed about one-quarter of the cost of the war (Kang and Rockoff 2015; Gilbert 1970; Sutch 2015).

In addition to relieving the burdens imposed by taxation, financing the war through borrowing offered a number of other advantages. It was hoped that selling bonds to American households would induce them to reduce their consumption and thereby reduce inflationary pressures during wartime. Owning war bonds was also seen as giving American households a financial stake in the war effort and increasing support for the war. McAdoo believed that people who were unable to support the country by fighting would welcome a chance to do their share in the "financial trenches" at home (1931).

Borrowing on such an enormous scale required extraordinary efforts to market bonds to institutions and households that had never previously purchased government debt. The usual underwriting and distribution networks for government bonds did not have the capacity to handle that level of borrowing on anything close to reasonable terms. For suggestions about how to organize an effort to market war bonds on a mass scale, McAdoo looked to the experience of the Civil War. As one method

---

4. This finding is underscored by the experience of Lisa Sevron, a New School public policy professor who worked as a teller at a check cashing establishment in the South Bronx. She reports that many of the store's regular customers developed a personal connection with her or the other tellers, trusting them more than the bankers who were just down the street (2013).

Table 1. Liberty Loan Subscriptions, by Loan

	First 1917	Second 1917	Third 1918	Fourth 1918	Victory 1919
Subscriptions ($billions)	2.000	3.809	4.177	6.959	4.500
Number of subscribers (millions)	4.0	9.4	18.4	22.8	11.8
Average subscription amount ($)	759	491	227	306	445

Source: Authors' compilation based on U.S. Department of the Treasury 1917, 1918, 1919.

of raising revenue, then Treasury Secretary Salmon Chase tapped the financier Jay Cooke to try his hand at selling government debt directly to ordinary Americans. Cooke did so by organizing a sales force paid on commission. Motivating sales agents through financial self-interest, McAdoo believed, was a "fundamental error.... Chase did not capitalize the emotion of the people, yet it was there and he might have put it to work" (1931, 374). McAdoo put the emotion of the American people to work by organizing four Liberty Loan drives conducted during the war. Rather than the continuous sale of bonds, the loans were marketed in a series of campaigns, each with a specific opening and closing date and sales goal, in order to keep engagement levels high. A final Victory Loan drive was conducted after the Armistice.

Table 1 presents summary data on each of the individual loan drives. The bonds were sold in denominations as low as $50, and subscriptions could be fulfilled through installment plans, both of which made the bonds accessible to a broad range of American households.[5] For example, a $50 Liberty Bond could be purchased by a payment of $4 up front, and then twenty-three weekly payments of $2. All told, the five bond drives raised around $24 billion. As a constant share of gross domestic product, this would be equivalent to more than $5 trillion today (calculation based on Williamson 2015). Sales of the fourth Liberty Loan alone totaled nearly $7 billion: nearly twenty-three million people, more than 20 percent of the U.S. population, bought bonds. During the third and fourth loan drives, more than two million people volunteered as foot soldiers for McAdoo's "financial front" (U.S. Treasury 1918).

Civil Society and the Liberty Loan Drives

The broad participation of the American public in the financing of the war was the result of a massive mobilization effort that left no corner of civil society untouched. The actual task of organizing McAdoo's financial army fell to the Federal Reserve System, which had been created by legislation passed in 1913. The Federal Reserve formed central Liberty Loan committees that in turn created state Liberty Loan committees. The state committees then arranged for local committees in counties and in urban areas. The federated nature of the Liberty Loan committees resembled the structure of U.S. civil society organizations at the time (Skocpol et al. 2002). Members of the committees were often drawn from the ranks of community notables: bankers, leaders of civic and business organizations, and newspaper publishers and editors.

Many of the reserve banks, through the publicity divisions of their central committees, circulated material about the bond selling efforts. The issues of the Minneapolis Fed's newsletter, *The Liberty Bell*, for example, contained inspirational stories, bond selling tips based on successful experiences in various locales, and an official Ninth District Song. The Chicago Fed distributed the *War Loan Reveille* to 3,600 local newspapers and the state's bankers, and specific appeals were written for inclusion in major trade journals and fraternal publications such as *Hoard's Dairyman*, the *Michigan Druggist, Modern Woodmen*, and *the Wisconsin Medical Journal* (McCutheon 1918).

---

5. Adjusting for inflation, $50 in 1919 is equivalent to $673 today. This is not an insignificant sum but an amount similar in magnitude to the cost of many common household appliances.

Civic and religious organizations were recruited by Liberty Loan committees to assist in bond sales. At the suggestion of the New York Fed, the Treasury Department recommended to President Wilson that the aid of the Boy Scouts of America be sought; in May 1917, Wilson officially called upon their service. Over the five loan drives, the Scouts secured tens of millions in subscriptions (Murray 1937). Also in that month, a separate women's-only organization, the National Women's Liberty Loan Committee, was created and chaired by Secretary McAdoo's wife Eleanor (who was also the daughter of President Wilson). The Women's Committee worked primarily through existing women's groups and fraternal organizations: the Ancient Order of the Hiberians Ladies' Auxiliary, the Daughters of the American Revolution, the National Grange, the Woman's Christian Temperance Union, the Women's Suffrage Association, the Young Women's Christian Association, and countless others. Under the aegis of the committee, the women of America became a formidable salesforce numbering in the hundreds of thousands, and they were frequently able to outraise their male counterparts (National Women's Liberty Loan Committee 1920). On Liberty Loan Sundays, America's clergy took their pulpits to preach the virtues of bond buying, and model sermons were distributed widely. For example, the Speaker's Bureau of the Seventh Federal Reserve published its own handbook, *Suggestions for Liberty Loan Sermons*, and the Chicago Fed sent more than a thousand copies of "The Legions of Christ" to Protestant and Catholic ministers in Cook County (McCutheon 1918).

The Committee on Public Information (CPI), created by executive order a few days after Congress made America's participation in the Great War official, was another important part of the bond drives. The person tapped to lead it, George Creel, was a muckraking journalist and vocal Wilson supporter. The Creel Committee, as the CPI was more commonly known, was a "gargantuan advertising agency the like of which the country had never known" (Mock and Larson 1939, 4). Through its News Division, it generated copy used by a largely cooperative press to inform the public of war goings-on. Its advertising division persuaded publishers to donate space for CPI propaganda; and its Division of Work with the Foreign Born had the all-important task of inspiring patriotism among the millions of people on American soil whose birthplace was someplace else. As a way to demonstrate their loyalty, members of some nationality groups, especially German Americans, were encouraged to buy Liberty Bonds. Failure to do so put them at risk of harassment or worse by zealous patriots (Breen 1984; Luebke 1974). Even the film industry was enlisted. Hollywood, for its part, understood that participating in the war effort was an opportunity that could further the industry's long-term interests, a sort of "practical patriotism" that married allegiance with prosperity (DeBauche 1997). Major stars such as Charlie Chaplin and America's sweetheart, Mary Pickford, helped promote Liberty Bonds through appearances at rallies and in patriotic films.

In addition to producing and distributing literature in multiple languages, creating news reels, recruiting American artists to design posters and billboards, and hosting war exhibitions in major cities, the CPI organized a volunteer speakers bureau known as the Four Minute Men (FMM), "the most unique and one of the most effective agencies developed during the war for the stimulation of public opinion and the promotion of unity" (Committee on Public Information 1920, 21). Supplied with material by the CPI, the volunteers wrote their own speeches and presented them during intermission at movie theaters. The speeches were calibrated to last no longer than the time it took the projectionist to change reels during a movie, and speakers were instructed to deliver them without notes (Axelrod 2009). Soon the work of the FMM expanded to include forums at churches, fraternal lodges, labor unions, and other gathering places. The FMM were issued talking points for each of the four Liberty Loan drives by the CPI. In addition to reminding their audiences of the principles for which the allies were fighting, the FMM were asked to provide information on the particulars of the issue, explain basic principles of investing, and exhort the virtues of savings and thrift.[6] According to Creel, seventy-five thousand volunteered for service as FMM across more than five thousand communities giving more than seven million speeches (1928).

Four Minute Men were found on 153 college campuses, and a junior division was created to sell War Savings Stamps (Committee on Public Information 1920). Marketed to households of modest means and to children, the stamps were distinct from Liberty Bonds and came in denominations as low as twenty-five cents. War Savings Stamps were designed to inculcate habits of thrift among the nation's schoolchildren and the general population (U.S. Treasury, National War-Savings Committee 1917),[7] and some of their features were later incorporated into the design of government savings bonds. The War-Savings Committee of the Treasury Department encouraged local communities to form war savings societies, small groups of ten or more individuals that were to "lay the foundations of thrift and economy throughout the United States" (1917, 6). By June 1918, more than seventy thousand such societies existed across the country (U.S. Treasury, National War-Savings Committee 1918a, 1918b). However, as a source of finance for the war, savings stamps were far less important than Liberty Bonds.

Commercial and Financial Institutions and Liberty Bonds

Financial institutions were critical to the success of the Liberty Loan drives. Banks that were members of the Federal Reserve System were given a powerful incentive to hold Liberty Bonds in that they could use them as collateral for loans from the Fed itself. But in addition to purchasing Liberty Bonds for their own accounts, banks and other financial institutions facilitated the payment of Liberty Loan subscriptions and extended credit to customers holding Liberty Bonds as collateral, effectively enabling individuals to purchase Liberty Bonds on credit.[8] Banks were also encouraged to offer to their customers a free place to keep their bonds (Leon 1918).

The Liberty Loan committees of the Federal Reserve districts actively monitored the subscriptions obtained through individual banks, and in some cases published bank-level subscription data for the financial community and the general public to scrutinize. For example, the Liberty Loan Committee of the Sixth Federal Reserve District published a series of pamphlets on the banks within each state in the district, with titles such as "What the Banks of Georgia Did in the Third Liberty Loan—Did Your Bank Do Its Part?" In that district, each bank was allocated a quota for subscriptions, and the pamphlets listed those quotas and the amount of actual subscriptions received for every bank.

Outside banking, American commercial enterprises were called on in a variety of ways to market the loans to their employees and their customers and to provide help with advertising and publicity. Department stores were turned into points of sale, and their store windows were given over to displays designed to inspire Liberty Loan purchases (*New York Times* 1918). Clerks were told to push Liberty Bonds in addition to merchandise, and in some stores, customers could use Liberty Bonds as credit against which to make purchases (Clifford 1917; *New York Times* 1917). Railroads, packing houses, and other large employers offered their employees an opportunity to buy bonds through payroll deductions. President Wilson

---

6. "For saving is the essence of these bond issues. The demand is that we, all of us, save out of our current earnings. We must save every week, every day from the money we get. . . . The appeal to save also involves this: Every man who saves (even if only a few dollars) becomes thereby a capitalist. . . . Fifty or a hundred dollars saved up instead of used hand to mouth means capital; and capital, even on the smallest scale, means freedom from the next day's worry, means independence, means power" (Committee on Public Information 1918).

7. "Thrift is conservation. Thrift is discrimination. Thrift is self-discipline, self-control, self-respect. Thrift is a foundation stone of character. Thrift is practical patriotism" (U.S. Treasury, National War-Savings Committee 1918a or b, 3)

8. Banks were instructed by the Federal Reserve to limit the rate of interest charged on loans with Liberty Bonds as collateral to the coupon rate of the bonds themselves.

Table 2. Liberty Bond Purchase Rates in Historical Perspective

1918–1919 Households		2013 Households	
1918–1919 Income	Liberty Bond Purchased in 1918–1919, Percent	Equivalent 2013 Income	Stock Ownership Rate, Direct or Indirect
Less than $1,020	36.7	Less than $13,800	11.4
$1,020 to $2,110	69.7	$13,800 to $28,399	26.4
$2,110 to $3,470	86.1	$28,400 to $46,699	49.7

Source: Authors' calculations from data collected in Olney 1995 and Board of Governors 2016.

designated April 26, 1918, as Liberty Day, and urged that every employee be released from service at noon to participate in Liberty Loan festivities (Whitney 1923).

Labor unions were also enlisted. The American Alliance for Labor and Democracy, headed by Samuel Gompers of the American Federation of Labor, was created to reach out to organized labor. Nominally independent, in fact the organization was a front for the CPI. The alliance established 150 branch offices across the country and orchestrated two hundred mass rallies (Axelrod 2009).

Subscriptions by Households of Modest Incomes

Some perspective on the success of the Liberty Bond drives in inducing ordinary households to make purchases can be found in data collected by the Bureau of Labor Statistics (BLS) in 1918 and 1919. In those years, the BLS conducted one of the first surveys of American households' incomes and expenditures. The survey was not intended to be nationally representative but instead focused on families in the middle of the earnings distribution headed by married couples and residing in urban areas.[9] The survey's comprehensive questions regarding the uses of households' funds revealed any purchases of Liberty Bonds.

Table 2 presents data on the rate at which the surveyed households had purchased Liberty Bonds within the previous year. This rate ranged from nearly 37 percent to more than 86 percent for the higher-income households in the survey.[10] Perhaps the best way to put these rates into perspective is to compare them with modern rates of ownership of financial assets. The most widely held financial asset today, besides a checking account, is common stock. Table 2 also presents data from the 2013 Survey of Consumer Finances on the rate at which households of different income levels owned stock, either directly or indirectly through mutual funds or retirement accounts. The income groups are the 2013 equivalent amounts of the incomes of the 1919 data—that is, the 1919 incomes adjusted for inflation into 2013 dollars. Comparing the data in the two panels shows that modern households own stock at far lower rates than 1919 households of equivalent income owned Liberty Bonds. The modern data also count all stock ownership, which presumably includes amounts purchased in earlier years, whereas the Liberty Bond data includes only purchases during the current year.[11] The Liberty Bond drives induced households to become owners of financial assets at extraordinary rates.

Further detail regarding the purchases of

---

9. The BLS surveyed 12,817 families residing in ninety-nine cities, mostly during late 1918 and 1919 (see Olney 1995).

10. The survey did not include any high-income households; these are the higher-income households among those actually sampled. James Feigenbaum (2015) documents the relationship between the incomes of surveyed households and the income of all households.

11. On the other hand, the BLS households may not have been representative of all households in their income groups, in that they were all married and living in urban areas.

Table 3. Liberty Bond Purchases

	(Families Making Liberty Bond Purchases)	
1919 Income	Median Value, Purchases	Median Percentage of Income
Less than $1,020	40	4.7
$1,020 to $2,110	60	4.4
$2,110 to $3,470	140	5.5

Source: Authors' calculations from data BLS Survey data collected in Olney 1995.

Liberty Bonds by ordinary households is presented in table 3, which shows the median value of the amount purchased, among those households that made purchases in the BLS survey. The smallest denomination Liberty Bond was $50, so the amounts in the table indicate that many households purchased Liberty Bonds in installment plans, and had not yet fully completed their purchases (the amounts in the table reflect actual expenditures on the bonds, rather than the amounts subscribed.) The data in the table indicate that households that purchased Liberty Bonds typically spent between 4.5 and 5.5 percent of their gross income on their purchases, a substantial amount for an asset that had not existed just two years before the survey was taken.

EMPIRICAL ANALYSIS OF VARIATION IN LIBERTY LOAN PARTICIPATION RATES

McAdoo succeeded in creating a popular financial movement. In doing so, he induced millions of ordinary Americans to save by investing in Liberty Bonds and introduced most of those households to the ownership of bonds for the first time. The movement, however, proved to be more popular and successful in some places than in others. For example, in the fourth, and largest, Liberty Loan drive, around 22 percent of the American population subscribed. But the success rates of McAdoo's financial troops varied widely, from 6.2 percent in North Carolina to 38.7 percent in Wyoming. In general, midwestern and western states had relatively high subscription rates, southern states had very low ones, and mid-Atlantic and New England states fell somewhere in between.

The success of the Liberty Bond drives in different places was clearly related to the level of wealth in general and banking resources in particular. However, the existence of strong civil society institutions and social capital likely also aided the campaign's success. In some places, citizens showed high civic engagement and established a broad and vibrant set of institutions that formed the backbone of local Liberty Bond sales efforts. In other places, fewer such institutions existed and the loan campaigns were not as well organized or staffed. Differences in the quality of institutions were therefore likely to have contributed to the variation in Liberty Loan subscription rates.

Data

No disaggregated data on Liberty Loan sales were ever published by the Federal Reserve or the Treasury. The annual Treasury reports include figures for sales and subscription rates at the state level and for larger cities, but those data conceal most of the geographical variation in Liberty Bond sales. For this paper, we assembled a new dataset of Liberty Bond subscriptions at the county level for several Federal Reserve districts from documents found in a number of different archives. These documents were published by the Federal Reserve Liberty Loan committees or by state-level Liberty Loan committees. The Minneapolis Federal Reserve, for example, published county tallies for the Ninth District in one of its *Liberty Bell* newsletters that we uncovered at the South Dakota Historical Society. Other reports turned up at the National Archives, in Princeton University's Liberty Loan Archive, the Library of Congress, and in books that individual states published on their World War I involvement.

Table 4. County Characteristics

Variable	Mean	Min	Max	SD	Observations
Liberty Bond subscription rate, fourth loan	0.14	0.00	0.57	0.10	1,378
Farm values per capita, 1920	$463.76	$0.08	$2,677	$414	1,378
Tax returns per capita, 1920	0.03	0.00	0.24	0.03	1,371
Log population, 1920	7.04	4.17	13.83	0.77	1,378
Percent urban, 1920	0.15	0.00	1.00	0.21	1,378
Sharecroppers as pct. of all farm tenants	0.49	0.00	1.00	0.21	1,378
Percent illiterate, 1910	0.09	0.00	0.57	0.08	1,378
Percent Catholic, 1910	0.07	0.00	0.85	0.10	1,378
Percent foreign born, 1910	0.09	0.00	0.49	0.10	1,378
Log banks per sq. mile, 1920 (000s)	7.37	0.00	4.23	6.01	1,366
Log banks per capita, 1920 (000s)	0.52	0.00	1.82	0.38	1,366
Boy Scouts per capita, 1917 (000s)	2.11	0.05	6.00	0.99	28
Women's clubs per capita, 1914 (000s)	0.08	0.01	0.19	0.05	28

Source: Authors' calculations from data collected in Haines 2010, U.S. Congressional Serial Set 1918, and Winslow 1914.

All told, we have data for Liberty Bond subscription rates for 1,378 counties, located within six of the twelve Federal Reserve districts.[12]

For the empirical analysis, we use the subscription rate for the largest (fourth) Liberty Loan, but in cases where we only have data for other loans, we substitute the subscription rate for the fifth loan, or for the third loan, where available. (In our empirical models, we include fixed effects for the different loans.) Our analysis focuses on the variation in this data across counties and in particular investigates whether measures of the strength of local civil society organizations or the presence of banks—both of which were enlisted in the loan drives to promote bond sales—were correlated with higher subscription rates, conditional on measures of wealth and other social characteristics. We therefore match these subscription data to contemporaneous data on local populations, wealth, and demographics from the federal census (Haines 2010). These data include measures of urbanization, illiteracy, farm values per capita, the share of farm tenants who were sharecroppers, and the prevalence of Catholics and the foreign born. No income data are available for the period, but we include the best available proxy, the number of tax returns filed as a percentage of a county's population, obtained from the U.S. Treasury.[13] We also include data we have collected on membership in civil society organizations. This produces a county-level dataset we can use to analyze the variation in Liberty Bond subscription rates.

Table 4 provides summary information on the variables in our analysis. Note the enormous variation across counties in subscription rates, from virtually zero to nearly 60 percent of a county's population. The counties included in the sample also varied quite significantly in their levels of wealth and social composition. On average, only 3 percent of the sample counties' populations filed income tax returns, and 49 percent of their farm tenants were share-

---

12. We have data for at least one Liberty Loan for all the counties in the Fourth (Cleveland), Fifth (Richmond), Eighth (Kansas City), Ninth (Minneapolis), and Twelfth (San Francisco) Federal Reserve districts, along with Iowa, located in the Seventh (Chicago) District. The publications of the Liberty Loan committees of the remaining Federal Reserve Districts do not appear to have included county-level data on subscription rates for any of the Liberty Loans.

13. For the 1920 tax year, a tax return was required only of individuals with a net income of $1,000, and married couples with a net income of $2,000. We thank Price Fishback and Paul Rhode for these data, which are drawn from a 1923 U.S. Treasury Department report.

Figure 2. Liberty Bond Participation, Sample Counties

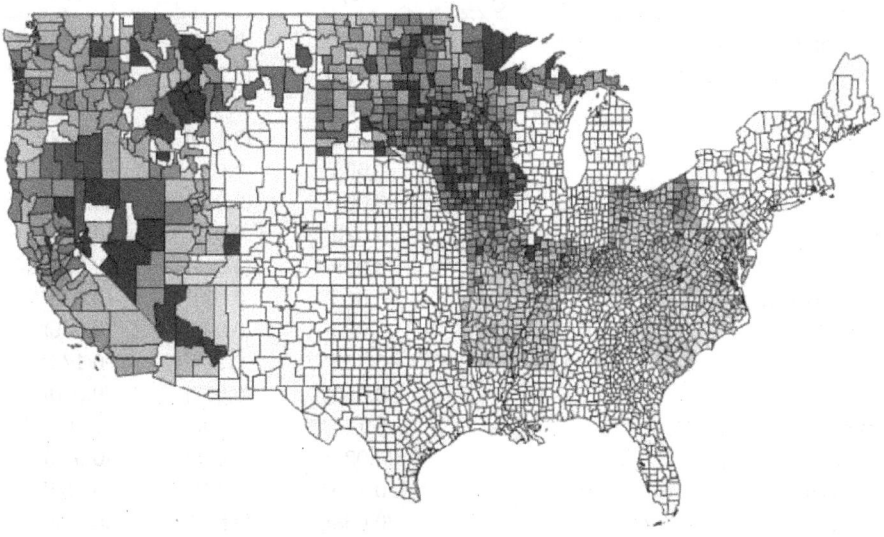

Source: Authors' calculations from data collected for the Fourth, Fifth, Eighth, Ninth, and Twelfth Federal Reserve Districts, and for the State of Iowa.

croppers. The mean values of the proportions illiterate, Catholic, and foreign born among the sample counties were 9, 7, and 9 percent, respectively. And the sample counties had on average 0.52 (log) banks per capita.

Before proceeding with the analysis, an illustration of the counties included in the sample, and the variation in Liberty Bond subscription rates across those counties, is presented in figure 2. In the figure, subscription rates are indicated by the darkness of the shading of the counties; counties for which we have no data are white. The figure clearly illustrates the higher subscription rates in the upper Midwest and West relative to the South. Subscription rates were particularly high in Iowa and Minnesota counties, places with both strong civil society institutions and large numbers of banks.

Findings

Table 5 presents estimates of cross-sectional regression models in which the economic and social determinants of Liberty Bond subscription rates are analyzed at the county level. The first column presents results of a simple specification in which only the available measures of wealth and income from the era are included—farm values per capita, which give the capitalized value of profits from farming, and the proportion of the population filing tax returns. Wealthier counties would obviously have had greater resources to commit to Liberty Bonds, and would likely also have had a greater capacity to participate in volunteer efforts to promote Liberty Bond purchases. Unsurprisingly, these variables are both very strongly correlated with Liberty Bond subscription rates and together explain just over 50 percent of the variation across counties. Richer counties clearly subscribed to Liberty Bonds at much higher rates.

We next add a number of variables related to economic and social characteristics of the counties. Both a county's population and its level of urbanization may have influenced the ease with which the bonds could be marketed. In particular, more densely populated communities may have made household canvassing much more efficient at a time when most families were without cars or telephones. The numerous promotional materials circulated about the bonds required that the targets of these appeals be able to read for the appeals to be effective, and thus bonds may have sold better among more literate populations. Literacy was

Table 5. Determinants of Liberty Bond Subscription Rates

	(1)	(2)	(3)	(4)
Farm values per capita (000s)	0.111***	0.077***	0.050**	0.045**
	(0.015)	(0.013)	(0.014)	(0.015)
Tax returns per capita	1.070**	0.486**	0.450*	0.439**
	(0.269)	(0.141)	(0.169)	(0.152)
Log population		−0.008	−0.011	−0.008
		(0.005)	(0.006)	(0.005)
Percent urban		0.070**	0.079**	0.071**
		(0.005)	(0.021)	(0.021)
Sharecroppers as percentage of tenants		−0.065**	−0.071**	−0.070**
		(0.020)	(0.021)	(0.019)
Percent illiterate		−0.235***	−0.224***	−0.174**
		(0.050)	(0.053)	(0.050)
Percent Catholic		0.114***	0.102***	0.100***
		(0.023)	(0.022)	(0.020)
Percent foreign born		0.190**	0.141	0.158**
		(0.068)	(0.088)	(0.054)
Log banks per square mile			1.027	0.730
			(0.608)	(0.503)
Log banks per capita			42.793**	41.688**
			(14.55)	(13.236)
Boy Scouts per capita (000s)				11.330*
				(5.000)
Women's clubs per capita (000s)				8.8032
				(105.319)
Constant	0.166*	0.175**	0.195**	0.131*
	(0.071)	(0.055)	(0.064)	(0.058)
Observations	1,367	1,367	1,358	1,358
R^2	0.510	0.675	0.671	0.701
Loan FE	Y	Y	Y	Y

Source: Authors' calculations.
Note: Robust standard errors in parentheses.
*p < 0.10, **p < 0.05, ***p < 0.01

also related to human capital and educational attainment, and therefore may also have reflected the income level of a county. To the extent that literacy rates reflected the quality and availability of local schools, these rates may also have indicated the degree to which public goods were provided in a county, and perhaps also the quality of institutions generally in that county.

We also include a measure of economic inequality: whether farm tenants were sharecroppers, as opposed to paying their rent with cash. Agricultural labor markets in early twentieth-century America were hierarchical: land owners at the top, cash tenants next, and sharecroppers and farm laborers at the bottom (Depew, Fishback, and Rhode 2013). Inequality hinders the production of public goods (Anderson, Mellor, and Milyo 2008), and thus we expect that participation in the Liberty Loan drives will be lower in more unequal counties. As noted, the foreign born were particular targets of CPI mobilization, and thus we include a measure of the proportion born abroad. Catholic organizations such as the Knights of Columbus and the National Catholic War Council promoted participation in the war effort, including buying Liberty Bonds. We therefore incorporate the Catholic percentage of the population in our specification.

The results, reported in the second column of the table, are strongly consistent with our expectations. More urbanized counties had higher subscription rates. Economic inequality reduced participation in the Liberty Loan drives. Literacy, on the other hand, appears to have been strongly correlated with Liberty Bond ownership. Counties with more Catholics and with larger foreign-born populations had higher subscription rates as well. These latter results provide at least suggestive evidence of the effects of the Liberty Bond sales campaigns. The presence of large numbers of Catholics was likely correlated with Catholic organizations that were enlisted in the sales effort. And the foreign born were specifically targeted in the campaigns. For these groups, Liberty Loans may also have had a compensatory effect, in that they had lower social status than Protestants and the native born.

In the third column of table 5 we add our data on banks: not total banking resources, which would be very closely related to income and wealth, but the total number of banks, scaled by both population and by county size in square miles (Rajan and Ramcharan 2015). These variables capture the reach of the banking system in the population; greater bank density should have facilitated more bond subscriptions, through more frequent and convenient contacts between local bankers and the surrounding population. Apparently, it did. The subscription rates in counties with above-average bank density were substantially higher than in other counties with no bank access. Conditional on income and wealth, and on a number of different social characteristics, counties with greater numbers of banks, which were actively involved in selling Liberty Bonds, had higher subscription rates.

Finally, in the last column, we add two indicators of social capital, both measured at the state level on a per capita basis: membership in the Boy Scouts and the number of women's clubs.[14] As noted, each of these groups played a significant role in marketing the bonds.

Therefore, we expect that in states where these organizations had a greater presence, more people would have bought Liberty Bonds. Both coefficients on our civil society variables are positive; however, only that of the Boy Scouts is statistically significant.

The most important insight that emerges from these regressions is that Liberty Bond subscriptions were not simply a matter of income and wealth, although both were quite important. Given the very strong correlation between financial asset ownership and income in modern household surveys, one might be tempted to believe that Liberty Bonds would have been purchased mainly in wealthy areas. Yet even conditional on measures of income and wealth, the local strength of the Liberty Loan campaigns clearly mattered. We cannot directly measure the size or structure of local Liberty Loan committees, but the regression estimates indicate that the presence of greater numbers of organizations that were enlisted in the campaigns was correlated with higher subscription rates. Moreover, the presence of greater numbers of individuals who were specifically targeted by the campaigns, such as the foreign born, was also correlated with higher levels of participation. Social conditions mattered as well; more urbanized counties, counties with lower rates of illiteracy, and counties with lower levels of inequality also had higher subscription rates. These measures likely indicate the extent to which counties were amenable to the efforts of the campaigns to promote participation in the Liberty Bond drives.

Taken together, these results suggest that the massive campaigns to market Liberty Bonds were effective. They also demonstrate that, at least in principle, it is possible to raise the savings of ordinary households by enlisting financial institutions and civil society organizations in efforts to promote savings vehicles. To be sure, the conditions that prevailed during World War I were unusual in many respects. We believe, however, that these results offer valuable lessons for the design of modern initiatives to promote savings. We discuss the specific implications of these findings in the con-

---

14. We collected data on Boy Scout membership from the *8th Annual Report of the Boy Scouts of America* (U.S. Congressional Serial Set 1918) and on women's clubs from the *Annual Directory* (Winslow 1914).

clusion; in the next section, we describe efforts to promote government bonds during and after World War II.

SERIES E BOND SALES DURING WORLD WAR II

In the decades following World War I, the federal government continued to market its bonds to ordinary households, with varying degrees of success. The most important of these efforts were the Series E bond sales undertaken during World War II.

In 1935, the Roosevelt administration created savings bonds. Unlike Liberty Bonds, these were not marketable securities—they could not be traded, and their value could not fluctuate. They were offered in denominations as small as $25 (purchase price, $18.75), and had a schedule of fixed redemption values, which amounted to the purchase price plus accumulated interest. These instruments were offered to provide a source of financing to the federal government but also to create an attractive savings vehicle to ordinary households. They proved quite popular.

At the outbreak of World War II, American policymakers faced the same menu of financing options as Secretary McAdoo had in the previous confrontation with Germany and her allies. President Roosevelt, for his part, favored heavy taxation and a forced savings program operating through regular payroll deductions. The latter would both raise money quickly and act as a brake on inflation. Treasury Secretary Henry Morgenthau Jr., however, believed that the public would voluntarily lend its money to the government from a sense of patriotism and shared sacrifice and sought to finance much of the war expenditures through borrowing. Although the government issued a number of different debt securities during the war, among the most important were the Series E savings bonds, denoted defense bonds. These were essentially savings bonds with a new name.[15] However, unlike ordinary savings bonds, the sales of Series E bonds were promoted quite aggressively in large-scale bond drives.

Morgenthau enlisted the help of Peter Odegard, a political scientist at Amherst College, to design the Treasury's bond selling program. In many respects, the plan simply reprised many of the features of the Liberty Loan campaign: selling efforts were concentrated in short drives; America's commercial banks, sometimes at the prodding of the American Bankers Association, agreed to participate, this time as issuing agents; publishers were expected to donate space for advertising; and legions of volunteers were recruited from the ranks of America's civic, religious, and business organizations (Morse 1971; Olney 1971). Once again, department stores were commandeered for war purposes. For example, whenever a bond was sold at a Younkers store in downtown Des Moines, a coffin of Adolf Hitler was lowered from the ceiling to the floor, where it came to rest by a poster entreating passersby the store window to "Help Us Bury Hitler" (Lindaman 2014). A propaganda apparatus, the Division of Press, Radio, and Advertising, was installed in the Treasury Department, as was a Women's Section headed by Harriet Elliott, dean of women at the University of North Carolina. Morgenthau volunteered his wife to serve in the Women's Section "to keep her from worrying too much" about their son in the armed services (Olney 1971, 56). During the loan drives, some five or six million volunteers canvassed their local communities, asking their neighbors to do their part to "buy our boys back" (Sparrow 2008, 263). Personal solicitation, in fact, proved highly effective, according to wartime research conducted by social psychologists employed in the Division of Program Surveys in the Department of Agriculture (Cartwright 1949).

Given the similarity in the roles of civil society and financial institutions in each of the wars, we might expect a resemblance in the geography of the mass financial mobilizations of World Wars I and II. This is precisely what

---

15. Sales of E Bonds were limited to individuals who could purchase, at most, $5,000 (at maturity) worth of bonds during any calendar year. Wealthier investors and institutions (except commercial banks) could buy Series F and G Bonds issued in larger denominations and with longer maturities. The Treasury Department also issued marketable short-term securities. In the end, 28 percent of war expenditures were financed by borrowing from the public (Rockoff 2012).

Figure 3. Series E Bond Purchases Per Capita, 1944

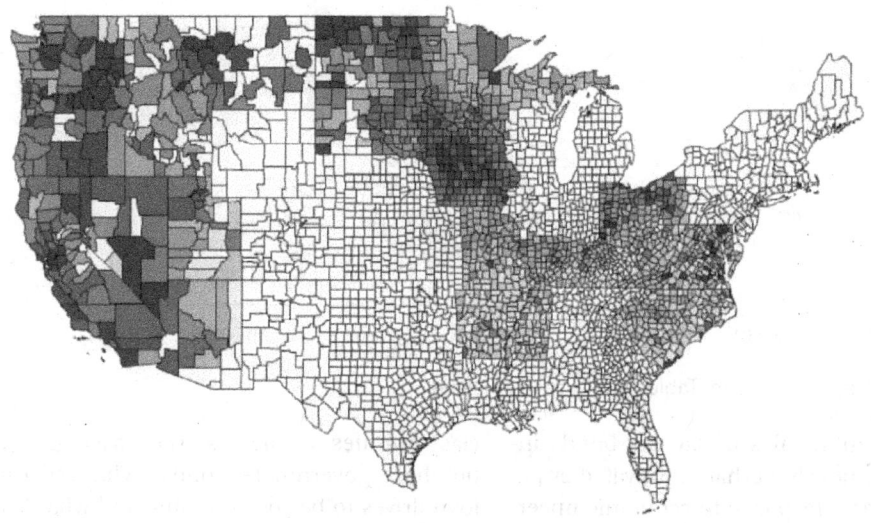

Source: Authors' calculations from data collected in Haines 2010.

we find. Figure 3 presents a map with counties shaded by the sales of Series E bonds per capita in 1944. The similarity between the geographical patterns exhibited in this map and that of figure 2 is striking. The raw correlation between Liberty Bond participation rates and county-level sales of Series E bonds per capita (logged) is an impressive 0.67. Counties with more effective Liberty Loan promotion also purchased Series E bonds at high rates.

U.S. Savings Bonds After World War II

After the war, the Series E Defense Bond became a peacetime security in which American families continued to invest, either at their workplaces through payroll deduction or over the counter. The Treasury developed new methods of promoting savings bonds, including a bond-a-month program in cooperation with the nation's banks. As they did during the two world wars, the Treasury also initiated periodic drives, centered on nonwar motives or as tie-ins with highly visible government initiatives such as the space program in the 1960s. During the Vietnam War, the Johnson administration launched in 1967 a new savings product, the Freedom Share, which was not particularly successful (U.S. Treasury, Savings Bond Division 1991), perhaps because the war itself, by that point, was not very popular.

In the months following the terrorist attacks of September 11, 2001, several members of Congress proposed legislation that would have authorized the U.S. Treasury to issue updated versions of war bonds (Makinen 2002). The Treasury responded to these proposals by introducing Patriot Bonds, based on the existing Series EE savings bonds. These Series EE bonds are the modern successors to the Series E defense bonds of World War II.

The Patriot Bonds were not a new financial instrument; they were simply traditional savings bonds with the words "Patriot Bond" and a profile of Thomas Jefferson printed on them. No major initiatives were introduced to promote the purchases of these bonds, beyond the change in the name. Individuals wishing to purchase a Patriot Bond could do so through a financial institution, and a few offices operated by the U.S. Treasury that promoted savings bonds. But no large-scale effort was made to appeal to Americans' patriotism to promote the bonds, and no engagement with civil society organizations was sought for help with the marketing. Based on our analysis of the campaigns to market Liberty Bonds, we would predict that the introduction of Patriot Bonds would have had little effect.

And this is precisely what happened. Figure 4 presents monthly sales of U.S. savings bonds.

Figure 4. Monthly Sales of U.S. Savings Bonds, in Millions

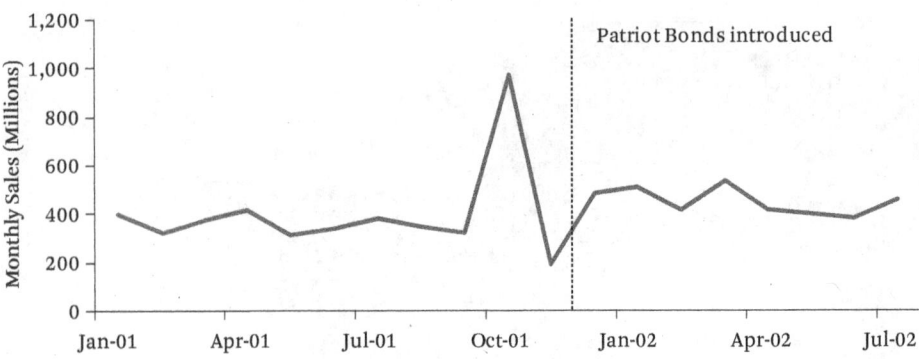

Source: U.S. Treasury Bulletin, Table SBN-3, various issues.

In October 2001, sales of savings bonds increased enormously, perhaps motivated by patriotism or as a response to economic uncertainty following the terrorist attacks of September. This surge preceded the introduction of Patriot Bonds in December 2001. In the months that followed, savings bond sales appear to have been slightly higher than during the same months of 2001, but the increase was extremely small.

In 2003, the U.S. Treasury eliminated its marketing efforts for savings bonds, and over the following years, changes to the savings bonds the government offered made them far less attractive to ordinary households (see Tufano and Schneider 2005). In 2011, paper savings bonds were eliminated; rather than going to a local financial institution to purchase a bond, individuals must now use the Treasury's website. This may have reduced the appeal of savings bonds as gifts, and made them less accessible to households without high-speed Internet access. All of these changes have been motivated by concerns that the costs of issuing and administering savings bonds may have exceeded their benefits for the borrowing costs of the federal government. However, these changes neglect the critically important role that savings bonds have played in encouraging savings among households with modest means.

CONCLUSION: LESSONS FOR PROGRAMS TO INCREASE SAVINGS

The Liberty Loan drives of World War I induced millions of American households, including a substantial fraction of urban working-class families, to increase their savings and purchase government bonds. What led the loan drives to be so successful, and what lessons do they hold for modern policymakers wishing to increase the savings rates of lower- and middle-income households?

First, the Liberty Bond drives enlisted the participation of all manner of civic and economic organizations, from women's clubs to the Boy Scouts to periodicals and businesses of every description, and worked closely with local banks. These organizations devoted considerable resources to the cause of marketing the bonds, and their achievements were publicized widely. Working together with offices created by the government to create and distribute marketing materials for the bonds, these organizations created what was probably the largest and most effective sales force in American history. But the local presence of this sales force, and its successes, varied significantly across counties. Our analysis has shown that in counties with more banks, higher literacy rates, and a greater presence of groups associated with the organization of the Liberty Loan campaigns, subscription rates were higher. The quality and character of local institutions, and likely the degree of social capital, influenced the rate of success of the campaigns.

Second, although the loan drives advertised heavily in periodicals, much of the selling was done through face-to-face contacts at individuals' homes and at places such as movie theaters and department stores. The considerable "shoe-leather" element to the bond selling was complemented by large rallies held in cities and towns led by celebrities and other notable figures. Again, our empirical analysis shows that in counties where the in-person presence of the loan campaigns was greater, subscription rates were higher.

Third, a variety of marketing messages were used in selling the bonds, but for the most part they did not appeal to individuals' financial self-interest. Rather than focusing on the rates of return offered by the bonds or the importance of saving for retirement, the loan drives appealed to individuals' patriotism, local pride, and the value of contributing to a greater cause (see figure 1). To be sure, some of these messages were quite xenophobic, and some elements of the campaign worked to shame the foreign born into demonstrating their loyalty by purchasing the bonds. But even though Liberty Bonds were reasonably attractive investments, the marketing efforts behind them did not emphasize financial motives for purchasing them, consistent with Secretary McAdoo's desire to lift bond sales "above the commercial plane" (1931, 378).

That these characteristics of the Liberty Loan drives would help make them successful is consistent with the findings of modern research on savings behavior. Impatience, cognitive biases, and an aversion to banks lead many households to choose to not save at all, even if it is in their interest to do so. By creating a massive marketing campaign, and using powerful face-to-face appeals to deliver messages related to patriotism and the greater causes associated with purchasing government bonds, the loan drives were able to overcome these biases and induce historically unprecedented numbers of lower- and middle-income households to subscribe.

Given that the Liberty Loan campaigns were conducted during extraordinary circumstances—World War I—one could not reasonably expect that any modern peacetime program to increase savings could hope to be as large or as effective or rely on similar marketing messages. No modern cause is as compelling as the defeat of the Germans to inspire individuals to save, or to enlist the volunteer participation of countless individuals to market savings vehicles. Yet we believe that the sources of the Liberty Loans' success offer valuable lessons that could help inform the design of programs to raise the savings rates of ordinary households.

In recent years, a growing number of initiatives have been proposed or implemented to increase savings rates. None of them have any of the attributes that made the Liberty Loan drives so successful. For example, some programs have sought to improve the financial literacy of ordinary individuals, in the hopes that this would increase their savings rates. But the results have been mixed at best (for reviews, see Fernandes, Lynch, and Netemeyer 2014; Lusardi and Mitchell 2014; Miller et al. 2015; Hastings, Madrian, and Skimmyhorn 2012). For example, state mandates requiring high school students to take a financial literacy course have not increased savings rates (Cole, Paulson, and Shastry 2015). The notion that greater financial literacy alone would not increase savings is consistent with the experience of the Liberty Bond drives, which promoted saving and investing using a variety of marketing messages unrelated to financial self-interest.

Others have sought to increase savings by marketing low-cost savings vehicles. For example, Peter Tufano and Daniel Schneider (2005) call for a renewal of efforts to promote savings bonds, which have been all but abandoned by the federal government. In response, the Treasury added investment in savings bonds as an option on Form 8888 that allows people to allocate their tax refunds to accounts at a financial institution. However, this feature is set to expire with the 2016 tax season and currently is not widely promoted. As we have seen, the lack of any effect from the mere designation of savings bonds as Patriot Bonds in 2001 illustrates the importance of a substantial marketing campaign to induce households to save.

In a related proposal, Mehrsa Baradaran advocates for reviving the postal savings banks that served immigrants and small savers in the United States from 1911 to 1966 (2015). In an era before deposit insurance and the automobile, the safety, convenience, and familiarity of the U.S. Postal Service (USPS) proved attractive to many working-class people (Baradaran 2015). And unlike many U.S. government agencies, the USPS is incredibly popular with the public.

In the Pew survey cited earlier, 84 percent of those interviewed had a favorable impression of USPS. In addition to their trustworthiness, local post offices offer the advantage of operating in virtually every neighborhood. We found in our cross-sectional analysis that the supply of financial institutions was an important factor in increasing subscription rates, and in a recent study, researchers demonstrated that supply-side factors influence savings rates, especially for those who are at risk for being "unbanked" (Célérier and Matray 2014). Increasing the supply of nonbank financial institutions—perhaps even working with the AFS companies that are frequented by LMI individuals—might be a mechanism for improving savings rates at the lower end of the wealth distribution.

Both of these ideas hold promise, and that they do not rely on traditional banks, which many low- and middle-income Americans distrust, adds to their appeal. But our historical analysis suggests that ultimately their success may depend on whether an effective marketing campaign can be created to persuade households to participate. Without such concerted efforts, take-up rates for any kind of savings program are likely to be low (Currie 2006).[16]

A potentially significant step toward actually implementing a program along these lines was announced in 2015 by the Treasury Department: the creation of a new savings account, the myRA. These accounts would function like a Roth IRA, but would be invested in government savings bonds and would therefore be guaranteed by the government. Currently, the Treasury Department is partnering with Intuit, the maker of TurboTax,[17] to advertise the new myRA to some of its customers via email. It is also using social media platforms to promote its availability both to individuals and to employers.

The myRA is an important step, but the experience of the Liberty Bond drives suggests that to be successful, its promotion should not only rely on e-marketing but also enlist the help of community groups, businesses, churches, and other organizations to reach the families who would benefit most from increased savings. Partnerships could be forged with organizations such as the National Association of Tax Professionals or with the Internal Revenue Service's Volunteer Tax Assistance Program (VITA), for example, to encourage LMI to invest their tax returns in myRA.[18]

Moreover, such a marketing campaign would likely need to be regionally targeted—in places

---

16. For example, several states are experimenting or have experimented with Children's Development Accounts, savings accounts that are established for children as early as birth with deposits from the state or charitable foundations. In 2008, Harold Alfond, a Maine philanthropist, launched a pilot program, the Harold Alfond College Challenge, to facilitate access to higher education by encouraging college savings as early as possible in a child's life. Using the state's 529 college savings plan as the platform, the Challenge offered a $500 grant to every Maine child less than a year old whose parents or other responsible adult opened an account. No initial contribution was required. The pilot program featured extensive outreach and recruited health professionals to encourage and facilitate sign-up. At the end of the pilot year, the enrollment rate was 53 percent. The following year, the challenge was implemented statewide, but fewer resources were invested in outreach and marketing. At the end of the first year of statewide availability, 39 percent of eligible children had been enrolled, a drop of nearly 15 percent from the previous year (Clancy and Lassar 2010). At the urging of policy advocates, in 2014 the Challenge was redesigned as an opt-out rather than an opt-in program (Clancy and Sherraden 2014).

17. Another partnership with TurboTax, the Refund-to-Save initiative, used motivational prompts embedded in the tax preparation software as a means to increase savings from tax refunds by users (Grinstein-Weiss et al. 2014). The intervention was moderately successful, inducing treated participants to deposit between $200 and 300 more from their refunds in various types of accounts compared with controls.

18. Treasury could build on, for example, the success of the SaveUSA program, a partnership between VITA and the Corporation for National and Community Service in four cities, New York, Tulsa, Newark, and San Antonio. SaveUSA allows tax filers working with trained volunteer tax preparers to open a special savings account with a local financial institution with an initial deposit of $200 or more from their tax refund. Participants then pledged to keep at least $200 in their account for a year. If they were successful in doing so, they received a 50 percent match on the pledged amount, up to $500 (Azurdia and Freedman 2016).

where civil society institutions are not as well developed, additional effort will need to be put forth. It is also worth underscoring that retirement is just one of many motives for saving. It is understandably one that preoccupies policymakers, but for many it may not have as much significance as advocates would hope. In fact, for LMI individuals, retirement ranks below unexpected expenses and even "just to save" as motives for savings (Board of Governors 2015). Thrift can be a virtue in its own right, not just the means to some material end. Perhaps we need to be more creative in the ways we currently answer the question of "saving for what?" drawing inspiration from the historical record to design appeals that would resonate with diverse audiences.

REFERENCES

Anderson, Lisa R., Jennifer M. Mellor, and Jeffrey Milyo. 2008. "Inequality and Public Good Provision: An Experimental Analysis." *Journal of Socio-Economics* 37(3): 1010–28. doi: 10.1016/j.socec.2006.12.073.

Axelrod, Alan. 2009. *Selling the Great War: The Making of American Propaganda*. New York: Palgrave Macmillan.

Azurdia, Gilda, and Stephen Freedman. 2016. "Encouraging Nonretirement Savings at Tax Time. Final Impact Findings from the SaveUSA Evaluation." New York: MDRC. Accessed May 9, 2016. http://mdrc.org/sites/default/files/SaveUSA_FinalReportpercent202015.pdf.

Baradaran, Mehrsa. 2015. *How the Other Half Banks: Exclusion, Exploitation, and the Threat to Democracy*. Cambridge, Mass.: Harvard University Press.

Barr, Michael S., and Rebecca M. Blank. 2011. "Savings, Assets, Credit, and Banking Among Low-Income Households: Introduction and Overview." In *Insufficient Funds*, edited by Rebecca M. Blank and Michael S. Barr. New York: Russell Sage Foundation.

Board of Governors of the Federal Reserve System (Board of Governors). 2015. "Report on the Economic Well-Being of U.S. Households in 2014." Washington: Federal Reserve System. Accessed May 9, 2016. http://www.federalreserve.gov/econresdata/2014-report-economic-well-being-us-households-201505.pdf.

———. 2016. "Survey of Consumer Finances, 2013." Washington: Federal Reserve System. Accessed May 31, 2016. http://www.federalreserve.gov/econresdata/scf/scfindex.htm

Breen, W. J. 1984. *Uncle Sam at Home: Civilian Mobilization, Wartime Federalism, and the Council of National Defense, 1917–1919*. Contributions in American Studies no. 70. Westport, Conn: Greenwood Press.

Brehm, John, and Wendy Rahn. 1997. "Individual-Level Evidence for the Causes and Consequences of Social Capital." *American Journal of Political Science* 41(3): 999–1023.

Burhouse, Susan, Karyen Chu, Ryan Goodstein, Joyce Northwood, Yazmin Osaki, and Dhruv Sharma. 2014. "2013 FDCI National Survey of Unbanked and Underbanked Households." Washington: Federal Deposit Insurance Corporation. Accessed May 9, 2016. https://www.fdic.gov/householdsurvey/2013report.pdf.

Carter, Susan, Scott Sigmund Gartner, Michael R. Haines, Alan L. Olmstead, Richard Sutch, and Gavin Wright, eds. 2006. *Historical Statistics of the United States*, millennial ed. New York: Cambridge University Press.

Cartwright, Dorwin. 1949. "Some Principles of Mass Persuasion: Selected Findings of Research on the Sale of United States War Bonds." *Human Relations* 2(3): 253–67.

Célérier, Claire, and Adrien Matray. 2014. "Unbanked Households: Evidence of Supply-Side Factors." *Les Cahiers de Recherche* research paper no. 1039. Paris: Hautes Etudes Commerciales de Paris.

Choi James J., David Laibson, Briggitte Madrian, and Andrew Metrick. 2004. "Saving for Retirement on the Path of Least Resistance." Working paper. Cambridge, Mass.: Harvard University.

Clancy, Margaret, and Terry Lassar. 2010. "College Savings Plan Accounts at Birth: Maine's Statewide Program." Center for Social Development policy brief no. 10–16. St. Louis, Mo.: Washington University, George Warren Brown School of Social Work.

Clancy, Margaret, and Michael Sherraden. 2014. "Automatic Deposits at Birth: Maine's Harold Alfond College Challenge." Center for Social Development policy report no. 14–05. St. Louis, Mo.: Washington University.

Clifford, Edward. 1917. "Selling the First Installment of the Liberty Loan in the Seventh Federal Reserve District, May 4th to June 15th, 1917." Chicago: Seventh Federal Reserve District, Liberty Loan Committee.

Cole, Shawn, Anna Paulson, and Gauri Kartini Shastry. 2015. "High School Curriculum and Financial Outcomes: The Impact of Mandated Personal Finance and Mathematics Courses." *Journal of Human Resources*, forthcoming. Published ahead of print November 30, 2015. doi: 10.3368/jhr.51.3.0113-5410R1.

Committee on Public Information. Division of Four Minute Men. 1918. "The Third Liberty Loan." Bulletin no. 29, April 6, 1918. Washington: Government Printing Office.

———. 1920. "Complete Report of the Chairman of the Committee on Public Information, 1917–1919." Washington: Government Printing Office.

Creel, George. 1928. *How We Advertised America*. New York: Harper & Brothers.

Currie, Janet. 2006. "The Take-Up of Social Benefits." In *Public Policy and the Income Distribution*, edited by Ian J. Auerbach, David Card, and John M. Quigley. New York: Russell Sage Foundation.

DeBauche, Leslie Midkiff. 1997. *Reel Patriotism: The Movies and World War I*. Madison: University of Wisconsin Press.

De Nardi, Mariacristina. 2015. "Quantitative Models of Wealth Inequality: A Survey." *NBER* working paper no. 21106. Cambridge, Mass.: National Bureau of Economic Research. Accessed May 9, 2016. http://www.nber.org/papers/w21106.

Depew, Briggs, Price V. Fishback, and Paul W. Rhode. 2013. "New Deal or No Deal in the Cotton South: The Effect of the AAA on the Agricultural Labor Structure." *Explorations in Economic History* 50(4): 466–86. doi: 10.1016/j.eeh.2013.06.004.

Feigenbaum, James. 2015. "Intergenerational Mobility During the Great Depression." Working paper. Cambridge, Mass.: Harvard University. Accessed May 9, 2016. http://scholar.harvard.edu/jfeigenbaum/publications/jmp.

Fernandes, Daniel, John G. Lynch, and Richard G. Netemeyer. 2014. "Financial Literacy, Financial Education, and Downstream Financial Behaviors." *Management Science* 60(8): 1861–83.

Garon, Sheldon M. 2012. *Beyond Our Means: Why America Spends While the World Saves*. Princeton, N.J: Princeton University Press.

Gilbert, Charles. 1970. *American Financing of World War I*. Westport, Conn: Greenwood Publishing.

Grinstein-Weiss, Michal, Krista Comer, Blair Russell, Clinton Key, Dana C. Perantie, and Dan Ariely. 2014. "Refund to Savings: 2013 Evidence of Tax-Time Saving in a National Randomized Control Trial." *Center for Social Development* research report no. 14–03. St. Louis, Mo.: Washington University.

Guiso, Luigi, Paola Sapienza, and Luigi Zingales. 2004. "The Role of Social Capital in Financial Development." *American Economic Review* 94(3): 526–56.

———. 2008. "Trusting the Stock Market." *Journal of Finance* 63(6)(December): 2557–600. doi: 10.1111/j.1540-6261.2008.01408.x.

Guiso, Luigi, and Paolo Sodini. 2013. "Household Finance: An Emerging Field." In *Handbook of the Economics of Finance*, vol. 2, edited by George M. Constantinides, Milton Harris, and Rene M. Stulz. Atlanta, Ga.: Elsevier.

Haines, Michael R., and Inter-University Consortium for Political and Social Research (Haines). 2010. *Historical, Demographic, Economic, and Social Data: The United States, 1790–2002*, vol. 3. ICPSR02896-v3. Ann Arbor, Mich.: Inter-University Consortium for Political and Social Research [distributor], 2010-05-21. http://doi.org/10.3886/ICPSR02896.v3.

Hastings, Justine S., Brigitte C. Madrian, and William L. Skimmyhorn. 2012. "Financial Literacy, Financial Education, and Economic Outcomes." *NBER* working paper no. 18412. Cambridge, Mass.: National Bureau of Economic Research. Accessed May 9, 2016. http://www.nber.org/papers/w18412.pdf.

Kang, Sung Won, and Hugh Rockoff. 2015. "Capitalizing Patriotism: The Liberty Bonds of World War I." *Financial History Review* 22(1): 45–78.

Karlan, Dean, Aishwarya Lakshmi Ratan, and Jonathan Zinman. 2014. "Savings by and for the Poor: A Research Review and Agenda." *Review of Income and Wealth* 60(1)(March): 36–78. doi: 10.1111/roiw.12101.

Laibson, David. 1997. "Golden Eggs and Hyperbolic Discounting." *Quarterly Journal of Economics* 112(2): 443–78.

Leon, Maurice. 1918. "Safe-Keeping of Bonds for Small Holders." *Journal of the American Bankers Association* 10(7): 514.

Lindaman, Matthew. 2014. "First the War, Then the Future: Younkers Department Store and the Project of a Civic Image During World War II." *Annals of Iowa* 73(1): 1–27.

Luebke, Frederick C. 1974. *Bonds of Loyalty: German-Americans and World War I*. DeKalb: Northern Illinois University Press.

Lusardi, Annamaria, and Olivia S. Mitchell. 2014, "The Economic Importance of Financial Literacy: Theory and Evidence." *Journal of Economic Literature* 52(1): 5–44. doi: 10.1257/jel.52.1.5.

Makinen, Gail. 2002. "The Economic Effects of 9/11: A Retrospective Assessment." Washington: Congressional Research Service. Accessed June 1, 2016. https://fas.org/irp/crs/RL31617.pdf.

Mani, Anandi, Sendhil Mullainathan, Eldar Shafir, and Jiaying Zhao. 2013. "Poverty Impedes Cognitive Function." *Science* 341 (6149): 976–80.

McAdoo, William G. 1931. *Crowded Years: The Reminiscences of William G. McAdoo*. Cambridge, Mass.: Riverside Press.

McCutheon, Ben F. 1918. "Report of the Publicity Department, Seventh Federal Reserve District." Chicago: Federal Reserve Bank.

Means, Gardiner C. 1930. "The Diffusion of Stock Ownership in the United States." *Quarterly Journal of Economics* 44(4): 561–600. http://www.jstor.org/stable/1884024.

Miller, Margaret, Julia Reichelstein, Christian Salas, and Bilal Zia. 2015. "Can You Help Someone Become Financially Capable? A Meta-Analysis of the Literature." *World Bank Research Observer* 30(2): 220–46. doi: 10.1093/wbro/lkv009.

Mitchell, Lawrence E. 2007. *The Speculation Economy: How Finance Triumphed Over Industry*. San Francisco: Berrett-Koehler.

Mock, James Robert, and Cedric Larson. 1939. *Words That Won the War: The Story of the Committee on Public Information, 1917–1919*. Princeton, N.J.: Princeton University Press.

Morse, Jarvis M. 1971. *Paying for a World War: The United States Financing of World War II*. Washington: Government Printing Office.

Murray, William D. 1937. *The History of the Boy Scouts of America*. New York: Boy Scouts of America.

National Women's Liberty Loan Committee. 1920. "Report of the National Women's Liberty Loan Committee for the Victory Loan Campaign, April 21st to May 10th." Washington: Government Printing Office.

New York Times. 1917. "Bond Sales in Stores Starts Tomorrow." May 20, 1917.

———. 1918. "Rainbow Division Aims to Raise $450,000. Keen Rivalry Marks Work of 81 Business Organizations Representing Many Industries." April 9, 1918, p. 4.

O'Brien, Rourke. 2012. "'We Don't Do Banks': Financial Lives of Families on Public Assistance." Washington, D.C.: New America Foundation. Accessed May 9, 2016. https://static.newamerica.org/attachments/3772-we-dont-do-banks/RourkeMarch2012.280c7e858336448499de926c84038108.pdf.

O'Donoghue, Ted, and Matthew Rabin. 1991. "Doing It Now or Later." *American Economic Review* 89(1): 103–24.

O'Sullivan, Mary. 2007. "The Expansion of the U.S. Stock Market, 1885 1930: Historical Facts and Theoretical Fashions." *Enterprise and Society* 8(3): 489–542.

Olney, Lawrence M. 1971. *The War Bond Story*. Washington: Government Printing Office.

Olney, Martha L. 1995. *Saving and Dissaving of 12,817 American Households, 1917–1919*. Amherst: University of Massachusetts [producer], 1993. Ann Arbor, Mich.: Inter-University Consortium for Political and Social Research [distributor]. http://doi.org/10.3886/ICPSR06276.v1.

Ott, Julia. 2011. *When Wall Street Met Main Street: The Quest for an Investors' Democracy*. Cambridge, Mass.: Harvard University Press.

Pew Charitable Trusts. 2015. "American's Financial Security." Issue Brief. Philadelphia, Pa.: Pew Charitable Trusts. Accessed May 9, 2016. http://www.pewtrusts.org/en/research-and-analysis/issue-briefs/2015/02/americans-financial-security-perceptions-and-reality.

Rajan, Raghuram, and Rodney Ramcharan. 2015. "The Anatomy of a Credit Crisis: The Boom and Bust in Farm Land Prices in the United States in the 1920s." *American Economic Review* 105(4): 1439–77. Accessed May 9, 2016. https://www.aeaweb.org/articles?id=10.1257/aer.20120525.

Rhine, Sherrie L.W., and Eric Robbins. 2012. "2011 FDIC Survey of Banks' Efforts to Serve the Unbanked and Underbanked." Washington: Federal Deposit Insurance Corporation. Accessed May 9, 2016. https://www.fdic.gov/unbankedsurveys/2011survey/2011report.pdf.

Rockoff, Hugh. 2012. *America's Economic Way of War*. New York: Cambridge University Press.

Saez, Emmanuel, and Gabriel Zucman. 2016. "Wealth Inequality in the United States Since 1913: Evidence from Capitalized Income Tax

Data." *Quarterly Journal of Economics* 131(2): 519–78.

Sevron, Lisa. 2013. "The High Cost, for the Poor, of Using a Bank." *New Yorker*, October 9, 2013. Accessed May 9, 2016. http://www.newyorker.com/business/currency/the-high-cost-for-the-poor-of-using-a-bank.

Skocpol, Theda, Ziad Munson, Andrew Karch, and Bayliss Camp. 2002. "Patriotic Partnerships: Why Great Wars Nourished American Civic Voluntarism." In *Shaped by War and Trade: International Influences on American Political Development*, edited by Ira Katznelson and Martin Shefter. Princeton Studies in American Politics. Princeton, N.J.: Princeton University Press.

Sparrow, James T. 2008. "'Buying Our Boys Back': The Mass Foundations of Fiscal Citizenship in World War II." *Journal of Policy History* 20(2): 263. doi: 10.1353/jph.0.0015.

Sutch, Richard. 2015. "Financing the Great War. A Class Tax for the Wealthy, Liberty Bonds for All." *Behl* working paper no. 2015-09. Berkeley: University of California.

Tufano, Peter, and Daniel Schneider. 2005. "Reinventing Savings Bonds. Doorways to Dreams Fund." Allston, Mass.: D2D Fund. Accessed May 9, 2016. http://www.d2dfund.org/files/publications/Reinventing-Savings-Bonds.pdf.

U.S. Congressional Serial Set, vol. 113. 1918. Washington: Government Printing Office.

U.S. Department of the Treasury (U.S. Treasury). 1917. "Annual Report of Secretary of the Treasury on the State of the Finances: 1917." Washington: Government Printing Office.

———. 1918. "Annual Report of Secretary of the Treasury on the State of the Finances: 1918." Washington: Government Printing Office.

———. 1919. "Annual Report of Secretary of the Treasury on the State of the Finances: 1919." Washington: Government Printing Office.

———. 1923. *Statistics of Income from Returns of Net Income for 1921*. Washington: Government Printing Office.

U.S. Treasury, National War-Savings Committee. 1917. *War-Savings Stamps: Handbook for Banking, Education, Industrial, and Other Interests*. Washington: Government Printing Office.

———. 1918a. *War Saver: A Bulletin for War Savings Societies of the United States* 1(2)(April). Washington: Government Printing Office.

———. 1918b. *War Saver: A Bulletin for War Savings Societies of the United States* 1(4)(June). Washington: Government Printing Office.

U.S. Treasury, Savings Bond Division. 1991. "A History of the United States Savings Bond Program," 50th anniversary issue. Washington: Government Printing Office. Accessed May 9, 2016. https://www.treasurydirect.gov/indiv/research/history/history_sb.pdf

Warshow, H. T. 1924. "The Distribution of Corporate Ownership in the United States." *Quarterly Journal of Economics* 39(1): 15–38.

Whitney, Nathaniel Ruggles. 1923. *The Sale of War Bonds in Iowa*. Iowa City: State Historical Society of Iowa.

Wilcox, Ronald T. 2008. *Whatever Happened to Thrift?: Why Americans Don't Save and What to Do About It*. New Haven, Conn.: Yale University Press.

Williamson, Samuel H. 2015. "Seven Ways to Compute the Relative Value of a U.S. Dollar Amount, 1774 to present." *Measuring Worth*. Accessed May 9, 2016. http://www.measuringworth.com/.

Winslow, Helen M, ed. 1914. *Official Register and Directory of Women's Clubs in America*, vol. 16. Boston, Mass.: Helen M. Winslow, publisher.

Wolkoitz, Eva, and Theresa Schmall. 2015. "2014 Underserved Market Size: Financial Opportunity in Dollars and Cents." Chicago: Center for Financial Services Innovation. Accessed May 9, 2016. http://www.cfsinnovation.com/Document-Library/2014-Underserved-Market-Size-Financial-Health-Oppo.

PART III
Social Dimensions of Wealth Inequality

Does Your Home Make You Wealthy?

ALEXANDRA KILLEWALD AND BRIELLE BRYAN

Estimating the lifetime wealth consequences of homeownership is complicated by ongoing events, such as divorce or inheritance, that may shape both homeownership decisions and later-life wealth. We argue that prior research that has not accounted for these dynamic selection processes has overstated the causal effect of homeownership on wealth. Using NLSY79 data and marginal structural models, we find that each additional year of homeownership increases midlife wealth in 2008 by about $6,800, more than 25 percent less than estimates from models that do not account for dynamic selection. Hispanic and African American wealth benefits from each homeownership year are 62 percent and 48 percent as large as those of whites, respectively. Homeownership remains wealth-enhancing in 2012, but shows smaller returns. Our results confirm homeownership's role in wealth accumulation and that variation in both homeownership rates and the wealth benefits of homeownership contribute to racial and ethnic disparities in midlife wealth holdings.

Keywords: wealth, homeownership, race, inequality

In the United States, net worth is highly unequally distributed (Keister and Moller 2000), showing strong persistence across generations (Charles and Hurst 2003; Pfeffer and Killewald 2015) and massive racial disparities (Kochhar, Fry, and Taylor 2011; Oliver and Shapiro 2006). Wealth disparities are consequential because wealth facilitates a variety of life chances, including marriage entry and stability (Eads and Tach, this issue; Schneider 2011) and children's educational and labor market outcomes (Conley 1999, 2001; Orr 2003).

Homeownership is hypothesized to be a key mechanism for wealth accumulation and therefore for the construction and reproduction of asset inequalities. Estimating the contribution of homeownership to wealth at midlife, however, poses substantial methodological and conceptual challenges because wealth is itself a determinant of transitions to homeownership (Di and Liu 2007). The positive association between homeownership and wealth, therefore, may merely reflect that wealthier individuals are more likely to purchase (and keep) homes. Thus, conventional regression models that estimate the association between current

Alexandra Killewald is professor of sociology at Harvard University. **Brielle Bryan** is a doctoral student in sociology and social policy at Harvard University.

This research was supported in part by an Emerging Scholars Small Grant from the University of Wisconsin Institute for Research on Poverty. An earlier version of this paper was presented at the 2015 annual meeting of the Population Association of America. We are grateful to Fangsheng Zhu for research assistance and to Vanesa Estrada-Correa, Fabian Pfeffer, Bob Schoeni, and anonymous reviewers for helpful comments. Direct correspondence to: Alexandra Killewald at killewald@fas.harvard.edu, 436 William James Hall, Harvard University, 33 Kirkland St., Cambridge, MA 02138; and Brielle Bryan at briellebryan@g.harvard.edu, 432 William James Hall, Harvard University, 33 Kirkland St., Cambridge, MA 02138.

wealth and homeownership history are likely to overestimate the causal role of homeownership in wealth accumulation.

We produce a more accurate estimate of the effect of homeownership patterns on midlife wealth, incorporating how prior wealth shapes transitions to homeownership and the likelihood of remaining a homeowner across the life course. We also estimate race differences in wealth gained through homeownership, considering race disparities in both rates of homeownership and the wealth benefits of each year spent as a homeowner.

THEORETICAL FRAMEWORK

The study of wealth is inherently the study of wealth accumulation. Individuals' current wealth holdings are the product of an unfolding set of pathways by which new resources are set aside in assets and previous assets increase (or decrease) in value. Particularly for Americans in the middle 60 percent of the wealth distribution, principal residence is the largest component of household assets (see Wolff, this issue). As a result, homeownership is often conceptualized as a key pathway by which wealth accumulation occurs. Housing markets are also an important site for the generation of race gaps in wealth (Oliver and Shapiro 2006), given that blacks are less likely to own homes than whites (Charles and Hurst 2002; Oliver and Shapiro 2006), are at higher risk of return to renting (Boehm and Schlottmann 2004, 2008; Herbert, McCue, and Sanchez-Moyano 2013), and experience fewer housing upgrades (Boehm and Schlottmann 2004).

Why Might Homeownership Facilitate Wealth Accumulation?

Homeownership will tend to encourage wealth accumulation when home values increase more rapidly than inflation, yielding a positive return on investment. In general, risky assets, such as stocks, are assumed to have higher rates of return than safer investments, such as cash (for example, Choudhury 2001). Whether homeownership is wealth enhancing or wealth depressing may therefore depend on the alternative use of financial resources, if not invested in housing. The wealth-enhancing effects of homeownership will also depend on location- and period-specific housing appreciation rates relative to inflation. When assets appreciate rapidly, high-leverage households—those with high gross debt relative to their net worth—will benefit from asset ownership, but declines in asset prices put high-leverage households at risk for substantial declines in net worth. In our context, home ownership will tend to increase leverage through mortgage debt. As Edward Wolff describes elsewhere in this volume, the housing market crash that accompanied the Great Recession led to substantial declines in net worth for the middle class in large part because these households were highly leveraged and much of their asset portfolio was in housing wealth.

In addition to direct effects of homeownership on wealth through appreciation or depreciation, homeownership may increase non-housing wealth by reducing housing costs. High rental prices and tax benefits for homeowners may make homeownership a less expensive option than renting, increasing disposable income that can be set aside for savings. Home equity can also be used to facilitate access to other wealth-enhancing investments, including entrepreneurial activity (Adelino, Schoar, and Severino 2015; Black, de Meza, and Jeffreys 1996).

Finally, homeownership may change individuals' earnings, savings rates, and other household behavior. Monthly mortgage payments may encourage saving (Boehm and Schlottmann 2008), increasing wealth more rapidly than would otherwise have occurred. Although the evidence is mixed, homeownership may also affect outcomes such as geographic mobility, health, and family structure (for a review, see Dietz and Haurin 2003), each of which may in turn affect wealth.

Each of the described mechanisms may lead to heterogeneity by race in the wealth benefits of homeownership. Home appreciation is less for black homeowners than white and slower in highly segregated minority neighborhoods than others (Boehm and Schlottmann 2008; Flippen 2004; Oliver and Shapiro 2006). Discrimination in lending markets, including for small business loans (Cavalluzzo and Wolken 2005), may mean minority homeowners are less able to leverage their home equity for investment in other wealth-enhancing assets. Less favorable mortgage terms for minority homeowners (Bocian, Ernst, and Li 2008; Oliver and Shapiro 2006; but see also Charles and Hurst 2002) and lower likelihood of refinancing during favorable interest periods (Nothaft and Chang 2005; Van Order and Zorn 2002) may also limit wealth gains for minority homeowners.

Estimating the Effect of Homeownership on Wealth

Despite homeownership's prominent position in Americans' asset portfolios and hypothesized pathways of wealth accumulation, evaluations of the effect of long-term homeownership patterns on wealth accumulation are rare (Di, Belsky, and Liu 2007). For example, Thomas Boehm and Alan Schlottmann (2008) document that wealth accumulation is concentrated in housing rather than nonhousing wealth but do not attempt to estimate the causal effect of homeownership on wealth.

The scarcity of causal estimates may stem in part from the challenge of modeling causal relationships in dynamic processes. Although homeownership is hypothesized to affect wealth, wealth also predicts subsequent home purchase (Di and Liu 2007). Thus, a cross-sectional examination of the association between current wealth and cumulative homeownership does not reveal the effect of home purchase on subsequent wealth but will be confounded with selection into homeownership on the basis of previous wealth. For example, Tracy Turner and Heather Luea (2009) estimate that each additional year of homeownership is associated with an average increase in wealth of about $13,700. Because they do not condition on wealth prior to the period over which homeownership is observed, their estimate of the wealth benefits of homeownership is likely to be upwardly biased.

Zhu Di, Eric Belsky, and Xiaodong Liu (2007) estimate the effect of homeownership on net worth over twelve years, controlling for both prior wealth and the household's tendency for wealth accumulation in the five years before the observation window. They allow the benefits of homeownership to vary nonlinearly with years of ownership and estimate average wealth returns to homeownership ranging from about $3,000 per year to about $14,000 per year. Christopher Herbert, Daniel McCue, and Rocio Sanchez-Moyano (2013) similarly estimate the association between years of homeownership and later wealth, controlling for wealth at the beginning of the period, and find that each year of homeownership is associated with an additional $9,500 in net worth, on average. They further find that the benefits of homeownership are about 20 percent lower for blacks ($8,500) than whites ($10,500); the variation between whites and Hispanics is not statistically significant.

Like Di, Belsky, and Liu (2007) and Herbert, McCue, and Sanchez-Moyano (2013), our analysis controls for wealth and other attributes of individuals prior to the period over which homeownership patterns are observed. However, we also adjust for spurious factors that occur during the observation window and may affect both homeownership and later-life wealth. For example, if homeownership is observed between 2000 and 2010 and an unexpected inheritance is received in 2002 and used to purchase a home in 2003, an individual will likely have higher wealth in 2010 than expected based on 2000 wealth and will also have spent substantial time in homeownership, but homeownership was the consequence of wealth gains, not the cause.

On the other hand, covariate values at the end of the observed homeownership period may be due not only to spurious intervening factors but also to homeownership status earlier in the period. For example, homeownership is associated with diminished risk of divorce (Cooke 2006; South 2001), and marriage is in turn associated with greater wealth (Addo and Lichter 2013; Zagorsky 2005). Thus, controlling for lifetime marital history when estimating the effects of homeownership on wealth may underestimate the wealth benefits of homeownership, because a portion of the causal pathway—that operates via marriage—is controlled away. This illustrates that standard regression models cannot properly account for the ongoing, reciprocal relationship between homeownership and other wealth-related characteristics. If these factors are controlled, homeownership's effect is likely to be understated, but if they are ignored the estimate of homeownership's effect is likely to be biased upward.

Using marginal structural models and inverse probability of treatment weights, we account for the fact that homeownership both affects and is affected by other characteristics, including previous wealth. Our analysis is designed to estimate the effect of homeownership on midlife wealth relative to likely behavior in the absence of homeownership. In other words, we do not compare the wealth outcomes of homeowners with best-case non-homeowner investors but with individuals who are otherwise similar but do not own a home. Our research question can be thought of as attempting to answer the following counterfactual question: "If an individual were randomly blocked from homeownership for a year, what would the estimated effect on his midlife wealth be?" We believe our approach provides the most accurate estimate to date of the cumulative effect of homeownership on adults' wealth outcomes, and we estimate this effect separately for whites, blacks, and Hispanics. We also recognize the possibility for variation in the wealth benefits of homeownership across even narrow time frames and explore in particular how the Great Recession altered the estimated net worth returns to homeownership.

DATA AND METHODS

Marginal structural models can account for intersecting causal relationships by extending inverse probability of treatment weights (IPTW) to a dynamic context (Robins, Hernán, and Brumback 2000). We use data on wealth and homeownership status collected by the National Longitudinal Survey of Youth 1979 (NLSY79) between 1985 and 2008. The IPTW approach estimates the probability that an individual would have experienced her actual pattern of homeownership between 1986 (treating 1985 as the baseline) and 2008. Thus, homeownership is the treatment and occurs as a series of statuses across the twenty-three years. We can express the probability that an individual (i) experiences a particular twenty-three-year homeownership pattern as the product of annual conditional probabilities:

$$w_i^{-1} = \prod_{t=1986}^{2008} w_{ti}^{-1}$$
$$= \prod_{t=1986}^{2008} P(E_t = e_{ti} \mid \bar{E}_{t-1} = \bar{e}_{(t-1)i}, \bar{X}_t = \bar{x}_{ti})$$

In each period (t), we estimate the probability (w_{ti}^{-1}) that the homeownership status was the actual status experienced by the individual (e_{ti}), given the history of homeownership ($\bar{e}_{(t-1)i}$) and other confounders, such as income, marital status, and prior wealth ($\bar{x}_{ti}$).

Multiplying across all years gives the probability that the individual experiences the observed sequence of homeownership outcomes. The IPTW (w_i) is the inverse of this probability. Regression models that weight the sample by the IPTWs create a pseudo-population in which homeownership status in each period is independent of prior confounding variables, making it unnecessary to condition on these variables (Robins, Hernán, and Brumback 2000).

Consistent with prior research (Sharkey and Elwert 2011; Wodtke, Harding, and Elwert 2011), we use stabilized IPTWs to reduce the variance of the weights. The stabilized weights can be expressed as

$$sw_i = \prod_{t=1986}^{2008} \frac{P(E_t = e_{ti} \mid \bar{E}_{t-1} = \bar{e}_{(t-1)i}, X_0 = x_0)}{P(E_t = e_{ti} \mid \bar{E}_{t-1} = \bar{e}_{(t-1)i}, \bar{X}_t = \bar{x}_{ti})}.$$

The denominator of the stabilized weight is the inverse of the original weight. The numerator is computed similarly, except that the model conditions on time-invariant baseline traits and prior homeownership status but not other time-varying confounding variables.

Data

The NLSY79 includes 12,686 men and women first interviewed in 1979, when they were ages fourteen to twenty-two. We exclude subsamples discontinued by NLSY79 prior to 2008, including the entire military sample. The remaining 9,763 individuals have subsequently been interviewed annually or biennially (U.S. Bureau of Labor Statistics 2016a), the response rate remaining over 75 percent (U.S. Bureau of Labor Statistics 2016b). Respondents were ages twenty to twenty-eight in the first year asset information was collected (1985) and forty-seven to fifty-six in the most recent year (2012).

Our final models are weighted regressions with years of homeownership between 1986 and 2008 as the main independent variable and midlife wealth, measured as net worth in 2008, as the dependent variable. We describe the wealth data collected by the NLSY79 in more detail later because net worth is one of the time-varying variables in our model of homeownership transitions. In general, net worth in a given survey wave is the sum of respondents' reported debts and assets of various kinds, including reported home value and mortgage debt. Respondents' reporting their net worth with error will not bias the estimated wealth benefits of homeownership, provided the error is classical, even if measurement error is greater for some components of net worth than others. However, our results could be biased upward if respondents' reports of home equity are disproportionately biased upward relative to those of other asset types. This might be true if respondents overestimate the values of their homes, which might be especially likely in the midst of the housing crisis, when home values were falling. However, research suggests that homeowners overestimate the value of their home by only about 6 percent, on average, and homeowners' errors are not strongly associated with traits of either the owners or the local housing market (Goodman and Ittner 1992). More recent comparisons of data from the Survey of Consumer Finances and the Panel Study of Income Dynamics do not indicate that reported equity in the primary residence is unusually error-prone relative to other components of net worth (Pfeffer et al. 2016).

Our measures of years spent in homeownership assume no homeownership status transitions between waves in which homeownership information is collected; the interwave period is between one and four years. Likewise, to create the estimated probability of a particular homeownership status in an interwave year, we use the most recent available set of covariate values for prediction. Because the stabilized weights include baseline covariates in both the numerator and denominator, the homeownership experiences of the weighted pseudo-population are not independent of these baseline traits, which must also be included in the final outcome model (Wodtke, Harding, and Elwert 2011). We estimate median regressions because they are less sensitive to outliers—a particularly important property given the heavily skewed wealth distribution. Thus, our results estimate the median wealth returns to each year of homeownership. Like ordinary least squares, median regression assumes a constant association between homeownership and wealth across the entire wealth distribution and does not allow us to identify whether the wealth gains of homeownership disproportionately accrue to those at the top of the wealth distribution, a point we return to later.

We estimate regression models pooled by race and also separate regression models for Hispanics, non-Hispanic blacks, and non-Hispanic whites, each of which uses IPTWs estimated from race-specific models of homeownership patterns. We do not have a large enough sample size to estimate race-specific models for other racial groups. Our analytic sample for the IPTW models includes 5,636 individuals. Our three race-specific IPTW models include 1,668 blacks, 2,396 whites, and 977 Hispanics.

One limitation of our analysis is that the estimates pertain to a specific birth cohort and period. Home prices fluctuate substantially in real terms and declined precipitously during the Great Recession, as Wolff describes elsewhere in this issue. To test the sensitivity of our results, we use the same model but replace the dependent variable with the respondent's net worth in 2012, close to the trough of housing values during the Great Recession (Federal Reserve 2016; Dow Jones 2016). We expect lower estimated wealth returns to homeownership in 2012 than in 2008.

Hazard Model Specification
Using discrete-time hazard models and a logit link function, we estimate the risks of entry into first-time homeownership in the next survey year for an individual who has never owned a home (50,180 person-years), entry into a subsequent homeownership spell for a person who has previously owned a home but is not a current homeowner (13,348 person-years), and exit from homeownership for current homeowners (transitions to new homes without intervening spells of non-ownership are not counted) (40,800 person-years). In each wave

of the NLSY79, we consider individuals to be homeowners if they report that they or their spouses or partners own or are making payments toward owning their homes. Standard errors are clustered at the individual level in each model. To increase statistical power, our hazard models include all respondents who participated in the current survey wave and provided homeownership data in the next survey wave, even if they do not qualify for our final analytic model because they subsequently attrit. In all models, we use an offset (the log of exposure time) to account for varying durations between homeownership reports due either to the switch from annual to biennial data collection after 1994 or the fact that homeownership was not collected in some post–1985 survey years (1991, 2002, 2006, and 2010). Because of the importance of wealth to our models of selection into homeownership, we use data only from years in which wealth information was collected by the NLSY79.

Although our period of wealth accumulation begins in 1985, we have information on homeownership status since the first wave of the NLSY79 in 1979. Because of the young age of the sample in 1979, we assume that anyone not observed to own a home between 1979 and 1985 has never previously owned a home. Individuals who already owned their homes in 1979 (less than 5 percent of the sample) are left-censored. For these individuals, we assume homeownership began at age eighteen if they were older than eighteen in 1979. If they were eighteen or younger in 1979, we assume they became homeowners in 1979. These assumptions do not affect our calculation of years of homeownership between 1986 and 2008 in our regression models, only the predictors of homeownership transitions used to generate the IPTWs.

The goal of the hazard models is to produce accurate predicted probabilities to use in the IPTWs. To this end, we experimented with model specification, using model fit statistics to adjudicate among alternative specifications of key control variables, such as income. Because of this data-mining process, we do not put great weight on the substantive interpretation of these models, particularly for specific functional forms.[1]

Age

In each hazard model, age is specified as a linear spline with one knot. The knot is at age thirty-five in the model of first-time transition to homeownership, at age thirty-four in the model of transition to a subsequent spell of homeownership, and at age twenty-seven in the model of exit from homeownership. We also control for birth cohort using the respondent's age in 1985.

Race

Race is captured with binary variables for whether the respondent is Hispanic, or, if not Hispanic, black, white, Asian American and Pacific Islander, or another race.

Education

We measure educational attainment in the current year in five categories: less than a high school diploma or GED (general educational development test), exactly a high school diploma or GED, some college education, a four-year college degree, or an advanced degree.

Social Origins

Respondents' social origins are measured with parental education, parental age, whether the respondent was born in the South, and the respondent's number of siblings, all measured at baseline in 1979. Parental education is measured in the same categories as the respondent's education and is the maximum among the respondent's residential parents, if more than one. Parental age is measured as the average between residential parents, if more than one. For respondents not living with any parent at age fourteen, maternal values are used when available. Otherwise, paternal values are used. A dummy variable is set to one if the respondent was born in the American South.

---

1. The hazard models used to create the numerator of the stabilized inverse probability of treatment weights and the attrition weights use only time-invariant covariates set to their baseline values in 1985. For these models we rely on linear specifications of the baseline covariates.

Independent Residence

By definition, homeowners live independently, homeownership being defined by whether the respondent and spouse or partner own or are making payments to own the home. We therefore include a measure of independent residence only in our models of transitions to homeownership. We define the respondent as living independently if in the current survey she is not residing in her parents' home or in a group home (such as fraternity or sorority house, juvenile detention center, or hospital). In all models, we also include a measure of the number of years since the respondent last lived non-independently.[2] Individuals already living independently in 1979 are left-censored. For these individuals, we assume that independent residence began at age eighteen or in 1979, whichever is earliest. In the model of first-time transition to homeownership, years of consecutive independent residence is modeled linearly. In the model of transition to a subsequent spell of homeownership, years of consecutive independent residence enters the model linearly but is top coded at 7. In the model of exit from homeownership, years of consecutive independent residence is modeled as a linear spline with a knot at 2.

Marriage, Gender, and Children

In each wave, we create a binary variable for whether the respondent is currently married. We distinguish between unmarried men and women, incorporating the possibility for a gender gap in homeownership. We recognize that having children may precipitate the decision to buy a home, so we include a dummy variable for whether the respondent has children in the home.

Prior Homeownership Experiences

In the model of repeat homeownership, we include the number of years since the individual was last a homeowner, top coded at 4. For the model of exit from homeownership, we control for the number of years the individual has spent in the current homeownership spell, specified as a linear spline with a knot at 4. To capture unobserved traits possibly associated with enduring risk of homeownership exit, we also include a dummy variable to indicate whether the individual has ever experienced a transition out of homeownership.[3]

Income

We construct a measure of all income received by the respondent and the respondent's spouse or partner in the prior calendar year, excluding income of other household members.[4] We adjust this measure by the square root of family size (including any cohabiting partner) to more accurately capture disposable income. For the transition to first-time homeownership, we specify income with a linear spline with knots at the 25th and 75th percentiles of the unweighted distribution. For transition to repeat homeownership, we use a linear spline with a knot at the 25th percentile of the unweighted distribution. For transitions out of homeownership, we use a linear spline with knots at the 25th and 50th percentiles of the unweighted distribution.

Wealth

In most years, the NLSY79 has collected information on the respondent's net worth (1985 through 1990, 1992 through 1994, 1996, 1998, 2000, 2004, 2008, and 2012). Net worth is generally the sum of: housing equity (market value less debt); vehicle equity; cash savings, individual retirement accounts, or stocks and bonds; equity of farms, businesses, or other property owned by the respondent or spouse; and other (residual) valuable items or debts. Beginning in 1988, respondents were also asked to report the value of any rights they hold to estates or trusts. In our models of transitions to homeownership, we log wealth for those

---

2. We assume stability in independent residence between reports for up to two years following a report.

3. We assume stability in homeownership status between reports, for up to three years following a report.

4. Our measure of income includes inheritance and gifts from relatives received in the last calendar year. It is possible that transfers are endogenous with intended home purchase. Estimates of the effect of homeownership on midlife wealth were nearly identical when inheritance and gifts were excluded from the income measure.

with positive net worth and include separate indicators for zero and negative net worth. In the model of transitions out of homeownership, we specify the log of positive net worth as a linear spline with a knot at the 50th percentile of the overall unweighted wealth distribution. We also include indicators for zero and negative wealth. Income and wealth are adjusted to 2012 dollars using the consumer price index. We also top and bottom code positive wealth and income at the 99th and 1st percentiles for each year.

Missing Data and Final Weights

We multiply impute item-missing data on covariates. If homeownership status, which is used to construct the outcome in the hazard models, is missing in any year from 1985 to 2008 in which wealth was also collected, we lack full information on homeownership patterns, so we consider the respondent to have attrited following the last wave in which homeownership information was available and exclude the individual from our IPTW-weighted regressions. We also consider individuals to have attrited if they do not provide information on wealth in 2008—our outcome variable. Following Geoffrey Wodtke, David Harding, and Felix Elwert (2011), we create stabilized weights that account for sample attrition between 1985 and 2008 in the same way as we created stabilized treatment weights, modeling the hazard of attrition at the next wave.

To account for varying probabilities of selection in the initial sample, varying rates of cooperation with the baseline interview, and attrition between 1979 and 1985, we use custom weights supplied by NLSY79 to make the sample of 1985 respondents nationally representative. The product of the stabilized treatment weight, the stabilized attrition weight, and the NLSY79 custom weight (normalized to average one) is the final weight for the individual. Prior to analysis, we also top and bottom code each of the three component weights at the 95th and 5th percentiles of the distribution to reduce the potential for unduly influential outliers.

RESULTS

Table 1 shows descriptive statistics in the sample of individuals and person-year observations used in the IPTW regressions. As expected, race differences in net worth in 2008, at midlife, are vast: an average of $434,000 for whites, versus $247,000 for Hispanics and $126,000 for blacks. Because the distribution of wealth is right-skewed, median values are substantially lower for all groups: $213,000 for whites, $92,000 for Hispanics, and $26,000 for African Americans. Homeownership patterns also differ substantially; whites spend, on average, 14.9 years in homeownership during the twenty-three-year period, versus 10.8 for Hispanics and 7.6 for blacks. Whites are also advantaged with respect to Hispanics and blacks in their social origins; they are less likely to have been born in the South, have fewer siblings, and have parents with higher average education. In terms of achieved characteristics, whites again are most advantaged, having the highest average family incomes, highest probabilities of independent residence, highest marriage rates, and most education.

The results of the hazard models for transitions into and out of homeownership are provided in table A1. We summarize only the most important findings here. First, prior wealth is strongly positively associated with entrance into both first-time and repeat homeownership and negatively associated with exits from homeownership. These strong associations demonstrate the importance of controlling for prior wealth when considering the association between homeownership patterns and later-life assets. Second, as expected, compared with otherwise similar whites, African Americans and Hispanics are less likely to enter both first and repeat homeownership and are at greater risk of exiting homeownership.

Table 2 presents the results of our regression models. For comparison, we present the results of unweighted regressions as well as our preferred weighted results. We anticipate that weighting will reduce the estimated association between homeownership and subsequent wealth, because the weights remove any association between midlife wealth and homeownership due to the effect of the time-varying variables in our model on both. In the pooled sample, the unadjusted models estimate an additional $9,280 in wealth for every year spent as a homeowner, even after taking into account

Table 1. Descriptive Statistics for the IPTW Sample

	All	White	Black	Hispanic
Persons	5,636	2,396	1,668	977
Wealth as of 2008 ($100,000)—mean	3.83	4.34	1.26	2.47
	(6.85)	(7.14)	(3.67)	(4.84)
Median	1.67	2.13	0.26	0.92
Years of homeownership between 1986 and	13.70	14.88	7.60	10.75
2008—mean	(7.82)	(7.33)	(7.54)	(8.11)
Median	16	17	5	11
Age in 1985	23.67	23.67	23.63	23.52
	(2.31)	(2.31)	(2.32)	(2.35)
Female	0.52	0.51	0.55	0.53
South	0.32	0.24	0.62	0.37
Number of siblings	3.28	2.99	4.62	4.38
	(2.21)	(1.90)	(2.84)	(2.91)
Parental age in 1978	45.25	45.49	44.34	44.56
	(6.89)	(6.67)	(7.60)	(7.16)
Parental education				
Less than a high school diploma or GED	0.25	0.16	0.48	0.62
Exactly a high school diploma or GED	0.42	0.46	0.35	0.21
Some college education	0.13	0.14	0.10	0.08
Four-year college degree	0.12	0.14	0.05	0.05
Advanced degree	0.08	0.10	0.03	0.04
Person-years	78,904	33,544	23,352	13,678
Age	32.56	32.56	32.52	32.43
	(7.11)	(7.11)	(7.11)	(7.15)
Family income ($100,000)—mean	0.73	0.79	0.45	0.57
	(2.22)	(1.94)	(2.41)	(0.52)
Median	0.57	0.62	0.30	0.44
Positive wealth ($100,000)—mean	1.71	1.88	0.63	1.12
	(3.93)	(4.08)	(1.99)	(2.86)
Median	0.50	0.60	0.13	0.28
Zero wealth	0.04	0.02	0.18	0.08
Negative wealth	0.10	0.09	0.13	0.11
Independent residence	0.88	0.90	0.78	0.85
Years since last dependent residence	9.19	9.56	6.91	8.30
	(7.37)	(7.34)	(6.99)	(7.25)
Years of homeownership	3.88	4.32	1.58	2.65
	(5.63)	(5.81)	(3.73)	(4.77)
Ever lost homeownership before	0.24	0.24	0.22	0.25
Years since last homeownership	0.51	0.43	0.80	0.74
	(1.85)	(1.68)	(2.43)	(2.29)
Male single	0.20	0.19	0.28	0.21
Female single	0.21	0.18	0.37	0.23
Education				
Less than a high school diploma or GED	0.10	0.07	0.16	0.23
Exactly a high school diploma or GED	0.41	0.41	0.44	0.38
Some college education	0.24	0.24	0.27	0.27
Four-year college degree	0.18	0.21	0.10	0.09
Advanced degree	0.06	0.07	0.03	0.03

Source: Authors' calculations.

Note: All samples are weighted by the 2008 NLSY79 weight. Standard deviations in parentheses.

Table 2. Estimated Effects of Homeownership on Wealth

	Coefficient	Robust S.E.	N	Marginal Effect at Mean
Absolute wealth (dollars)				
2008 wealth				
All—unweighted	9,279.8***	(350.4)	5,636	
All—weighted	6,786.7***	(672.9)	5,636	
White—unweighted	11,264.7***	(675.8)	2,396	
White—weighted	7,602.1***	(1,073.1)	2,396	
Black—unweighted	5,792.2***	(443.7)	1,668	
Black—weighted	3,644.5***	(442.7)	1,668	
Hispanic—unweighted	9,662.0***	(868.0)	977	
Hispanic—weighted	4,684.3***	(948.9)	977	
2012 wealth				
All—weighted	4,424.1***	(563.5)	5,227	
White—weighted	5,139.9***	(1,037.1)	2,220	
Black—weighted	2,574.9***	(395.1)	1,557	
Hispanic—weighted	3,168.5***	(841.4)	909	
Nonhousing wealth (2008)—weighted	2,085.6***	(282.8)	5,595	
Logged positive wealth				
2008 wealth				
All—unweighted	0.100***	(0.004)	4,805	12,879
All—weighted	0.049***	(0.006)	4,805	6,196
White—weighted	0.045***	(0.007)	2,211	9,338
Black—weighted	0.068***	(0.010)	1,245	3,195
Hispanic—weighted	0.069***	(0.010)	817	6,793
2012 wealth				
All—weighted	0.047***	(0.006)	4,266	5,505
White—weighted	0.039***	(0.008)	2,001	7,621
Black—weighted	0.055***	(0.008)	1,054	2,433
Hispanic—weighted	0.080***	(0.011)	733	6,368

Source: Authors' calculations.
Note: Weights are top and bottom coded at the 5th and 95th percentiles.
* $p < 0.05$, ** $p < 0.01$, *** $p < 0.001$

variation in baseline characteristics, including 1985 wealth. Adjusting for time-varying spurious characteristics, however, reduces the estimated effect by 27 percent, to a benefit of $6,787 per year of homeownership, substantially less than the estimates of Herbert, McCue, and Sanchez-Moyano (2013) and Turner and Luea (2009), which are respectively $9,500 and $13,700. A regression weighted with our attrition weight and the NLSY79 custom weight, but not the treatment weight, increases the estimated association between homeownership and midlife wealth compared to the unweighted model, confirming that the treatment weight is what reduces the estimated association, not the attrition weight or sampling weight.[5] Thus, failure to account for dynamic selection into homeownership leads to substantially inflated

---

5. In a supplemental model, we replaced the product of our attrition weight and NLSY79 custom weight for 1985 respondents with a single NLSY79 custom weight designed to make the sample of respondents observed in every wave between 1985 and 2008 (inclusive) in which wealth data were collected nationally representative.

estimates of the wealth benefits of owning a home.[6]

We also find that each additional year of homeownership is associated with an increase of $2,086 in midlife nonhousing wealth, consistent with Di and colleague's (2007) finding that nonhousing wealth is positively associated with prior homeownership. Thus, although the majority of the wealth benefits of homeownership accrue to housing wealth, the wealth benefits of homeownership do not appear to be limited to home-equity gains.

Our race-specific results show substantial disparities in the wealth returns to homeownership. Whites are estimated to accumulate median wealth gains of $7,602 for every year of homeownership, versus $4,684 for Hispanics and only $3,645 for blacks. Thus the wealth benefits of each year of homeownership are 48 percent as large for blacks as for whites and 62 percent as large for Hispanics. Although adjustments for selection reduce the estimated return to homeownership for each group, the change is proportionally largest for Hispanics. In other words, the differences between Hispanic owners and nonowners, in terms of characteristics conducive to wealth accumulation, are not well captured by baseline covariates alone; differences in circumstances over the observation period also need to be considered. Failure to adjust for the processes by which individuals enter into and maintain homeownership thus not only overstates the wealth benefits of homeownership but also understates the race gap in these benefits; adjusting for dynamic selection processes reduces the Hispanic to white ratio of wealth benefits from homeownership from 86 percent to 62 percent. Our estimate of the relative disadvantage of African Americans' wealth benefits of homeownership relative to whites' is also substantially larger than that of Herbert, McCue, and Sanchez-Moyano (2013), who find only a 20 percent gap.

As expected, the estimated wealth returns to homeownership are lower when wealth is measured in 2012. In the pooled sample, each additional year of homeownership is associated with an increase in midlife wealth of $4,424 in 2012, 35 percent less than when the outcome is 2008 wealth. This decline is not primarily due to declines in the relative value of homeownership but to declines in overall wealth levels, compressing absolute gains; when we replicate the models using the log of net worth as the outcome, restricting the sample to those with positive net worth, we see that, on average, the proportional benefits of homeownership for wealth declined only modestly between 2008 and 2012, from about 4.9 percent to about 4.7 percent.

Given that Hispanics and African Americans were hit particularly hard by the Great Recession in terms of proportional declines in wealth and home equity (Grinstein-Weiss, Key, and Carrillo 2015; McKernan et al. 2013), we might expect that variation by race in the wealth returns to homeownership would be even larger in 2012 than in 2008. However, we find similar disparities in 2012 as 2008. In 2012, the wealth benefits of each year of homeownership are 50 percent as large for blacks and 62 percent as large for Hispanics as for whites.

One natural question is whether the absolute wealth benefits of homeownership are lower for racial minorities simply because overall wealth levels are lower.[7] Furthermore, our estimates of the median wealth benefits of homeownership may mask greater absolute returns to homeownership for high-wealth indi-

---

In other words, we used the NLSY79's combined sampling and attrition weight rather than our own. The results were similar: an estimated gain of $6,311 in midlife wealth per year of homeownership, versus $6,787 in the main model.

6. Furthermore, without adjustments for dynamic selection, controls for wealth at baseline have a relatively small effect on the estimated wealth benefits of homeownership. In a supplemental unweighted model that further omitted wealth in 1985 from the baseline model, the estimated wealth benefit for each year of homeownership was $9,783. Adjusting for wealth at baseline therefore reduces this naïve estimate by only 5 percent, versus 31 percent relative to the naïve model when we implement our preferred adjustment for dynamic selection.

7. Similarly, we find that the absolute wealth returns to homeownership were lower for less-educated than more-educated whites (the sample is not large enough to do a similar analysis for Hispanics and African Americans).

viduals. To investigate this possibility, we repeat our models using the log of net worth among those with positive net worth as the outcome rather than raw wealth values. In proportional terms, among those with positive net worth, whites have the lowest wealth returns to homeownership in both 2008 and 2012. It is tempting to interpret these results as estimating the returns for every $1 invested in home purchase, but this is not the case: the models predict 2008 (or 2012) wealth with years of homeownership, not the return on dollars invested in housing. The absolute models assume that an extra year of homeownership has a constant effect on midlife wealth across the wealth distribution, whereas the proportional models assume that it benefits individuals by a constant proportion across the wealth distribution. Given that wealth levels are substantially lower for racial minorities than whites, regardless of homeowner status, similar proportional gains from homeownership will translate into larger absolute gains for whites; this is a purely mechanical relationship and does not by itself reveal anything about the social process underlying racial variation in the wealth benefits of homeownership.[8]

A more challenging question is whether equality in the wealth benefits of homeownership should be interpreted as a statement about absolute or proportional equality. If the goal is to assess whether the housing market is biased against minority homeowners, proportional equality might be the preferred standard. However, even if the wealth returns to homeownership are proportional to wealth and homogeneous by race, it tells us only that the pervasive wealth disadvantage that racial minorities experience relative to whites in both housing and nonhousing wealth limits minority homeowners' abilities to keep pace with the absolute wealth accumulation rates of their white peers. Beyond standard income and investment considerations, recent research highlights that African American families' wealth positions are disadvantaged by negative health shocks (Thompson and Conley, this volume) and incarceration (Schneider and Turney 2015; Sykes and Maroto, this volume).

To explore the role of homeownership in racial wealth gaps, we decompose how closing the race gap in homeownership rates would change the race gap in the total wealth benefits of homeownership, versus the effect of eliminating the gap in the returns to each year of homeownership. As shown in table 3, we begin by simulating the wealth gains from homeownership for whites, blacks, and Hispanics who experienced the race-specific median years of homeownership and race-specific median returns to each year of homeownership between 1986 and 2008. Disparities are large; in this simulation, whites accumulate a total of $129,000 for homeownership, versus $52,000 for Hispanics and $18,000 for blacks. In other words, the gains are only 40 percent as large for Hispanics and only 14 percent as large for blacks. Now we simulate the total midlife wealth gains from homeownership under the counterfactual scenario that each group owns a home for seventeen years during the period—the median for whites—but experiences race-specific wealth benefits for each year of homeownership. The gaps in accumulated wealth due to homeownership decrease for both groups; the cumulative gains for Hispanics are now 62 percent and for blacks 48 percent as large as for whites. When we alternatively hold constant the wealth returns to a year of homeownership at the estimated level for whites ($7,602) but allow each race to have different exposure to homeownership, Hispanics accumulate 65 percent and blacks 29 percent as much as whites. Thus, for both blacks and Hispanics, race disparities in

---

8. Restricting the log of net worth models to respondents with positive net worth omits 15 and 18 percent of respondents in 2008 and 2012, respectively. If this selection process varies by race, differences in the sample could contribute to the white advantage in absolute but not proportional wealth returns to homeownership. We do not find support for this possibility in 2008: absolute wealth returns estimated on a sample of respondents with positive net wealth show wealth returns to homeownership about twice as large for whites as for either Hispanics or African Americans. However, in 2012, when the sample is restricted to respondents with positive net worth, we find that Hispanics have absolute wealth returns to homeownership similar to those of whites, and the black-white gap in the returns to homeownership is somewhat diminished. Therefore, in 2012 race differences in selection into positive net worth may contribute to the lower proportional returns to homeownership for whites.

Table 3. Simulated Total Wealth Benefits of Homeownership

	White	Black	Hispanic	White	Black	Hispanic
Median years homeownership	17	5	11			
Estimated median wealth gain/ year of homeownership	7,602	3,645	4,684			
	Simulated Total Wealth Benefits of Homeownership			Simulated Midlife Wealth		
Absolute						
Current	129,234	18,225	51,524	212,900	26,145	91,684
No homeownership	0	0	0	83,666	7,920	40,160
Equal years (seventeen)	129,234	61,965	79,628	212,900	69,885	119,788
Equal returns ($7,602)	129,234	38,010	83,622	212,900	45,930	123,782
Equals years and returns	129,234	129,234	129,234	212,900	137,154	169,394
Relative to whites						
Current		0.14	0.40		0.12	0.43
No homeownership		N/A	N/A		0.09	0.48
Equal years (seventeen)		0.48	0.62		0.33	0.56
Equal returns ($7,602)		0.29	0.65		0.22	0.58
Equals years and returns		1.00	1.00		0.64	0.80

Source: Authors' calculations.

rates of homeownership and returns to homeownership are both substantial contributors to the race gap in wealth accumulated from homeownership. For Hispanics, the two factors contribute approximately equally, and, for blacks, the role of differences in rates of homeownership is larger.

The three rightmost columns of table 3 simulate the role of homeownership in the race gap in midlife wealth. We simulate median midlife wealth levels by race in the absence of homeownership by subtracting from observed median wealth levels the simulated total wealth benefits of homeownership given race-specific homeownership rates and returns to homeownership, as calculated in the left-hand columns. To these baseline levels, we then add wealth gains from homeownership in three alternative scenarios: years of homeownership equalized at the white median; returns to years of homeownership equalized at the white median; and total wealth benefits of homeownership equalized setting both years of homeownership and the returns to years of homeownership to the white median for all respondents. At midlife, the observed median wealth of Hispanics and African Americans is 43 percent and 12 percent that of whites, respectively. In the counterfactual simulation of no homeownership, the analogous numbers are 48 percent and 9 percent, respectively. Although whites are advantaged in wealth in part because of their higher rates of homeownership and greater wealth returns per year of homeownership, these gains are similar to whites' advantage in other wealth-generating processes; disparities in homeownership experiences contribute to the race gap in wealth, but not uniquely so.

Equalizing homeownership rates and the wealth benefits per year of homeownership, however, could substantially narrow race gaps in wealth. Under this simulated scenario, Hispanic median midlife wealth is 80 percent and African American 64 percent that of whites. Although substantial race gaps in midlife wealth remain even in this optimistic scenario, the results show that equality in wealth benefits of homeownership could substantially narrow them.

Our analyses are, of course, imperfect. Although our models are designed to account for dynamic selection into homeownership, they have the same limitations as all observational studies and depend on the assumption that we have captured wealth-relevant differences between homeowners and renters with our control variables. Although prior research does not suggest substantial bias due to reporting error, overestimates of home values relative to other assets could upwardly bias the homeownership wealth returns. Our results suggest that prior estimates have overstated the wealth benefits of homeownership, and the true effect could be even lower than our results suggest.

Our results also apply to the experiences of a particular cohort at a particular point in their lives and in a particular macroeconomic context. Although we find substantial wealth benefits from homeownership regardless of whether wealth is measured in 2008 or 2012, cohorts of homeowners entering the housing market after the Great Recession may have different experiences. The observed variation in the wealth benefits of homeownership by race may also be context-specific and sensitive to the overall wealth gap between whites, African Americans, and Hispanics. For example, the Hispanics included in our sample were all observed in the United States in 1979, when they were young adults, so the estimates may not reflect the benefits of homeownership for recent Hispanic immigrants.

Finally, the simulations in table 3 are descriptive rather than causal. They illustrate how race gaps in wealth would change under various illustrative counterfactual scenarios, but they are not designed to incorporate, for example, the possibility that changes in homeownership rates would also change the returns to homeownership.

CONCLUSIONS

Home equity is the largest component of most American asset portfolios, and homeownership is widely assumed to be a pathway to wealth accumulation. Yet prior estimates of the long-term benefits of homeownership for later-life wealth have typically ignored the possibility of spurious events during the observation window that affect both transitions into and out of homeownership and subsequent wealth. Our results confirm that homeownership has substantial wealth benefits. Each additional year spent as a homeowner is associated with about $6,800 more in midlife wealth in 2008. Comparing our weighted and unweighted results, we find that accounting for the dynamic relationships between wealth, homeownership, and other wealth-enhancing characteristics reduces the wealth benefits of homeownership by 27 percent. In 2012, each year of homeownership between 1986 and 2008 is associated with about $4,400 more in midlife wealth. Thus, even in the midst of the housing crisis, time spent in homeownership positively affected wealth. However, our estimates of the wealth benefits of homeownership are smaller than previous estimates (Herbert, McCue, and Sanchez-Moyano 2013; Turner and Luea 2009).

Although housing markets do not appear to uniquely disadvantage African Americans and Hispanics—eliminating homeownership would not substantially change the race gap in wealth—altering their homeownership experiences to be comparable to those of whites would substantially narrow race gaps in midlife wealth. We find that, compared with whites, blacks and Hispanics are disadvantaged in three distinct ways. First, as shown in our descriptive results, they have, on average, characteristics that are less likely to facilitate entering and maintaining homeownership. As a result, they participate less in this wealth-generating state. Programs and policies designed to reduce racial disparities in other domains, including education and income, may thus have spillover effects on the race gap in homeownership and wealth.

Second, even holding other determinants of homeownership constant, blacks and Hispanics have lower rates of entry into homeownership and higher rates of exit than whites, further depressing their accumulated years of homeownership. Stricter enforcement of antidiscrimination laws in housing markets might help close the race gap in access to homeownership, particularly given evidence that blacks face higher rates of rejection for mortgage applications than comparable whites (Charles and Hurst 2002). Recent analyses have also implicated residential segregation in the concentration of subprime lending among black and Hispanic homeowners (Hwang, Hankinson, and Brown 2015). It is possible that stricter regulations in subprime lending would reduce race disparities in risk of homeownership exit.

Third, for every year they spend as homeowners, blacks and Hispanics receive lower median wealth returns than whites do. Disparities in homeownership rates and in the returns to homeownership both contribute substantially to the gaps by race in long-term wealth accumulation from homeownership. One possible mechanism for equalizing returns is to invest in predominantly black and Hispanic neighborhoods, given that other scholars have attributed lower rates of home appreciation for black homeowners in part to racial segregation (Flippen 2004; Oliver and Shapiro 2006). However, the results from our models of log wealth demonstrate that minority homeowners do not experience lower proportional wealth returns to homeownership, but the substantially lower average wealth positions of nonwhite owners and nonowners alike imply that these proportional returns translate into far smaller absolute wealth benefits. Policies aimed only at housing markets, therefore, may have limited effect on equalizing the wealth returns to years of homeownership without also addressing other sources of the residual race gap in wealth above and beyond race differences in income. Future research is needed to further investigate the sources of this residual gap and identify policy levers to narrow it.

Table A1. Discrete-Time Hazard Models of Entry to and Exit from Homeownership

	First	Repeat	Exit
Age in 1985	0.00539	0.0163	0.0497***
	(0.00905)	(0.0135)	(0.00903)
Age			
Thirty-five or younger	0.0107		
	(0.00677)		
Older than thirty-five	−0.0633***		
	(0.0108)		
Thirty-four or younger		0.0116	
		(0.00937)	
Older than thirty-four		−0.0518***	
		(0.00934)	
Twenty-seven or younger			−0.123***
			(0.0181)
Older than twenty-seven			−0.0645***
			(0.00525)
Race (reference: white)			
Black	−0.515***	−0.612***	0.551***
	(0.0516)	(0.0775)	(0.0584)
Hispanic	−0.316***	−0.273***	0.338***
	(0.0531)	(0.0815)	(0.0552)
Asian American or Pacific Islander	−0.211	0.289	0.234
	(0.225)	(0.464)	(0.232)
Other	0.0743	0.00964	0.0900
	(0.0621)	(0.0901)	(0.0627)
Log family income			
Bottom quartile	−0.0261**	−0.0180	0.0323**
	(0.00853)	(0.0127)	(0.0119)
Second quartile			−0.582***
			(0.0796)

Table A1. (*continued*)

	First	Repeat	Exit
Middle two quartiles	0.510***		
	(0.0407)		
Top quartile	−0.137		
	(0.0708)		
Top three quartiles		0.247***	
		(0.0434)	
Top two quartiles			−0.0962
			(0.0547)
Log positive wealth		0.234***	0.202***
		(0.0146)	(0.0194)
Bottom two quartiles			−0.152**
			(0.0493)
Top two quartiles			−0.0357
			(0.0220)
Zero wealth (dummy)	1.158***	1.059***	−1.794**
	(0.148)	(0.208)	(0.633)
Negative wealth (dummy)	1.700***	1.445***	−1.095*
	(0.139)	(0.196)	(0.465)
Independent residence	−0.146**	−0.284**	
	(0.0523)	(0.109)	
Years since last reported non-independent residence	−0.00724		
	(0.00486)		
Top coded at seven		0.0587***	
		(0.0149)	
Two or less			−0.597***
			(0.0531)
More than two			0.000595
			(0.00495)
Years since last homeownership (top coded at four)		−0.0328*	
		(0.0147)	
Years of homeownership			
Four or less			−0.175***
			(0.0195)
More than four			−0.0698***
			(0.00890)
Ever lost homeownership before			0.0427
			(0.0567)
Male single (reference: married couple)	−0.818***	−0.413***	0.736***
	(0.0498)	(0.0786)	(0.0601)
Female single (reference: married couple)	−0.611***	−0.422***	0.428***
	(0.0456)	(0.0683)	(0.0568)
Has children	0.149***	0.296***	−0.0816
	(0.0441)	(0.0659)	(0.0478)
Education (reference: less than high school)			
High school diploma or GED	0.144**	0.132	−0.353***
	(0.0556)	(0.0831)	(0.0587)

(*continued*)

Table A1. (continued)

	First	Repeat	Exit
Some college education	0.274***	0.269**	-0.460***
	(0.0617)	(0.0944)	(0.0670)
Four-year college degree	0.495***	0.452***	-0.844***
	(0.0710)	(0.122)	(0.0848)
Advanced degree	0.617***	0.724***	-0.779***
	(0.103)	(0.182)	(0.112)
Parental education (reference: less than high school)			
High school diploma or GED	-0.0163	-0.0976	0.0855
	(0.0441)	(0.0727)	(0.0480)
Some college education	0.0308	-0.145	0.215**
	(0.0601)	(0.0999)	(0.0684)
Four-year college degree	-0.177*	-0.187	0.147
	(0.0699)	(0.126)	(0.0840)
Advanced degree	-0.192*	-0.152	0.229*
	(0.0807)	(0.145)	(0.0924)
Parental age	-0.000585	-0.00220	-0.00707*
	(0.00262)	(0.00420)	(0.00300)
Born in South	0.228***	0.196**	0.00131
	(0.0388)	(0.0602)	(0.0437)
Number of siblings	0.0151*	-0.00289	-0.00769
	(0.00742)	(0.0128)	(0.00849)
N (person-years)	50,180	13,348	40,800

Source: Authors' calculations.
Note: Standard errors in parentheses.
* $p < 0.05$, ** $p < 0.01$, *** $p < 0.001$

REFERENCES

Addo, Fenaba R., and Daniel T. Lichter. 2013. "Marriage, Marital History, and Black-White Wealth Differentials Among Older Women." *Journal of Marriage and Family* 75(2): 342-62.

Adelino, Manuel, Antoinette Schoar, and Felipe Severino. 2015. "House Prices, Collateral, and Self-Employment." *Journal of Financial Economics* 117(2): 288-306.

Black, Jane, David de Meza, and David Jeffreys. 1996. "House Prices, the Supply of Collateral and the Enterprise Economy." *Economic Journal* 106(434): 60-75.

Bocian, Debbie Gruenstein, Keith S. Ernst, and Wei Li. 2008. "Race, Ethnicity and Subprime Home Loan Pricing." *Journal of Economics and Business* 60(1-2): 110-24.

Boehm, Thomas P., and Alan M. Schlottmann. 2004. "The Dynamics of Race, Income, and Homeownership." *Journal of Urban Economics* 55(1): 113-30.

———. 2008. "Wealth Accumulation and Homeownership: Evidence for Low-Income Households." *Cityscape* 10(2): 225-56.

Cavalluzzo, Ken, and John Wolken. 2005. "Small Business Loan Turndowns, Personal Wealth, and Discrimination." *Journal of Business* 78(6): 2153-78.

Charles, Kerwin Kofi, and Erik Hurst. 2002. "The Transition to Home Ownership and the Black-White Wealth Gap." *Review of Economics and Statistics* 84(2): 281-97.

———. 2003. "The Correlation of Wealth Across Generations." *Journal of Political Economy* 111(6): 1155-82.

Choudhury, Sharmila. 2001. "Racial and Ethnic Differences in Wealth and Asset Choices." *Social Security Bulletin* 64(4): 1-15.

Conley, Dalton. 1999. *Being Black, Living in the Red: Race, Wealth, and Social Policy in America.* Berkeley: University of California Press.

———. 2001. "Capital for College: Parental Assets

and Postsecondary Schooling." *Sociology of Education* 74(1): 59–72.

Cooke, Lynn Prince. 2006. "'Doing' Gender in Context: Household Bargaining and Risk of Divorce in Germany and the United States." *American Journal of Sociology* 112(2): 442–72.

Di, Zhu Xiao, Eric Belsky, and Xiaodong Liu. 2007. "Do Homeowners Achieve More Household Wealth in the Long Run?" *Journal of Housing Economics* 16(3-4): 274–90.

Di, Zhu Xiao, and Xiaodong Liu. 2007. "The Importance of Wealth and Income in the Transition to Homeownership." *Cityscape* 9(2): 137–51.

Dietz, Robert D., and Donald R. Haurin. 2003. "The Social and Private Micro-Level Consequences of Homeownership." *Journal of Urban Economics* 54(3): 401–50.

Eads, Alicia, and Laura Tach. 2016. "Wealth and Inequality in the Stability of Romantic Relationships." *RSF: The Russell Sage Foundation Journal of the Social Sciences* 2(6). doi: 10.7758/RSF.2016.2.6.10.

Federal Reserve Bank of New York (Federal Reserve). 2016. "Distribution of Home Price Changes by County." New York: Federal Reserve Bank. Accessed June 2, 2016. https://www.newyorkfed.org/home-price-index/index.html.

Flippen, Chenoa. 2004. "Unequal Returns to Housing Investments? A Study of Real Housing Appreciation Among Black, White, and Hispanic Households." *Social Forces* 82(4): 1523–51.

Goodman, John L., Jr., and John B. Ittner. 1992. "The Accuracy of Home Owners' Estimates of House Value." *Journal of Housing Economics* 2(4): 339–57.

Grinstein-Weiss, Michal, Clinton Key, and Shannon Carrillo. 2015. "Homeownership, the Great Recession, and Wealth: Evidence from the Survey of Consumer Finances." *Housing Policy Debate* 25(3): 419–45.

Herbert, Christopher E., Daniel T. McCue, and Rocio Sanchez-Moyano. 2013. "Is Homeownership Still an Effective Means of Building Wealth for Low-Income and Minority Households? (Was It Ever?)." *Joint Center for Housing Studies* working paper. Cambridge, Mass.: Harvard University. Accessed June 9, 2016. http://jchs.harvard.edu/sites/jchs.harvard.edu/files/hbtl-06.pdf.

Hwang, Jackelyn, Michael Hankinson, and Kreg Steven Brown. 2015. "Racial and Spatial Targeting: Segregation and Subprime Lending within and across Metropolitan Areas." *Social Forces* 93(3): 1081–108.

Keister, Lisa A., and Stephanie Moller. 2000. "Wealth Inequality in the United States." *Annual Review of Sociology* 26: 63–81.

Kochhar, Rakesh, Richard Fry, and Paul Taylor. 2011. *Wealth Gaps Rise to Record Highs Between Whites, Blacks, and Hispanics*. Washington, D.C.: Pew Research Center. Accessed May 25, 2016. http://www.pewsocialtrends.org/files/2011/07/SDT-Wealth-Report_7-26-11_FINAL.pdf.

McKernan, Signe-Mary, Caroline Ratcliffe, Eugene Steuerle, and Sisi Zhang. 2013. "Less Than Equal: Racial Disparities in Wealth Accumulation." Washington, D.C.: Urban Institute.

Nothaft, Frank E., and Yan Chang. 2005. "Refinance and the Accumulation of Home Equity Wealth." In *Building Assets, Building Credit: Creating Wealth in Low-Income Communities*, edited by Nicholas P. Retsinas and Eric S. Belsky. Washington, D.C.: Brookings Institution Press.

Oliver, Melvin L., and Thomas M. Shapiro. 2006. *Black Wealth/White Wealth: A New Perspective on Racial Inequality*, 2nd edition. New York: Routledge.

Orr, Amy J. 2003. "Black-White Differences in Achievement: The Importance of Wealth." *Sociology of Education* 76(4): 281–304.

Pfeffer, Fabian T., and Alexandra Killewald. 2015. "How Rigid Is the Wealth Structure and Why? Inter- and Multigenerational Associations in Family Wealth." *PSC* research report no. 15-845. Ann Arbor: Population Studies Center at the Institute for Social Research, University of Michigan.

Pfeffer, Fabian T., Robert F. Schoeni, Arthur Kennickell, and Patricia Andreski. 2016. "Measuring Wealth and Wealth Inequality." *Journal of Economic and Social Measurement* 41(2): 103–20.

Robins, James M., Miguel Ángel Hernán, and Babette Brumback. 2000. "Marginal Structural Models and Causal Inference in Epidemiology." *Epidemiology* 11(5): 550–60.

S&P Dow Jones Indices (Dow Jones). 2016. "S&P/Case-Shiller U.S. National Home Price Index." New York: S&P Dow Jones Indices LLC. Accessed June 2, 2016. http://us.spindices.com/indices/real-estate/sp-case-shiller-us-national-home-price-index.

Schneider, Daniel. 2011. "Wealth and the Marital Divide." *American Journal of Sociology* 117(2): 627–67.

Schneider, Daniel, and Kristin Turney. 2015. "Incarceration and Black-White Inequality in Homeownership: A State-Level Analysis." *Social Science Research* 53: 403–14.

Sharkey, Patrick, and Felix Elwert. 2011. "The Legacy of Disadvantage: Multigenerational Neighborhood Effects on Cognitive Ability." *American Journal of Sociology* 116(6): 1934–81.

South, Scott J. 2001. "Time-Dependent Effects of Wives' Employment on Marital Dissolution." *American Sociological Review* 66(2): 226–45.

Sykes, Bryan L., and Michelle Maroto. 2016. "A Wealth of Inequalities: Mass Incarceration, Employment, and Racial Disparities in U.S. Household Wealth, 1996 to 2011." *RSF: The Russell Sage Foundation Journal of the Social Sciences* 2(6). doi: 10.7758/RSF.2016.2.6.07.

Thompson, Jason, and Dalton Conley. 2016. "Health Shocks and Social Drift: Examining the Relationship Between Acute Illness and Family Wealth." *RSF: The Russell Sage Foundation Journal of the Social Sciences* 2(6). doi: 10.7758/RSF.2016.2.6.08.

Turner, Tracy M., and Heather Luea. 2009. "Homeownership, Wealth Accumulation and Income Status." *Journal of Housing Economics* 18(2): 104–14.

U.S. Bureau of Labor Statistics, Department of Labor. 2016a. National Longitudinal Survey of Youth 1979 cohort, 1979-2012 (rounds 1-25). Produced and distributed by the Center for Human Resource Research, The Ohio State University. Columbus, OH.

———. 2016b. National Longitudinal Survey of Youth, Retention & Reasons for Noninterview. Accessed June 2, 2016. https://nlsinfo.org/content/cohorts/nlsy79/intro-to-the-sample/retention-reasons-noninterview.

Van Order, Robert, and Peter Zorn. 2002. "Performance of Low-Income and Minority Mortgages." In *Low-Income Homeownership: Examining the Unexamined Goal*, edited by Nicholas P. Retsinas and Eric S. Belsky. Washington, D.C.: Brookings Institution Press.

Wodtke, Geoffrey T., David J. Harding, and Felix Elwert. 2011. "Neighborhood Effects in Temporal Perspective: The Impact of Long-Term Exposure to Concentrated Disadvantage on High School Graduation." *American Sociological Review* 76(5): 713–36.

Wolff, Edward N. 2016. "Household Wealth Trends in the United States, 1962 to 2013: What Happened over the Great Recession?" *RSF: The Russell Sage Foundation Journal of the Social Sciences* 2(6). doi: 10.7758/RSF.2016.2.6.02.

Zagorsky, Jay L. 2005. "Marriage and Divorce's Impact on Wealth." *Journal of Sociology* 41(4): 406–24.

A Wealth of Inequalities: Mass Incarceration, Employment, and Racial Disparities in U.S. Household Wealth, 1996 to 2011

BRYAN L. SYKES AND MICHELLE MAROTO

Despite the strong relationship between the rise in mass incarceration over the last forty years and racial inequality in employment and wages, few studies have examined the long-term consequences and spillover effects of criminal justice contact on the black-white wealth gap in the United States. In this paper, we investigate the mechanisms whereby the local and distal incarceration of a family member affects household wealth, focusing on wealth disparities by race and education. Using data from the Survey of Income and Program Participation (SIPP), the Current Population Survey, and the Survey of Inmates in State and Federal Correctional Facilities and Local Jails, we apply fixed-effects and probit models to estimate how a family member's incarceration influences household assets and debt over panel waves. We find that having an incarcerated family member reduced household assets by 64.3 percent and debt by 85.1 percent after we adjusted for the underrepresentation of institutionalization in SIPP data. We also discuss these findings in the context of broader racial disparities in wealth and employment. Our findings demonstrate how contemporary patterns of mass incarceration contribute to the maintenance of social inequality in wealth and form barriers to economic security for other household members.

Keywords: wealth, incarceration, families, stratification

It is well established that the detrimental effects of incarceration extend into many areas of social life (Wakefield and Uggen 2010). Incarceration limits future employment prospects and earnings (Western and Pettit 2005; Western 2006; Pettit 2012), blocks political participation (Manza and Uggen 2006), and can lead to physical and mental health issues for former offenders (Schnittker, Massoglia, and Uggen 2011). These far-reaching effects have led some to characterize incarceration as a criminal credential or absorbing status that results in continuing disadvantage for former prisoners (Pager 2003, 2007).

The consequences of incarceration spread beyond the formerly incarcerated as well. Incarceration increases material hardship and familial stress, exacerbates marital instability by straining family ties, and is associated with a variety of adverse outcomes for children (Wildeman and Muller 2012). In this study we investigate the relationship between incarcera-

Bryan L. Sykes is assistant professor in the Department of Criminology, Law & Society at the University of California, Irvine. **Michelle Maroto** is assistant professor in the Department of Sociology at the University of Alberta.

An earlier version of this paper was presented at the Russell Sage Wealth Inequality Meeting in October 2015 and the 2016 Annual Meeting of the Population Association of America. We thank Fabian Pfeffer, Robert Schoeni, Sheldon Danziger, Robert Hauser, Alexandra Killewald, anonymous reviewers, and participants of the RSF Wealth Inequality Meeting for comments on previous versions of our paper. Direct correspondence to: Bryan L. Sykes at blsykes@uci.edu, 3317 Social Ecology II, University of California, Irvine, CA 92697; and Michelle Maroto at maroto@ualberta.ca, 6-23, Tory Building, University of Alberta, Edmonton, AB T6G 2H4, Canada.

tion and the wealth profiles of ex-offenders and other family members, who include parents, romantic partners, and dependents.

Although researchers have shown that incarceration influences a variety of economic outcomes for former offenders and those around them, research on the relationship between incarceration and wealth accumulation is relatively new. The few studies on this topic indicate that incarceration is associated with decreased rates of homeownership and net worth for former offenders (Maroto 2015; Zaw, Hamilton, and Darity 2016); it is a particularly salient factor in explaining black-white disparities in homeownership (Schneider and Turney 2015). Additional research points to increasing debt for former offenders through the courts' use of heavy pre- and post-conviction fines and fees that many individuals simply cannot afford to pay (Harris, Evans, and Beckett 2010, 2011).

Despite the growing research on mass incarceration and the importance of wealth for economic well-being, little is known about the long-term consequences of imprisonment for the wealth accumulation of former inmates and their families. We focus on how the negative effects of incarceration can infect households through economic disadvantage in the form of declining wealth. In doing so, we combine data from the 1996 to 2008 panels of the Survey of Income and Program Participation (SIPP), the Current Population Survey (CPS), the Survey of Inmates in State and Federal Correctional Facilities (SISFCF), and the Survey of Inmates in Local Jails (SILJ) to address the following research questions: How does the incarceration of one individual influence overall household wealth accumulation, as measured by total assets and debt? What happens to the racial wealth gap once we account for incarceration? And, on a more methodological level, does institutionalization in national household surveys provide a good proxy for incarceration?

In addition to demonstrating how the consequences of incarceration extend to families and household members, we also show how incarceration influences the racial wealth gap in the United States. With racial wealth disparities that greatly exceed income gaps, African Americans and Hispanics face continuing disadvantage in housing and credit markets (Conley 1999; Oliver and Shapiro 2006). Wealth inequality has also widened along racial lines since the recent economic downturn and its uneven recovery (Pfeffer, Danziger, and Schoeni, 2013; Wolff 2014), which further necessitates studies of the potential mechanisms behind racial inequality in wealth accumulation. Thus, this study offers a larger theoretical contribution in its investigation of incarceration's place within a broader system of racial inequality by demonstrating incarceration's contagious nature.

THEORETICAL FRAMEWORK AND BACKGROUND

We combine multiple conceptions of incarceration and its consequences within our theoretical framework. This framework highlights two key components related to incarceration's negative effects. First, incarceration's consequences are lasting and diffuse across the life course to implicate employment opportunities, educational attainment, and old-age dependency. Serving time in prison or jail acts as an absorbing status that feeds into a process of cumulative disadvantage. Second, incarceration influences more than just the formerly incarcerated individual; it harms families, children, friends, and even entire neighborhoods. Together, these components demonstrate incarceration's contagious nature, which routinely disadvantages entire households in the United States within a broader system of inequality, hallmarked by discrimination (Lum et al. 2014; Reskin 2012).

The Consequences of Incarceration

By the end of 2013, almost 6.9 million adults were under correctional supervision, 2.23 million of whom were in prison or jail (Glaze and Kaeble 2014). Current estimates indicate that approximately 65 million Americans (27.8 percent) have a criminal record (Rodriguez and Emsellem 2011). The risk of incarceration is not uniform, given that young black men with little education are most likely to spend time behind bars (Pettit and Western 2004; Pettit, Sykes, and Western 2009; Pettit 2012; Western and Wildeman 2009). Among cohorts born in the late 1970s, 68 percent of African American men with less than a high school education served time in state or federal prison by the height of the prison boom in 2010 (Western and Travis 2014; Pettit, Sykes, and Western 2009). Although rates of incarceration are much lower for other racialized groups, 20 percent of less-educated Hispanic men and 28 percent of less-educated white men in this cohort had a record in the same period. These disproportionate rates of incarceration stem from the criminal justice system's varying enforcement efforts, as well as the implementation of mandatory minimum sentencing, three strikes, and other laws in the 1980s and 1990s (Western and Travis 2014; Wacquant 2001).

The racial and educational disproportionality in incarceration is compounded by its numerous and well-documented social and economic consequences. In the labor market, incarceration acts a stigmatized status that creates barriers to employment and affects later earnings for former offenders, which furthers economic disadvantage (Pager 2003; Pager and Quillian 2005; Western and Pettit 2005; Western 2006; Pettit 2012). Although incarceration can shelter inmates from violence and provide them some access to health care (Patterson 2010), inmates have higher rates of certain diseases and psychological problems than the rest of the population (Schnittker, Massoglia, and Uggan 2011; Sykes, Hoppe, and Maziarka 2016; Wildeman and Muller 2012). Incarceration is also associated with increased morbidity, stress, and the risk of infectious disease, creating additional long-term health problems for former prisoners (Johnson and Raphael 2009; Massoglia 2008a, 2008b; Schnittker and John 2007; Sykes and Piquero 2009).

The Contagious Nature of Imprisonment

The consequences of incarceration are not limited to the formerly incarcerated individual. They are contagious and extend beyond the individual offender to disadvantage families, contacts, and communities (Lum et al. 2014; Wildeman and Muller 2012). As a result, families share in the social, economic, and health consequences of the former inmate. Parental incarceration is associated with increased material hardship and downward mobility for families (Geller, Garfinkel, and Western 2011; Schwartz-Soicher, Geller, and Garfinkel 2011; Sykes and Pettit 2015), along with child homelessness (Wildeman 2014) and a larger reliance on government programs (Sugie 2012; Sykes and Pettit 2015). For couples, incarceration is associated with an increased probability of single parenthood, separation, and divorce for current inmates (Apel et al. 2010; Lopoo and Western 2005), as well as repartnering (Turney and Wildeman 2013) and having children with multiple partners after incarceration (Sykes and Pettit 2014). Given that about half of all inmates are parents and approximately 2.6 million children under the age of eighteen have a parent in prison or jail, the collateral consequences of incarceration extend to children as well (Sykes and Pettit 2014; Western and Wildeman 2009).

Thus, previous research on the effects of incarceration for families, households, and communities shows how the consequences of incarceration are as contagious as incarceration itself. Many researchers have come to refer to these consequences as "collateral damage" (Foster and Hagan 2015; Hagan and Foster 2012) because the incarceration of one family member affects the economic well-being of other members through the loss of employment and income. However, wealth and asset ownership present another often-overlooked component of economic well-being. Wealth, in all of its many forms, creates more stability than income, particularly in times of economic distress (Keister and Moller 2000; Spilerman 2000). Wealth is associated with better outcomes for children (Keister 2000a), particularly when financial transfers fund and enable postsecondary educational attainment (Rauscher, this issue), and it is related to increased stability in romantic relationships (Eads and Tach, this issue). The benefits associated with assets, investments, and homeownership, the largest wealth component for most households, compound over time (Killewald and Bryan, this issue). Thus, the importance of wealth accumulation for many social, economic, and romantic outcomes requires an investigation into the relationship between incarceration and household assets and debt.

Incarceration and Household Wealth

Spending time in prison or jail creates a stigmatized legal status that limits access to and advancement within multiple areas of society, including credit markets. Recent studies on legal financial obligations (LFOs) show that former offenders face added debt burdens from heavy pre- and post-conviction fines and fees within the criminal justice system (Harris, Evans, and Beckett 2010, 2011). Payments can be particularly high because courts rarely consider offenders' abilities to pay in assessing these fines and fees (Beckett and Harris 2011). The failure to pay fees on time can lead to accruing debts and even additional jail time for the former offender (Bannon, Nagrecha, and Diller 2010). In addition, county clerks can garnish the wages of a spouse and seize joint assets in cases of nonrepayment (Harris, Evans, and Beckett 2010).

Researchers have also found connections between wealth and incarceration. Using NLSY79 data and fixed-effects models to help account for selection, Michelle Maroto shows that the likelihood of homeownership declined by an additional 28 percentage points after incarceration, and an ex-offender's net worth decreased by an average of $42,000 after incarceration. These declines compounded already low levels of wealth and coincided with additional labor market consequences that also limited ex-offenders' abilities to earn income (Maroto 2015). Using state-level data from 1985 to 2005, Daniel Schneider and Kristin Turney (2015) also find that higher state-level incarceration rates are associated with decreased black homeownership rates, which leads to larger black-white wealth disparities. Khaing Zaw, Darrick Hamilton, and William Darity (2016) show that wealth is associated with lower rates of incarceration, but, when compared with whites, the likelihood of future incarceration was higher for blacks at every level of wealth. In light of incarceration's effects on the wealth of former offenders, our framework is based in a contagion model of incarceration that leads to the expectation that the consequences of incarceration will spread to households, limiting both assets and debt.

Long before changes to American criminal justice policies resulted in the massive expansion of prisons and jails, sociological theory predicted the very relationship between penal practices, employment, and wealth. Michel Foucault (2015) shows that the origins of a punitive society rest on social beliefs about the nature of work, leisure, and power. These three elements converge to shape capital and household wealth, individual delinquency, and extrajuridical rules that maintain dominance over the poor and working class through penal codes. The "illegalisms" of idleness and employment irregularity during the early nineteenth century produced structural responses by government agents that resulted in "a de facto arrangement with the police that meant that a worker without a work record book was not arrested if he possessed a saving bank book," thereby allowing the worker to escape further policing and institutionalization (Foucault 2015, 193). Thus the relationship between incarceration and household wealth has its antecedents in the modes of production and the structure of employment.

Just as multiple mechanisms help explain incarceration's negative consequences on employment, multiple direct and indirect pathways tie incarceration and household wealth outcomes together. Incarceration limits a person's ability to make payments, which can increase debt delinquency and negatively affect credit scores. Incarceration can then directly impede access to credit markets by making it more difficult for former offenders to access banks and lending, which leads to decreases in both assets and debt. Like employers, lenders may interpret a previous incarceration as a signal of untrustworthiness or instability, thereby limiting a previously incarcerated person's access to investment and lending opportunities (Holzer, Raphael, and Stoll 2003; Pager and Quillian 2005). In addition, former offenders often also try to avoid mainstream financial institutions for fear of the extra surveillance (Brayne 2014; Goffman 2009).

A previous incarceration can also affect wealth through other indirect mechanisms. By limiting education, employment, and earnings, which are highly connected to wealth building

(Bricker et al. 2014; Semyonov and Lewin-Epstein 2013), incarceration limits wealth for ex-offenders, along with their family members. Partners of incarcerated persons must also find ways to make up for a missing member of the household, which influences income flows and childcare options. These strains, along with changes in economic well-being and the physical and mental health of former offenders, can all lead to asset losses, less access to lending, and lower overall debt.

Connections to Racial Inequality
Given the overrepresentation of young black and Hispanic men in the criminal justice system, incarceration's effects on wealth also factor into broader wealth disparities. Although imprisonment rates in the United States have declined slightly in recent years, racial wealth gaps, strengthened by differential returns to resources that largely benefit white households, have been increasing since the Great Recession (Kochhar, Fry, and Taylor 2011; Pfeffer, Danziger, and Schoeni, 2013; Wolff 2014). According to Survey of Consumer Finances data, the median net worth in 2013 for white non-Hispanic households was approximately 7.8 times greater than that of nonwhite or Hispanic households (Bricker et al. 2014). Even after accounting for variation in education and income, large racial wealth gaps remain in the United States (Oliver and Shapiro 2006). Black households are less likely to own their homes, have less net worth, and accumulate fewer assets over time than whites (Gittleman and Wolff 2004; Killewald 2013; Kuebler and Rugh 2013). Additional research has also shown significant disparities in wealth accumulation, home ownership rates, and home equity between white and Hispanic households (Campbell and Kaufman 2006; Flippen 2001, 2004; Krivo and Kaufman 2004). Yet, homeownership itself is a key marker of racial inequality: Killewald and Bryan (this issue) show that the wealth generating returns to homeownership are greatest for whites (at about $11,000 for each year of ownership) compared with Hispanics and blacks (about $9,000 and $5,000, respectively).

Multiple individual and structural mechanisms contribute to racial wealth disparities and general wealth inequality. On an individual level, these disparities stem from demographic differences contained in life cycle and microeconomic models (Addo and Lichter 2013; Keister 2004). In addition to family structure differences, lower levels of education, inadequate income, poor job prospects, and family poverty impede minorities' transitions into homeownership and limit wealth accumulation (Bricker et al. 2014; Hall and Crowder 2011; Heflin and Pattillo 2006; Semyonov and Lewin-Epstein 2013). However, income and wealth are not perfectly correlated because other factors, particularly credit market access and behavior, also matter for wealth outcomes (Keister 2000a; McCloud and Dwyer 2011). Finally, differences in the incidence and amount of intergenerational transfers further work to maintain racial wealth gaps (Keister 2000b, 2003; Oliver and Shapiro 2006).

These mechanisms have all been supported by historical and contemporary discrimination in multiple markets, combined with residential segregation (Massey 2015; Massey and Denton 1993; Shapiro 2004). Although the process of redlining originally resulted in the greatest disadvantages to segregated minority communities through the denial of services, reverse redlining, where lenders target these communities for the sale of subprime loans, now leads to larger wealth disparities (Fisher 2009; Squires 2003; Williams, Nesiba, and McConnell 2005). This serial displacement of capital, as Jacob Rugh, Len Albright, and Douglas Massey (2015) describe it, very much played into the widening of racial wealth inequality since the recent economic downturn (Pfeffer, Danziger, and Schoeni 2013; Wolff 2014).

In the discussion of these broader mechanisms of racial wealth inequality, many researchers overlook a key explanation—the differential rates and experiences of incarceration that black and white households face. Although continuing racial wealth gaps likely remain due to direct discrimination, it is possible that the different rates of incarceration across groups (that is, racial minorities' higher rates of incarceration) will also partially explain these lingering wealth disparities. When they are searching for housing and attempting to access lending markets, black and Hispanic former offenders likely face the double jeopardy of racial discrimination and prejudice against those with criminal records. Incarceration, therefore, provides us with an additional structural-level explanation for racial wealth inequality at the household level.

ESTIMATING THE EFFECTS OF INCARCERATION

Researchers often face certain challenges in studying the consequences of incarceration because our forms of recordkeeping, which generate knowledge, often undercount disadvantaged members of society. Although Michel Foucault states that "it is a society that links to this permanent activity of punishment a closely related activity of knowledge" through "a recording" of the individual (2015, 196), recent research suggests that such recordings are at best incomplete. Since the Great Recession, scholars have drawn increasing attention to the underestimation of program participation and markers of social disadvantage in household surveys. Even though the forms, specifics, and solutions vary across studies, the arguments and conclusions are broadly consistent: national household data, when compared with official statistics, underreport or exclude members of the population, thereby obscuring important metrics of social inequality. For instance, Bruce Meyer and his colleagues (2009) compare weighted household program estimates to administrative data to show how five major nationally representative household surveys underreport transfers in food stamps, Temporary Assistance for Needy Families, and worker's compensation. They suggest a series of adjustment methods to address take-up rates—the fraction of eligible individuals or families that receive a given transfer.

Similarly, Becky Pettit (2012) finds that by excluding institutionalized populations, mainly those who are in prisons and jails, national surveys distort our understanding of racial inequality in employment, wages, educational completion, and political participation. As a solution to this problem, she includes inmates in the numerator or denominator of specific measures and then reestimates racial inequality in those social indicators to understand how sampling bias has grown in tandem with the rise in mass incarceration. Other scholars raise similar concerns and use alternative solutions (see Heckman and LaFontaine 2010; Neal and Rick 2014).

We propose a different, hybridized solution to these issues. We address the incorporation of the institutionalized population by constructing new weights for national surveys. Using data from a standard national survey that measures wealth and debt in the United States, we show how our incarceration-adjusted national weights for this survey track the overall penal representation when benchmarked to published statistics. Further, we estimate weighted models (unadjusted and adjusted for incarceration) to explore how institutionalization affects inequality in household assets and debt.

DATA

We use data from four sources to estimate the relationship between institutionalization and household wealth and debt. Our primary source is the Survey of Income and Program Participation. SIPP is a longitudinal, household-based survey that captures the noninstitutionalized population through a continuous series of nationally representative panels. We rely on the 1996, 2001, 2004, and 2008 panels. Each includes a sample that captures information on the socio-demographic characteristics of household members, including measures of employment, wealth, program participation, and life-course transitions over multiple years. SIPP oversamples residences from high poverty areas to boost survey representation in places where household underreporting is more prevalent. Every panel comprises an independent sample that interviewers followed for two to four years. The core data were retrospectively collected every four months during waves until the 2008 panel, when cost concerns led to a redesign that now contains annual recalls with an event history calendar.

Each SIPP wave contains four randomly selected rotation groups staggered across waves within panels. To minimize seam bias between reference months, we draw on data from the fourth reporting month in each panel wave when survey responses are most accurate (for more detail on seam issues in SIPP, see Ham, Li, and Shore-Sheppard 2016). Data on assets and liabilities are drawn from topical modules and matched to core data using a unique person identifier that indexes the panel, sampling unit (or household), and person number. Table A1 displays the household interview dates for the asset and liabilities topical modules across panel waves.

We then leverage periodic survey data from the SISFCF and the SILJ to measure institutionalization in the United States. These data are collected by the U.S. Census Bureau and distributed by the Bureau of Justice Statistics (BJS). Data for the SILJ were collected in 1972, 1978, 1983, 1989, 1996, and 2002, and for the SISFCF in 1974, 1979, 1986, and 1991. Inmates in federal facilities were surveyed in 1991, and state and federal data on inmates were jointly collected in 1997 and 2004. These surveys contain socio-demographic information that can be used to construct annual race, sex, age, and education specific incarceration rates.

We also draw on published correctional population totals from BJS. These data provide annual counts on the number of adult inmates in state, federal, and local (or jail) custody. Correctional totals are benchmarked using data from the National Prisoner Statistics Program, Annual Survey of Jails, Census of Jail Inmates, and the Annual Probation and Parole Surveys.

Additionally, we use data from the March Current Population Survey since 1972 to obtain population totals that will be used in the denominator of the incarceration rate. CPS data are collected by the Census Bureau and the Bureau of Labor Statistics (BLS) in March of each year, and the CPS samples approximately fifty thousand to sixty thousand non-institutionalized respondents attached to households. These data are used to generate the race, sex, age, and educational distribution of the civilian population.

Finally, we use BLS data to adjust wealth and debt dollars throughout the period. We standardize the buying power across panels and interview years using the consumer price index (CPI) inflation calculator. All income, wealth, and debt statistics are expressed in 2015 dollars.

CONCEPTUAL MEASURES

Table 1 displays the operationalization and coding of measures in our study. Our main variable, *institutionalized*, shows that 0.2 percent of all respondents in the 1996 SIPP panel report the institutionalization of a household member between December 1996 and March 2000. This percentage dips to 0.1 percent in the 2001 panel and returns to 0.2 percent during the 2004 and 2008 panels. Between the 1996 and 2004 panels, average monthly household income rose from $6,815 to $7,171. However, during the 2008 panel, average monthly household income declined to roughly $6,750 due to the onset of the Great Recession.

Our two key outcome measures—*total assets* and *total debt*—present complementary measures of wealth. Like total household income, the Great Recession also eliminated a significant amount of household wealth. Total average household assets during the 1996 panel amounted to almost $189,000, rising to over $272,000 by the 2004 panel. The economic slowdown that began in December 2007 and ended in June 2009 had devastating consequences for household wealth. The 2008 panel shows that mean household assets had declined to almost $246,000. Average household debt, however, shows a steady increase across the four panels, going from almost $85,000 in 1996 to almost $116,000 by the close of 2011.

In our models, we also account for additional explanations of wealth inequality by using person- and household-level control variables related to demographic, family, education, and employment dynamics. We control for the respondent's reported *age, gender, marital status, number of children,* and *education*. We measure age in years and include a quadratic age-squared term to account for any nonlinear relationships with wealth. We measure gender with an indicator variable of male or female and marital status with a variable indicating whether the respondent was never married. We incorporate a variable for the respondent's *race and ethnicity* that includes four categories: non-Hispanic white (the referent), non-Hispanic black, Hispanic, and non-Hispanic other. Education is a categorical variable with three categories: less than high school, high school diploma, and some college

Table 1. Variable Operationalization and Descriptive Statistics by Panel Year

		Panel Year							
		1996		2001		2004		2008	
Variable	Coding	Mean	SD	Mean	SD	Mean	SD	Mean	SD
Institutionalized	1 = yes; 0 = no	0.002	0.040	0.001	0.040	0.002	0.040	0.002	0.040
Monthly household income	continuous	6,815	6,383	7,086	6,604	7,171	6,880	6,750	6,342
Total household wealth	continuous	188,921	1,052,520	234,898	1,576,812	272,241	977,487	245,661	759,743
Total household debt	continuous	84,495	168,187	101,526	164,356	111,430	156,383	115,692	184,707
Non-Hispanic white	1 = yes; 0 = no	0.73	0.44	0.71	0.45	0.72	0.45	0.68	0.47
Non-Hispanic black	1 = yes; 0 = no	0.12	0.32	0.12	0.32	0.12	0.32	0.12	0.32
Hispanic	1 = yes; 0 = no	0.10	0.31	0.12	0.33	0.10	0.30	0.13	0.33
Non-Hispanic other	1 = yes; 0 = no	0.04	0.21	0.05	0.22	0.07	0.25	0.08	0.27
Less than high school (LTHS)	1 = yes; 0 = no	0.15	0.36	0.14	0.35	0.12	0.32	0.11	0.31
High school (HS) diploma	1 = yes; 0 = no	0.32	0.47	0.30	0.46	0.27	0.44	0.27	0.45
Some college (SC)	1 = yes; 0 = no	0.53	0.50	0.56	0.50	0.61	0.49	0.62	0.48
Male	1 = yes; 0 = no	0.48	0.50	0.48	0.50	0.48	0.50	0.48	0.50
Age	# years	39.29	12.43	39.89	12.70	40.49	12.93	41.43	13.46
Age²	# years squared	1698.00	1006.00	1752.00	1029.00	1806.00	1055.00	1897.00	1109.00
Never married	1 = yes; 0 = no	0.43	0.49	0.43	0.49	0.43	0.50	0.44	0.50
Female-headed household	1 = yes; 0 = no	0.21	0.41	0.22	0.41	0.23	0.42	0.23	0.42
# of family members in household	# members	3.09	1.61	3.05	1.66	3.02	1.62	3.05	1.67
# of children in household	# children	0.90	1.18	0.88	1.19	0.86	1.17	0.81	1.16
Employed	1 = yes; 0 = no	0.79	0.41	0.77	0.42	0.78	0.41	0.73	0.45
Average household poverty	continuous	1197	358	1330	415	1425	436	1617	511
Live in metro area	1 = yes; 0 = no	0.80	0.40	0.76	0.43	0.76	0.42	0.77	0.42
N		188,509		123,926		117,031		154,417	

Source: Authors' calculations based on SIPP data.
Note: All dollar estimates are scaled for inflation and in 2015 dollars.

or higher. We also control for labor market variables of *employment status* and *monthly household income*, along with measures of *average household poverty* and an indicator for whether the person lives in a *metro area*.

These other demographic and educational measures display considerable consistency across panels, although the percentage of non-Hispanic whites declines and that of Hispanic and non-Hispanic others increases. Additionally, over time, the sample has become more educationally advantaged, as the percentage of respondents with at least some college education increased from 53 percent during the 1996 panel to 62 percent during the 2008 panel.

METHODS

We merge population totals from the SISFCF, the SILJ, and the CPS by race, sex, age, and education to construct annual group-specific incarceration rates. Weighted group proportions from inmate surveys are linearly interpolated by facility type between survey years and applied to correctional population totals by facility type to construct national, group-specific incarceration counts. These aggregate inmate totals represent the numerator of the incarceration rate, while the denominator is obtained from non-institutionalized totals associated with the race-sex-age-education distribution of the civilian population. Further information on this method is provided in multiple published studies on mass incarceration (see Pettit, Sykes, and Western 2009; Pettit 2012; Sykes and Pettit 2014; Western and Beckett 1999; Western and Pettit 2005; Western 2006).

The 1996 SIPP panel contains entry and exit dates for each household member and the reason for departure or reentry. Consequently, subsequent panels do not include the month and day of entry or exit from the household. Therefore, we only leverage information on the reason for entering and departing the household. Respondents who report "institutionalization" as the explanation for household entry and exit are used to compare the race-sex-age-education distributions of adults currently institutionalized in American prisons and jails. We estimate race-sex-age-education group means for SIPP respondents who report institutionalization and match the incarceration rates to this socio-demographic distribution in SIPP. We calculate an institutionalization rate adjustment (IR_{ADJ}) factor that is the ratio of the incarceration rate derived from CPS and inmate data (IR_{CPS}) relative to the institutionalized rate in SIPP (IR_{SIPP}), as displayed in equation 1.[1]

$$IR_{ADJ} = \frac{IR_{CPS}}{IR_{SIPP}} \quad (1)$$

Because SIPP contains multiple weights (for example, individual, household, and family weights), we elect to use the individual weights for our analysis because we are interested in the relationship between having a family member institutionalization and household wealth and debt. We then estimate a new, adjusted SIPP institutionalized weight (SI_W) that accounts for national incarceration rates (in equation 2) by multiplying the adjusted institutionalization rate factor (IR_{ADJ}) with individual SIPP weights (S_W) if the respondent reported being institutionalized during a specific month during that calendar year.

$$SI_W = S_W * IR_{ADJ} \quad (2)$$

The unadjusted and adjusted SIPP weights are then benchmarked to published institutionalization rates (Pettit and Western 2004). We also apply these unadjusted and adjusted weights to our statistical models to understand how estimates of inequality change over time with growth in incarceration.

Because SIPP is a longitudinal dataset with multiple panels and waves, we use the fixed-effects estimator to measure the association between the institutionalization of a family member and household assets and debt. Jack Johnston and John DiNardo (1997, 399) show that fixed-effects estimation solves problems of omitted variable bias by "throwing away" parts of the variance that contaminate ordi-

---

1. Although institutionalization is usually conceptualized to include respondents who exited and entered the home due to military enlistment and assisted-care living environments, our measure based on SIPP data does not include active military personnel, students living in dormitories, or old-age assisted group quarters.

Table 2. Civilian Institutionalization Rates, 1999

	Education				B-W Magnitude Difference
	Less Than High School	High School	Some College	Total	
Pettit & Western (2004): Table 4					
NH-white	2.9	1.7	0.2	1	8.5
NH-black	21.0	9.4	1.7	8.5	
SIPP weighted					
NH-white	1.7	0.2	0.05	0.3	2.7
NH-black	3.1	0.6	0.11	0.8	
SIPP incarceration weighted					
NH-white	9.5	1.5	0.14	1.4	6.0
NH-black	28.6	6.2	0.70	8.4	

Source: Authors' calculations based on SIPP, Survey of Inmates, and Current Population data.
Note: U.S. men ages twenty to thirty-four.

nary least squares or random-effects estimators. The Wu-Hausman test confirms that the error is correlated with our explanatory variables, indicating that the fixed-effects estimator is consistent, efficient, and preferred over the random-effects estimator.

We also estimate a series of probit models that quantify whether institutionalization affects having any household assets or debt between panel waves. We then report marginal effects—the rate of change in the dependent variable (that is, the predicted probability) relative to a unit change in an independent variable (Long 1997; Powers and Xie 2000)—with all models evaluated at their mean values.

FINDINGS

According to our results, the institutionalization of one family member is associated with declines in assets and debt and the household level. In addition to showing how institutionalization relates to wealth outcomes, these findings also demonstrate its contagious nature. The incarceration of one family member can have lasting consequences for the entire household.

Patterns of Institutionalization

Table 2 presents civilian institutionalization rates by race and education among U.S. men ages twenty to thirty-four in 1999. We compare published estimates of race and educational inequality in incarceration to institutionalization rates contained in SIPP using unadjusted SIPP weights and our incarceration-adjusted SIPP weights. The first horizontal panel presents published estimates from Becky Pettit and Bruce Western's (2004) work on mass imprisonment and the life course; the middle panel displays estimates using normal SIPP weights; and the final panel displays our SIPP-incarceration weighted statistics.

First, the pattern of institutionalization in the unadjusted SIPP weighted data follows a racial and educational distribution similar to that of Pettit and Western (2004). However, racial and educational inequality is largely underestimated using unadjusted SIPP weights to measure institutionalization. For instance, whereas Pettit and Western find that 21 percent of young, black men with less than a high school diploma were institutionalized in 1999, unadjusted SIPP weights underestimate this group by almost sevenfold. The magnitude of this problem intensifies across levels of educational attainment. Sykes and Pettit (2014) observe similar racial and educational gradients when comparing parental incarceration estimates from the National Survey of Children's Health with inmate surveys and official statistics. Overall, inequality in institutionalization is 2.7 times higher among blacks than among whites using unadjusted SIPP weights, versus the 8.5 factor difference in Pettit and Western (2004).

By contrast, estimates from SIPP-incarceration weighted data are much closer in the aggregate but highly variable by educational level. Among those with less than a high school diploma, our measure overshoots the estimates that Pettit and Western report (2004). One possibility for this discordance is that the age distribution of institutionalized respondents in SIPP does not perfectly align with the range of twenty to thirty-four reported in Pettit and Western, resulting in weighted averages that give greater weight to individuals closer to age thirty-four. Another possibility is that the educational distribution in SIPP overrepresents undereducated respondents during the 1996 panel, which may explain why estimates for respondents with a high school diploma and some college converge with statistics reported in Pettit and Western (2004). Nevertheless, our total estimates for institutionalization are much closer than the unadjusted SIPP weights.

Patterns in Assets, Debt, and Institutionalization

Figure 1 plots average household assets by race and institutionalization in the United States from 1996 to 2011. The top panel is for households without an incarcerated member; the bottom panel is for households with an incarcerated member.[2] The top panel shows significant racial gaps in wealth among households without an incarcerated family member. In 1996, white households held nearly $221,000 in wealth at the mean versus $60,000 among blacks, resulting in a black-white gap of $160,000 in 1996. This gap in wealth reached its zenith at roughly $230,000 in 2004 and declined to $179,000 by the close of 2011.

By contrast, households with an institutionalized family member are much closer and more volatile in their wealth patterns. In 1996, white households with an institutionalized member held approximately $183,000 in assets, versus the paltry $51,000 among similarly situated black households, resulting in a black-white wealth gap of almost $132,000, similar to that between households without an institutionalized family member. White assets fall below those of blacks in 1999, but the gap surges to almost $270,000 in 2002, stabilizes in 2009, and then settles at approximately $45,000 by 2011. The volatility between 2002 and 2009 could be the result of indictments and convictions following high-profile corporate crimes and malfeasance during this period, particularly for non-Hispanic whites.[3]

Figure 2 displays average household debt by race and institutionalization. Non-Hispanic whites without a family member institutionalized have greater debt than similar black households, as displayed in the top panel. In 1996, white families had around $92,400 of debt to the $50,300 of debt in black households, a debt gap of $42,100. The black-white debt gap climbs to almost $59,000 in 2002 and soars to nearly $64,300 in 2009.

Among households with an institutionalized family member (lower panel), black and white debt levels begin the series fairly even. However, by 1998, black household debt declined to about $14,000 as white debt levels rose. The slow increase in debt among black families with a household respondent institutionalized means that the debt gap remained fairly stable after 2005 and much smaller than the gaps for households without institutionalized family members.

Estimating Household Assets and Debt

Table 3 presents fixed-effects estimates of household wealth and debt by SIPP weighted and SIPP-incarceration weighted adjustments. Columns 1 through 4 present unlogged estimates of wealth and debt; columns 5 through

---

2. The y-axes of these panels have been scaled similarly to facilitate comparisons of within-race and between-group differences in wealth (figure 1), debt (figure 2), and employment (figure 3) among households with and without a member institutionalized.

3. For instance, in 2003 one non-Hispanic white household with an institutionalized member actually held more than $3 million in assets, which skewed the results for this year. SIPP data limitations for measuring wealth, in combination with the low number of respondents institutionalized, may explain this variation.

Figure 1. Average Household Wealth by Race and Institutionalization

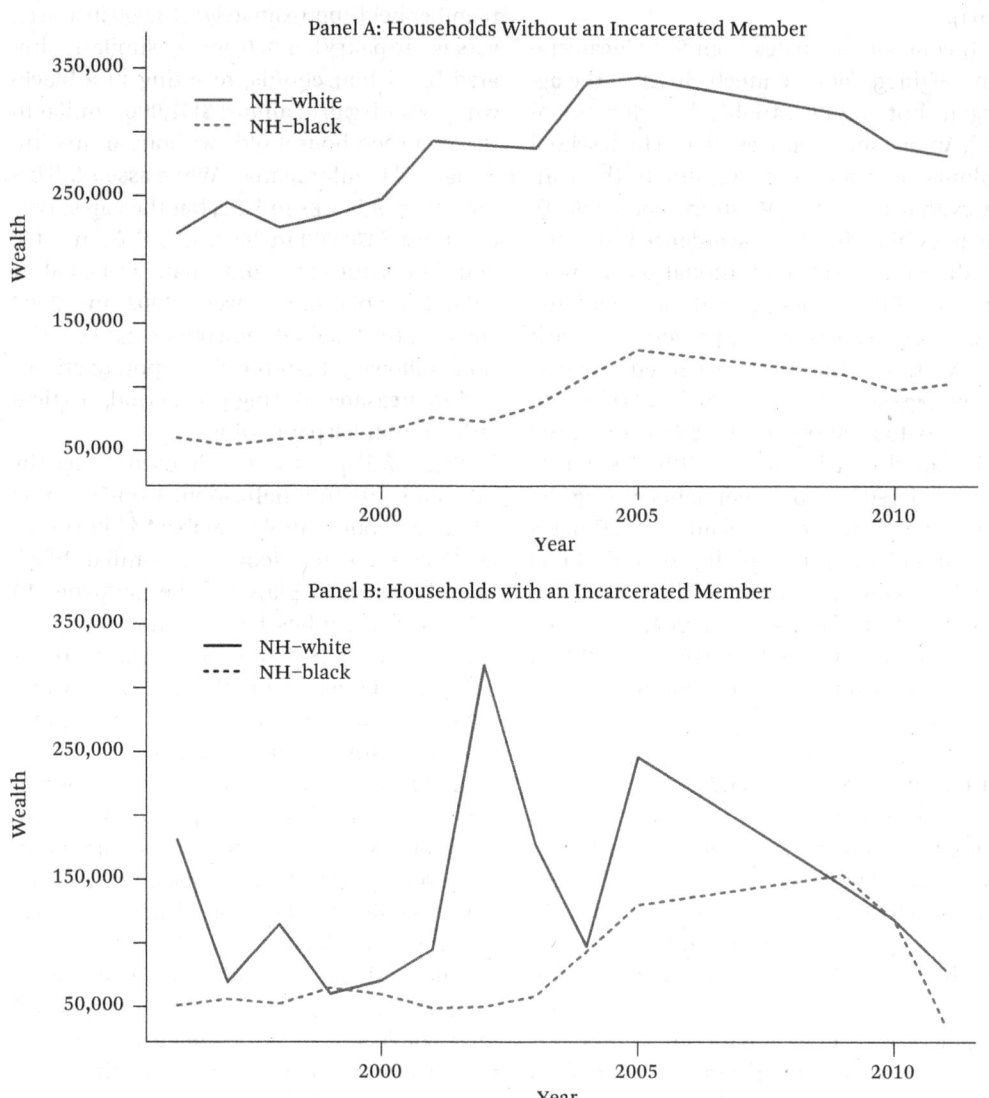

Source: Authors' calculations based on SIPP data with adjusted incarceration rates.

8 display logged differences. The institutionalization of a family member is not associated with lower assets or debt using either unadjusted or adjusted SIPP weights. However, the SIPP-incarcerated weights display larger differences for both assets and debt. Having any assets and debt in the previous wave is significantly related to having wealth and debt in the current wave. The estimated black-white wealth gap is almost $148,000 (column 2) and the debt gap about $45,200.

We also logged assets and debts to address data skewing and the nonlinear association between incarceration and components of household wealth.[4] The unadjusted SIPP weights (column 5) indicate that, holding all other vari-

---

4. Model fit improved considerably with the functional form transformation, even though this leads to a truncated distribution. To account for this, we also assess the relationship between institutionalization and the presence of any assets or debt in subsequent models.

Figure 2. Average Household Debt by Race and Institutionalization

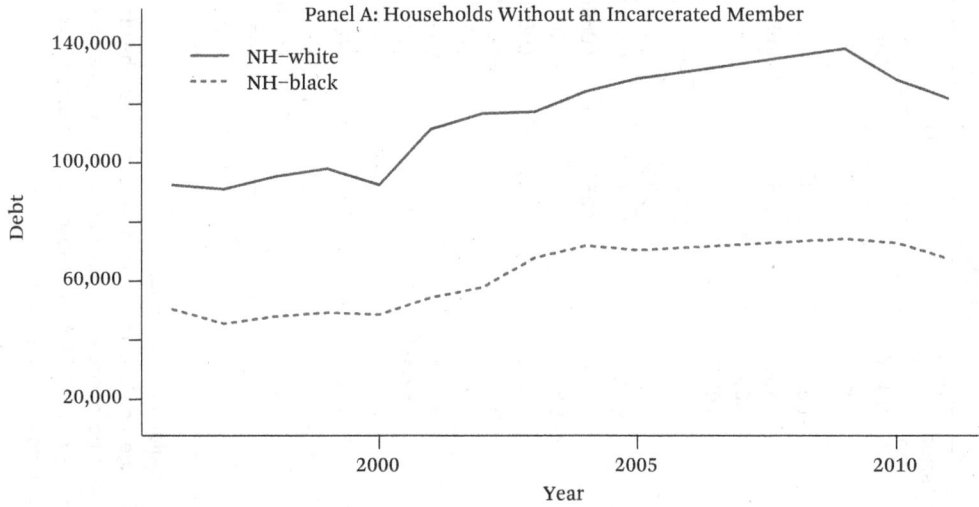

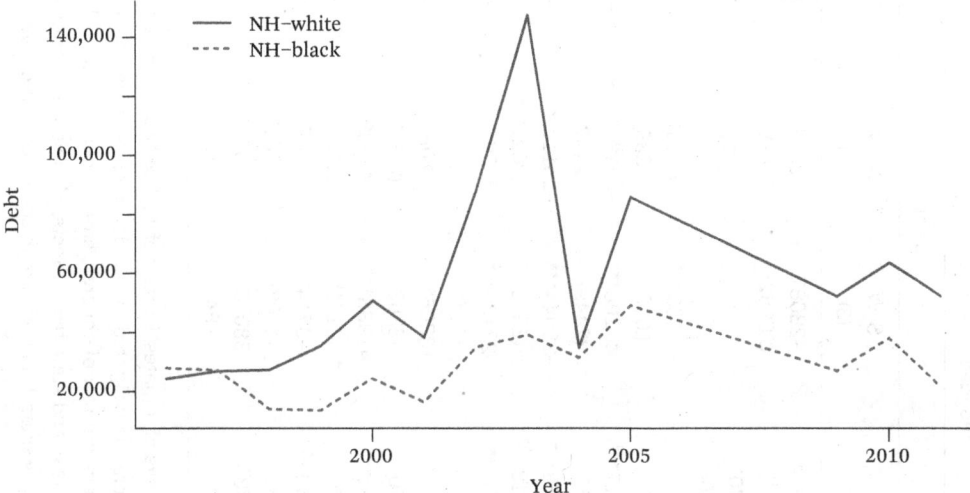

Source: Authors' calculations from SIPP data with adjusted incarceration rates.

ables constant, having an institutionalized family member is moderately associated with a 57.3 percent reduction in total household assets.[5] The SIPP-incarceration adjusted weights reveal a larger disparity; having a family member incarcerated reduces household assets by 64.3 percent using these weights.

Logged debt levels display greater magnitude differences. Even though unadjusted SIPP weights show that institutionalization is linked with lower household debt by 84.1 percent compared with households unexposed to institutionalization, the SIPP-incarceration weight adjustments (column 8) indicate a stronger association, at 86.1 percent. Thus, estimates of institutionalization in logged scales reveal how

---

5. Because many of these coefficients exceed 0.1, we use the following formula to determine the percentage change in assets and debt for a one-unit change in each predictor variable: %Δ(y) = 100*(e^b − 1) (Gelman and Hill 2007; Wooldridge 2009, 190).

Table 3. Estimated Household Wealth and Debt Levels

	Unlogged								Logged							
	Net Wealth		Debt						Assets				Debt			
	S-W (1)	S-I-W (2)		S-W (3)	S-I-W (4)				S-W (5)	S-I-W (6)			S-W (7)	S-I-W (8)		
Institutionalization	−24980 (41728)	−41614 (40037)		−28087 (26982)	−33974 (27310)				−0.85+ (.500)	−1.03* (.466)			−1.84* (.738)	−1.97** (.684)		
Any previous assets	−0.230** (.77)	−0.230** (.77)		—	—				0.05*** (.005)	0.05*** (.005)			—	—		
Any previous debt	—	—		−0.163*** (.039)	−0.163*** (.039)				—	—			−0.04*** (.004)	−0.04*** (.004)		
NH-black	−147904*** (9455)	−147917*** (9457)		−45200*** (2449)	−45197*** (2447)				−1.63*** (.054)	−1.63*** (.054)			−1.38*** (.069)	−1.37*** (.069)		
Hispanic	−122169*** (20336)	−122858*** (20313)		−35044*** (2826)	−35110*** (2821)				−1.03*** (.053)	−1.03*** (.053)			−1.10*** (.070)	−1.10*** (.069)		
NH-other	−78781*** (19569)	−78477*** (19555)		−23139*** (3279)	−23095*** (3278)				−0.56*** (.055)	−0.56*** (.055)			−0.83*** (.081)	−0.83*** (.081)		
High school	51136*** (5901)	50977*** (5890)		13305*** (2303)	13208*** (2297)				0.95*** (.048)	0.95*** (.048)			1.28*** (.065)	1.28*** (.064)		
Some college or more	136236*** (8037)	136003*** (8029)		41988*** (2191)	41938 (2189)				1.64*** (.047)	1.64*** (.047)			2.12*** (.064)	2.12*** (.064)		
Male	−14008+ (8600)	−14071+ (8585)		−3714* (1708)	−3645* (1708)				−0.12*** (.023)	−0.12*** (.023)			−0.31*** (.037)	−0.32*** (.037)		
N	380786	380786		380786	380786				344782	344782			380770	380770		
R²	.62	.62		.64	.64				.79	.80			.70	.70		

Source: Authors' calculations based on SIPP, Surveys of Inmates, Bureau of Justice Statistics, and Current Population (CPS) data.

Note: S-W = SIPP weighted; S-I-W = SIPP incarceration weighted. All models include additional controls for age, age squared, marital status, female-headed household designations, number of children, number of family members, employment, household monthly income, average household poverty, metro status, race-institutionalization interactions, and month, year, and state fixed effects. Models were estimated using areg in STATA 14 and absorbed by households. Robust standard errors are reported. Non-Hispanic whites, less than a high school education, and women are the reference groups.

+$p < 0.10$, *$p < 0.05$, **$p < 0.01$, ***$p < 0.001$

Table 4. Marginal Effects of Current Institutionalization on Whether a Household Has Any Assets or Debt

	Assets		Debt	
	S-W	S-I-W	S-W	S-I-W
Institutionalization	-0.018	-.027+	-0.036*	-0.039*
	(.013)	(.015)	(.018)	(.019)
Any previous assets	0.127***	0.128***	—	—
	(.001)	(.001)		
Any previous debt	—	—	0.250***	0.250***
			(.002)	(.002)
NH-black	-0.054***	-0.054***	-0.053***	-0.054***
	(.001)	(.001)	(.002)	(.002)
Hispanic	-0.039***	-0.039***	-0.064***	-0.065***
	(.002)	(.002)	(.002)	(.002)
NH-other	-0.018***	-0.018***	-0.048***	-0.048***
	(.002)	(.002)	(.002)	(.002)
High school	0.023***	0.022***	0.051***	0.050***
	(.001)	(.002)	(.002)	(.002)
Some college or more	0.051***	0.052***	0.097***	0.097***
	(.001)	(.001)	(.002)	(.002)
Male	-0.006***	-0.005***	-0.027	-0.026
	(.001)	(.001)	(.001)	(.001)
N	380786	380786	380786	380786

Source: Authors' calculations based on SIPP, Surveys of Inmates, Bureau of Justice Statistics, and Current Population (CPS) data.
Note: S-W = SIPP weighted; S-I-W = SIPP incarceration weighted. All models include additional controls for age, age squared, marital status, female-headed household designations, number of family members, number of children, employment, household monthly income, average household poverty, metro status, race-institutionalization interactions, and month, year, and state fixed effects. Standard errors are clustered on households. All marginal effects are evaluated at their mean values. Non-Hispanic whites, less than a high school education, and women are the reference groups.
+$p < 0.10$, *$p < 0.05$, **$p < 0.01$, ***$p < 0.001$

the SIPP-incarcerated weights correct for large differences in magnitude that result from undercounting and excluding inmates.

Racial gaps in assets and debt also appear in these models. We estimate that black household assets are 80.4 percent lower than white households, and household debt was approximately 74.6 percent lower among black households. In addition, Hispanic households held 64.3 percent less in assets and 66.7 percent less in debt than otherwise similar non-Hispanic white households. Together with the effects of institutionalization, these results indicate that institutionalization and race can both block access to credit markets, limiting wealth accumulation, as well as families' abilities to borrow.

Table 4 presents marginal effects of current institutionalization on whether a household has any assets or debt. Although the SIPP unadjusted weights do not detect a significant association between institutionalization and the likelihood of having assets, the SIPP-incarcerated weight model shows that incarceration is moderately associated with a 2.7 percentage point reduction in the probability of having assets, holding all other variables at their mean values. When held at their mean values, non-Hispanic blacks, Hispanics, and other non-Hispanic racial groups

Table 5. Marginal Effects of Changes in Household Wealth and Debt on Changes in Institutionalization

	Change in Probability of Institutionalization (Asset Model)		Change in Probability of Institutionalization (Debt Model)	
	S-W	S-I-W	S-W	S-I-W
Any previous assets	−0.00006*	−0.00007	—	—
	(.00003)	(.00005)		
Any previous debt	—	—	−0.00009***	−0.0001**
			(.00002)	(.00003)
NH-black	−0.000005	−0.00003	−0.000003	−0.00003
	(.00003)	(.00004)	(.00003)	(.00004)
Hispanic	0.00006*	0.00001	0.00005	0.000006
	(.00003)	(.00004)	(.00003)	(.00004)
NH-other	0.000009	−0.00003	0.000004	−0.00003
	(.00004)	(.00007)	(.00004)	(.00007)
High school	0.00006+	0.00006	0.00006*	0.00007
	(.00003)	(.00004)	(.00003)	(.00004)
Some college or more	0.00002	0.00003	0.00003	0.00004
	(.00003)	(.00004)	(.00003)	(.00004)
Male	−0.00001	−0.00002	−0.00001	−0.00002
	(.00002)	(.00003)	(.00002)	(.00003)
N	373023	373023	373023	373023

Source: Authors' calculations based on SIPP, Surveys of Inmates, Bureau of Justice Statistics, and Current Population (CPS) data.

Note: S-W = SIPP weighted; S-I-W = SIPP incarceration weighted. All models include additional controls for age, age squared, marital status, female-headed household designations, number of family members, number of children, employment, household monthly income, average household poverty, metro status, race-institutionalization interactions, and month, year, and state fixed effects. Standard errors are clustered on households. All marginal effects are evaluated at their mean values. Non-Hispanic whites, less than a high school education, and women are the reference groups.
+$p < 0.10$, *$p < 0.05$, **$p < 0.01$, ***$p < 0.001$

are 5.4, 3.9, and 1.8 percentage points less likely to have assets than non-Hispanic whites, respectively.

Households with an incarcerated family member are about 3.6 percentage points less likely to have debt when using the SIPP unadjusted weights. However, the SIPP-incarceration adjusted weights widen this disparity by 10 percent, resulting in the likelihood of having debt being 3.9 percentage points lower in households with a family member incarcerated. This association is likely driven by reduced access to credit markets among disadvantaged households.

Our first set of models shows that institutionalization is associated with lower assets and debt across households; however, the presence of assets and debt might also influence a household member's likelihood of institutionalization. Table 5 presents the marginal effects of changes in household wealth and debt on changes in institutionalization between panel waves. Although having previous assets is associated with a reduced probability of institutionalization, the effect is too small to be meaningful. Furthermore, the SIPP-incarceration adjusted weights do not show any association between previous wealth affecting changes in institutionalization.

Similarly, having previous debt is strongly associated with a lower probability of becoming incarcerated, and the model with adjusted

Figure 3. Average Household Employment by Race and Institutionalization

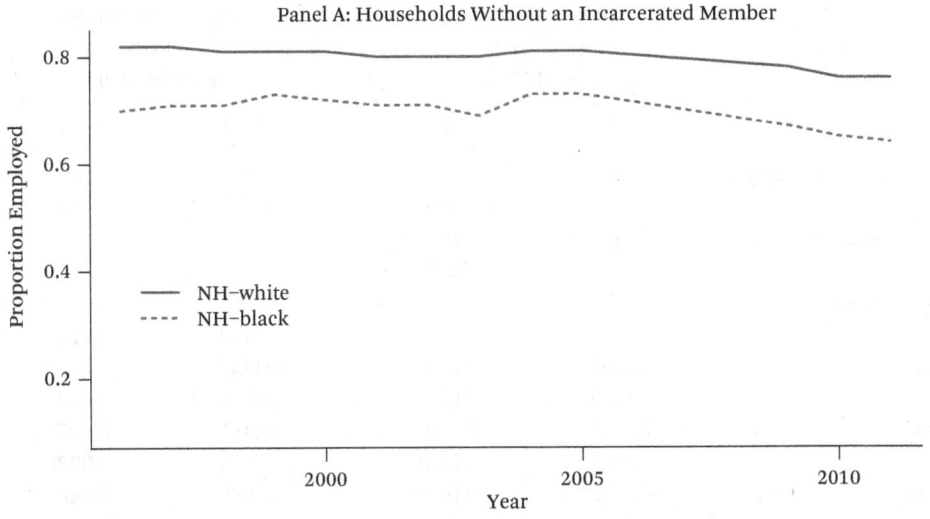

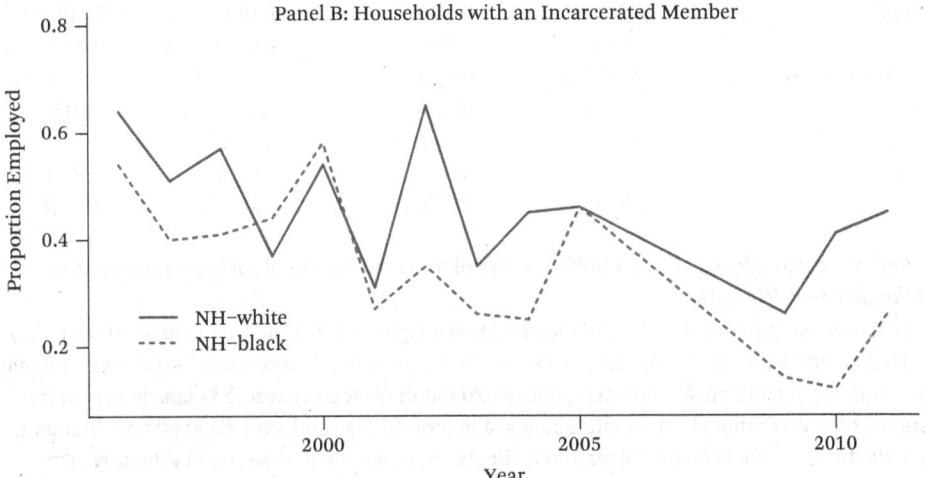

Source: Authors' calculations based on SIPP data with adjusted incarceration rates.

SIPP-incarcerated weights confirms this association. However, like the wealth model, the effect is too small to be meaningful.

Employment and Institutionalization

Figure 3 plots average household employment by race and institutionalization. In the first panel, nearly 82 percent of non-Hispanic whites without an institutionalized family member were employed in 1996. By the close of 2011, this figure had fallen 6 percentage points to 76 percent.[6] In comparison, black households without an institutionalized family member saw their employment rates rise from 70 percent in 1996 to 73 percent in 2005. However, by the end of 2011, only 64 percent of respondents

---

6. We benchmarked these estimates to employment to population ratios (EPR) presented in Becky Pettit, Bryan Sykes, and Bruce Western's study (2009, table 17). Because 2008 is the last year in the report before the 2008 SIPP panel began interviewing respondents for wave 4 in 2009 (see table A1), we can only compare estimates of our SIPP-incarceration adjusted EPR with that in Pettit, Sykes, and Western for 2005. Pettit and her colleagues report an EPR of 80.6 in 2005 for men; our comparable EPR is 80.8 using the SIPP-incarcerated adjusted weights.

Table 6. Marginal Effects of Changes in Institutionalization on Employment

	Change in Probability of Employment (Asset Model)		Change in Probability of Employment (Debt Model)	
	S-W	S-I-W	S-W	S-I-W
Previous institutionalization	0.004	0.052	0.007	0.051
	(.038)	(.049)	(.038)	(.051)
Any previous assets	0.081***	0.081***	—	—
	(.003)	(.003)		
Any previous debt	—	—	0.130***	0.130***
			(.002)	(.022)
NH-black	-0.054***	-0.054***	-0.050***	-0.050***
	(.003)	(.003)	(.003)	(.003)
Hispanic	-0.002	-0.001	0.007*	0.007*
	(.003)	(.004)	(.003)	(.003)
NH-other	-0.058***	-0.057***	-0.050***	-0.050***
	(.004)	(.004)	(.004)	(.004)
High school	0.106***	0.106***	0.095***	0.095***
	(.003)	(.003)	(.003)	(.003)
Some college or more	0.177***	0.178***	0.159***	0.160***
	(.003)	(.003)	(.003)	(.003)
Male	0.130***	0.131***	0.134***	0.134***
	(.002)	(.002)	(.002)	(.002)
N	380786	380786	380786	380786

Source: Authors' calculations based on SIPP, Surveys of Inmates, Bureau of Justice Statistics, and Current Population (CPS) data.

Note: S-W = SIPP weighted; S-I-W = SIPP incarceration weighted. All models include additional controls for age, age squared, marital status, female-headed household designations, number of family members, number of children, employment, household monthly income, average household poverty, metro status, race-institutionalization interactions, and month, year, and state fixed effects. Standard errors are clustered on households. All marginal effects are evaluated at their mean values. Non-Hispanic whites, less than a high school education, and women are the reference groups.

+$p < 0.10$, *$p < 0.05$, **$p < 0.01$, ***$p < 0.001$

in black households without an incarcerated member were employed.

The lower panel shows the employment rates among households with an incarcerated family member. The employment rates are much lower among whites and blacks in residences exposed to incarceration. Between 1996 and 2011, white households with an incarcerated family member had an employment rate that fell from 64 percent to 45 percent over the period. Household employment is much more dire among blacks when a family member is incarcerated. In 1996, 54 percent were employed, but only 26 percent were employed by the close of 2011, a drop of nearly 28 percentage points.

Finally, table 6 presents marginal effects of changes in institutionalization on employment. A previous incarceration was not statistically associated with an increased probability of employment when the household held any assets. However, a comparison of estimates using the unadjusted SIPP weights and the adjusted SIPP-incarceration weights shows a large point-estimate change for previous institutionalization. The debt model confirms that this positive change is real, suggesting that perhaps a previous incarceration and increases in the probability of employment may be mandated by parole, probation, or court agents.

CONCLUSIONS AND IMPLICATIONS

Recent statistics from a Gallup poll indicate that two-thirds of Americans are dissatisfied with the way income and wealth are distributed in the United States (Newport 2015). At the same time, concern is growing about the reach and pull of mass incarceration in America, particularly for measuring socioeconomic progress among families (Pettit 2012; Pettit and Sykes 2015; Sykes and Pettit 2014, 2015). However, no scholarship has linked these two disparate social problems to better understand the relationship between mass incarceration and household wealth over time. Our paper addresses this issue using longitudinal data on incarceration, assets, and debt among household members to explore the spillover effects of incarceration on wealth accumulation.

We find that incarceration not only influences the wealth and assets of the formerly incarcerated person but also spreads across households to affect the assets and debt of family members. The institutionalization of a family member was associated with a 64.3 percent decrease in asset levels and an 86.1 percent decrease in debt levels, as reported in our weighted models in table 3. Families with an institutionalized member were also 2.7 percentage points less likely to report owning any assets and 3.9 points less likely to report owning any debt, compared to otherwise similar households without institutionalized members (see table 4). With these findings, we provide additional evidence for the collateral damage associated with incarceration's spillover effects for non-incarcerated household members, show support for incarceration's contagious consequences for families, and bring together conversations of wealth inequality and mass incarceration.

In these relationships, incarceration directly and indirectly influences wealth. By reducing employment and increasing economic strain on families, incarceration can also limit any opportunities for asset accumulation. Institutionalization's negative association with both assets and debt also indicates that it blocks access to credit markets and lending institutions. It can do so through its negative effects on credit scores, which most lenders use to make credit-based lending decisions, and the potential use of a household family member's incarceration itself in a lender's decision. Former offenders might also be choosing to avoid mainstream lending institutions, which further impedes their ability to build wealth.

In addition to highlighting incarceration's relationship with household wealth, our findings also contribute to studies of racial inequality in wealth. Racial wealth disparities that continue after accounting for education and income are well documented in the United States. For instance, non-Hispanic black households held about 80.4 percent less in assets and 74.6 percent less in debts than similar non-Hispanic white households in our study (see table 3). Although these large disparities could be compounded by the institutionalization of a family member, we did not find support for this relationship, partly because most non-Hispanic black households held little wealth before the family member was institutionalized.[7]

In fact, because the association between institutionalization and assets was weaker than the associations for race, a non-Hispanic white household with an institutionalized member would actually hold more in assets than an otherwise similar black or Hispanic household without an institutionalized member. This finding mirrors that of Thompson and Conley (this issue), who show that white families facing health shocks still had greater wealth than

---

7. We are cautious in this conclusion because to test this proposition may require exogenous variation in exposure to incarceration at the household level. We used day of entry into the household, day of exit from the household, and job training and job seeking programs that were subsidized by welfare and social service agencies as instrumental variables for institutionalization within the 1996 panel (the only panel that had these variables) to assess this proposition. Despite various model specifications for institutional endogeneity, our instruments were not very strong. Douglas Staiger and James Stock (1997) recommend an F-value of 10 or greater for strong instruments; ours was 7.3.

black families who did not. Overall, by highlighting the associations across institutionalization, race, and wealth, we show that the disproportionate incarceration of young black men with limited education also helps explain these wealth disparities at a household level.

Our study has a few potential limitations. First, wealth estimates tend to be inconsistent because of the complexity of measuring the various components of wealth, a lack of standardization across surveys, and the difficulty many respondents have in estimating their wealth (Spilerman 2000). To help account for inconsistencies, SIPP includes questions about different types of assets and debt, regularly incorporates reinterview checks, and compares results with Flow of Funds and Survey of Consumer Finances data from the Federal Reserve Board (Czajka, Jacobson, and Cody 2003; Kalton et al. 1998). A second potential limitation is that we cannot control for selection into incarceration because measures of delinquency and low self-control—risk factors for future institutionalization—are not included in SIPP.

Despite these possible drawbacks, we provide a methodological contribution by using institutionalization as a proxy for incarceration in household surveys. National surveys, like SIPP, that report lower estimates of institutionalization may also underestimate the impact of incarceration on asset accumulation and debt reduction. We provide one possible solution for incorporating inmates into national surveys, but to do so requires at least one measure with which to benchmark incarceration statistics to official records. Foucault (2015, 196) highlights how the production of knowledge requires adequate record keeping (or "recordings"). Yet the social exclusion inherent in national surveys that render inmates invisible (Pettit 2012) and undercount families receiving government aid (Meyer, Mok, and Sullivan 2009) leads to what he calls the *penalization of existence*: "a diffuse, everyday penalty, with para-penal extensions introduced into the social body itself, prior to the judicial apparatus" that shapes "rewards and punishments" (Foucault 2015, 193). We show that the penalization of existence conferred to former inmates is dispersed throughout the household, affecting the components of wealth for everyone in residence and further concentrating social disadvantage at a residential level.

Table A1. Interview Dates for Assets and Liabilities Topical Modules by SIPP Panel

Wave	1996	2001	2004	2008
w3	12/1996 to 03/1997	10/2001 to 01/2002	10/2004 to 01/2005	
w4				09/2009 to 12/2009
w6	12/1997 to 03/1998	10/2002 to 01/2003	10/2005 to 01/2006	
w7				09/2010 to 12/2010
w9	12/1998 to 03/1999	10/2003 to 01/2004		
w10				09/2011 to 12/2011
w12	12/1999 to 03/2000			

Source: Authors' calculations.

REFERENCES

Addo, Fenaba R., and Daniel T. Lichter. 2013. "Marriage, Marital History, and Black-White Wealth Differentials Among Older Women." *Journal of Marriage and Family* 75(2): 342–62.

Apel, Robert, Arjan A. J. Blokland, Paul Niewbeerta, and Marieke van Schellen. 2010. "The Impact of Imprisonment on Marriage and Divorce: A Risk Set Matching Approach." *Journal of Quantitative Criminology* 26(2): 269–300.

Bannon, Alicia, Mitali Nagrecha, and Rebekah Diller. 2010. *Criminal Justice Debt: A Barrier to Re-Entry*. New York: Brennan Center for Justice.

Beckett, Katherine, and Alexis Harris. 2011. "On Cash and Conviction: Monetary Sanctions as Misguided Policy." *Criminology & Public Policy* 10(3): 505–37.

Brayne, Sarah. 2014. "Surveillance and System Avoidance: Criminal Justice Contact and Institutional Attachment." *American Sociological Review* 79(3): 367–91.

Bricker, Jesse, Lisa J. Dettling, Alice Henriques, Joanne W. Hsu, Kevin B. Moore, John Sabelhaus, Jeffrey Thompson, and Richard A. Windle. 2014. "Changes in U.S. Family Finances from 2010 to 2013: Evidence from the Survey of Consumer Finances." *Federal Reserve Bulletin* 100(4): 1–41. Accessed May 13, 2016. http://www.federalreserve.gov/pubs/bulletin/2014/pdf/scf14.pdf.

Campbell, Lori Ann, and Robert L. Kaufman. 2006. "Racial Differences in Household Wealth: Beyond Black and White." *Research in Social Stratification and Mobility* 24(2): 131–52.

Conley, Dalton. 1999. *Being Black, Living in the Red: Race, Wealth, and Social Policy in America*. Berkeley: University of California Press.

Czajka, John L., Jonathan E. Jacobson, and Scott Cody. 2003. "Survey Estimates of Wealth: A Comparative Analysis and Review of the Survey of Income and Program Participation." Washington, D.C.: Mathematica Policy Research.

Eads, Alicia, and Laura Tach. 2016. "Wealth and Inequality in the Stability of Romantic Relationships." *RSF: The Russell Sage Foundation Journal of the Social Sciences* 2(6). doi: 10.7758/RSF.2016.2.6.10.

Fisher, Linda. 2009. "Target Marketing of Subprime Loans: Racialized Consumer Fraud and Reverse Redlining." *Brooklyn Journal of Law and Policy* 18(1): 121–55.

Flippen, Chenoa A. 2001. "Racial and Ethnic Inequality in Homeownership and Housing Equity." *Sociological Quarterly* 42(2): 121–49.

———. 2004. "Unequal Returns to Housing Investments? A Study of Real Housing Appreciation among Black, White, and Hispanic Households." *Social Forces* 82(4): 1523–51.

Foster, Holly, and John Hagan. 2015. "Punishment Regimes and the Multi-Level Effects of Parental Imprisonment: Inter-Generational, Intersectional, and Inter-Institutional Models of Social Inequality and Exclusion." *Annual Review of Sociology* 41: 135–58.

Foucault, Michel. 2015. *The Punitive Society: Lectures at the College de France 1972–1973*. New York: Palgrave Macmillian.

Geller, Amanda, Irwin Garfinkel, and Bruce Western. 2011. "Paternal Incarceration and Support for Children in Fragile Families." *Demography* 48(1): 25–47.

Gelman, Andrew, and Jennifer Hill. 2007. *Data Analysis Using Regression and Multilevel/Hierarchical Models*. Cambridge: Cambridge University Press.

Gittleman, Maury, and Edward N. Wolff. 2004. "Racial Differences in Patterns of Wealth Accumulation." *Journal of Human Resources* 39(1): 193–227.

Glaze, Lauren, and Danielle Kaeble. 2014. "Correctional Populations in the United States, 2013." Washington: Bureau of Justice Statistics. Accessed May 13, 2016. http://www.bjs.gov/content/pub/pdf/cpus13.pdf.

Goffman, Alice. 2009. "On the Run: Wanted Men in a Philadelphia Ghetto." *American Sociological Review* 74(3): 339–57.

Hagan, John, and Holly Foster. 2012. "Intergenerational Educational Effects of Mass Imprisonment in America." *Sociology of Education* 83(2): 259–86.

Hall, Matthew, and Kyle Crowder. 2011. "Extended-Family Resources and Racial Inequality in the Transition to Homeownership." *Social Science Research* 40(6): 1534–46.

Ham, John, Xianghong Li, and Lara Shore-Sheppard. 2016. "The Employment Dynamics of Disadvantaged Women: Evidence from the SIPP." *Journal of Labor Economics* 34(4)(October). doi: 10.1086/686274.

Harris, Alexes, Heather Evans, and Katherine Beckett. 2010. "Drawing Blood from Stones: Legal Debt and Social Inequality in the Contemporary United States." *American Journal of Sociology* 115(6): 1753–99.

———. 2011. "Courtesy Stigma and Monetary Sanctions: Toward a Socio-Cultural Theory of Punishment." *American Sociological Review* 76(2): 234–64.

Heckman, James, and Paul LaFontaine. 2010. "The American High School Graduation Rate: Trends and Levels." *Review of Economics and Statistics* 92(2): 244–62.

Heflin, Colleen M., and Mary Pattillo. 2002. "Kin Effects on Black-White Account and Home Ownership." *Sociological Inquiry* 72(2): 220–39.

Holzer Harry J., Steven Raphael, and Michael A. Stoll. 2003. "Employment Barriers Facing Ex-offenders." Paper presented at the Urban Institute Reentry Roundtable, "Employment Dimensions of Reentry: Understanding the Nexus Between Prisoner Reentry and Work." New York University Law School (May 19–20, 2003).

Johnston, Jack, and John DiNardo. 1997. *Econometric Methods*, 4th ed. New York: McGraw-Hill.

Johnson, Rucker, and Steven Raphael. 2009. "The Effect of Male Incarceration Dynamics on AIDS Infection Rates Among African-American Women and Men." *Journal of Law and Economics* 52(2): 251–93.

Kalton, Graham, Marianne Winglee, Louis Rizzo, Thomas Jabine, and Daniel Levine. 1998. "SIPP Quality Profile 1998." SIPP working paper no. 230. Washington: U.S. Department of Commerce, Bureau of the Census. Accessed May 13, 2016. http://www.census.gov/sipp/workpapr/wp230.pdf.

Keister, Lisa A. 2000a. *Wealth in America: Trends in Wealth Inequality*. New York: Cambridge University Press.

———. 2000b. "Race and Wealth Inequality: The Impact of Racial Differences in Asset Ownership on the Distribution of Household Wealth." *Social Science Research* 29(4): 477–502.

———. 2003. "Sharing the Wealth: The Effect of Siblings on Adults' Wealth Ownership." *Demography* 40(3): 521–42.

———. 2004. "Race, Family Structure, and Wealth: The Effect of Childhood Family on Adult Asset Ownership." *Sociological Perspectives* 47(2): 161–87.

Keister, Lisa A., and Stephanie Moller. 2000. "Wealth Inequality in the United States." *Annual Review of Sociology* 26(1): 63–81.

Killewald, Alexandra. 2013. "Return to Being Black, Living in the Red: A Race Gap in Wealth That Goes Beyond Social Origins." *Demography* 50(4): 1177–95.

Killewald, Alexandra, and Brielle Bryan. 2016. "Does Your Home Make You Wealthy?" *RSF: The Russell Sage Foundation Journal of the Social Sciences* 2(6). doi: 10.7758/RSF.2016.2.6.06.

Kochhar, Rakesh, Richard Fry, and Paul Taylor. 2011. "Twenty-to-One: Wealth Gaps Rise to Record Highs Between Whites, Blacks and Hispanics." Washington, D.C.: Pew Research Center.

Krivo, Lauren J., and Robert L. Kaufman. 2004. "Housing and Wealth Inequality: Racial-Ethnic Differences in Home Equity in the United States." *Demography* 41(3): 585–605.

Kuebler, Meghan, and Jacob S. Rugh. 2013. "New Evidence on Racial and Ethnic Disparities in Homeownership in the United States from 2001 to 2010." *Social Science Research* 42(5): 1357–74.

Long, J. Scott. 1997. *Regression Models for Categorical and Limited Dependent Variables*. Thousand Oaks, Calif.: Sage Publications.

Lopoo, Leonard M., and Bruce Western. 2005. "Incarceration and the Formation and Stability of Marital Unions." *Journal of Marriage and Family* 67(3): 721–34.

Lum, Kristian, Samarth Swarup, Stephen Eubank, and James Hawdon. 2014. "The Contagious Nature of Imprisonment: An Agent-Based Model to Explain Racial Disparities in Incarceration Rates." *Journal of the Royal Society* 11(98): 1–12.

Manza, Jeff, and Christopher Uggen. 2006. *Locked Out: Felon Disenfranchisement and American Democracy*. New York: Oxford University Press.

Maroto, Michelle Lee. 2015. "The Absorbing Status of Incarceration and Its Relationship with Wealth Accumulation." *Journal of Quantitative Criminology* 31(2): 207–36.

Massey, Douglas S. 2015. "The Legacy of the 1968 Fair Housing Act." *Sociological Forum* 30(S1): 571–88.

Massey, Douglas S., and Nancy Denton. 1993. *American Apartheid: Segregation and the Making of the Underclass*. Cambridge, Mass.: Harvard University Press.

Massoglia, Michael. 2008a. "Incarceration, Health, and Racial Disparities in Health." *Law & Society Review* 42(2): 275–306.

———. 2008b. "Incarceration as Exposure: The Prison, Infectious Disease, and Other Stress-Related Illnesses." *Journal of Health and Social Behavior* 49(1): 56–71.

McCloud, Laura, and Rachel E. Dwyer. 2011. "The Fragile American: Hardship and Financial Troubles in the 21st Century." *Sociological Quarterly* 52(1): 13–35.

Meyer, Bruce, Wallace K.C. Mok, and James X. Sullivan. 2009. "The Under-Reporting of Transfers in Household Surveys: Its Nature and Consequences." *NBER* working paper no. 15181. Cambridge, Mass.: National Bureau of Economic Research.

Neal, Derek and Armin Rick. 2014. "The Prison Boom & the Lack of Black Progress after Smith & Welch." Unpublished manuscript. Accessed October 17, 2015. https://drive.google.com/file/d/0B82YTFxQDWpjd1BvYzl6bVhtRnM/edit?pli=1.

Newport, Frank. 2015. "In U.S., 60% Satisfied With Ability to Get Ahead." Gallup. Accessed May 13, 2016. http://www.gallup.com/poll/181340/satisfied-ability-ahead.aspx?utm_source=Politics&utm_medium=newsfeed&utm_campaign=tiles.

Oliver, Melvin, and Thomas Shapiro. 2006. *Black Wealth/White Wealth: A New Perspective on Racial Inequality*, 2nd ed. New York: Routledge.

Pager, Devah. 2003. "The Mark of a Criminal Record." *American Journal of Sociology* 108(5): 937–75.

———. 2007. *Marked: Race, Crime, and Finding Work in an Era of Mass Incarceration*. Chicago: University of Chicago Press.

Pager, Devah, and Lincoln Quillian. 2005. "Walking the Talk: What Employers Say Versus What They Do." *American Sociological Review* 70(3): 355–80.

Patterson, Evelyn J. 2010. "Incarcerating Death: Mortality in U.S. State Correctional Facilities, 1985–1998." *Demography* 47(3): 587–607.

Pettit, Becky. 2012. *Invisible Men: Mass Incarceration and the Myth of Black Progress*. New York: Russell Sage Foundation.

Pettit, Becky, and Bryan Sykes. 2015. "Civil Rights Legislation and Legalized Exclusion: Mass Incarceration and the Masking of Inequality." *Sociological Forum* 30(S1): 589–611.

Pettit, Becky, Bryan Sykes, and Bruce Western. 2009. *Technical Report on Revised Population Estimates and NLSY 79 Analysis Tables for the Pew Public Safety and Mobility Project*. Cambridge, Mass.: Harvard University Press.

Pettit, Becky, and Bruce Western. 2004. "Mass Imprisonment and the Life Course: Race and Class Inequality in U.S. Incarceration." *American Sociological Review* 69(2): 151–69.

Pfeffer, Fabian T., Sheldon Danziger, and Robert F. Schoeni. 2013. "Wealth Disparities Before and After the Great Recession." *The Annals of the American Academy of Political and Social Science* 650(1): 98–123.

Powers, Daniel, and Yu Xie. 2000. *Statistical Methods for Categorical Data Analysis*. San Diego, Calif.: Academic Press.

Rauscher, Emily. 2016. "Passing It On: Parent-to-Adult Child Financial Transfers for School and Socioeconomic Attainment." *RSF: The Russell Sage Foundation Journal of the Social Sciences* 2(6). doi: 10.7758/RSF.2016.2.6.09.

Reskin, Barbara F. 2012. "The Race Discrimination System." *Annual Review of Sociology* 38: 17–35.

Rodriguez, Michelle, and Maurice Emsellem. 2011. "65 Million Need Not Apply: The Case for Reforming Criminal Background Checks for Employment." New York: National Employment Law Project. Accessed May 13, 2016. https://www.nelp.org/content/uploads/2015/03/65_Million_Need_Not_Apply.pdf.

Rugh, Jacob S., Len Albright, and Douglas S. Massey. 2015. "Race, Space, and Cumulative Disadvantage: A Case Study of the Subprime Lending Collapse." *Social Problems* 62(2): 186–218.

Schneider, Daniel, and Kristin Turney. 2015. "Incarceration and Black-White Inequality in Homeownership: A State-Level Analysis." *Social Science Research* 53(September): 403–14.

Schnittker, Jason, and Andrea John. 2007. "Enduring Stigma: The Long-Term Effects of Incarceration on Health." *Journal of Health and Social Behavior* 48(2): 115–30.

Schnittker Jason, Michael Massoglia, and Christopher Uggen. 2011. "Incarceration and the Health of the African American Community." *Du Bois Review* 8(1): 133–41.

Schwartz-Soicher, Ofira, Amanda Geller, and Irwin Garfinkel. 2011. "The Effect of Paternal Incarceration on Material Hardship." *Social Service Review* 85(3): 447–73.

Semyonov, Moshe, and Noah Lewin-Epstein. 2013. "Ways to Richness: Determination of Household Wealth in 16 Countries." *European Sociological Review* 29(6): 1134–48.

Shapiro, Thomas M. 2004. *The Hidden Cost of Being African American: How Wealth Perpetuates Inequality*. New York: Oxford University Press.

Spilerman, Seymour. 2000. "Wealth and Stratification Processes." *Annual Review of Sociology* 26: 497–524.

Squires, Gregory D. 2003. "The New Redlining: Predatory Lending in an Age of Financial Service Modernization." *Sage Race Relations Abstracts* 28(3-4): 5–18.

Staiger, Douglas, and James H. Stock. 1997. "Instrumental Variables Regression with Weak Instruments." *Econometrica* 65(3): 557–86.

Sugie, Naomi F. 2012. "Punishment and Welfare: Paternal Incarceration and Families' Receipt of Public Assistance." *Social Forces* 90(4): 1403–27.

Sykes, Bryan L. 2014. "Documentation and Methods for Incarceration Rates in the United States, 1972–2010." In *The Growth of Incarceration in the United States: Exploring Causes and Consequences*, edited by Jeremy Travis, Bruce Western, and Steve Redburn. Washington, D.C.: National Academies Press.

Sykes, Bryan, Trevor Hoppe, and Kristen Maziarka. 2016. "Cruel Intentions? HIV Prevalence and Criminalization during an Age of Mass Incarceration, U.S. 1999–2012." *Medicine* 95(16):e3352. doi: 10.1097/MD.0000000000003352.

Sykes, Bryan L., and Becky Pettit. 2014. "Mass Incarceration, Family Complexity, and the Reproduction of Childhood Disadvantage." *The Annals of the American Academy of Political and Social Science* 654(1): 127–49.

———. 2015. "Severe Deprivation and System Inclusion Among Children of Incarcerated Parents in the United States After the Great Recession." *RSF: The Russell Sage Foundation Journal of the Social Sciences* 1(1): 108–32.

Sykes, Bryan L., and Alex Piquero. 2009. "Structuring and Recreating Inequality: Health Testing Policies, Race, and the Criminal Justice System." *The Annals of the American Academy of Political and Social Science* 623(1): 214–27.

Thompson, Jason, and Dalton Conley. 2016. "Health Shocks and Social Drift: Examining the Relationship Between Acute Illness and Family Wealth." *RSF: The Russell Sage Foundation Journal of the Social Sciences* 2(6). doi: 10.7758/RSF.2016.2.6.08.

Turney, Kristin, and Christopher Wildeman. 2013. "Redefining Relationships: Explaining the Countervailing Consequences of Parental Incarceration for Parenting." *American Sociological Review* 78(6): 949–79.

Wacquant, Loic. 2001. "Deadly Symbiosis: When Ghetto and Prison Meet the Mesh." *Punishment and Society* 3(1): 95–134.

Wakefield, Sara, and Christopher Uggen. 2010. "Incarceration and Stratification." *Annual Review of Sociology* 36: 387–406.

Western, Bruce. 2006. *Punishment and Inequality in America*. New York: Russell Sage Foundation.

Western, Bruce, and Katherine Beckett. 1999. "How Unregulated Is the U.S. Labor Market? The Penal System as a Labor Market Institution." *American Journal of Sociology* 104(4): 1030–60.

Western, Bruce, and Becky Pettit. 2005. "Black-White Wage Inequality, Employment Rates, and Incarceration." *American Journal of Sociology* 111(2): 553–78.

Western, Bruce, and Jeremy Travis, eds.. 2014. *The Growth of Incarceration in the United States*. Washington, D.C.: National Academies Press.

Western, Bruce, and Christopher Wildeman. 2009. "The Black Family and Mass Incarceration." *The Annals of the American Academy of Political and Social Science* 621(1): 221–42.

Wildeman, Christopher, and Christopher Muller. 2012. "Mass Imprisonment and Inequality in Health and Family Life." *Annual Review of Law and Social Science* 8: 11–30.

Williams, Richard, Reynold Nesiba, and Eileen Diaz McConnell. 2005. "The Changing Face of Inequality in Home Mortgage Lending." *Social Problems* 52(2): 181–208.

Wolff, Edward N. 2014. "Household Wealth Trends in the United States, 1983–2010." *Oxford Review of Economic Policy* 30(1): 21–43.

Wooldridge, Jeffrey M. 2009. *Introductory Econometrics: A Modern Approach*, 4th ed. Cincinnati, Oh.: South-Western College Publishing.

Zaw, Khaing, Darrick Hamilton, and William Darity Jr. 2016. "Race, Wealth, and Incarceration: Results from the National Longitudinal Survey of Youth." *Race and Social Problems* 8(1): 103–15.

Health Shocks and Social Drift: Examining the Relationship Between Acute Illness and Family Wealth

JASON THOMPSON AND DALTON CONLEY

This paper analyzes the extent to which health shocks play a role in black-white wealth inequality. Deploying data from the Panel Study of Income Dynamics, we implement a first-differences identification strategy in estimating the effects of acute health events on changes in wealth for couples across waves of data from 1999 to 2011. We find that although such shocks affect both white and black families, they make black families more vulnerable financially as family heads near retirement. In comparison with their white counterparts, black families that experience an acute health shock are more likely to rely on social safety nets, such as food stamps and Social Security Disability Insurance. Findings hold implications across multiple policy arenas, including health-care and labor law.

Keywords: health, race, wealth inequality

The gap in wealth between black families and white families in the United States has been well documented since the 1990s (Oliver and Shapiro 1995; Conley 1999). In 1998, the median wealth of white families was six times that of black families. By 2013, this disparity had nearly doubled as assets and debts evolved in the wake of the Great Recession (Thompson and Suarez 2015; Wolff, this issue). A considerable literature notes the origins of this inequality and the roles of residential segregation, discrimination in mortgage markets, and returns on investments in either sustaining or widening the black-white wealth disparity over time (Oliver and Shapiro 1995; Conley 1999; Keister 2000; Keister and Moller 2000; Smith 2001; Krivo and Kaufman 2004). Absent from this literature, however, is an attempt to link disparities in family wealth with research on prevalent racial disparities in health. If racial disparities in health exist at all levels of socioeconomic status (Williams et al. 2010) and the onset of poor health associates with drains in family wealth (Smith 1999, 2004; Wu 2003), health may be added to the list of factors contributing to the persistent black-white inequality in wealth.

The existing literature on the connections between health and socioeconomic status details the depletion of family wealth following the onset of severe illnesses for Americans older than fifty (Smith 1999; Wu 2003). The search for mechanisms behind this "asset cost of poor health" (Poterba, Venti, and Wise 2010) has pointed toward increased medical costs and changes in labor market participation as factors driving this relationship. Although prior studies detail the impact of health shocks on family wealth, most fail to examine this relationship in terms of racial inequality in the United States. To address this deficit,

---

Jason Thompson is a doctoral candidate in sociology at New York University. **Dalton Conley** is Henry Putnam University Professor of Sociology at Princeton University. He is also research associate at the National Bureau of Economic Research.

Direct correspondence to: Jason Thompson at jason.thompson@nyu.edu, 295 Lafayette Street, Fourth Floor, New York, NY, 10012; and Dalton Conley at dconley@princeton.edu, 153 Wallace Hall, Princeton, NJ, 08544.

we analyze the extent to which health shocks for older men and women affect net worth for married and cohabitating couples. In doing so, we take careful note of the likelihood of experiencing an acute health shock, the consequent changes in labor market participation, and the resultant drain on family wealth as additional factors behind the black-white wealth disparity.

Deploying data from the Panel Study of Income Dynamics (PSID), we implement a first-differences identification strategy in estimating the effects of health events on changes in wealth for couples across waves of data from 1999 to 2011. Further, we apply this approach to both acute and chronic health conditions—the former where we expect the relationship from health to wealth to be more causal and the latter where we expect it to be more spurious. Lower levels of baseline wealth among black couples, in comparison with white couples, place them at an increased risk of financial hardship when facing health complications. Following the experience of an acute health shock, the drain on wealth for black families increases their likelihood of falling into total net debt and widens the black-white divide in total family wealth. The economic vulnerability of black families who experience a severe health event also increases their likelihood of reliance on social safety nets as couples near retirement. Findings from this study hold potential implications for multiple arenas of social policy, including health-care and labor legislation.

BACKGROUND

An extensive literature has documented a robust correlation between socioeconomic status (SES)—measured in a variety of ways—and health outcomes. Most studies favor a social causation hypothesis, in which the short- and long-term stressors of lower SES lead to a variety of health concerns over the life course (Ross and Wu 1995; Link and Phelan 1995; Adler and Ostrove 1999; Haas 2006). A significant body of literature also highlights persistent health inequality between blacks and whites: that black individuals at all age, education, and income levels experience higher mortality, earlier onset, and greater severity of many diseases (Williams and Collins 1995; Bibbins-Domingo et al. 2009; Braveman et al. 2010; Williams et al. 2010).

Despite the weight of evidence in support of social causation hypotheses, associations between SES and health prove more complex than a unidirectional causal relationship. Literature on health selection reverses the direction of the SES-health relationship and details that poor health may spur "social drift," in which the ill individual drains family resources (Adler and Ostrove 1999; Haas 2006) via diminished labor market participation (Smith 1999; Wu 2003) and increased debt (Himmelstein et al. 2005, 2009; Mohanan 2013). If black men and women are disproportionately likely to experience adverse health events at all levels of income, then the consequent social drift may further widen the black-white divide in SES, especially in terms of wealth.

Many existing analyses of health shocks and social drift use the Health and Retirement Study (HRS). Launched in 1992, the HRS has collected longitudinal data every two years on the income, assets, and health of individuals older than fifty in the first wave. The research produced using the HRS presents significant evidence in support of social drift in the aging population. Using the first three waves of the HRS, James Smith (1999) finds that those with cancers, heart conditions, strokes, and lung diseases experienced an estimated drain on wealth of $16,846. In comparison, those reporting milder health conditions experienced a drain of only $3,620 (Smith 1999, 154). James Poterba and his colleagues (2010) use the HRS and operationalize health by constructing an index variable from twenty-seven health-related questions. The authors find that couples in the top third of the health distribution in continuing two-person households (that is, those not experiencing widowhood or divorce) accumulated, on average, over 50 percent more assets than those in the lowest third.

Studies on the financial consequences of poor health also examine the pathways through which health shocks drain wealth. Findings show that poor health decreases labor market participation and increases the likelihood of retirement (Bound et al. 1999; Smith 2004; Wu 2003; Himmelstein et al. 2005; Conley and

Thompson 2013; Zajacova et al. 2015). Poor health also relates to decreased wealth via medical expenses (Smith 1999, 2004; Wu 2003; Himmelstein et al. 2005, 2009). David Himmelstein and his colleagues (2009) find that 57 percent of families filing for bankruptcy in early 2007 cited difficulty paying medical bills as a leading reason for their filing. Health-care burdens also affect wealth through the residential mobility needed to care for the ill individual (Choi et al. 2014). These changes in labor force participation and increased medical expenses are especially pronounced for more serious health shocks (Smith 1999).

Existing studies on health-related social drift motivate this analysis, but prior research largely ignores racial disparities in the impact of health on wealth and the potential for health shocks to drive wealth inequality. This dearth of research is startling in light of pronounced racial inequalities in wealth (Conley 1999), access to health care, and health outcomes (Williams and Collins 1995; Williams et al. 2010). The limited literature discussing racial disparities in social drift finds no significant differences between black and white individuals in the HRS (Wu 2003). However, given the prominence of race in analyses of social causation in health (Williams et al. 2010), these potential disparities require further attention.

This study briefly touches on the trends in black wealth and white wealth from 1999 to 2011 before focusing on the drains in family wealth following the onset of an acute illness. In doing so, we draw attention to the oversight of these relationships across a wider range of the working-age population and persistent black-white disparities in health and wealth. Our first-differences regression models identify changes in health status from the previous wave. We expect this identification strategy to attenuate bias introduced by time-constant omitted variables. When an acute illness strikes the man or woman in a couple, we expect that to negatively influence net worth during the same period. We then analyze health-care costs and family dynamics in labor market participation following acute health shocks as mechanisms by which health affects wealth across race and gender. In conclusion, we provide descriptive evidence that the disproportionately vulnerable economic position of black families who experience an acute illness relates with an increased likelihood of reliance on social safety nets.

DATA

The Panel Study of Income Dynamics is the world's longest-running longitudinal household survey, tracking family economic histories every year from 1968 through 1997 and biennially since. The initial study wave consists of a nationally representative sample of families in 1968 along with an oversample of low-income families, totaling approximately eighteen thousand individuals in five thousand families. Unique to the PSID, the survey follows children of sample members into adulthood as they form their own households. Partly because of extensive follow-up measures, the sample size has grown to nearly twenty-five thousand individuals in more than 8,500 families as of 2011. Important for the study of family dynamics in health and labor market decisions, the PSID codes information at both the family and individual levels.

To examine the relationship between health shocks and changes in wealth, we construct a panel of data collected biennially from 1999 to 2011 (n = 7,422 couple-years). Because the sample of nonblack racial minorities in the PSID is small, we include only those who are black or white. Further work is necessary to examine heterogeneity within and across a more comprehensive list of racial categories. Those eligible for analysis include married or cohabitating couples who remain in their relationship for at least two consecutive waves of data between 1999 and 2011. We restrict the sample to couples in which both individuals are ages forty-five to sixty-four to better gauge the effects of health shocks on wealth for a portion of the working-age population prior to eligibility for full Social Security benefits and typical retirement age.

To eliminate the confounding factor of asset reallocation in divorce or separation, we choose to limit our analyses to couples who continue in relationships across contiguous waves. It is likely that individuals without a partner face different constraints on assets and labor market decisions following the onset of poor health. However, restricting analyses to single individuals in contiguous waves decreases the sample to a problematically small size for analysis. Additionally, the PSID does not code data on the deceased, precluding the ability to examine the impact of health shocks on wealth for families who experience the death of either member of the couple following the onset of an illness. In the discussion, we review the potential for these sources of bias to augment research findings.

The structure of the PSID between 1999 and 2011 is well suited for this analysis. First, from 1999 onward, the PSID codes a series of health events for family heads. Second, it also includes extensive data on family health-care costs and patterns of labor force participation for each partner. Finally, to examine the relationship between the onset of health conditions and short-term changes in family wealth, we need a window of time brief enough to attenuate potential bias due to unobserved variables and spurious correlation. The two-year spans between waves and the PSID variables coded since 1999 provide a viable data structure to address these issues.

The primary dependent variable in this analysis is total family wealth. In every survey year from 1999 onward, the PSID calculates wealth by summing the values of family business or farm, checking and savings, real estate other than main home, stocks and mutual funds, vehicles, bonds and life insurance policies, individual retirement accounts and annuities, and main home, minus any debts. This variable is standardized to 2011 dollars. Given the high skew of the wealth distribution, we log-transform these standardized values.[1] A primary concern of the log transformation is that the log of wealth does not permit analysis of negative values or total net debt. Therefore, we also examine a dichotomous dependent variable equal to 1 if the family holds negative net wealth.[2] If we were concerned with aggregate wealth levels, then the selection of certain years would be critical to our estimations given their potential association with different points in the business cycle. However, because we are interested in comparing patterns of change across two periods rather than overall levels of wealth, we find cyclical concerns less troubling. As a precaution, we include survey year indicator variables to account for the potential presence of idiosyncrasies in any wave.

Our primary independent variables distinguish acute health shocks from the onset of chronic illnesses based on wave-to-wave changes in the incidence of nine physical health conditions coded in the PSID.[3] We define an acute health shock as the occurrence of cancer, heart attack, heart disease, or a stroke between waves. We code the onset of a chronic illness as a new diagnosis of asthma, arthritis, diabetes, high blood pressure, or lung disease from one wave to the next. These distinctions subsume self-reported health and provide analyses of separate tiers of health complications. We code men and women as one in each wave the individual is diagnosed with a new acute or chronic illness. Research on the health and wealth connection varies in the terminology and criteria to distinguish between categories of health conditions. With few exceptions, our definition of acute shocks largely overlaps with severe and major illnesses in other studies (but see Wu 2003; Smith 1999, 2004; Coile and Milligan 2009). For a full discussion of our rationale for including each illness under its category, see the appendix.

Although all of these shocks may have developed over the course of years, they are

---

1. Analyses run using the inverse hyperbolic sine transformation of all monetary values increase standard errors but fail to significantly alter results. These results are available on request.

2. Unfortunately, the main interview of the PSID only codes the occurrence of bankruptcy in the 1996 interview, prior to the addition of survey questions regarding health histories. This precludes us from examining the relationship between acute health shocks and bankruptcy filings.

3. Although the onset of mental health conditions may adversely affect family wealth, we argue that the directionality of the relationship between health and wealth is more difficult to discern for a mental illness, such as depression, than it is with a physical illness, such as a stroke.

largely asymptomatic until an event affects an individual's behavior. We intend the terms acute and chronic to signal the severity of the illness and the degree of medical treatment that the illness necessitates. For instance, it is likely that an individual experiencing a heart attack will undergo initial treatment, including surgeries and hospital stays, within a short period following the health event. The subsequent complications of an acute shock will likely continue beyond the initial health event and result in changes to diet and medications. However, it is arguable that the primary impact of such a health event on wealth will occur relatively soon after the event and initial treatment. Given this rationale, we allow each member of a couple to experience more than one acute health shock during the study. For instance, if a family head experiences a stroke between 1999 and 2001 and then has a heart attack between 2007 and 2009, the individual would be coded as having an acute health shock twice between 1999 and 2011.

On the other hand, a disease such as diabetes will likely require more regular maintenance over a longer period following the diagnosis and result in effects on wealth that are not necessarily discernible in the short term. Because we feel that the effects of chronic health conditions on wealth will be less discernible in a span of two years, we permit the man or woman to be coded as having the onset of a chronic condition only once. It may be that the onset of an additional chronic illness may compound economic hardships for the family of the ill individual. We argue that this additional hardship remains difficult to measure in the span of two years. Alternate analyses that code each new incidence of a chronic illness for family heads fail to significantly alter results.

In our primary regression models, we include a series of control variables for changes in labor market participation. The PSID codes employment status history by month and constructs a variable representing the total number of weeks spent out of the labor force (unemployed and not looking for work) in a given year. We collapse these into dichotomous measures equal to 1 if the man or woman spent any time out of the labor force. To control for retirement decisions, we also include an indicator variable for each member of the couple noting if either retired between waves of data. In preliminary models, we included the change in log-transformed family income standardized to 2011 dollars. These models produced similar results. We omit this variable in our presented analyses to estimate the direct effect of health on wealth.

In subsequent models, we deploy variables on total health expenses and labor market participation to analyze how changes in health may affect family wealth. First, we estimate total health expenses for families in which a man or woman experienced the onset of an acute or chronic illness. These expenses include costs associated with doctor's visits, outpatient surgery, prescription medication, hospitalization, and nursing home care; they are standardized to 2011 dollars for analysis. Next, we estimate the change in weeks worked, the change in weeks spent out of the labor force, and the likelihood of entering retirement to examine the severity of the impact of health shocks on labor supply. Finally, to examine policy-relevant outcomes of wealth depletion due to acute illness, we analyze descriptive statistics regarding receipt of food stamps and Social Security benefits.

All ordinary least squares regression models implement a first-differences identification strategy to factor out all unobserved, time-constant variables potentially related to changes in wealth.[4] These include many of the behavioral measures, such as exercise and tobacco and alcohol use, so long as the individual does not change their behavior in a significant manner across waves.[5] Key to our identification strategy is the hypothesis that the

---

4. A commonly used alternative to first-differences is a fixed-effects identification strategy. However, two separate tests show autocorrelation in our data, suggesting that the more efficient option is first-differences. Analyses implementing a fixed-effects approach yield similar results.

5. We included these behavioral measures in prior models with no significant changes in results, likely due to lack of variation for individuals and families across waves.

causal arrow in the health-wealth relationship will point from the experience of an acute health shock to consequent drains on family wealth in the short term and that this causality may be less clear when examining chronic conditions. Our first-differences approach decreases the likelihood of reverse causation because the short span of two years between waves reduces the time in which changes in wealth may affect health. It may be, for example, that changes in wealth relate to increased stress, higher blood pressure, and a greater likelihood of heart conditions. To test this hypothesis, we regress the onset of acute and chronic illnesses on the log of baseline wealth and the change in log-transformed wealth from t–2 to t–1 (see appendix). Results show that baseline wealth and changes in wealth do not predict acute health events in the short term. We therefore argue that it is more likely that the onset of acute illnesses leads to changes in wealth over a two-year period because unexpected health shocks cause changes in labor market participation and health-care expenses, among other wealth-draining phenomena.[6]

The general model to examine the effects of changes in health on changes in wealth takes the following form:

$$\Delta \log wealth_i = \beta_0 + \beta_1 acute\ man_i \\ + \beta_2 acute\ woman_i \\ + \beta_3 chronic\ man_i \\ + \beta_4 chronic\ woman_i \\ + \beta_5 \Delta controls_i + \beta_6 \log wealth_{it-1} \\ + \beta_6 X_t + \Delta \varepsilon_i$$

where $\Delta \log wealth_i$ is the change in log-transformed total family wealth for family i across two waves of the PSID. The subsequent four variables indicate the onset of an acute or chronic illness from the prior wave for each member of the couple. $\Delta controls_i$ is the wave-to-wave change in a vector of control variables for family i, including absence from the labor force and retirement for each member of the couple. Log-transformed wealth at t–1 controls for whether overall changes in logged family wealth are conditional on baseline wealth.[7] Finally, X_t represents a vector of dummy variables for each wave of differenced data, the second wave being the suppressed category, and $\Delta \varepsilon_i$ represents the change in the idiosyncratic error. Further, we perform ordered logit regressions of entering into net debt on the onset of acute and chronic illnesses and the control variables. We run each model for black and white families with men and women ages forty-five to sixty-four. In models examining the pathways through which health affects wealth, we substitute the wave-to-wave changes in the log of family wealth with between-wave changes in weeks of work missed and weeks of work out of the labor force. Finally, we perform first-differences ordered logit regressions of a man or woman entering retirement on acute health shocks for each member of the couple.

FINDINGS
Median levels of wealth in our sample follow the general trends outlined by Edward Wolff (this issue) and Jeffrey Thompson and Gustavo Suarez (2015).[8] Median wealth for married and cohabitating couples between the ages of forty-five and sixty-four in the PSID rose steadily from 1999 to 2007 with an increase of 61.8 percent for black families and 28.6 percent for white families (figure 1). With the onset of the

---

6. Lagging the measure of health shocks by one wave would potentially address issues of temporal ordering, but doing so significantly reduces the number of cases we are able to analyze by depleting a full wave of family-years. Furthermore, if we were to lag the indicator for a health shock by a wave, we would be attempting to measure the change in wealth up to four years after the health event, leaving greater room for confounding influences in the health-wealth relationship.

7. Interaction terms between the log of baseline wealth and acute illness failed to prove significant.

8. The precise values of racial wealth disparities depend on the measurement of wealth and the sampling within the chosen set of data. As Fabian Pfeffer and Robert Schoeni note in this issue, data sets vary in the extent to which they include vehicle wealth in the calculation of total net assets. Furthermore, the calculation of family wealth in 2007 from a representative sample of families in 1968 (as is the case with the PSID) may provide dif-

Figure 1. Median Family Wealth

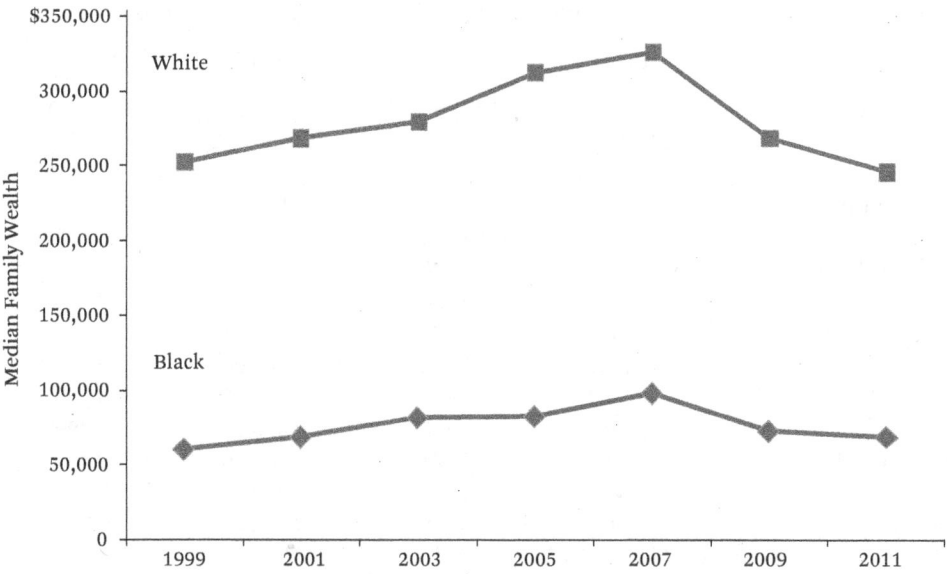

Source: Authors' calculation based on PSID.

Great Recession, wealth dropped precipitously, with black and white median wealth retreating to 2001 levels within the subsequent two years. Figure 1 portrays this unique span of time for wealth accumulation and volatility in the United States. Although this study bridges a distinct era in the early 2000s, our findings regarding the impact of acute health shocks on wealth are not sensitive to the general trends of boom or bust from 1999 to 2011.[9] This is not to say that individual family dynamics in response to health shocks do not differ during periods of prosperity and economic recession. However, it appears with the data at hand that the drain on wealth following an acute health shock does not differ between an era of general economic growth and one of economic decline.

Table 1 shows weighted descriptive statistics of our sample separated by race. As a point of comparison, we also include descriptive statistics for married and cohabitating couples between the ages of thirty and forty-four. As expected, a gap in mean and median wealth between black and white couples is clear. It also increases in magnitude across the life course. The mean wealth for white couples is more than three times that of black couples among those age thirty to forty-four. This disparity increases to four to one later in adulthood; the pattern is similar when measuring median wealth. Older men and women in our sample are significantly more likely to experience an acute health shock or the onset of a chronic illness later in life than between the

---

ferent values than a calculation rendered from a representative cross-section in the year 2007, such as the Survey of Consumer Finances (SCF). Despite these potential discrepancies, the trends in wealth from 1999 to 2011 for black and white families in our sample are similar to those detailed by Jeffrey Thompson and Gustavo Suarez (2015) using waves of SCF data from 1998 to 2013.

9. Interaction terms between the wave of data and the onset of acute and chronic illnesses were insignificant, suggesting that our findings are not an artifact of a unique downturn in the economy (results available on request). This null finding may be attributed to a variety of factors, including the types of assets families draw upon in times of economic crisis and bankruptcy exemptions for home equity. Future research should address the health-wealth connection in the recovery from the Great Recession with additional data regarding the continued evolution of assets beyond 2011.

Table 1. Descriptive Statistics

	Ages Thirty to Forty-Four		Ages Forty-Five to Sixty-Four	
	Black	White	Black	White
Mean family wealth	$83,409	$269,850	$179,854	$711,481
	($210,384)	($755,654)	($290,142)	($1,996,052)
Median family wealth	$31,904	$94,019	$68,831	$271,873
Mean family income	$81,294	$114,207	$83,262	$132,408
	($44,349)	($101,509)	($42,275)	($167,621)
Man acute health shock	0.022	0.040	0.219	0.194
	(0.146)	(0.196)	(0.414)	(0.395)
Woman acute health shock	0.068	0.063	0.161	0.150
	(0.252)	(0.244)	(0.368)	(0.357)
Man chronic illness	0.220	0.250	0.445	0.469
	(0.415)	(0.433)	(0.497)	(0.499)
Woman chronic illness	0.302	0.221	0.526	0.442
	(0.459)	(0.415)	(0.500)	(0.497)
N	606	1,724	514	1,608

Source: Authors' compilation based on PSID.
Note: Statistics weighted by mean family survey weight across all waves of valid data. Monetary values standardized to 2011 dollars.

ages of thirty and forty-four. This discrepancy is most prominent for the experience of acute health shocks among black men. The incidence among partnered black men between forty-five and sixty-four is ten times that among their younger married and cohabitating counterparts (21.9 percent to 2.2 percent). Among partnered older white men, the incidence increases fivefold, from 4 percent to 19.4 percent. Older black and white women also experience an elevated incidence of acute health shocks in comparison with their younger counterparts, but the differences are not as stark, with a 2.4 times increased risk. We call attention to the increased incidence of severe health events and growing wealth disparity later in the life course to highlight the potential role of acute health shocks in the widening black-white wealth gap among older couples.

Likely because so few younger couples experience acute illnesses, regressions of change in the log of family wealth on acute health shocks produce null findings for those ages thirty to forty-four.[10] However, in table 2 we see a significant drain on the log of family wealth following acute health shocks for couples between forty-five and sixty-four. In black families, an acute health shock for a man relates with a 60 percent decrease in family wealth. In white families, an acute health shock for a man does not associate with a significant change in the log of family wealth, but for a woman corresponds with a 25 percent drop.[11] These significant decreases in family wealth following

10. Analyses available on request.

11. We argue that the marginal significance of these coefficients is likely due to the small sample size, given the mean of 233 black families per wave and 827 white families per wave. Unfortunately, widening the age span of respondents eligible for this study is untenable, as the incidence of acute illnesses drops significantly with age. It is likely that heterogeneous effects of health on wealth exist across the types of illnesses categorized as acute in this study. In results not shown, we perform separate regressions of change in the log of family wealth on each acute illness (cancers, heart attacks, heart diseases, and strokes). Unfortunately, disaggregating acute health shocks into the component illnesses increases the standard errors for the estimates of the effect of illness on wealth, rendering the coefficients for most illnesses insignificant. For black families, heart diseases and strokes significantly predict drops in the log of wealth for men and women, respectively. In white families, the onset of

Table 2. First-Differences OLS Regressions of Log Total Family Wealth on Couples' Health

	Black	White
Man acute illness	−0.596+	−0.166
	(0.354)	(0.125)
Woman acute illness	−0.619	−0.247+
	(0.390)	(0.139)
Man chronic illness	−0.178	−0.055
	(0.285)	(0.088)
Woman chronic illness	−0.300	−0.090
	(0.231)	(0.096)
Observations	1,631	5,791
R^2	0.240	0.130

Source: Authors' compilation based on PSID.
Note: Robust standard errors clustered by family in parentheses. Models include controls for log family wealth at t−1, changes in employment status, and dummy variables for each wave of data. Monetary values standardized to 2011 dollars.
+p < 0.1, *p < 0.05, **p < 0.01, ***p < 0.001

Table 3. First-Differences Ordered Logit Regressions of Net Debt on Couples' Health

	Black	White
Man acute illness	0.700*	0.485+
	(0.354)	(0.288)
Woman acute illness	0.745+	0.486
	(0.444)	(0.330)
Man chronic illness	0.517	0.251
	(0.331)	(0.238)
Woman chronic illness	0.263	0.190
	(0.268)	(0.263)
Observations	1,631	5,791

Source: Authors' compilation based on PSID.
Note: Robust standard errors clustered by family in parentheses. Models include controls for log family wealth at t−1, changes in employment status, and dummy variables for each wave of data. Monetary values standardized to 2011 dollars.
+p < 0.1, *p < 0.05, **p < 0.01, ***p < 0.001

acute health shocks contrast with the null associations between the onsets of chronic conditions and changes in wealth. For black and white men and women, diagnosis of a chronic illness does not significantly reduce log-transformed family wealth.

Although the coefficients for acute health shocks do not differ across race by a statistically significant margin, the magnitude of this difference is compelling. To place these elasticities in context, refer to the median family wealth for black and white couples age forty-five to sixty-four. Following an acute health shock for a man, a black family at the median level of wealth would drop from $68,831 to $27,808 in total assets. In contrast, a white family at the median level of wealth with a woman experiencing an acute health shock would see their wealth change from $271,873 to $204,720. Given the baseline racial wealth disparity, white families would see a larger drop in terms of dollar amount ($67,153 versus $41,023). However, the white to black ratio of wealth actually increases from 3.95 to 7.36 following the onset of an acute illness in a white and a black family at their respective levels of median wealth. Additionally, a white couple at the median level of wealth who experienced an acute health shock would maintain nearly three times the median wealth of black families who did not ($204,720 versus $68,831).

The effects of acute illnesses on wealth also appear in an examination of the likelihood of falling into negative net worth, or net debt. Table 3 shows results of first-differences ordered logit regressions of holding negative net worth on the onset of health conditions and changes in control variables. Following an acute health shock, black couples are twice as likely to develop net debt than those unaffected by such illness [exp(0.700) for black men and exp(0.745) for black women]. Although black families are at an increased risk of negative net worth regardless of who experiences the health shock, white families face a greater likelihood of net debt only if a man experiences a severe illness.

cancers for men relates with decreased family wealth. However, the differences between coefficients for each acute illness are not significant and, with few exceptions, the relationship between each acute illness and change in wealth is in the same direction. These results are available on request.

Table 4. First-Differences OLS Regressions of Labor Force Participation on Change in Couples' Health

	Black		White	
	Man	Woman	Man	Woman
	Weeks Worked			
Acute illness	−9.131***	−1.964	−4.510***	−0.565
	(1.931)	(1.529)	(0.855)	(1.064)
Observations	1,631	1,631	5,791	5,791
	Weeks out of Labor Force			
Acute illness	6.692***	−0.973	0.467	−0.640
	(1.816)	(2.410)	(0.938)	(1.265)
Observations	1,631	1,631	5,791	5,791

Source: Authors' compilation based on PSID.
Note: Robust standard errors clustered by family in parentheses. Models include a control for onset of a chronic illness and dummy variables for each wave of data.
+$p < 0.1$, *$p < 0.05$, **$p < 0.01$, ***$p < 0.001$

Table 5. First-Differences Ordered Logit Regressions of Retirement on Change in Couples' Health

	Black		White	
	Man	Woman	Man	Woman
Acute illness	1.613***	1.333**	0.707***	0.135
	(0.269)	(0.403)	(0.194)	(0.314)
Observations	1,631	1,631	5,791	5,791

Source: Authors' compilation based on PSID.
Note: Robust standard errors clustered by family in parentheses. Models include a control for onset of a chronic illness, log family wealth at t−1, and dummy variables for each wave of data. Monetary values standardized to 2011 dollars.
+$p < 0.1$, *$p < 0.05$, **$p < 0.01$, ***$p < 0.001$

A white family is 1.6 times [exp(0.485)] more likely to find itself in net debt following an acute health shock for a man.

In line with the literature, the drains on wealth following acute health shocks in our sample far outweigh the costs incurred from medical expenses (Smith 1999; see also the appendix). To examine the ways in which acute illness may affect wealth, we present the predicted change in weeks of work per year following an acute health shock for either member of a couple (table 4). The changes in weeks worked in the same wave as experiencing an acute illness are significant for black and white men but not for women of either race. Married and cohabiting black men lose an additional nine weeks of work after an acute health event, whereas married and cohabitating white men lose four and a half weeks. The difference between these two coefficients is significant at the $p < 0.05$ level. Furthermore, only black men show an increase in weeks out of the labor force following an acute health shock. Black men spend an average of 6.7 more weeks out of the labor force following an acute health event. At the same time, black women, white men, and white women see no significant change.

Another strong black-white disparity in labor market participation following an acute health shock is evident in retirement decisions. In table 5, we present results of first-differences ordered logit regressions of retirement on acute and chronic illnesses. As a

Figure 2. Median Family Wealth at Retirement of First Member of Couple

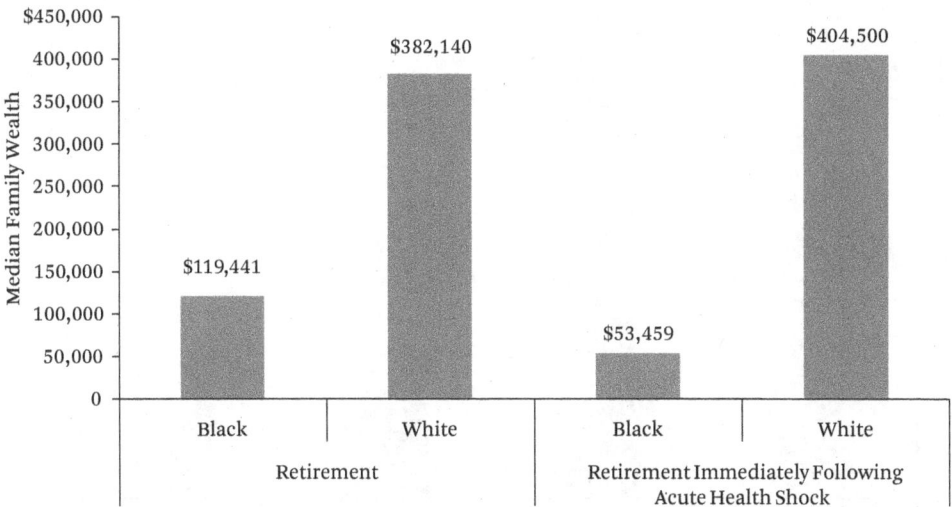

Source: Authors' compilation based on PSID.

reminder, these retirements would be considered early in the sense that our sample is restricted to individuals younger than the age at which they would be eligible for full Social Security benefits in retirement. Acute illnesses significantly predict retirement for black men, black women, and white men. In all, retirement following acute health shocks is more prevalent among married and cohabitating black couples. Black men are significantly more likely than white men [exp(1.613) = 5.02 for black men and exp(0.707) = 2.03 for white men] to retire in the same wave in which they experience a severe illness. For white women, an acute illness is not a significant predictor of retirement. However, black women are 3.8 times [exp(1.333)] more likely to retire in the same wave in which they experience an acute health shock.

Early retirement decisions have significant consequences for families as they begin to rely on accrued assets for consumption in later stages of the life course. In figure 2, we show the median family wealth for black and white couples in our sample as the first member of the couple enters retirement. The median of black couples with a retiree following an acute health shock is less than half that of their counterparts with a healthy retiree ($53,459 versus $119,441). In contrast, the median wealth for white families varies only slightly ($382,140 versus $404,500). Whereas white families may opt into retirement at relatively the same economic standing regardless of health status, black families enter illness-induced retirement with increased financial strain. Indeed, black families with an early retiree following an acute health shock have one-third less median wealth than the mean annual income of black couples in our sample: $53,459 (figure 2) versus $83,262 (table 1). Furthermore, the white to black ratio of median wealth on retirement increases dramatically among families with an ill retiree. The median wealth of a white couple with an early retiree is more than three times that of a black couple with at least one member entering retirement ($382,140 versus $119,441). This ratio more than doubles, from 3.2 to 1 up to 7.6 to 1, among families with a retiree who experienced an acute illness within the two years before retirement.

This impact of health on wealth has implications for families' future reliance on social safety nets. With smaller nest eggs than white families, black families are more likely to rely on social safety nets following an acute health shock. After an acute illness, seventeen percent of black families in our sample received government assistance via food stamps for the first time, whereas only 7 percent of white families did so (figure 3). This racial disparity is

Figure 3. Receiving Food Stamps for First Time Following Acute Health Shock

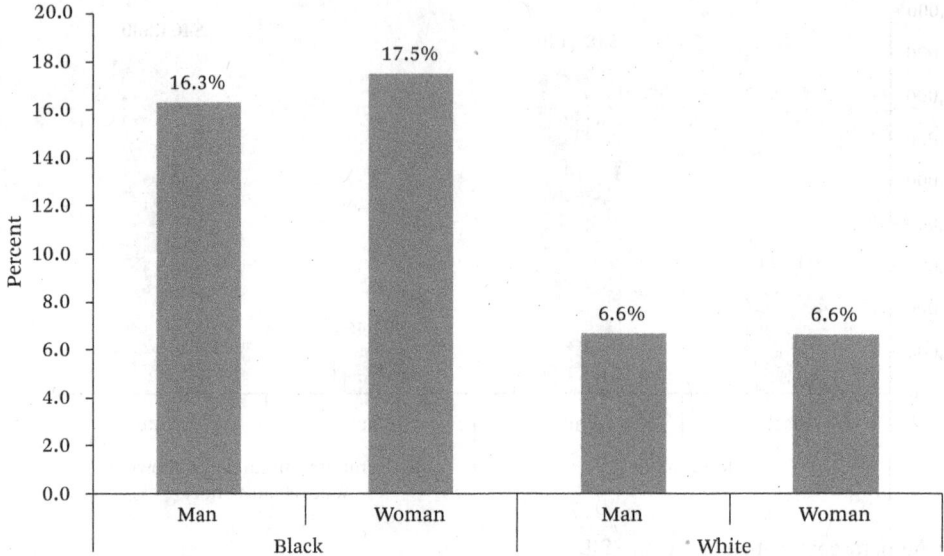

Source: Authors' compilation based on PSID.

Figure 4. Receiving SSDI Following Acute Health Shock

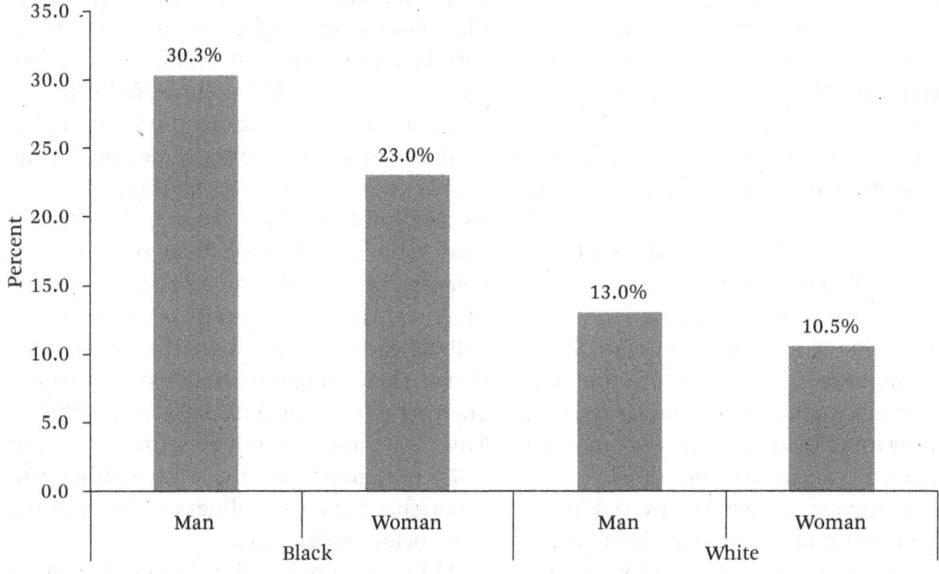

Source: Authors' compilation based on PSID.

also seen among families receiving Social Security Disability Insurance (SSDI) following an acute health shock of either the man or the woman (figure 4). Conditional on not already receiving SSDI, black men and women who experience a severe illness are significantly more likely to consequently rely on SSDI (30.3 percent versus 13.0 percent for men and 23.0 percent versus 10.5 percent for women). In all, drains on wealth are seen for black and white families who experience an acute health shock, black families being disproportionately vulnerable to net debt and reliance on social safety nets following time off of work, time out of the labor force, and early retirement.

DISCUSSION

Our findings show significant depletions of family wealth following acute health shocks for black and white couples. Given the baseline racial disparities in wealth, the percentage drain on total assets is greater for black families in the wake of severe illnesses for a man. Furthermore, acute health shocks for men and women predict net debt for black couples. Although white couples do lose a significant percentage of their net worth after a health shock, the median wealth of white families with an acutely ill man or woman is multiple times that of black families who did not experience a severe health event. In this paper, we highlight differential patterns of labor market participation as a way black families become financially more vulnerable and more likely to rely on social safety nets following health shocks.

As addressed in the literature (Smith 1999), it appears as though the brunt of the impact of health on wealth occurs through changes in labor market participation, rather than increased health-care expenses (Smith 1999, 2004; Wu 2003). Receipt of SSDI or Old-Age and Survivors Insurance (OASI) potentially plays an important role in the connections between health shocks, wealth depletion, and retirement decisions. It may be that the greater likelihood of entering retirement following an acute health shock for a black family is associated with the greater SSDI and OASI replacement rate among lower earners. Greater replacement rates among the lowest earning men and women (and, likely the families with the least wealth) may allow families with less wealth to retire following an acute health shock without experiencing a dramatic loss of annual income in retirement. However, the lower annual Social Security income among these families would likely fail to safeguard them in the event of future health complications. Compounding this issue, families with fewer economic resources are less likely to also hold additional retirement wealth in a defined contribution retirement fund (Devlin-Foltz, Henriques, and Sabelhause, this issue) to serve as an additional buffer against further financial hardship.

Although we uncover significant disparities between black and white families, data limitations may underestimate the drains on wealth for both black and white families, along with the racial disparity in wealth depletion following acute health events. First, the examination of changes in wealth in a two-year window of time is intended to reduce the impact of confounding factors in the health-wealth relationship and narrow in on a causal estimate of health shocks on family wealth. It is likely that health-care costs and lost labor may linger beyond two years in the case of illnesses such as cancers, severe heart conditions, and strokes. Supplemental analyses of changes in family wealth over multiple waves of data (four-plus years) following acute health shocks show that drains in wealth possibly persist beyond this two-year window. However, diminished sample sizes in these analyses and increased standard errors render the point estimates insignificant. Given larger sample sizes over a longer span, the total loss of wealth may surpass that estimated with the data at hand.

Second, the limitation of our sample to continuing married and cohabitating couples also likely underestimates the impact of health shocks on family wealth by ignoring couples who divorce or separate between two waves of data. Alicia Eads and Laura Tach, elsewhere in this issue, detail the connection between economic hardship and marital strain. If the link between financial hardship and likelihood for the dissolution of a relationship is similar for those experiencing health complications, our findings would underestimate the impact of health on wealth for families reallocating assets as well as losing wealth from health-care expenses and diminished labor market participation. Less than 2 percent of individuals in our sample who experience an acute health shock also divorce within the same wave of data. Although this sequence of events is possible, the frequency at which it occurs is minimal and presents too small of a sample to properly estimate changes in wealth following such a sequence.

Finally, the coding of the PSID precludes the

ability to measure mortality in the same wave as the onset of severe health conditions. It is likely that mortality following acute health shocks would increase drains on wealth and potentially increase the black-white disparity in wealth. The loss of a partner would increase health-related costs associated with acute illnesses via funeral expenses. Additionally, loss of life ensures that the partner cannot return to a job or reenter the labor force after an absence. Therefore, families would continue to drain wealth throughout the remaining time between waves of data, rather than level out as the once-ill partner returns to work. Furthermore, if black individuals face a greater risk of mortality due to cancers, severe heart conditions, and strokes (Williams and Jackson 2005; Siegel, Naishadham, and Jemal 2012), then including families experiencing the death of an ill partner may increase the growing black-white disparity in wealth following acute health shocks.

Despite these limitations, our findings offer directions for future research and empirical data for policy discussions. From a health-care policy perspective, our findings do not depend on health insurance status. This is not to say, however, that health-care coverage plays no role in the relationship between acute health events and family wealth. If insurance coverage increases the likelihood of seeking preventive medicine and leads to a reduction in the onset of acute illnesses later in the life course (Hadley 2003), then expanded coverage would indeed play a role in reducing the impact of severe health events on family wealth. Implementation of the Affordable Care Act presents the opportunity to examine the impact of a new health-care regime on medical care and how this might dampen the effects of health on wealth.

Beyond future research agendas analyzing expanded health-care and health outcomes, further work toward labor policy may also address the role of health in wealth accumulation, along with the existing black-white disparities. Our findings corroborate prior literature in that the majority of the impact of health on wealth stems from a decrease in labor market participation and leaving the labor force altogether. Our findings show that an acute illness decreases the number of weeks worked for black and white men. This may be an unfortunate but necessary step for recovery from cancers, heart conditions, and strokes. However, at least among black families, acute illnesses also predict an increase in weeks spent out of the labor force. Although policy may not be able to address the severity of acute health shocks via work missed because of illness, legislation may soften the blow of health on wealth for those forced out of the labor market on the basis of acute health conditions. Revisions to current policy, such as the Family and Medical Leave Act, may expand coverage for the most vulnerable, underemployed workers so that jobs are held for the individuals while they recover. This might cut down on the amount of time families go without a paycheck, because families would not be forced to combine a job search with the time necessary to recover from an illness.

CONCLUSION

It is likely that health is both "a cause and a consequence of larger processes of stratification" (Haas 2006, 349). In this vein, those at the lower end of the socioeconomic spectrum may be more likely to experience adverse health outcomes leading to further diminished socioeconomic status. We test this hypothesis to determine the impact of acute health shocks on wealth for black and white families. Black families experience a significant drain in wealth and are at an increased risk of net debt following an acute health shock. Although health affects wealth in white families, the existing wealth disparities are such that the ratio of median white wealth to median black wealth among married and cohabitating couples increases among families experiencing acute health shocks. Strikingly, median wealth of white couples following an acute health shock remains three times greater than that of healthy black couples.

The results from this study have implications for our understanding of family dynamics in response to health crises and shed light on factors contributing to economic security and insecurity in adulthood. Loss of labor market participation and reliance on stored economic resources following acute health shocks inhibit families' ability to accumulate assets in the future (Poterba, Venti, and Wise 2010). This lost opportunity for asset accumulation places families in vulnerable economic positions as heads of the household age. Furthermore, this loss of family wealth at a point in the life course when couples are nearing retirement places black families in a particularly insecure position as they end their working careers. Our findings link health shocks and family wealth on the micro level with macro-level issues of inequality and social policy, because wealth depletion can lead to a greater burden on social safety nets.

Because full implementation of the Affordable Care Act is under way, this micro-macro connection may indeed evolve. Expanding health-care coverage may relate to better preventive care, higher quality treatment, and positive health outcomes (for a review, see Hadley 2003). Better health may then relate to better economic security as individuals face fewer medical costs (Smith 1999) and are able to avoid illness-induced retirement and work later into the life course (Bound et al. 1999). As more recent data become available, research should examine whether the relationship between health shocks and family wealth also evolves throughout the recovery from the Great Recession and the implementation of quasi-universal health care in the United States.

APPENDIX

Coding of Chronic and Acute Illnesses

We categorize an illness as acute if it meets at least one of two criteria. First, as discussed in the main text, the illnesses defined as acute for this study are likely more severe in terms of initial treatment following the onset of the adverse health condition. Second, although the socioeconomic status-health gradient is noted for many of the illnesses operationalized as acute and chronic in this study (for a review, see Lang et al. 2012), we sought to minimize the likelihood for endogeneity in the relationship between acute illnesses and family wealth. Therefore, a second criterion is satisfied if the illness is not strongly related with baseline wealth for families in our sample.

Each illness we define as acute in this study satisfies both criteria, with the exception of heart attacks and strokes for white women. This may upwardly bias the estimate of the drain on family wealth following a diagnosis for white women in our sample, because less money would represent a larger change in the percentage of family net worth when analyzing log-transformed wealth. Despite this potential bias, we classify heart attacks and strokes as acute illnesses for two reasons. First, they meet the first criterion regarding the severity of the initial treatment following the onset of the illness. Second, any upward bias in estimating drains on family wealth for white families would result in underestimating the black-white wealth disparity following acute health shocks, which is the key contribution of this paper. We feel that the potential for this bias is less troubling, given findings on the null associations involving baseline wealth, changes in wealth, and the onset of acute health shocks.

Based on these criteria, we depart from prior literature in coding lung diseases and diabetes. Stephen Wu (2003) and James Smith (1999, 2004) use the Health and Retirement Survey and include lung diseases (such as chronic bronchitis and emphysema) as severe illnesses. We argue that this category may gloss over significant variation between types of noncancerous lung diseases that differ substantially in terms of their impact on labor market participation and, consequently, family wealth. Furthermore, we define lung disease as a chronic illness given that log-transformed baseline wealth significantly predicts the onset of such diseases for black women, white men, and white women (table A1). Stephen Wu also includes the diagnosis of diabetes as a "health shock" (2003). In our study, diabetes is included as a chronic illness for the same theoretical and empirical reasons as lung disease. Log baseline family wealth significantly predicts the onset of diabetes for black women, white men, and white women in our sample (table A1). Our definitions of acute and chronic illnesses most closely align with those that Courtney Coile and Kevin Milligan outline (2009), with the exception of our inclusion of heart disease as an acute illness, which satisfies our criteria for severity of treatment and

Table A1. Logit Regressions of Diabetes, Lung Disease, and Heart Disease on Log Family Wealth

	Diabetes		Lung Disease		Heart Disease	
	Man	Woman	Man	Woman	Man	Woman
Black Couples						
Log family wealth at time t−1	0.005	−0.051+	−0.061	−0.118***	0.000	−0.050
	(0.034)	(0.028)	(0.040)	(0.033)	(0.046)	(0.046)
Observations	1,631	1,631	1,631	1,631	1,631	1,631
White Couples						
Log family wealth at time t−1	−0.090***	−0.110***	−0.104***	−0.112***	−0.039	−0.049
	(0.023)	(0.027)	(0.027)	(0.023)	(0.028)	(0.036)
Observations	5,791	5,791	5,791	5,791	5,791	5,791

Source: Authors' compilation based on PSID.
Note: Robust standard errors clustered by family in parentheses. Models include dummy variables for each wave of data. Monetary values standardized to 2011 dollars.
+$p < 0.1$, *$p < 0.05$, **$p < 0.01$, ***$p < 0.001$

Table A2. Logit Regressions of Chronic and Acute Illnesses on Log Family Wealth

	Black		White	
	Man	Woman	Man	Woman
Onset of Chronic Illness				
Log family wealth at time t−1	−0.038+	−0.016	−0.036**	−0.025
	(0.020)	(0.021)	(0.014)	(0.015)
Observations	1,631	1,631	5,791	5,791
Onset of Acute Illness				
Log family wealth at time t−1	−0.012	−0.013	0.005	−0.028
	(0.029)	(0.030)	(0.022)	(0.023)
Observations	1,631	1,631	5,791	5,791

Source: Authors' compilation based on PSID
Note: Robust standard errors clustered by family in parentheses. Models include dummy variables for each wave of data. Monetary values standardized to 2011 dollars.
+$p < 0.1$, *$p < 0.05$, **$p < 0.01$, ***$p < 0.001$

lack of association with baseline family wealth in our sample.

Directionality in the Health-Wealth Relationship

Tables A2 and A3 test the extent to which the onset of chronic illnesses and acute health shocks are related with baseline family wealth and prior changes in family wealth. In table A2, we regress the experience of either type of health event on the log of family wealth at time t−1. Results show that baseline family wealth predicts the onset of chronic illnesses for men but fails to predict acute health shocks for men and women in our sample. Table A3 assesses whether changes in family wealth may spur the onset of chronic conditions and acute health events. Although an increase in the log of family wealth from t−2 to t−1 predicts the onset of chronic illnesses between t−1 and t, we see that prior changes in the log of family wealth are not related with the experience of an acute health shock for married and cohabitating men and women.

Table A3. Logit Regressions of Chronic and Acute Illnesses on Changes in Log Family Wealth

	Black		White	
	Man	Woman	Man	Woman
	\multicolumn{4}{c}{Onset of Chronic Illness}			
Change in log family wealth from time t–2 to t–1	−0.008 (0.030)	0.025 (0.030)	0.046+ (0.027)	0.007 (0.025)
Observations	1,369	1,369	4,870	4,870
	\multicolumn{4}{c}{Onset of Acute Illness}			
Change in log family wealth from time t–2 to t–1	0.037 (0.036)	0.054 (0.041)	0.031 (0.029)	0.043 (0.040)
Observations	1,369	1,369	4,870	4,870

Source: Authors' compilation based on PSID.
Note: Robust standard errors clustered by family in parentheses. Models include dummy variables for each wave of data. Monetary values standardized to 2011 dollars.
+$p < 0.1$, *$p < 0.05$, **$p < 0.01$, ***$p < 0.001$

Figure A1. Median Health-Care Expenses Following Acute Health Shock

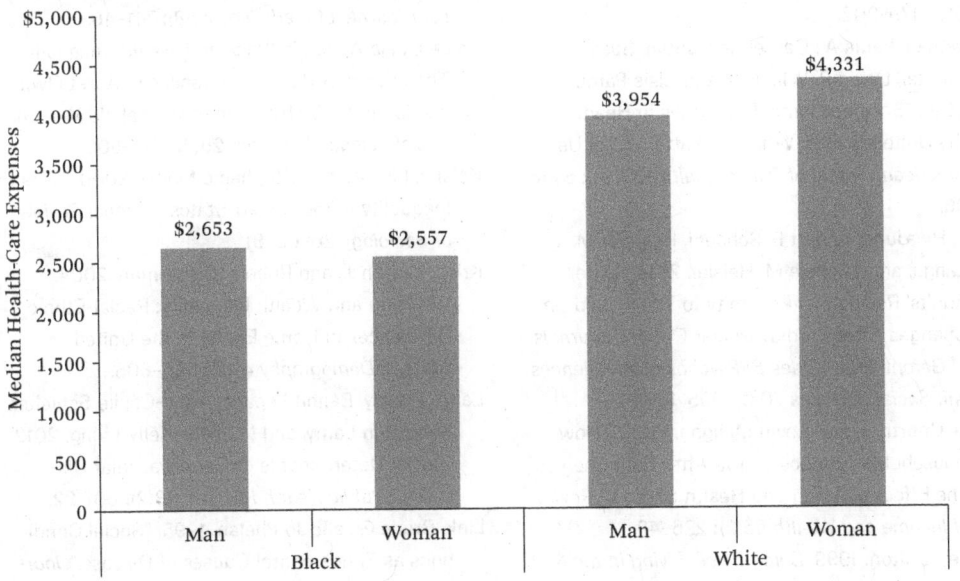

Source: Authors' compilation based on PSID.

Health-Care Expenses Following Acute Health Shocks

Prior literature highlights health-care costs as a way in which acute health shocks may affect family wealth (Smith 1999; Wu 2003). However, the health-care costs shown in figure A1 are relatively small in comparison with the total drain in family wealth. Following acute health shocks, the median health-care expenditure for black families is nearly $2,600, whereas that for white families is between $4,000 and $4,300. In contrast, a black family with median wealth after an acute health shock would lose approximately $40,000 and a white family more than $65,000. These findings corroborate earlier studies suggesting that the drain on wealth following the experience of a severe illness far outweighs the costs incurred from medical expenses (Poterba, Venti, and Wise 2010).

REFERENCES

Adler, Nancy, and Joan Ostrove. 1999. "Socioeconomic Status and Health: What We Know and What We Don't." *Annals of the New York Academy of Sciences* 896(1): 3–15.

Bibbins-Domingo, Kirsten, Mark J. Pletcher, Feng Lin, Eric Vittinghoff, Julius M. Gardin, Alexander Arynchyn, Cora E. Lewis, O. Dale Williams, and Stephen B. Hulley. 2009. "Racial Differences in Incident Heart Failure Among Young Adults." *New England Journal of Medicine* 360(12): 1179–90.

Bound, John, Michael Schoenbaum, Todd R. Stinebrickner, and Timothy Waidmann. 1999. "The Dynamic Effects of Health on the Labor Force Transitions of Older Workers." *Labour Economics* 6(2): 179–202.

Braveman, Paula A., Catherine Cubbin, Susan Egerter, David R. Williams, and Elsie Pamuk. 2010. "Socioeconomic Disparities in Health in the United States: What the Patterns Tell Us." *American Journal of Public Health* 100(S1): S186–96.

Choi, HwaJung, Robert F. Schoeni, Kenneth M. Langa, and Michele M. Heisler. 2014. "Older Adults' Residential Proximity to Their Children: Changes After Cardiovascular Events." *Journals of Gerontology, Series B: Psychological Sciences and Social Sciences* 70(6): 995–1004.

Coile, Courtney, and Kevin Milligan. 2009. "How Household Portfolios Evolve After Retirement: The Effect of Aging and Health Shocks." *Review of Income and Wealth* 55(2): 226–48.

Conley, Dalton. 1999. *Being Black, Living in the Red: Race, Wealth, and Social Policy in America.* Berkeley: University of California Press.

Conley, Dalton, and Jason Thompson. 2013. "The Effects of Health and Wealth Shocks on Retirement Decisions." *Federal Reserve Bank of St. Louis Review* 95(5): 389–404.

Devlin-Foltz, Sebastian, Alice Henriques, and John Sabelhaus. 2016. "Is the U.S. Retirement System Contributing to Rising Wealth Inequality." *RSF: The Russell Sage Foundation Journal of the Social Sciences* 2(6). doi: 10.7758/RSF.2016.2.6.04.

Eads, Alicia, and Laura Tach. 2016. "Wealth and Inequality in the Stability of Romantic Relationships." *RSF: The Russell Sage Foundation Journal of the Social Sciences* 2(6). doi: 10.7758/RSF.2016.2.6.10.

Haas, Steven A. 2006. "Health Selection and the Process of Social Stratification: The Effect of Childhood Health on Socioeconomic Attainment." *Journal of Health and Social Behavior* 47(4): 339–54.

Hadley, Jack. 2003. "Sicker and Poorer—The Consequences of Being Uninsured: A Review of the Research on the Relationship Between Health Insurance, Medical Care Use, Health, Work, and Income." *Medical Care Research and Review* 60(2): 3–75.

Himmelstein, David U., Elizabeth Warren, Deborah Thorne, and Steffie Woolhandler. 2005. "Illness and Injury as Contributors to Bankruptcy." *Health Affairs* W5-63-73.

———. 2009. "Medical Bankruptcy in the United States, 2007: Results of a National Study." *American Journal of Medicine* 122(8): 741–46.

Keister, Lisa A. 2000. "Race and Wealth Inequality: The Impact of Racial Differences in Asset Ownership on the Distribution of Household Wealth." *Social Science Research* 29(4): 477–502.

Keister, Lisa A., and Stephanie Moller. 2000. "Wealth Inequality in the United States." *Annual Review of Sociology* 26: 63–81.

Krivo, Lauren J., and Robert L. Kaufman. 2004. "Housing and Wealth Inequality: Racial-Ethnic Differences in Home Equity in the United States." *Demography* 41(3): 585–605.

Lang, Thierry, Benoit Lepage, Anne-Cécile Schieber, Sébastien Lamy, and Michelle Kelly-Irving. 2012. "Social Determinants of Cardiovascular Diseases." *Public Health Reviews* 33(2): 601–22.

Link, Bruce G., and Jo Phelan. 1995. "Social Conditions as Fundamental Causes of Disease." *Journal of Health and Social Behavior* 35(1): 80–94.

Mohanan, Manoj. 2013. "Causal Effects of Health Shocks on Consumption and Debt: Quasi-Experimental Evidence from Bus Accident Injuries." *Review of Economics and Statistics* 95(2): 673–81.

Oliver, Melvin, and Thomas Shapiro. 1995. *Black Wealth/White Wealth: A New Perspective on Racial Inequality.* New York: Routledge.

Pfeffer, Fabian T., and Robert F. Schoeni. 2016. "How Wealth Inequality Shapes Our Future." *RSF: The Russell Sage Foundation Journal of the Social Sciences* 2(6). doi: 10.7758/RSF.2016.2.6.01.

Poterba, James, Steven Venti, and David Wise. 2010. "The Asset Cost of Poor Health." *NBER* working paper series no. 16389. Cambridge, Mass.: National Bureau of Economic Research.

Ross, Catherine E., and Chia-ling Wu. 1995. "The Links Between Education and Health." *American Sociological Review* 60(5): 719–45.

Siegel, Rebecca, Deepa Naishadham, and Ahmedin Jemal. 2012. "Cancer Statistics, 2012." *CA: A Cancer Journal for Clinicians* 62(1): 10–29.

Smith, James P. 1999. "Healthy Bodies and Thick Wallets: The Dual Relation Between Health and Economic Status." *Journal of Economic Perspectives* 13(2): 145–66.

———. 2001. "Why Is Wealth Inequality Rising?" In *The Causes and Consequences of Increasing Inequality*, edited by Finis Welch. Chicago: University of Chicago Press.

———. 2004. "Unraveling the SES-Health Connection." *Population and Development Review* 30 (Supplement): 108–32.

Thompson, Jeffrey P., and Gustavo A. Suarez. 2015. "Exploring the Racial Wealth Gap Using the Survey of Consumer Finances." *FEDS* working paper no. 2015-76. Washington: Federal Reserve System. doi: 10.17016/FEDS.2015.076.

Williams, David R., and Chiquita Collins. 1995. "U.S. Socioeconomic and Racial Differences in Health: Patterns and Explanations." *Annual Review of Sociology* 21: 349–86.

Williams, David R., and Pamela B. Jackson. 2005. "Social Sources of Racial Disparities in Health." *Health Affairs*. 24(2): 325–34.

Williams, David R., Selina A. Mohammed, Jacinta Leavell, and Chiquita Collins. 2010. "Race, Socioeconomic Status, and Health: Complexities, Ongoing Challenges, and Research Opportunities." *Annals of the New York Academy of Sciences* 1186(1): 69–101.

Wolff, Edward N. 2016. "Household Wealth Trends in the United States, 1962 to 2013: What Happened over the Great Recession?" *RSF: The Russell Sage Foundation Journal of the Social Sciences* 2(6). doi: 10.7758/RSF.2016.2.6.02.

Wu, Stephen. 2003. "The Effects of Health Events on the Economic Status of Married Couples." *Journal of Human Resources* 47(3): 219–30.

Zajacova, Anna, Jennifer B. Dowd, Robert F. Schoeni, and Robert B. Wallace. 2015. "Employment and Income Losses Among Cancer Survivors: Estimates from a National Longitudinal Survey of American Families." *Cancer* 121(24): 4425–32.

Passing It On: Parent-to-Adult Child Financial Transfers for School and Socioeconomic Attainment

EMILY RAUSCHER

As wealth inequality increases, the importance of parental financial transfers for socioeconomic attainment may also rise. Using data from the 2013 Panel Study of Income Dynamics Rosters and Transfers Module, this study investigates two questions: how parental financial transfers for education have changed over time, and what the relationship is between these transfers and adult socioeconomic outcomes. Results suggest that transfers for education have increased, have become more commonplace, and have become more dependent on parental wealth over time. Holding constant several individual and parental measures, the relationship between parental transfers for school and adult socioeconomic attainment is positive. This relationship holds when using three-stage least squares models to account for potential endogeneity of financial transfers for school. Overall, results support arguments that parental financial transfers for education facilitate the intergenerational transmission of socioeconomic standing.

Keywords: financial transfers, socioeconomic attainment, intergenerational inequality, education

Receiving financial help from parents after reaching adulthood contradicts American individualistic explanations for status attainment (Davis and Moore 1945; Sewell and Shah 1977). Yet, according to one estimate, 34 percent of young adults receive financial transfers from parents at some point during their transition to adulthood, and these transfers are more common among high-income families (Schoeni and Ross 2005, 402).

As wealth inequality increases (Piketty 2014; Keister 2000; Wolff 1995, 2006, this volume), the importance of parental financial transfers for individual outcomes may also rise. Coupled with rising college tuition costs, the unequal ability of parents to pay for their children's postsecondary education could increase inequality in graduation rates, student loan debt, or educational quality (Armstrong and Hamilton 2013; Houle 2013; Carnevale and Strohl 2010; Hoxby and Avery 2013). Unequal access to education has broad and enduring implications for adult outcomes, including income and wealth (Card 1999; Boshara, Emmons, and Noeth 2015). Thus, one potential consequence of wealth inequality could be unequal financial support for education and, in turn, increasingly unequal outcomes in the next generation of adults.

How have parental financial transfers for school changed over time? Have they increased or become more dependent on wealth as wealth inequality has increased? Furthermore, what is the relationship between these transfers for school and adult socioeconomic outcomes, including education, income, and wealth? If fed-

Emily Rauscher is assistant professor of sociology at the University of Kansas.

This research was supported by the Center on Assets, Education, and Inclusion in the School of Social Welfare of the University of Kansas. I am grateful to the participants of the Russell Sage Foundation workshop, the volume editors, and anonymous reviewers for helpful comments. Direct correspondence to: Emily Rauscher at emily.rauscher@ku.edu, 716 Fraser Hall, 1415 Jayhawk Blvd. Lawrence, KS 66045.

eral or institutional support makes up for lower parental support among low-wealth students, there may be no relationship between parental transfers and socioeconomic outcomes. Wealthy families may provide more financial support for their children's education because they qualify for less need-based aid or their children attend more expensive institutions. At the same time, however, students from wealthy backgrounds may qualify for more academic scholarships because they had higher quality early education; they also may be savvier about applying to multiple schools and choosing the one that offers the best financial award package—reducing the amount of financial support from parents. In other words, the relationships between parental wealth, parental financial transfers to young adults for education, and socioeconomic attainment in adulthood are unclear.

Existing research on parental financial transfers tends to rely on older data. I address these questions using recently released data from the 2013 Panel Study of Income Dynamics (PSID) Rosters and Transfers Module. The PSID data allow analysis of changes in parental financial transfers over time as well as examination of the relationship between these transfers and adult socioeconomic outcomes.

THEORETICAL AND EMPIRICAL BACKGROUND

To provide background for this study, I review research on parent-to-adult child transfers, the relationship of these transfers to inequality and education, the transition to adulthood, and the relationship between wealth and child outcomes.

Parent-to-Adult Child Transfers

A financial transfer from a living parent is called an *inter vivos* transfer, to distinguish it from financial transfers or bequests to adult children after the death of a parent. A long line of research theorizes and investigates relationships—including transfers—between parents and their adult children (Parsons 1943; Stack 1974; Becker 1981; Hogan, Eggebeen, and Clogg 1993; Sarkisian and Gerstel 2004; for reviews, see Lye 1996; Swartz 2009; Seltzer and Bianchi 2013). Much of the research on transfers attempts to understand the motivation for *inter vivos* transfers (Becker 1981; Hogan, Eggebeen, and Clogg 1993; Eggebeen and Hogan 1990; Kohli and Kunemund 2003; Yamada 2006), document the consequences of divorce (Furstenberg, Hoffman, and Shrestha 1995; White 1992; Eggebeen 1992), or explain variation by race, gender, or other demographic characteristics (Sarkisian and Gerstel 2004; Berry 2006; Eggebeen and Hogan 1990). In a related area of research, evidence from Europe documents the relationship between *inter vivos* transfers and welfare regimes or state support for the elderly (Attias-Donfut, Ogg, and Wolff 2005; Albertini, Kohli, and Vogel 2007), echoing evidence from the United States that parental financial transfers differ by parental income. For example, Robert Schoeni and Karen Ross find that compared with young adults (ages eighteen to thirty-four) from families in the bottom half of the income distribution, those in the top quartile received nearly three times as much financial support from parents (2005, 411).

Only recently has research begun to investigate the potential consequences of parent-to-adult child transfers. For example, Claire Scodellaro, Myriam Khlat, and Florence Jusot (2012) find that transfer receipt is associated with health in a French sample. Others find evidence that parental transfers are associated with unequal living standards and adult socioeconomic outcomes (Semyonov and Lewin-Epstein 2001; Swartz 2008, 2009). These unequal outcomes make sense in light of the evidence showing substantial differences in financial transfers from parents to young adult children by parental income (McGarry and Schoeni 1995). This and other evidence, however, is based on relatively old data. For example, Schoeni and Ross rely on data from the 1988 PSID for their transfer analyses (2005). As Judith Seltzer and Suzanne Bianchi note, "A surprising number of articles on intergenerational relationships still rely on the first two waves of the NSFH [National Survey of Families and Households] begun in 1987–1988" (2013, 285). Thus, descriptive information on intergenerational financial transfers in the United States would benefit from more recent information, such as that available in the 2013 PSID Rosters and Transfers Module.

A small literature examines financial transfers for specific purposes, including education. Moshe Semyonov and Noah Lewin-Epstein (2001), for example, examine the association between adult living standards and parental transfers for education or the purchase of a house. Relying on an Israeli sample, however, their findings may not be generalizable to the United States. Other evidence suggests families with more children provide less college financial support for each one (Henretta et al. 2012; Steelman and Powell 1989, 1991; Yilmazer 2008) or that parental financial support for college may depend on the sex composition of children (Powell and Steelman 1989). Research, however, tends not to investigate variation in intergenerational transfers over time.

Thus, although class inequality in transfers is well documented (Eggebeen and Hogan 1990; McGarry and Schoeni 1995; Schoeni and Ross 2005), in many cases this evidence relies on data from two decades ago, and little research investigates changes in transfers over time or the relationship between transfers for education and socioeconomic attainment.

Inequality, Education, and Parental Transfers
Unequal parental financial transfers for education have potentially long-lasting consequences. For example, research suggests intergenerational mobility varies by level of education. Comparing mobility among college graduates with that among others, evidence shows greater mobility among those with a degree (Torche 2011; Hout 1988). Not surprisingly, however, a college degree is not equally available to all (Carnevale and Strohl 2010; Haskins 2008). At the admission stage, student SAT scores are correlated with family income (Balf 2014), youth from families with lower socioeconomic status (SES) are less likely to apply to highly selective schools that provide more financial aid (Hoxby and Avery 2013), and higher SES families enjoy advantages in admission, grooming children from a young age to ensure acceptance to a selective postsecondary school (Stevens 2007).

After admission, the likelihood of graduating within six years remains unequal by socioeconomic background (Bowen, Chingos, and McPherson 2009). Enjoying financial support from parents, young adults from higher SES families can forgo work to focus on studies or social activities (Walpole 2003; Hamilton 2013). Alternatively, those from working-class backgrounds can borrow to pay for college but face daunting student loans, which can encourage dropout or limit choices after graduation (Armstrong and Hamilton 2013; Houle 2013).

By influencing the quantity and quality of education received, parental financial transfers for education may have meaningful implications for adult outcomes. Using survey data from Europe, Marco Albertini and Jonas Radl (2012) find evidence that financial transfers help reproduce inequality of occupational status across generations. Given higher costs of postsecondary education in the United States, parental transfers for education may play a similar role in reproducing inequality across generations in the United States.

Extended Adolescence
Parental transfers for education may be particularly important for adult socioeconomic outcomes in the contemporary context, which offers limited opportunity for early economic independence. Life-course theorists argue that the period between adolescence and adulthood has extended in recent decades and is now a distinct life stage, which some refer to as "emerging adulthood" or "extended adolescence" (Arnett 2000; Settersten, Furstenberg, and Rumbaut 2005). Evidence suggests this extension may be due to economic changes (Danziger and Rouse 2007). Regardless of the causes, however, young adults are undoubtedly struggling to establish themselves in the current social context (Silva 2013; Danziger and Rouse 2007; Newman 2013). Furthermore, this extended period of dependence on parental resources seems unlikely to shrink in the near future, given economic trends and the erosion of the social safety net (Kalleberg 2009; Hacker 2006).

As contemporary young adults struggle to complete their education, find a job that pays a living wage, pay off student loans, or afford health insurance (Danziger and Rouse 2007), those who received parental financial support for school may face fewer barriers to independence and greater opportunity to capitalize on their education. For example, parental transfers could prevent young adults from having to accrue student debt, which could allow them to take better advantage of their school experience, pursue further education, or accept a coveted but unpaid internship. At the same time, college tuition costs have risen and wealth inequality has increased in recent decades (College Board 2015; Piketty 2014; Keister 2000; Wolff 1995, 2006, this volume). Along with these economic changes, parental financial transfers for school may have increased over time, playing a greater role in the lives of contemporary emerging adults.

Wealth Inequality and Child Outcomes
Wealth has implications for a wide variety of outcomes, including health (Thompson and Conley, this volume; Pollack et al. 2007), intelligence (Mani et al. 2013), and educational attainment (Conley 2001; Pfeffer 2011, 2015). In fact, Fabian Pfeffer and Alexandra Killewald (2015) find that children's educational attainment plays a major role in the intergenerational transmission of wealth. Wealth gaps in education may reflect differences in parenting behaviors, preschool attendance, school quality at the elementary and secondary level, parental financial support for postsecondary education, or "real and psychological safety nets" (Shapiro 2004, 11), among other things. Although evidence suggests the importance of parental wealth for postsecondary education (Conley 2001; Pfeffer 2015), it is unclear to what extent this reflects parental transfers for college as opposed to earlier investments in education or some other factor. Learning more about the mechanisms involved will help in understanding the potential consequences of growing wealth inequality and policies that could improve equality of opportunity. As the distribution of wealth and therefore of families' ability to support their young adult children becomes increasingly unequal (Piketty 2014), parental transfers may become more unequal and their importance for individual outcomes may also rise.

Although some suggest that recent increases in wealth inequality are driven largely by gains among the top 0.1 percent of wealth holders (Saez and Zucman 2015), Fabian Pfeffer and Robert Schoeni point out (in this volume) that inequality has increased throughout the distribution and particularly for families with children. Thus, the growing wealth gap has implications for the ability of families throughout the wealth distribution to finance postsecondary education.

At the same time, parental transfers could contribute to wealth inequality. As of 1983, for example, evidence from Edward Wolff (1992) suggests that financial transfers from living parents accounted for half of the wealth of those born after 1933. More recently, Lingxin Hao (1996) finds evidence that financial transfers are positively associated with wealth among families with children. Thus, the relationship between parental financial transfers for education and wealth inequality may be reciprocal. I address potential endogeneity in this study but focus on assessing whether an association exists.

Several questions remain. How have parental financial transfers for school changed over time? Wealthier parents have more funds to transfer to their adult children, so their transfers will likely be higher. To what extent, however, is wealth related to transfers? Have transfers increased or become more dependent on parental wealth as wealth inequality increased? Furthermore, what is the relationship between these transfers for school and adult socioeconomic attainment, including education, income, and wealth?

HYPOTHESES
A growing body of evidence illustrates that early childhood investment is critical for successful development (Heckman and Masterov 2007; Heckman 2006). If early childhood is so critical, perhaps any meaningful benefits of parental support occur earlier in life and transfers in adulthood are redundant, with no bearing on adult outcomes. Hypothesis 1 is that parental transfers to young adult children for education are not associated with adult socioeconomic outcomes when holding parental SES measures constant.

Alternatively, parental transfers could promote a sense of entitlement, sap motivation, or promote laziness. For example, Laura Hamilton (2013) finds that parental support for college encourages students to adopt a strategy of "satisficing"—doing the minimum acceptable amount of school work and earning lower grades to meet graduation requirements. If parental financial transfers encourage satisficing behavior in school or other realms of life, young adults receiving transfers could find themselves outstudied and outearned on the job market by young adults who did not enjoy parental financial support. In other words, parental transfers could be negatively associated with adult SES outcomes. Hypothesis 2 is that parental transfers for education are negatively associated with adult socioeconomic outcomes.

The difficulties and experiences of contemporary young adults, however, suggest that parental support during young adulthood may have nontrivial consequences for adult outcomes (Silva 2013). Consistent with findings from Europe (Albertini and Radl 2012), parental transfers may help to reproduce inequality across generations. In the context of rising tuition costs and extended adolescence, parental transfers for education may be particularly important for young adult outcomes. Hypothesis 3 is that parental financial transfers for education are positively associated with adult socioeconomic outcomes.

DATA AND METHODS

The Rosters and Transfers Module of the Panel Study of Income Dynamics provides recent and long-term transfer information between parents and adult children from 9,107 families who participated in the 2013 survey. These data are linked to individual and household information from the regular PSID surveys using the child's 1968 interview and person number. Individual and household information for mothers and fathers are also linked using the Family Identification Mapping System provided by the PSID.

The sample is limited to those with parental transfer information who were older than twenty-two in 2013, the year income and financial transfers were measured. The sample therefore includes cohorts born between 1943 and 1990, who turned eighteen between 1961 and 2008. The main analyses include those with maternal measures, including education, household income and wealth, marital status, age, race, and ethnicity. These measures are calculated separately for each parent in case of divorce or separation. Sensitivity analyses using paternal measures allow a smaller sample size (because 23 percent of the main sample is missing paternal measures) but yield similar results (see the online supplement, tables 1 through 10).

I limit the sample to those over age twenty-two to ensure that all individuals are beyond the traditional college completion age, the period during which the majority of parent-to-child transfers for school likely occur. One potential concern is that children from wealthier or higher SES families may have received transfers for school after that age—to complete graduate degrees, for example. To address this concern, I conduct two sets of sensitivity analyses limited to those who were older than thirty and older than thirty-four in 2013. These results are consistent with the main analyses and are presented in table A1. In a second step to address concern that those from wealthier families received transfers after college, I compare the amount of financial transfers for any purpose between parents and children in 2012 (the year before the 2013 Rosters and Transfers Module) by cohort and parental wealth. The comparisons suggest low-wealth parents (below the median) gave their young adult children (ages twenty-three through twenty-nine) more money and received less money from them in 2012 than high-wealth parents (see table A2). Among cohorts in their thirties, those with wealthier parents received slightly more money from their parents on average than those with poorer parents ($10 more among those age thirty to thirty-four and $28 more among those age thirty-five to thirty-nine) but gave their parents quite a bit more than those with poorer parents ($1,712 among those age thirty to thirty-four and $1,569 among those age thirty-five to thirty-nine). Thus, young adults from wealthier families do not appear to receive more from their parents than others, whether before or after age thirty. In fact, at least in 2012, adult children from both high- and low-wealth backgrounds gave their parents more than they received.

The modest average transfer amounts suggest the PSID transfer data may not capture large transfers among the very wealthy. Individuals in the data may fail to report all transfers or very wealthy individuals may fail to appear in the data. These are limitations of the data and results should be interpreted with these limitations in mind.

Measures

Parental transfers for school measure the total amount of money parents report giving their child for school since age eighteen in the 2013 Rosters and Transfers Module. Transfers are adjusted for inflation based on the year in which the child turned eighteen, but results are similar using unadjusted values (see table A3). In some cases, children appear more than once in the data (if their parents are divorced and both parents completed the survey, for example). In those cases, the total amount of transfers from both parents is calculated. The long-term transfer question in the 2013 module requires parents to recall how much financial support they gave their child for education since that child turned eighteen. Depending on the child's age, this could be a long period. Given the potential for recall bias, this retrospective reporting is less than ideal. The 2013 data provide more recent information over a longer range of cohorts than available in most existing research on parental transfers, which similarly relies on retrospective reports. Nevertheless, parental transfers may be measured with error.

In an effort to address concern about potential measurement error, I conduct sensitivity analyses limited to those who were younger than thirty in 2013. The recall period is shorter for these cohorts and transfers should therefore be measured with less error. However, because these cohorts are young, they are unlikely to have reached full earning potential and may not be employed. Financial transfers for school have had little time to generate any implications for income or wealth among young cohorts. The results, presented in table A4, are consistent with the main analyses, but the coefficients for parental transfers predictably do not reach significance in models predicting wealth (and in one model predicting household income).

Education is measured in years for both individuals and their parents and represents the highest grade or year of school completed. Individual education is measured in 2013. Father's and mother's education are the highest education reported for each parent from any previous wave of the PSID (1968 to 2011). Maximum parental education provides the best measure of parental educational attainment, even if it occurred after the traditional age.

Individual income is total household income in 2012 (reported in the 2013 survey and converted to 2013 dollars using the Bureau of Labor Statistics Consumer Price Index Inflation Calculator) and includes income of all members in the family unit. Parental income is the total household income of the mother's or father's household (measured separately in case parents are divorced or separated) the year the individual was seventeen years old (converted to 2013 dollars). Income is measured when the child was seventeen because it provides the parental income measure closest to but before the year the child turned eighteen. This parental income measure partially assesses parents' ability to support their child's postsecondary education and would be the year of income reported on initial financial aid applications for those attending college at the traditional age. Because parental income and ability to support a child could vary by parental age, I also measure (and control for) parental age when the child was seventeen.

Individual wealth is the sum of all family assets in 2013, including home equity and net of debt. Parental wealth is the same statistic in the year with available wealth data closest to the year the child was seventeen (converted to 2013 dollars). The PSID collected wealth in 1984, 1989, 1994, 1999, and every two years after that through 2013. For the earliest cohorts, the measure of parental wealth is just over twenty years after the child was seventeen. Fewer individuals are in the earlier cohorts of the sample; however, for approximately 27 percent of the sample, parental wealth is measured more than two years from when the individual was seventeen. Because of the potential measurement error, I do not control for parental wealth in the main analyses. Supplemental analyses controlling for parental wealth are presented in the online supplement (tables 11 through 13) and yield similar results. Models using parental wealth to predict the amount of financial transfers for school yield similar results when limited to those who turned eighteen after 1981 (for whom parental wealth is measured within two years of when the individual was seventeen).

Because financial transfers for school, household income, and wealth are skewed, I use transformed measures in regressions. I take the natural log of transfers and total individual and parental household income plus one, to include those with zero values. Some households have negative values for wealth. To reduce skewness without excluding those with zero or negative wealth values, I take the inverse hyperbolic sine (IHS) of wealth. Research suggests that the IHS transformation is methodologically sound and superior to other transformations in its retention of negative wealth values (Burbidge, Magee, and Robb 1988; MacKinnon and Magee 1990; Pence 2006). All currency is either measured in or converted to 2013 dollars to adjust for inflation using the Bureau of Labor Statistics consumer price index inflation calculator.

I also measure and control for the child's number of siblings. Parental financial support for education is related to the number of siblings a child has, likely because parental assets are typically divided among all their children (Henretta et al. 2012; Steelman and Powell 1989, 1991; Yilmazer 2008). Beyond number of siblings, I use family birth information to measure whether the first two children born to the individual's mother are the same sex and whether her first child is male. Dalton Conley and Rebecca Glauber note that parents in the United States prefer to have children of both sexes: "Families with two same-sex children (either two boys or two girls) are about seven percentage points more likely to have a third child than are families with two opposite sex children" (2008, 723). Conley and Glauber use the sex mix of the first two children in a family as an instrument for sibship size to estimate its effect on educational outcomes. Others use sibling sex composition as an instrument to investigate adult labor market (Angrist and Evans 1998) and educational outcomes (Goux and Maurin 2005; Currie and Yelowitz 2000).

Furthermore, some evidence suggests parental financial support for college and child educational outcomes may depend on the sex composition of children (Powell and Steelman 1989, 1990). I use indicators for whether the first two children born to the individual's mother are the same sex and whether the first child is male, along with indicators for each birth year, as exogenous variables in three-stage least squares (3SLS) analyses to help address potential endogeneity of parental financial transfers.

Parental ability to offer their children financial assistance also depends on marital status (Amato, Rezac, and Booth 1995) and race (Conley 1999; Shapiro 2004). I therefore control for parental marital status when the child was age seventeen and parental identification as African American, other nonwhite race, or Latino. Because many of the financial benefits of marriage accrue to cohabiters as well, marital status is an indicator for whether the mother or father was married or permanently cohabiting when the child was seventeen. Parental race and ethnicity are based on self-report. However, self-reported race depends on a variety of factors, including social context and question wording and—as in previous research (Kramer, Burke, and Charles 2015; Saperstein 2006)—is not consistent over time. Therefore, I average each self-reported race category (white, African American, other, and Latino) over all waves with nonmissing information and assign the parent to the category if the parent so identified at least half the time. For example, if a parent identified as Latino in at least half of the waves for which data are available, that individual is assigned a 1 for the Latino indicator. The process is the same for each racial category. Additional controls include individual birth year and gender.

Analysis

To address the first question about how parental financial transfers for school have changed over time, I aggregate transfer information by cohort and graph the pattern over time. I also examine differences in parental financial transfers for school by wealth and whether parental wealth has become more important for predicting transfers over time.

To address the second question about the relationship between transfers for school and adult SES outcomes, I use ordinary least squares (OLS) and 3SLS regression models. In OLS models, I regress individual outcomes (including education, income, and wealth) on the amount of parental financial transfers for education, an indicator for whether parents gave the individual no money for school, and control variables (including birth year, gender, number of siblings, parental education, parental income when child was seventeen, parental age when child was seventeen, parental marital status when child was seventeen, and parental race and ethnicity). The OLS model is as follows:

$$\text{Outcome}_i = \alpha + \beta_1 \text{Transfer Amount}_i + \beta_2 \text{No Transfers}_i + \beta_k \text{Controls}_i + \varepsilon_i$$

The coefficients of interest, β_1 and β_2, measure the relationship between the outcome and parental transfer amount and receipt, adjusted for individual and parental differences. All analyses are weighted using the 2013 PSID longitudinal weight, and standard errors are robust to potential heteroskedasticity.

In some cases, control measures limit the sample size or may raise concerns about multicollinearity, particularly between amount of parental transfers for education and the indicator for receipt of any transfers for education. I therefore show results from models limited to those who received at least some financial assistance from parents. As a sensitivity analysis, I also fit the models with controls limited to birth year, gender, and parental education, age, and income or further limited to only birth year and gender. Results are consistent in both cases, and the latter results are shown in table A5.

This study investigates whether an association exists between parental transfers for education and adult socioeconomic outcomes. It cannot establish a causal relationship because multiple unobserved factors, including parental characteristics or individual ability, could influence both parental transfers and child attainment as an adult. An association is of interest because it would suggest that parental transfers are one mechanism through which parents may pass advantage on to their children. However, in an attempt to address concern about a potential spurious relationship, I also conduct 3SLS analyses, using two measures of sibling sex composition and birth year indicators as exogenous variables to adjust for endogeneity of parental financial transfers for school and number of siblings. As in previous analyses using sibling sex composition as an instrument (Conley and Glauber 2008), to increase precision, I limit the 3SLS sample based on number of siblings. Because sibling sex composition affects whether families with two children have more children, I limit the sample to those with one to three siblings.

Briefly, 3SLS uses the exogenous variables in the model to predict instrumented values of the endogenous variables (Zellner and Theil 1962). Similar to an instrumental variable analysis, the instrumented values are the predicted values of the endogenous variables after regressing them on all of the exogenous variables in the model. 3SLS uses these instrumented values to estimate a consistent covariance matrix and uses them both to fit the final model. The 3SLS results provide a more precise estimate of the relationship, after adjusting for potential endogeneity of parental transfers and number of siblings.

RESULTS

Table 1 presents descriptive information for the sample used in the main analyses. Descriptive information for paternal measures is provided in the online supplement table 1. These tables provide raw information about income, wealth, and parental transfers, because it is more meaningful than the transformed versions used in all regressions. On average, table 1 shows that individuals received over $13,000 from parents for school since they turned eighteen (in 2013 dollars). However, 75 percent received no educational transfers from parents.

Based on table 1, the sample completed an average of just over fourteen years of education. This reflects that nearly 34 percent of the sample did not complete more than a high school diploma and may therefore have accrued no postsecondary educational expenses. Approximately 26.6 percent completed more than twelve but fewer than sixteen years of ed-

Table 1. Descriptive Statistics

	Mean	SD	No Money for School	Any Money for School	T-test
Highest grade completed	14.17	2.12	13.67	15.69	**
Wealth ◊	$240,278.90	920423.20	$218,709.70	$303,991.50	**
Total household income •	$94,769.05	154050.10	$84,983.37	$123,648.70	**
Parental transfers for school	$13,117.77	40610.60	$0.00	$52,748.74	**
Received no transfers for school	0.75	0.43	1.00	0.00	N/A
Mother years of education	13.21	2.48	12.65	14.88	**
Mother age ‡	42.16	5.24	41.66	43.67	**
Mother household income ‡	$106,786.00	133906.90	$88,532.82	$161,931.90	**
Mother wealth ‡	$345,626.70	1450527.00	$257,080.60	$611,567.30	**
Mother married ‡	0.81	0.39	0.79	0.90	**
Mother white	0.82	0.38	0.79	0.93	**
Mother black	0.13	0.33	0.16	0.04	**
Mother other race	0.05	0.22	0.05	0.03	**
Mother Latino	0.06	0.24	0.07	0.02	**
Birth year	1972.19	11.74	1970.72	1976.63	**
Male	0.49	0.50	0.50	0.48	
Number of siblings	2.62	2.04	2.83	2.00	**
First two children same sex	0.51	0.50	0.51	0.50	
First child male	0.50	0.50	0.49	0.53	+
Married	0.54	0.50	0.54	0.53	
Family size	2.78	1.51	2.77	2.79	
Head of household white	0.83	0.38	0.80	0.92	**
Head of household black	0.13	0.34	0.16	0.04	**
Head of household other race	0.04	0.20	0.04	0.04	
Head of household Latino	0.08	0.27	0.09	0.05	**
N	4118		3200	918	
N ◊	4238		3277	961	
N •	4234		3273	961	

Source: Author's compilation based on PSID.
Note: The sample is limited to individuals who were older than twenty-two in 2013 with parental, transfer, sibling, and socioeconomic information. All currency is measured in 2013 dollars. Mother wealth, first two children same sex, first child male, head of household race, and head of household Latino have smaller sample sizes: N = 4092, 3843, 4036, 4099, and 4107, respectively. Descriptive statistics including paternal measures are shown in the online supplement table 1.
‡ Indicates measured when individual was seventeen years old (or the closest available time point in the case of parental wealth)
T-test indicates the significance level of a two-tailed t-test of the difference between those who received transfers for school and those who did not.
+p < 0.10, *p < 0.05, **p < 0.01

ucation, 22.6 percent completed sixteen years, and 17 percent completed more than sixteen. On average, the sample completed slightly more education but have lower household incomes than their parents (after adjusting for inflation).

Figure 1 graphs mean financial transfers for school (in both raw and 2013 dollars) by the year cohorts turned eighteen (in five-year cohort categories). The figure also shows changes in the proportion receiving no transfers for education by cohort. The figure illus-

Figure 1. Mean Parental Financial Transfers for School and Proportion Receiving No Money from Parents for School

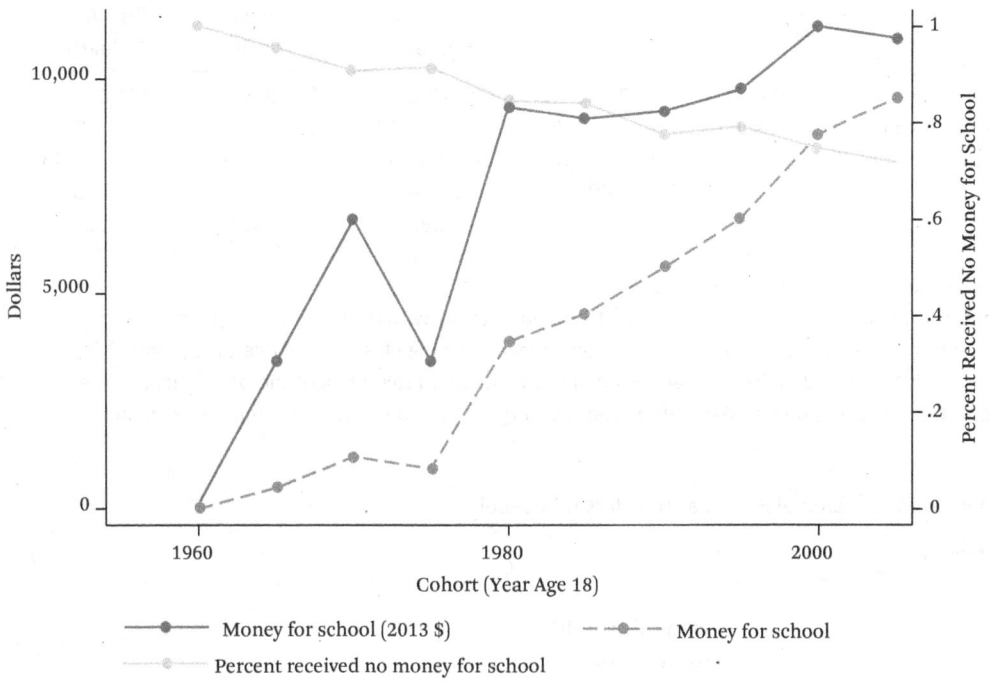

Source: Author's compilation based on PSID.
Note: Based on the sample in table 1. Money for School (2013 $) represents mean parental financial transfers for school by cohort, adjusted for inflation to 2013 dollars based on the year in which the individual turned eighteen.

trates that average parental financial transfers for school have increased over time—whether adjusting for inflation or not. At the same time, the proportion receiving no transfers for education has declined, suggesting parental assistance for education is becoming more common.

Table 1 compares mean values of those who received financial assistance from parents for education with those who did not. Educational attainment, wealth, and household income are significantly higher among those who received financial transfers ($p < 0.01$). Nearly all other measures differ significantly as well. For example, children who received transfers have fewer siblings and are from later cohorts ($p < 0.01$). Parents who gave their children money for school were older, completed more education, had higher income, and were more likely to be married when the child was seventeen years old ($p < 0.01$). These parents were also more likely to be white and less likely to be black or Latino ($p < 0.01$).

Table 2 shows differences in the amount and prevalence of transfers for school among those above and below median parental wealth as well as those in the top wealth quartile (see also figure 2). Young adults whose parental household wealth was above the median received more than seven times more money for school than those below. Excluding those who received no help for school, those above the median still received more than double those below. The gap is even wider when comparing transfers below the median with the top quartile. Those in the top quartile of parental wealth received more than eleven times more transfers for education than those below the median and more than three times more when limited to those who received some financial help for school. The proportion receiving transfers also differs by parental wealth. Only 13 percent of

Table 2. Transfers for School by Parental Wealth

	All	Below Median Wealth	Above Median Wealth	Top Wealth Quartile
Parental transfers for school	$13,035.20	$3,026.56	$23,048.32	$34,013.38
Received no transfers for school	0.75	0.87	0.63	0.57
Any money for school ◊	$52,185.30	$22,883.50	$62,739.27	$78,212.43
N	4092	2474	1618	775
N ◊	915	283	632	367

Source: Author's compilation based on PSID.
Note: Sample is the same as that in table 1, limited to those with parental wealth. Parental wealth is measured when the individual was seventeen years old (or the closest available time point). All currency is measured in 2013 dollars. Statistics are weighted to represent the population, so the proportion receiving no transfers differs slightly from calculation based on sample sizes alone.

Figure 2. Mean Parental Financial Transfers for School

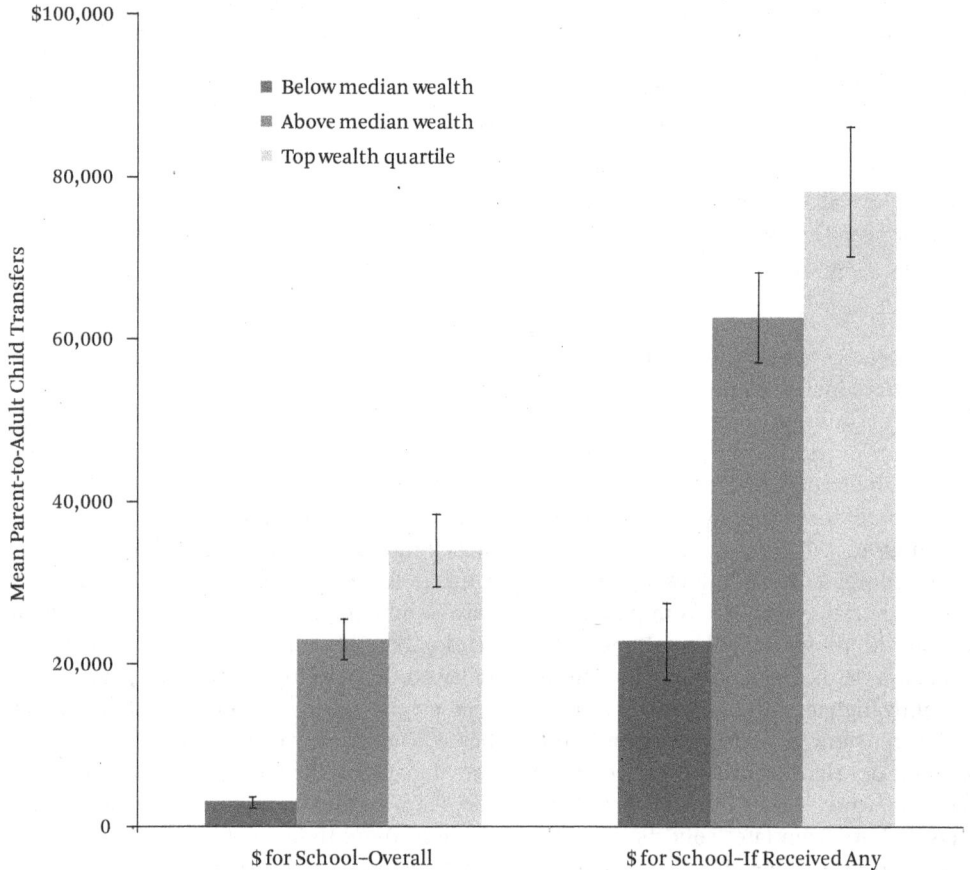

Source: Author's compilation based on PSID.
Note: Based on table 2.

Table 3. Predicted Parental Transfers for School

	Log Parental Transfers for School				
Variables	(1) <1963	(2) 1963-1973	(3) 1974-1982	(4) >1982	(5) All
IHS mother wealth ‡	-0.01	0.05+	0.07**	0.07**	-0.19**
	(0.03)	(0.03)	(0.02)	(0.02)	(0.04)
IHS mother wealth x birth year					0.01**
					(0.00)
Mother years of education	0.43**	0.67**	0.61**	0.39**	0.52**
	(0.08)	(0.09)	(0.06)	(0.06)	(0.03)
Mother age ‡	-0.03	0.03	0.00	0.15**	0.05**
	(0.03)	(0.03)	(0.03)	(0.03)	(0.01)
Log mother household income ‡	0.70**	0.47**	0.74**	1.07**	0.65**
	(0.23)	(0.12)	(0.19)	(0.21)	(0.10)
Mother married ‡	-0.06	0.53	0.41	0.77*	0.53**
	(0.41)	(0.43)	(0.36)	(0.37)	(0.20)
Mother black	-0.35	-0.48	-0.61+	-1.30**	-0.85**
	(0.24)	(0.35)	(0.34)	(0.36)	(0.17)
Mother other race	-1.27**	2.54	0.89	0.85	1.58**
	(0.28)	(2.56)	(0.94)	(0.64)	(0.50)
Mother Latina	-2.44**	-1.51**	0.02	-1.00+	-1.31**
	(0.76)	(0.51)	(0.95)	(0.58)	(0.38)
Male	0.30	-0.45	-0.28	-0.43	-0.20
	(0.25)	(0.33)	(0.27)	(0.27)	(0.14)
Number of siblings	-0.01	-0.18*	-0.14*	-0.13*	-0.11**
	(0.05)	(0.08)	(0.06)	(0.06)	(0.03)
Birth year (centered)	0.04	0.03	0.07	0.11	-0.01
	(0.03)	(0.05)	(0.06)	(0.07)	(0.01)
Constant	-11.73**	-14.14**	-16.79**	-25.82**	-13.56**
	(2.73)	(2.42)	(2.89)	(3.84)	(1.19)
Observations	733	819	1,353	1,307	4,212
R^2	0.13	0.20	0.24	0.36	0.26

Source: Author's compilation based on PSID.
Note: Sample is the same as that in table 1, limited to those with parental wealth. All currency is measured in 2013 dollars. Robust standard errors in parentheses
‡ Indicates measured when individual was seventeen years old.
+$p < 0.1$, *$p < 0.05$, **$p < 0.01$

young adults below the median received parental transfers for school, compared with 37 percent above the median and 43 percent in the top quartile.

Table 3 shows results of OLS regressions predicting the amount of parental transfers for school. Comparing the coefficient for household wealth over successive cohorts suggests that transfers became more dependent on parental wealth over time. All currency measures used in the regressions are adjusted to 2013 dollars, so changes over time are not due to inflation. Further supporting the increasing importance of wealth, the interaction term between household wealth and birth year in the final model is positive and significant ($p < 0.01$). Results using paternal measures are consistent (see online supplement table 3).

Table 4. Parental School Transfers and Adult Outcomes

Variables	(1) Highest Grade All	(2) Highest Grade Received Transfers	(3) IHS Wealth All	(4) IHS Wealth Received Transfers	(5) Log Hh Income All	(6) Log Hh Income Received Transfers
Log money for school	0.24**	0.39**	0.45*	0.21	0.07**	0.09**
	(0.04)	(0.04)	(0.20)	(0.24)	(0.02)	(0.02)
No money for school	1.10**		3.44+		0.44*	
	(0.41)		(2.06)		(0.21)	
Mother years of education	0.20**	0.07*	-0.02	-0.17	0.04**	0.01
	(0.02)	(0.03)	(0.08)	(0.17)	(0.01)	(0.02)
Mother age ‡	0.03**	0.00	0.11**	0.05	-0.00	-0.01
	(0.01)	(0.01)	(0.03)	(0.08)	(0.00)	(0.01)
Log mother household income ‡	0.22**	-0.01	0.43*	2.42**	0.13**	0.22**
	(0.06)	(0.08)	(0.19)	(0.50)	(0.04)	(0.06)
Mother married ‡	0.19+	0.17	1.11*	-0.38	0.24**	-0.02
	(0.11)	(0.23)	(0.49)	(1.22)	(0.07)	(0.12)
Mother black	-0.17	0.02	-1.99**	-0.99	-0.51**	-0.32*
	(0.11)	(0.32)	(0.52)	(1.78)	(0.08)	(0.14)
Mother other race	0.75**	0.15	-0.05	1.94	0.08	0.15
	(0.22)	(0.28)	(1.07)	(1.76)	(0.13)	(0.25)
Mother Latina	0.00	0.02	1.68+	-0.95	-0.02	0.06
	(0.24)	(0.50)	(0.88)	(2.56)	(0.11)	(0.20)
Birth year	-0.02**	-0.00	-0.20**	-0.23**	-0.01**	-0.02**
	(0.00)	(0.01)	(0.01)	(0.03)	(0.00)	(0.00)
Male	-0.31**	-0.26**	1.15**	0.30	0.08+	0.03
	(0.07)	(0.09)	(0.31)	(0.62)	(0.04)	(0.06)
Number of siblings	-0.10**	-0.03	0.04	0.16	-0.01	0.03
	(0.02)	(0.04)	(0.07)	(0.19)	(0.01)	(0.02)
Constant	37.15**	17.84	377.80**	430.69**	32.79**	45.02**
	(6.73)	(11.92)	(25.46)	(52.95)	(4.52)	(7.63)
Observations	4,118	918	4,238	961	4,234	961
R^2	0.29	0.21	0.10	0.09	0.12	0.13

Source: Author's compilation based on PSID.
Note: Sample is the same as that in table 1. Even-numbered models labeled Received Transfers are limited to those who received parental transfers for school. All currency is measured in 2013 dollars. Robust standard errors in parentheses.
‡ Indicates measured when individual was seventeen years old.
+$p < 0.1$, *$p < 0.05$, **$p < 0.01$

Parental differences between those who received or did not receive educational transfers seem to reflect financial differences in ability to assist children with their education. Racial differences in wealth are well established (Conley 1999; Shapiro 2004) and parents with higher wealth, income, and education are better able to support their children's education (Lareau and Cox 2011; Conley 2001). Holding these factors constant, is there still a relationship between parental transfers and socioeconomic outcomes?

Regression results—shown in table 4—suggest that financial support from parents for school is positively associated with educational attainment, wealth, and household income,

Figure 3. Adult Household Income and Parental Financial Transfers for Education

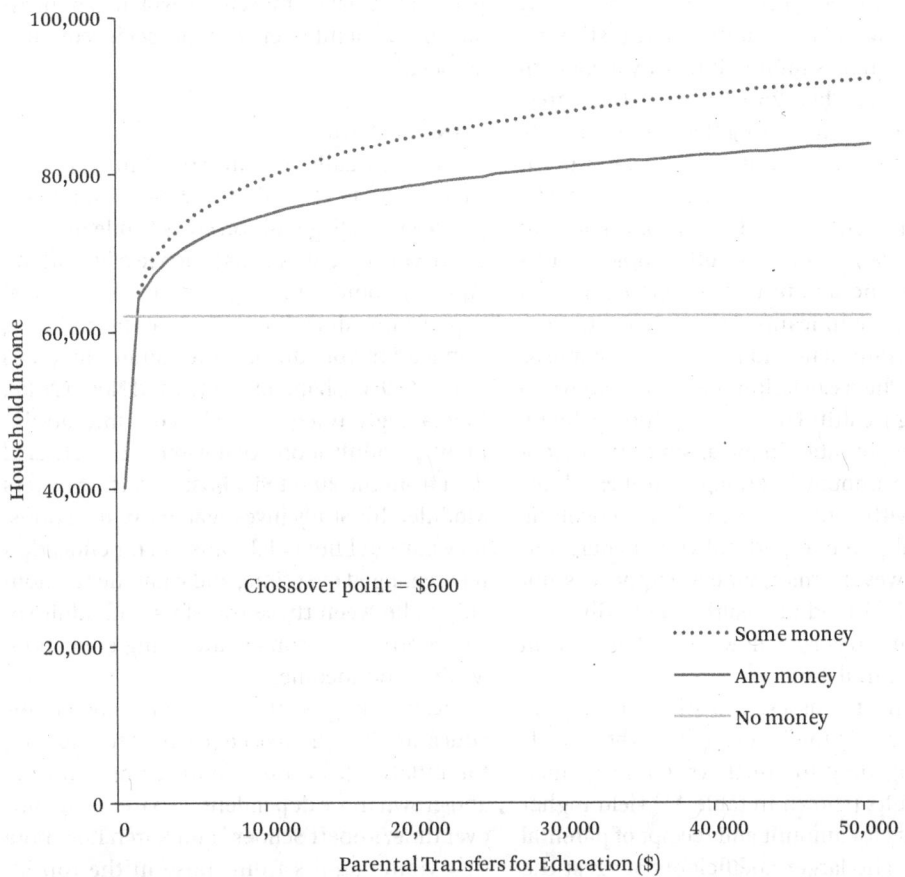

Source: Author's compilation based on PSID.
Note: No Money represents those who received no transfers from education (based on table 4, model 5). *Any Money* represents everyone (who received any amount, zero and above) (based on table 4, model 5). *Some Money* represents those who received more than zero dollars in transfers (based on table 4, model 6).

even when holding constant several parental measures, including income, age, and marital status when the child was seventeen, as well as parental educational attainment, race, and ethnicity. The indicator for whether parents gave an individual no money for school is positively associated with socioeconomic attainment measures. This suggests that individuals who received no financial transfers had higher socioeconomic attainment than those who received only a small amount of parental transfers. Receiving no financial assistance for education could reflect greater financial independence, other sources of financial support for education such as scholarships, or some other

factor. However, the crossover point at which receipt of financial transfers is associated with higher socioeconomic outcomes is generally quite low. For example, figure 3 illustrates predicted household income based on models 5 (solid lines) and 6 (dotted lines) from table 4. The graph shows that predicted household income is higher than for those receiving no parental transfers when parental transfers exceed a relatively modest $600. The crossover point is also low ($250) when predicting education but is higher when predicting wealth ($2,200).

I include the indicator for receiving no parental transfers because three quarters of the sample fall into this category, and the model may not accurately reflect the relationship without it. However, this indicator is negatively correlated with the amount of transfers received and makes multicollinearity a concern in regressions. Therefore, I also run the regression models when limiting the sample to those who received some money from parents for education. These results are shown in the even-numbered models in table 4. Consistent with the results from the full sample, results show that the amount of parental financial transfers is significantly associated with educational attainment and household income as an adult. The association does not hold when predicting wealth. Thus, among those who received any parental financial support for education, the amount received is significantly associated with adult SES even when controlling for several parental and individual characteristics. However, this financial support is not associated with adult wealth, suggesting that the amount received may play little role in wealth accumulation.

In an effort to assess sensitivity to the controls included in the model, I rerun the models controlling only for birth year and gender. These results (shown in table A5) yield higher coefficients for amount and receipt of parental transfers. The larger coefficients suggest the controls included in table 4 partially account for factors related to both parental transfers and individual SES attainment. To further address potential endogeneity of parental transfers, table 5 presents 3SLS results. The results suggest that parental transfers increase educational attainment and household wealth ($p < 0.05$). The coefficient for parental transfers only reaches marginal significance ($p < 0.10$) when predicting household income.

Finally, table 6 compares the intergenerational association of education, wealth, and income with and without controlling for parental transfers. That is, it provides coefficients for parental education, wealth, and household income in models predicting the same outcome in the next generation. Controlling for parental transfers accounts for between 5 and 29 percent of the parent-child association. Parental transfers reduce the intergenerational wealth association the least (5 percent), educational association the most (29 percent), and income association moderately (20 percent). Overall, parental transfers for school explain a nontrivial amount of intergenerational socioeconomic association.

CONCLUSION

Wealth inequality has increased in recent decades (Piketty 2014; Keister 2000; Wolff 2006), along with college tuition costs (College Board 2015). One potential consequence of wealth inequality could be unequal parental financial support for education and, given the enduring implications of education for adult outcomes (Card 1999; Boshara, Emmons, and Noeth 2015), increasingly unequal socioeconomic attainment in adulthood. Using recently released data from the 2013 PSID Rosters and Transfers Module, this study investigated two questions: how parental financial transfers for education have changed over time; and what the relationship is between these transfers and adult socioeconomic outcomes, including education, wealth, and income.

Results suggest that parental transfers for education have increased (even after adjusting for inflation), become more commonplace, and grown more dependent on parental wealth over time. Robert Schoeni and Karen Ross note that young adults from those in the top income quartile received nearly three times as much financial support from their parents as those in the bottom half of the income distribution (2005, 411). The difference by wealth is even more striking: young adults from families in the top wealth quartile received more than eleven times more money for school than those below the median. Excluding those who received no help, those in the top quartile still received more than triple the amount received by those below the median. These statistics echo Jonathan Fisher and his colleagues in this volume, who show that wealth inequality surpasses inequality of other financial measures.

Holding constant several individual and parental measures—including education, income, and wealth (see online supplement)—the relationship is positive between parental transfers for school and individual socioeconomic attainment, including education, household income, and wealth. The positive relation-

Table 5. Parental School Transfers and Adult Outcomes, Three-Stage Least Squares

Variables	(1) Highest Grade	(2) IHS Wealth	(3) Log Hh Income
Log money for school	0.15**	0.74**	0.06+
	(0.05)	(0.28)	(0.04)
Mother years of education	0.22**	−0.46*	0.01
	(0.04)	(0.20)	(0.02)
Mother age ‡	0.03**	0.05	0.01
	(0.01)	(0.04)	(0.01)
Log mother household income ‡	0.20**	0.21	0.10*
	(0.06)	(0.32)	(0.04)
Mother married ‡	0.39**	0.58	0.18*
	(0.11)	(0.58)	(0.07)
Mother black	−0.15	−0.92	−0.39**
	(0.14)	(0.73)	(0.09)
Mother other race	0.47+	−0.89	−0.03
	(0.24)	(1.31)	(0.16)
Mother Latina	0.15	2.01+	0.21
	(0.22)	(1.15)	(0.14)
Birth year	−0.02**	−0.22**	−0.02**
	(0.01)	(0.03)	(0.00)
Male	−0.30**	1.12**	0.06
	(0.07)	(0.35)	(0.04)
Number of siblings	−0.41	2.06	−0.33+
	(0.28)	(1.46)	(0.18)
Constant	53.30**	442.61**	57.95**
	(11.36)	(59.54)	(7.43)
Observations	2,766	2,824	2,823
R-squared	0.31	−0.01	0.07

Source: Author's compilation based on PSID.
Note: Sample is the same as that in table 1, further limited to those with one to three siblings. Exogenous variables in first stages: *First Two Children Same Sex; First Child Male; Birth Year* indicators. Endogenous variables predicted in first stages: *Log Money for School; # of Siblings*. All currency is measured in 2013 dollars. Robust standard errors in parentheses.
‡ Indicates measured when seventeen years old.
+$p < 0.1$, *$p < 0.05$, **$p < 0.01$

ship holds when predicting education and wealth in 3SLS models, which account for endogeneity of transfers.

Overall, results are consistent with hypothesis 3 and suggest that parental financial transfers for education may be one mechanism through which inequality is transmitted across generations. These findings support evidence that parental wealth is an important predictor of children's education (Conley 2001; Pfeffer 2015; Pfeffer and Killewald 2015) but add empirical evidence that parental transfers are one mechanism of that relationship. In addition, results raise further concern that rising inequality in parental wealth—and therefore in ability to finance postsecondary education—may exacerbate inequality of income and wealth as well as educational opportunity. Furthermore, if parents of lower means extend themselves to help their children pay for college, they may sacrifice saving for retirement and contribute to even greater inequality in retirement savings (Devlin-Foltz, Henriques, and Sabelhaus, this volume).

Table 6. Intergenerational Socioeconomic Association Accounted for by Parental Transfers for School

	Original Coefficient	Coefficient Controlling for Transfers	% Reduction	N
Years of education	0.31	0.22	29.03	4118
IHS wealth	0.21	0.20	4.76	4212
Log household income	0.20	0.16	20.00	4234

Source: Author's compilation based on PSID.
Note: Sample is the same as that in table 1, limited to those with parental wealth for the wealth regressions. Years of education coefficient is the coefficient for parental education when predicting child education, controlling for birth year, sex, number of siblings, parental race, parental ethnicity, and parental age and marital status when the child was seventeen years old. IHS wealth coefficient is the coefficient for parental wealth when predicting child IHS wealth, including the same controls. Log household income coefficient is the coefficient for parental income when predicting child log household income, including the same controls. All currency is measured in 2013 dollars.

This study has important limitations. First, I can only identify an associational relationship. An association between transfers and attainment is of interest in its own right because it suggests one mechanism through which inequality may be transmitted between generations. However, controls for parental characteristics and 3SLS analyses offer steps toward reducing concern about a spurious relationship. Second, the long period of recall required by the PSID parental transfer question provides a less than ideal measurement of parental transfers. Although examination of younger cohorts (see table A4) yields consistent results for education and helps mitigate this concern, error in the parental transfer measure is likely to result in attenuation bias. Third, this study does not identify mechanisms. Because children from wealthy families are more likely to receive scholarships for college, parental expenditures on tuition may be lower. However, these same children tend to enroll in more expensive, higher quality schools. Therefore, one potential mechanism for the relationship between parental transfers for school and socioeconomic attainment may be school quality. Other potential mechanisms include student loans, student employment, and social connections developed in college. However, definitively identifying mechanisms is beyond the scope of this paper. Finally, this study examines only parental financial transfers to adult children for school, which excludes other transfers, including those of time, for other purposes, or from children to parents.

Despite these limitations, results suggest parental financial transfers for education are increasing (even after accounting for inflation) and may play a nontrivial role in the intergenerational transmission of inequality. In fact, controlling for parental transfers accounts for between 5 and 29 percent of the parent-child association of socioeconomic status, depending on the measure. Although early childhood inputs are critical, evidence suggests that financial transfers in young adulthood are not redundant but instead provide important benefits.

If we aim to improve equality of opportunity—and allow individual effort and ability to play a larger role in socioeconomic attainment—results raise at least two policy-related questions. First, to what extent would additional financial assistance for education improve the socioeconomic attainment of young adults from disadvantaged backgrounds? Some sources of financial assistance exist, including federal Pell Grants for students with financial need, the McNair Scholars Program intended to help first generation college students succeed, and the federal Work-Study Program. Other options include state or federal financial matching in college savings accounts, subsidized living expenses or paid student internships for those with unmet financial need, free community college tuition, or student debt relief.

Second, Caroline Hoxby and Christopher Avery note that most high-achieving, low-income youth do not apply for selective colleges, which provide better financial aid and therefore often cost less than less selective colleges (2013). To what extent could information campaigns and increased counseling efforts—that target disadvantaged youth and encourage applications to selective colleges—improve financial outcomes in adulthood? Informed policy decisions require empirical evidence comparing the costs and benefits of each of these programs, including their effects on equality of opportunity.

Table A1. Parental Transfers for School and Adult Outcomes, Older Cohorts

Variables	(1)	(2)	(3)	(4)	(5)	(6)
	Highest Grade		IHS Wealth		Log Hh Income	
	>Age 30	>Age 34	>Age 30	>Age 34	>Age 30	>Age 34
Log money for school	0.28**	0.24**	0.41	0.52+	0.09**	0.09*
	(0.05)	(0.06)	(0.27)	(0.29)	(0.03)	(0.04)
No money for school	1.51**	1.08	2.71	3.71	0.58*	0.62+
	(0.56)	(0.66)	(2.77)	(2.99)	(0.29)	(0.35)
Mother years of education	0.22**	0.22**	-0.00	0.06	0.05**	0.05**
	(0.02)	(0.03)	(0.10)	(0.11)	(0.02)	(0.02)
Mother age ‡	0.04**	0.04**	0.09*	0.09*	-0.00	-0.00
	(0.01)	(0.01)	(0.04)	(0.04)	(0.01)	(0.01)
Log mother household income ‡	0.20**	0.17*	0.24	0.21	0.12**	0.10*
	(0.07)	(0.08)	(0.19)	(0.19)	(0.04)	(0.04)
Mother married ‡	0.16	0.13	1.68**	1.69*	0.26**	0.24*
	(0.14)	(0.16)	(0.59)	(0.66)	(0.08)	(0.10)
Mother black	-0.29*	-0.20	-2.27**	-2.48**	-0.44**	-0.54**
	(0.13)	(0.15)	(0.63)	(0.69)	(0.08)	(0.11)
Mother other race	0.85*	0.55	-0.59	0.25	0.06	0.26
	(0.34)	(0.48)	(1.97)	(3.29)	(0.18)	(0.32)
Mother Latina	-0.04	-0.28	0.56	0.83	0.03	0.03
	(0.35)	(0.45)	(1.23)	(1.44)	(0.15)	(0.21)
Birth year	-0.01*	-0.02**	-0.23**	-0.23**	-0.00	0.00
	(0.01)	(0.01)	(0.02)	(0.02)	(0.00)	(0.00)
Male	-0.29**	-0.25*	0.89*	1.06**	0.07	0.08
	(0.09)	(0.10)	(0.37)	(0.41)	(0.05)	(0.06)
Number of siblings	-0.10**	-0.12**	-0.09	-0.04	-0.04*	-0.04+
	(0.03)	(0.03)	(0.09)	(0.09)	(0.02)	(0.02)
Constant	27.52**	41.42**	451.13**	444.76**	17.53**	8.52
	(10.11)	(13.22)	(36.28)	(43.63)	(6.48)	(8.39)
Observations	2,591	1,933	2,620	1,951	2,617	1,950
R^2	0.27	0.25	0.11	0.11	0.11	0.09

Source: Author's compilation based on PSID.
Note: Sample is the same as that in table 1, limited to individuals older than thirty or older than thirty-four in 2013. All currency is measured in 2013 dollars. Robust standard errors in parentheses.
‡ Indicates measured when individual was seventeen years old.
+$p < 0.1$, *$p < 0.05$, **$p < 0.01$

Table A2. Intergenerational Financial Transfers in 2012

	Money Received from Parents		Money Given to Parents		
Age Group	Below Median Wealth	Above Median Wealth	Below Median Wealth	Above Median Wealth	N
23 to 24	$29.38	$18.92	$331.25	$1,927.82	325
25 to 29	69.69	29.45	445.75	1,689.77	997
30 to 34	44.95	55.26	411.40	2,123.39	821
35 to 39	23.96	51.97	869.71	2,438.82	506
40 to 44	78.30	42.26	455.89	696.30	346
45 to 49	35.69	46.15	481.95	1,493.41	332
50 to 54	24.61	29.28	790.23	1,571.23	299
55 to 59	21.70	31.63	566.16	545.45	207
60 to 64	256.55	44.36	34.53	920.24	136
65+	0.00	20.79	0.56	619.90	25
N	2426	1568	2426	1568	3994

Source: Author's compilation based on PSID.

Note: Sample is the same as that in table 1, limited to those with parental wealth. *Below Median Wealth* includes those below the median for mother's household wealth when the individual was seventeen years old (or the closest available time point). *Above Median Wealth* is limited to those above maternal median wealth. Equivalent measures based on paternal wealth are provided in the online supplement, table 10. All currency is measured in 2013 dollars.

Table A3. Parental Transfers for School and Adult Outcomes, Not Adjusted for Inflation

	(1)	(2)	(3)	(4)	(5)	(6)
	Highest Grade		IHS Wealth		Log Hh Income	
Variables	All	Received Transfers	All	Received Transfers	All	Received Transfers
Log money for school (unadjusted)	0.24** (0.04)	0.39** (0.04)	0.36+ (0.20)	0.19 (0.24)	0.06** (0.02)	0.10** (0.02)
No money for school	0.92* (0.39)		2.33 (1.89)		0.29 (0.19)	
Mother years of education	0.20** (0.02)	0.07* (0.03)	-0.01 (0.08)	-0.17 (0.17)	0.04** (0.01)	0.01 (0.02)
Mother age ‡	0.03** (0.01)	0.00 (0.01)	0.11** (0.03)	0.05 (0.08)	-0.00 (0.00)	-0.01 (0.01)
Log mother household income ‡	0.22** (0.06)	-0.01 (0.08)	0.44* (0.19)	2.43** (0.50)	0.14** (0.04)	0.22** (0.06)
Mother married ‡	0.18 (0.11)	0.18 (0.23)	1.11* (0.49)	-0.37 (1.22)	0.24** (0.07)	-0.02 (0.12)
Mother black	-0.17 (0.11)	0.02 (0.32)	-1.98** (0.52)	-0.99 (1.78)	-0.51** (0.08)	-0.32* (0.14)
Mother other race	0.76** (0.22)	0.15 (0.28)	-0.00 (1.07)	1.95 (1.77)	0.08 (0.13)	0.15 (0.25)
Mother Latina	0.01 (0.24)	0.03 (0.49)	1.67+ (0.88)	-0.95 (2.56)	-0.02 (0.11)	0.07 (0.20)
Birth year	-0.02** (0.00)	-0.02** (0.01)	-0.20** (0.01)	-0.24** (0.03)	-0.01** (0.00)	-0.02** (0.00)
Male	-0.31** (0.07)	-0.26** (0.09)	1.16** (0.31)	0.30 (0.62)	0.08+ (0.04)	0.03 (0.06)
Number of siblings	-0.10** (0.02)	-0.02 (0.04)	0.04 (0.07)	0.16 (0.20)	-0.01 (0.01)	0.03+ (0.02)
Constant	41.07** (6.68)	47.87** (11.46)	384.87** (25.22)	446.10** (52.79)	33.88** (4.49)	52.23** (7.63)
Observations	4,118	918	4,238	961	4,234	961
R^2	0.29	0.21	0.10	0.09	0.12	0.13

Source: Author's compilation based on PSID.
Note: Sample is the same as that in table 1. Similar to table 4, but money for school is not adjusted for inflation in these models. Even-numbered models labeled Received Transfers are limited to those who received parental transfers for school. *Money for School* is not adjusted for inflation; all other currency is measured in 2013 dollars. Robust standard errors in parentheses.
‡ Indicates measured when individual was seventeen years old.
+$p < 0.1$, *$p < 0.05$, **$p < 0.01$

Table A4. Parental Transfers for School and Adult Outcomes, Cohorts Younger than Thirty in 2013

	(1)	(2)	(3)	(4)	(5)	(6)
	Highest Grade		IHS Wealth		Log Hh Income	
Variables	All	Received Transfers	All	Received Transfers	All	Received Transfers
Log money for school	0.20**	0.24**	0.36	0.26	0.02	0.07*
	(0.05)	(0.05)	(0.30)	(0.36)	(0.03)	(0.03)
No money for school	0.49		3.62		0.03	
	(0.56)		(3.00)		(0.30)	
Mother years of education	0.14**	0.12*	0.00	−0.04	0.03*	0.02
	(0.03)	(0.05)	(0.12)	(0.25)	(0.01)	(0.02)
Mother age ‡	0.03**	0.04*	0.18**	0.10	0.01	−0.00
	(0.01)	(0.02)	(0.06)	(0.11)	(0.01)	(0.01)
Log mother household income ‡	0.33**	0.15	1.10**	2.25**	0.28**	0.19*
	(0.08)	(0.13)	(0.39)	(0.79)	(0.07)	(0.08)
Mother married ‡	0.20	0.07	−0.36	−0.99	0.08	0.11
	(0.17)	(0.34)	(0.84)	(1.93)	(0.09)	(0.13)
Mother black	0.19	0.45	−1.05	0.83	−0.54**	−0.12
	(0.18)	(0.47)	(0.86)	(2.16)	(0.12)	(0.16)
Mother other race	0.56*	0.56	−0.31	1.57	0.09	−0.01
	(0.28)	(0.37)	(1.31)	(2.52)	(0.16)	(0.33)
Mother Latina	0.13	−0.38	2.51*	−1.53	−0.09	−0.03
	(0.31)	(0.54)	(1.19)	(2.86)	(0.16)	(0.31)
Birth year	−0.12**	−0.08*	0.30*	0.52*	0.01	0.03
	(0.03)	(0.03)	(0.13)	(0.22)	(0.01)	(0.02)
Male	−0.31**	−0.41**	1.32*	0.60	0.08	0.11
	(0.11)	(0.14)	(0.57)	(0.97)	(0.06)	(0.09)
Number of siblings	−0.09**	−0.08	0.24+	0.58**	0.06**	0.09**
	(0.03)	(0.05)	(0.14)	(0.22)	(0.02)	(0.02)
Constant	239.19**	165.87*	−605.36*	−1,064.80*	−6.65	−60.87
	(50.03)	(64.72)	(258.94)	(429.45)	(28.33)	(42.69)
Observations	1,420	409	1,528	463	1,527	463
R^2	0.39	0.27	0.05	0.06	0.16	0.09

Source: Author's compilation based on PSID.

Note: Sample is the same as that in table 1, but limited to individuals under age thirty in 2013. Even-numbered models labeled Received Transfers are limited to those who received parental transfers for school. All currency is measured in 2013 dollars. Robust standard errors in parentheses.

‡ Indicates measured when individual was seventeen years old.

+$p < 0.1$, *$p < 0.05$, **$p < 0.01$

Table A5. Parental Transfers for School and Adult Outcomes, Minimum Controls

Variables	(1) Highest Grade	(2) IHS Wealth	(3) Log Hh Income
Log money for school	0.43**	0.61**	0.13**
	(0.04)	(0.19)	(0.02)
No money for school	2.21**	4.30*	0.77**
	(0.41)	(2.02)	(0.20)
Birth year	−0.01**	−0.20**	−0.02**
	(0.00)	(0.01)	(0.00)
Male	−0.26**	1.24**	0.10*
	(0.07)	(0.31)	(0.05)
Constant	33.47**	402.21**	40.93**
	(6.69)	(23.22)	(4.33)
Observations	4,118	4,238	4,234
R^2	0.20	0.08	0.05

Source: Author's compilation based on PSID.
Note: Sample is the same as that in table 1. Robust standard errors in parentheses. All currency is measured in 2013 dollars.
+$p < 0.1$, *$p < 0.05$, **$p < 0.01$

REFERENCES

Albertini, Marco, Martin Kohli, and Claudia Vogel. 2007. "Intergenerational Transfers of Time and Money in European Families: Common Patterns—Different Regimes?" *Journal of European Social Policy* 17(4): 319–34.

Albertini, Marco, and Jonas Radl. 2012. "Intergenerational Transfers and Social Class: Inter-vivos Transfers as Means of Status Reproduction?" *Acta Sociologica* 55(2): 107–23.

Amato, Paul R., Sandra J. Rezac, and Alan Booth. 1995. "Helping Between Parents and Young Adult Offspring: The Role of Parental Marital Quality, Divorce, and Remarriage." *Journal of Marriage and the Family* 57(2): 363–75.

Angrist, Joshua D., and William N. Evans. 1998. "Children and Their Parents' Labor Supply: Evidence from Exogenous Variation in Family Size." *American Economic Review* 88(3): 450–77.

Armstrong, Elizabeth A., and Laura T. Hamilton. 2013. *Paying for the Party: How College Maintains Inequality*. Cambridge, Mass.: Harvard University Press.

Arnett, Jeffrey Jensen. 2000. "Emerging Adulthood: A Theory of Development from the Late Teens Through the Twenties." *American Psychologist* 55(5): 469–80.

Attias-Donfut, Claudine, Jim Ogg, and Francois-Charles Wolff. 2005. "European Patterns of Intergenerational Financial and Time Transfers." *European Journal of Ageing* 2(3): 161–73.

Balf, Todd. 2014. "The Story Behind the SAT Overhaul." *New York Times*, March 6, 2014. Accessed May 11, 2016. http://www.nytimes.com/2014/03/09/magazine/the-story-behind-the-sat-overhaul.html.

Becker, Gary S. 1981. *A Treatise on the Family*. Cambridge, Mass.: Harvard University Press.

Berry, Brent. 2006. "What Accounts for Race and Ethnic Differences in Parental Financial Transfers to Adult Children in the United States?" *Journal of Family Issues* 27(11): 1583–604.

Boshara, Ray, William R. Emmons, and Bryan J. Noeth. 2015. "The Demographics of Wealth: How Age, Education and Race Separate Thrivers from Strugglers in Today's Economy." *Education and Wealth* essay no. 2. St. Louis, Mo.: Federal Reserve Bank of St. Louis.

Bowen, William G., Matthew M. Chingos, and Michael S. McPherson. 2009. *Crossing the Finish Line: Completing College at America's Public Universities*. Princeton, N.J.: Princeton University Press.

Burbidge, John B., Lonnie Magee, and A. Leslie Robb. 1988. "Alternative Transformations to Handle Extreme Values of the Dependent Variable." *Journal of the American Statistical Association* 83(401): 123–27.

Card, David. 1999. "The Causal Effect of Education on Earnings." In *Handbook of Labor Economics*, vol. 3A, edited by Scott Ashenfelter and David Card. Amsterdam: Elsevier.

Carnevale, Anthony P., and Jeff Strohl. 2010. "How Increasing College Access Is Increasing Inequality, and What to Do About It." In *Rewarding Strivers: Helping Low-Income Students Succeed in College*, edited by Richard D. Kahlenberg. New York: Century Foundation.

College Board. 2015. "Tuition and Fees and Room and Board over Time, 1974–75 to 2014–15." *Trends in College Pricing*. London, Ky.: College Board Publications.

Conley, Dalton. 1999. *Being Black, Living in the Red: Race, Wealth, and Social Policy in America.* Berkeley: University of California Press.

———. 2001. "Capital for College: Parental Assets and Postsecondary Schooling." *Sociology of Education* 74(1): 59–72.

Conley, Dalton, and Rebecca Glauber. 2008. "Parental Educational Investment and Children's Academic Risk: Estimates of the Impact of Sibship Size and Birth Order from Exogenous Variation in Fertility." *Journal of Human Resources* 41(4): 722–37.

Currie, Janet, and Aaron Yelowitz. 2000. "Are Public Housing Projects Good for Kids?" *Journal of Public Economics* 75(1): 99–124.

Danziger, Sheldon, and Cecilia Elena Rouse, eds. 2007. *The Price of Independence: The Economics of Early Adulthood.* New York: Russell Sage Foundation.

Davis, Kingsley, and Wilbert E. Moore. 1945. "Some Principles of Stratification." *American Sociological Review* 10: 242–49.

Devlin-Foltz, Sebastian, Alice Henriques, and John Sabelhaus. 2016. "Is the U.S. Retirement System Contributing to Rising Wealth Inequality." *RSF: The Russell Sage Foundation Journal of the Social Sciences* 2(6). doi: 10.7758/RSF.2016.2.6.04.

Eggebeen, David J. 1992. "Family Structure and Intergenerational Exchanges." *Research on Aging* 14(4): 427–47.

Eggebeen, David J., and Dennis P. Hogan. 1990. "Giving Between Generations in American Families." *Human Nature* 1(3): 211–32.

Fisher, Jonathan, David Johnson, Jonathan P. Latner, Timothy Smeeding, and Jeffrey Thompson. 2016. "Inequality and Mobility Using Income, Consumption, and Wealth for the Same Individuals." *RSF: The Russell Sage Foundation Journal of the Social Sciences* 2(6). doi: 10.7758/RSF.2016.2.6.03.

Furstenberg, Frank F., Jr., Saul D. Hoffman, and Laura Shrestha. 1995. "The Effect of Divorce on Intergenerational Transfers: New Evidence." *Demography* 32(3): 319–33.

Goux, Dominique, and Eric Maurin. 2005. "The Effect of Overcrowded Housing on Children's Performance at School." *Journal of Public Economics* 89(5–6): 797–819.

Hacker, Jacob. 2006. *The Great Risk Shift: The New Economic Insecurity and What Can Be Done About It.* New York: Oxford University Press.

Hamilton, Laura. 2013. "More Is More or More Is Less? Parental Financial Investments During College." *American Sociological Review* 78(1): 70–95.

Hao, Lingxin. 1996. "Family Structure, Private Transfers, and the Economic Well-Being of Families with Children." *Social Forces* 75(1): 269–92.

Haskins, Ron. 2008. "Education and Economic Mobility." In *Getting Ahead or Losing Ground: Economic Mobility in America*, edited by Julia B. Isaacs, Isabel V. Sawhill, and Ron Haskins. Washington, D.C.: Brookings Institution.

Heckman, James J. 2006. "Skill Formation and the Economics of Investing in Disadvantaged Children." *Science* 312(5782): 1900–2.

Heckman, James J., and Dimitriy V. Masterov. 2007. "The Productivity Argument for Investing in Young Children." *Review of Agricultural Economics* 29(3): 446–93.

Henretta, John C., Douglas A. Wolf, Matthew F. Van Voorhis, and Beth J. Soldo. 2012. "Family Structure and the Reproduction of Inequality: Parents' Contribution to Children's College Costs." *Social Science Research* 41(4): 876–87.

Hogan, Dennis P., David J. Eggebeen, and Clifford C. Clogg. 1993. "The Structure of Intergenerational Exchanges in American Families." *American Journal of Sociology* 98(6): 1428–58.

Houle, Jason N. 2013. "Disparities in Debt: Parents' Socioeconomic Resources and Young Adult Student Loan Debt." *Sociology of Education* 87(1): 53–69.

Hout, Michael. 1988. "More Universalism, Less Structural Mobility: The American Occupational Structure in the 1980s." *American Journal of Sociology* 93(6): 1358–400.

Hoxby, Caroline, and Christopher Avery. 2013. "The Missing 'One-Offs': The Hidden Supply of High-Achieving, Low-Income Students." *Brookings Papers on Economic Activity* 46(1): 1–65.

Kalleberg, Arne L. 2009. "Precarious Work, Insecure Workers." *American Sociological Review* 74(1): 1–22.

Keister, Lisa A. 2000. *Wealth in America: Trends in Wealth Inequality*. Cambridge: Cambridge University Press.

Kohli, Martin, and Harald Kunemund. 2003. "Intergenerational Transfers in the Family: What Motivates Giving?" In *Global Aging and Challenges to Families*, edited by V. L. Bengtson and A. Lowenstein. New York: Aldine de Gruyter.

Kramer, Rory, Ruth Burke, and Camille Z. Charles. 2015. "When Change Doesn't Matter: Racial Identity (In)Consistency and Adolescent Well-Being." *Sociology of Race and Ethnicity* 1(2): 270–86.

Lareau, Annette, and Amanda Cox. 2011. "Social Class and the Transition to Adulthood: Differences in Parents' Interactions with Institutions." In *Social Class and Changing Families in an Unequal America*, edited by M. Carlson and Paula England. Stanford, Calif.: Stanford University Press.

Lye, Diane N. 1996. "Adult Child-Parent Relationships." *Annual Review of Sociology* 22(1): 79–102.

MacKinnon, James G., and Lonnie Magee. 1990. "Transforming the Dependent Variable in Regression Models." *International Economic Review* 31(2): 315–39.

Mani, Anandi, Sendhil Mullainathan, Eldar Shafir, and Jiaying Zhao. 2013. "Poverty Impedes Cognitive Function." *Science* 341(6149): 976–80.

McGarry, Kathleen, and Robert F. Schoeni. 1995. "Transfer Behavior in the Health and Retirement Study: Measurement and the Redistribution of Resources Within the Family." *Journal of Human Resources* 30: S184–226.

Newman, Katherine. 2013. *The Accordion Family: Boomerang Kids, Anxious Parents, and the Private Toll of Global Competition*. Boston, Mass.: Beacon Press.

Parsons, Talcott. 1943. "The Kinship System of the Contemporary United States." *American Anthropologist* 45(1): 22–38.

Pence, Karen M. 2006. "The Role of Wealth Transformations: An Application to Estimating the Effect of Tax Incentives on Saving." *Contributions to Economic Analysis & Policy* 5(1): 1–26.

Pfeffer, Fabian T. 2011. "Status Attainment and Wealth in the United States and Germany." In *Persistence, Privilege, and Parenting: The Comparative Study of Intergenerational Mobility*, edited by Timothy Smeeding, R. Erikson, and Marcus Jäntti. New York: Russell Sage Foundation.

———. 2015. "Growing Wealth Gaps in Education." Unpublished manuscript, University of Michigan.

Pfeffer, Fabian T., and Alexandra Killewald. 2015. "How Rigid Is the Wealth Structure and Why? Inter- and Multigenerational Associations in Family Wealth." PSC working paper 15-845. Ann Arbor: University of Michigan. Accessed May 10, 2016. www.psc.isr.umich.edu/pubs/pdf/rr15-845.pdf.

Pfeffer, Fabian T., and Robert F. Schoeni. 2016. "How Wealth Inequality Shapes Our Future." *RSF: The Russell Sage Foundation Journal of the Social Sciences* 2(6). doi: 10.7758/RSF.2016.2.6.01.

Piketty, Thomas. 2014. *Capital in the Twenty-First Century*. Cambridge, Mass.: Harvard University Press.

Pollack, Craig Evan, Sekai Chideya, Catherine Cubbin, Brie Williams, Mercedes Dekker, and Paula Braveman. 2007. "Should Health Studies Measure Wealth? A Systematic Review." *American Journal of Preventive Medicine* 33(3): 250–64.

Powell, Brian, and Lala Carr Steelman. 1989. "The Liability of Having Brothers: Paying for College and Sex Composition of the Family." *Sociology of Education* 62(2): 134–47.

———. 1990. "Beyond Sibship Size: Sibling Density, Sex Composition, and Educational Outcomes." *Social Forces*. 69(1): 181–206.

Saez, Emmanuel, and Gabriel Zucman. 2015. "Wealth Inequality in the United States since 1913: Evidence from Capitalized Income Tax Data." NBER working paper no. 20625. Cambridge, Mass.: National Bureau of Economic Research.

Saperstein, Aliya. 2006. "Double-Checking the Race Box: Examining Inconsistency between Survey Measures of Observed and Self-Reported Race." *Social Forces* 85(1): 57–74.

Sarkisian, Natalia, and Naomi Gerstel. 2004. "Kin Support Among Blacks and Whites: Race and Family Organization." *American Sociological Review* 69: 812–37.

Schoeni, Robert F., and Karen E. Ross. 2005. "Material Assistance from Families during the Transition to Adulthood." In *On the Frontier of Adulthood*, edited by Richard A. Settersten Jr., Frank F. Furstenberg Jr., and Rubén G. Rumbaut. Chicago: University of Chicago Press.

Scodellaro, Claire, Myriam Khlat, and Florence Jusot. 2012. "Intergenerational Financial Transfers and Health in a National Sample from France." *Social Science and Medicine* 75(7): 1296–302.

Seltzer, Judith A., and Suzanne M. Bianchi. 2013. "Demographic Change and Parent-Child Relationships in Adulthood." *Annual Review of Sociology* 39: 275–90.

Semyonov, Moshe, and Noah Lewin-Epstein. 2001. "The Impact of Parental Transfers on Living Standards of Married Children." *Social Indicators Research* 54(2): 115–37.

Settersten, Richard A., Jr., Frank F. Furstenberg Jr., and Rubén G. Rumbaut, eds. 2005. *On the Frontier of Adulthood: Theory, Research, and Public Policy*. Chicago: University of Chicago Press.

Sewell, William, and Vimal Shah. 1977. "Socioeconomic Status, Intelligence, and Attainment of Higher Education." *Sociology of Education* 40(1): 1–23.

Shapiro, Thomas M. 2004. *The Hidden Cost of Being African American: How Wealth Perpetuates Inequalities*. New York: Oxford University Press.

Silva, Jennifer M. 2013. *Coming Up Short: Working-Class Adulthood in an Age of Uncertainty*. New York: Oxford University Press.

Stack, Carol B. 1974. *All Our Kin: Strategies for Survival in a Black Community*. New York: Harper and Row.

Steelman, Lala Carr, and Brian Powell. 1989. "Acquiring Capital for College: The Constraints of Family Configuration." *American Sociological Review* 54(5): 844–55.

———. 1991. "Sponsoring the Next Generation: Parental Willingness to Pay for Higher Education." *American Journal of Sociology* 96(6): 1505–29.

Stevens, Mitchell. 2007. *Creating a Class: College Admissions and the Education of Elites*. Cambridge, Mass.: Harvard University Press.

Swartz, Teresa Toguchi. 2008. "Family Capital and the Invisible Transfer of Privilege: Intergenerational Support and Social Class in Early Adulthood." In *Social Class and Transitions to Adulthood: New Directions for Child and Adolescent Development*, edited by J. T. Mortimer. New York: John Wiley & Sons.

———. 2009. "Intergenerational Family Relations in Adulthood: Patterns, Variations, and Implications in the Contemporary United States." *Annual Review of Sociology* 35: 191–212.

Thompson, Jason, and Dalton Conley. 2016. "Health Shocks and Social Drift: Examining the Relationship Between Acute Illness and Family Wealth." *RSF: The Russell Sage Foundation Journal of the Social Sciences* 2(6). doi: 10.7758/RSF.2016.2.6.08.

Torche, Florencia. 2011. "Is a College Degree Still the Great Equalizer? Intergenerational Mobility Across Levels in the United States." *American Journal of Sociology* 117(3): 763–807.

Walpole, MaryBeth. 2003. "Socioeconomic Status and College: How SES Affects College Experiences and Outcomes." *Review of Higher Education* 27(1): 45–73.

White, Lynn. 1992. "The Effect of Parental Divorce and Remarriage on Parental Support for Adult Children." *Journal of Family Issues* 13(2):234–50.

Wolff, Edward N. 1992. "Changing Inequality of Wealth." *American Economic Review* 82(2): 552–58.

———. 1995. *Top Heavy: A Study of the Increasing Inequality of Wealth in America*. New York: Twentieth Century Fund Press.

———. 2006. "Changes in Household Wealth in the 1980s and 1990s in the United States." In *International Perspectives on Household Wealth*, edited by Edward Wolff. Cheltenham: Edward Elgar.

———. 2016. "Household Wealth Trends in the United States, 1962 to 2013: What Happened over the Great Recession?" *RSF: The Russell Sage Foundation Journal of the Social Sciences* 2(6). doi: 10.7758/RSF.2016.2.6.02.

Yamada, Ken. 2006. "Intra-Family Transfers in Japan: Intergenerational Co-Residence, Distance, and Contact." *Applied Economics* 38(16): 1839–61.

Yilmazer, Tansel. 2008. "Saving for Children's College Education: An Empirical Analysis of the Trade-Off Between the Quality and Quantity of Children." *Journal of Family and Economic Issues* 29(2): 307–24.

Zellner, Arnold, and Henri Theil. 1962. "Three-Stage Least Squares: Simultaneous Estimation of Simultaneous Equations." *Econometrica* 30(1): 54–78.

Wealth and Inequality in the Stability of Romantic Relationships

ALICIA EADS AND LAURA TACH

The family is a key institution that transmits inequality, and racial and socioeconomic inequalities in family life have grown markedly. We use data from the 1996 to 2008 panels of the Survey of Income and Program Participation to offer a comprehensive account of how wealth relates to family stability and how that relationship varies by union type, age cohort, and both type and amount of wealth. We find that liquid and illiquid assets and secured debts are associated with a decrease in the likelihood of dissolution, and that large unsecured debts are associated with an increase. These associations do not differ significantly for married and cohabiting couples. We find evidence of both the material and the symbolic importance of wealth for stability. We also find that wealth explains a significant degree of the racial inequality in family stability.

Keywords: wealth inequality, marriage, cohabitation, family stability

The Great Recession of 2008–2009 raised public awareness about inequality in American society and invigorated scholarly activity into the causes and consequences of extreme and rising wealth inequality (Piketty 2014; Pfeffer, Danziger, and Schoeni 2013). The family is a key institution that transmits inequality across generations, and racial and socioeconomic inequalities in family life have grown markedly over the past half century (McLanahan 2004; Pfeffer and Schoeni, this issue). Most research has examined how family processes reproduce income inequality (Western et al. 2012), but wealth may influence the formation and stability of family relationships in distinct ways (Keister 2000, 6–16, 225–29). In this paper, we use longitudinal data from the 1996, 2001, 2004, and 2008 panels of the Survey of Income and Program Participation (SIPP) to offer a comprehensive account of how wealth relates to family stability and how that association varies by relationship type, age cohort, and type and amount of wealth. After examining both the material and symbolic significance of wealth for relationship stability, we consider whether wealth inequalities contribute to population-level inequalities in family stability by race and by macroeconomic context.

BACKGROUND

Family structure and family stability are profoundly unequal along the lines of race and class (McLanahan and Percheski 2008; Ellwood and Jencks 2004; Kennedy and Bumpass 2008). These inequalities have grown substantially over the past half century, contributing to what Sara McLanahan (2004) and others refer to as the "diverging destinies" of children. The so-

Alicia Eads is a graduate student in sociology at Cornell University. **Laura Tach** is assistant professor of policy analysis and management at Cornell University.

The authors thank Fabian Pfeffer, Bob Schoeni, and participants at the Russell Sage Foundation conference on wealth inequality for feedback on an earlier version of this manuscript. Direct correspondence to: Alicia Eads at ade25@cornell.edu, Department of Sociology, 376 Uris Hall, Cornell University, Ithaca, NY 14853; and Laura Tach at lauratach@cornell.edu, 253 Martha van Rensselaer Hall, Cornell University, Ithaca, NY 14853.

cioeconomic gradient in marriage and childbearing was minimal in the 1960s, but today most children of college-educated parents grow up in households characterized by stable married families and stable finances, whereas the children of less-educated parents are increasingly exposed to unstable family and economic situations. Socioeconomically disadvantaged adults are less likely to form marital relationships, are more likely to have children outside of marriage, and have less stable relationships than their more advantaged counterparts (McLanahan 2004; Tach, Mincy, and Edin 2010; Ventura and Bachrach 2000). As a result, the children of married parents spend the vast majority (84 percent) of their childhoods with both parents, whereas the children of unmarried parents can expect to spend only about half (52 percent) (Bumpass and Lu 2000). These patterns also fuel racial inequality in family life: African American couples are significantly less likely to marry or to have stable romantic relationships and more likely to have children outside marriage than whites; patterns for Latino families are more variable (Kennedy and Bumpass 2008; McLanahan and Percheski 2008).

The growing educational and racial gradients in family formation and stability are particularly consequential because they overlap with a period of growing income and wealth inequality. Part of changing dynamics in income inequality comes from rising incomes for those in the top decile of the income distribution. Emmanuel Saez (2009) calculates that from the 1940s until the early 1980s, the top decile accounted for just over 33 percent of total income in the United States. However, from the early 1980s forward, the percentage of income going to the top 10 percent rose such that by 2007, it accounted for fully half of total income. Wealth inequality has also been driven by the top of the distribution pulling away from the rest: the top 0.1 percent owned a staggering 22 percent of total wealth in 2012 (Saez and Zucman 2014). This growth at the top was accompanied by stagnation and even decline among the lower quintiles. These trends were exacerbated by the 2008 recession, when median wealth plummeted and wealth inequality increased sharply (Wolff, this issue).[1]

Socioeconomic status structures the formation, progression, and dissolution of romantic relationships. Much of the work on family dynamics and economic inequality has focused on education- or income-based measures of inequality (for a review, see McLanahan and Percheski 2008). We argue that wealth is an important but understudied dimension of family relationships. Wealth is not simply a function of income or education (Hurst et al. 1998; Keister 2000). First, wealth is a stock rather than a flow. It is transmitted across generations in very tangible and unequal ways. It buys access to elite social settings such as neighborhoods, schools, and colleges (Keister 2000; Oliver and Shapiro 1995; Rauscher, this issue). It also allows families to insure against economic risks in other domains of life and may serve as a buffer against adverse effects of income volatility on consumption (Fisher et al., this issue). Further, income and wealth are not highly correlated. Although those with long-term low income may begin to look like those with low wealth, this is not necessarily the case. The very wealthy may have low earnings and support consumption with income from assets (Wolff 1995) and differences in saving and investment are large at all income levels (Brimmer 1988). Because of these important distinctions, wealth may shape the progression and stability of family relationships in distinct and consequential ways.

Wealth and the Progression of Romantic Relationships

The institution of marriage is held in high esteem by Americans of all races and classes (Axinn and Thornton 2000; Thornton and Young-DeMarco 2001), and it is increasingly viewed as a coveted social status, or capstone, in the life course (Cherlin 2004). Today, most Americans believe that they should have not just steady employment but also some assets—money saved, a car, or even a home—before they marry (Dew and Price 2011; Edin and Kefalas 2005; Gibson-Davis, Edin, and McLanahan

---

1. Exactly how much inequality in income (Armour, Burkhauser, and Larrimore 2014) and in wealth (Bricker et al. 2015) has increased during the recession is debated.

2005; Lloyd and South 1996). These prerequisites for marriage—the "marriage bar"—are held by rich and poor alike, but the poor are significantly less likely to be able to realize them (Gibson-Davis, Edin, and McLanahan 2005). Researchers have used the idea of the marriage bar to explain racial and socioeconomic gaps in entry into marriage. Although wealth figures strongly in qualitative narratives (Edin and Kefalas 2005), only a handful of studies have examined it as an independent component. These studies find that wealth, particularly homeownership, increases the likelihood of marriage (Lloyd and South 1996; Gibson-Davis 2009), and that racial inequalities in wealth explain a significant part of the racial gap in the decision to marry (Schneider 2011).

Daniel Schneider (2011) argues that wealth may influence the decision to marry because of its symbolic value or its use value. Wealth has use value because it can be deployed to boost material well-being by mitigating material hardship and insuring against future economic uncertainty (Fisher, this issue; Oppenheimer, Kalmijn, and Lim 1997). The symbolic value of wealth inheres in what wealth signifies to others (Lamont and Molnár 2002; Cherlin 2004). To the extent that marriage has become a status marker, displays of wealth—a big wedding, purchasing a house—signal that the couple has achieved the requisite social status deemed worthy of marriage (Veblen 1973; Zelizer 1997; Cherlin 2004). The decision to hold assets jointly or solely may also hold symbolic meaning within the relationship as a signal of a couple's commitment, independence, or expectations about the future stability of their relationship (Addo and Sassler 2010; Kenney 2004; Treas 1993).

Compared with the accumulation of research on wealth and marriage entry, we know less about how wealth influences the stability of marriages. The family stress model predicts that economic hardships lead to feelings of economic pressure, which undermine interpersonal interactions and emotions within marriages, resulting in increased marital conflict (Conger and Elder 1994; Conger et al. 1990; Gudmunson et al. 2007). Marital conflict, in turn, is a key predictor of divorce (Amato and Rogers 1997). Economic hardship has been conceptualized in various ways—including income, poverty, and indicators of specific hardship experiences such as food or housing insecurity—and the associations with marital distress are robust to the specific indicator of hardship used (Conger, Conger, and Martin 2010).

Although wealth is moderately correlated with other indicators of socioeconomic status, it is not reducible to them, and scholars have only recently begun to untangle the unique effects of asset and debt accumulation on marital satisfaction and divorce (Dew 2011). Liquid assets (which can be converted to cash relatively easily) and illiquid assets (houses, cars, property) could promote marital stability because couples can draw on them to buffer against transitory shocks to income, which could reduce the marital strain that tends to accompany economic shocks. Asset holdings may have symbolic benefits as well: financial assets are associated with a positive future orientation, enhanced personal efficacy, and greater social participation (Sherraden 1991; Yadama and Sherraden 1996), which could have positive repercussions for interpersonal interactions and commitment within romantic relationships. Joint ownership of assets might signal particularly committed relationships (Addo and Sassler 2010; Treas 1993). Additionally, significant asset holdings might deter divorce because of the transaction costs associated with adjudicating the division of assets in divorce proceedings.

In contrast, predictions about how debt might influence marital stability are less clear. According to life-cycle theories of debt, secured debts, such as mortgages or educational loans, are investments that individuals (or couples) make to boost their long-term economic well-being.[2] In the long term, the financial ben-

---

2. During the recent housing boom, this relationship between secured debt and long-term economic well-being may have been more tenuous as homeowners increasingly cashed in home equity to finance consumption. We thank a reviewer for pointing this out. This became more prevalent beginning in 1999 (Brown et al. 2010). We confirm that relationships between secured debt and the likelihood of relationship dissolution are not significantly different for respondents in the 1996 and 2008 SIPP panels.

efits are expected to outweigh the short-term financial costs (Modigliani and Brumberg 1954). Such debts may have little short-term influence on relationships and may ultimately promote marital quality and stability in the long term. The meaning of secured debts may also have a life-cycle component, with greater secured debt at young ages being less troubling than it is at older ages.

Unsecured debts, such as consumer or credit card debt, also have ambiguous associations with relationship stability. They may be used to smooth consumption, thus averting financial hardships, and preserving relationship quality and stability. But they may also signal financial hardship or even cause it directly by diverting household income to debt repayment. Consistent with this latter hypothesis, consumer debt is associated with feelings of anxiety, economic pressure, and marital conflict (Conger and Elder 1994; Dew 2007; Drentea 2000).

Variation by Union Type
Virtually all the literature focuses on how wealth shapes decisions to start or end a marriage. Given the retreat from marriage and the concomitant growth of cohabitation over the past half century (Lundberg and Pollak 2013), whether economic forces influence the stability of cohabiting unions in the same way they influence the stability of marriages is significant. Hypotheses conflict. On one hand, ending a marriage has greater symbolic and financial costs than ending a cohabiting union. Divorce is a legal procedure that requires retaining a lawyer and undergoing court-mediated division of assets and belongings, which can be lengthy, costly, and emotionally painful. Divorce also has symbolic costs, given that partners lose their place in a legally recognized kinship system and the support that system provides. Thus, one might predict that married couples will be less likely to end their relationships in the face of low or declining levels of wealth than cohabiting couples, net of other economic characteristics.

On the other hand, given the marriage bar standards described, married couples might be more responsive to wealth than cohabiting couples when deciding to end relationships. If marriage is a coveted social status that signifies that a couple has made it financially, perhaps married couples will be more likely to break up than cohabiting couples when adverse economic conditions cause them to fall below the marriage bar. In fact, qualitative researchers have found that couples do not hold the same standards for their cohabiting relationships that they do for marital relationships, and they tolerate adverse economic and interpersonal conditions in cohabitation they say they would not tolerate within marriage (Edin and Kefalas 2005). Indeed, research examining the relative importance of economic conditions across union types has found that socioeconomic factors are more important predictors of relationship stability for marital unions than for cohabiting unions (Tach and Edin 2013).

Racial Inequality
Racial differences are large in the formation and stability of marital relationships. African American couples are less likely to enter marriage and have less stable marriages than white couples, even taking into account differences in economic characteristics such as income and employment (Kennedy and Bumpass 2008; McLanahan and Percheski 2008). Because racial inequalities in wealth are stark (Oliver and Shapiro 1995; Conley 1999; Bucks, Kennickell, and Moore 2006; Killewald and Bryan, this issue), if wealth shapes the progression of romantic relationships via the identified mechanisms—serving a use value by buffering financial hardships or serving a symbolic value by signaling the achievement and maintenance of the marriage bar—racial wealth gaps might explain some of the racial inequality in the stability of family relationships. Schneider (2011) finds that including measures of wealth as use value and symbolic value in models of first marriage reduced the black-white gap in marriage by about 30 percent, which was more than conventional economic covariates like employment and income explained. We know less about whether differences in wealth can help explain racial gaps in the stability of romantic relationships after they form.

Macroeconomic Contexts and Relationship Instability

Macroeconomic downturns—characterized by some combination of high unemployment rates, stock market volatility, falling gross domestic product, and declining housing values—have the potential to shape the economic well-being of large segments of the population and to have cascading effects on family dynamics. Under normal macroeconomic conditions, we might expect family-level economic hardship to reduce family stability by heightening economic strain, reducing marital quality, and thereby increasing divorce rates. But the effects of family-level economic hardship may be different during macroeconomic downturns, when many others are experiencing hardship as well. In particular, it may be more costly for couples to dissolve their unions (Modestino and Dennett 2013). Couples may face greater constraint in their housing and employment options. They may lack the financial wherewithal to set up two households or to cover the cost of a divorce. They may also find it more difficult to divide certain assets, such as homes or stock market holdings, if the value of those assets declined.

These forces may be one reason researchers have found mixed effects of macroeconomic conditions on divorce rates (Cherlin et al. 2013; Chowdhury 2013; Harknett and Schneider 2012). Divorce rates dropped during the Great Depression (Cherlin et al. 2013), but recessionary periods after World War II were associated with greater divorce risk (South 1985). Recent estimates from work on the Great Recession that began in 2008 found that rising unemployment rates were associated with reductions in the divorce rate (Amato and Beattie 2010; Hellerstein and Morrill 2011; Schaller 2012; Harknett and Schneider 2012; Cherlin et al. 2013; but see Arkes and Shen 2014). However, evidence from the Great Recession on the effect of foreclosure rates—another indicator of macroeconomic conditions—and marital stability is mixed. Kristen Harknett and Daniel Schneider (2012) find that higher foreclosure rates reduced divorce rates, but Philip Cohen (2014) finds that they increased them.

To our knowledge, research on the macroeconomic contexts of relationship stability has focused exclusively on marital stability. Even though the empirical record on marital stability is mixed, we predict that recessions might boost the stability of cohabiting unions, in part because the financial benefits to pooling incomes may be particularly necessary during macroeconomic hardship. Individuals are more likely to double up (share living arrangements) during recessionary times (Mykyta and Macartney 2011; Bitler and Hoynes 2015; Cherlin et al. 2013); cohabitation is one form of doubling up, and many cohabiting couples cite economic reasons for moving in together (Sassler 2004).

DATA AND METHOD

We use data from multiple panels of the Survey of Income and Program Participation, starting with the 1996 panel and ending with the 2008 panel, which concludes in 2013. The SIPP is a nationally representative survey designed to provide comprehensive information about the sources of income and government program participation of individuals and households in the United States on a subannual basis. The survey is designed as a series of national panels, each lasting three to four years. Together, the panels provide almost-continuous coverage of the U.S. household population since 1996. Unlike most other longitudinal surveys, each panel draws a new nationally representative sample rather than focusing on a single cohort (for which age and period effects are confounded).

In each SIPP panel, every member of the household age fifteen or older was interviewed every four months and asked about the previous four months. All were interviewed directly if possible or by proxy response from another household member otherwise. The SIPP imputes item—and person—nonresponse in all waves (Westat 2001, chapter 4). A household roster indicates the relationship of each household member to the household head, and monthly changes in the household roster are assessed at each survey. The SIPP follows all original sample members (who are present at the first survey wave) regardless of where they move in subsequent survey waves (unless they are institutionalized, in military barracks, or abroad). The SIPP also surveys new individuals who live in households with original sample members over the course of the panel; these new individuals are not followed after they stop living with an original sample member. The SIPP also includes topical modules that are a separate set of questions asked in addition to the regular core survey questions during two or three waves of each panel. One set of topical modules asks detailed questions about asset and debt types and values, which we use for this analysis.[3]

In this article, we construct an analytic subsample of families by identifying the household reference person, who we follow until the survey ends. By following just the reference person, we avoid having both parties to a single union in the data. We restrict the sample to working-age adults, ages eighteen to sixty-four. We further restrict the sample to opposite-sex couples, because there are too few same-sex couples in our sample, especially in earlier panels, for separate analyses. This results in a sample of 1,613,586 married family observations (67,460 distinct relationships) and 124,846 cohabiting family observations (8,632 distinct relationships) across all four panels of the SIPP. We observe about 8 percent of married couples, and 37 percent of cohabiting couples, ending their unions during the SIPP panels.

Measures

Family Structure and Dissolution

In each month of the SIPP, we assess family structure by identifying adults living in the same household and classifying them as household head, spouse of the household head, or unmarried partner of the household head. Households are coded as married if a spouse of the household head is listed on the household roster, or cohabiting if an unmarried partner of the household head is. In all of the SIPP panels used in this paper, participants were asked directly about the presence of an unmarried partner. We identify a *marital dissolution* as occurring in the month in which the household reference person's family structure changes from married to any other household type and either a separation or a legal divorce occurred. We identify *cohabitation dissolution* as occurring in the month in which one of the cohabiting partners no longer lives in the household. Because the SIPP includes no direct questions about the start and end dates of nonmarital romantic relationships in these panels, we must measure the start and end of cohabitations based on the household roster.

Family Wealth and Debt Components

We create four measures of wealth that mirror John Czajka, Jonathan Jacobson, and Scott Cody's (2003) measures using SIPP (for a detailed list of the SIPP variables comprising each measure, see table A1). First, we calculate the value of all *secured debt*. For most participants, this is largely their mortgage. Some have business debts secured by the value of the business. Second, we calculate the value of *unsecured debt*. This is largely store and credit card debt. Third, we calculate *liquid assets*, which includes saving and checking account balances. Fourth, we calculate *illiquid assets*, which include the values of participants' car or cars and the value of their house or business.[4] Information is collected on assets and debts held individually by each adult in the household, as well as some assets and debts jointly held by spouses. We add individual and jointly held assets and debts together for each person in the union to create family-level measures. The dollar value of these measures is adjusted to 2013 dollars using data from the Bureau of Labor Statistics CPI inflation calculator. Table 1 shows the mean and median values of each measure of wealth by union type and stability. We construct standard deviation measures of

---

3. The assets and debt topical modules were asked in the following waves: 3, 6, 9, and 12 for the 1996 panel; 3, 6, and 9 for the 2001 panel; 3 and 6 for the 2004 panel; and waves 4, 7, and 10 for the 2008 panel.

4. The SIPP does not have reliable data on life insurance, defined contribution pensions, annuities, or trusts and thus underestimates assets (Czajka, Jacobson, and Cody 2003).

Table 1. Demographic and Economic Characteristics, 1996–2013

	Full Sample	Married No Dissolution	Married Dissolution	Cohabiting No Dissolution	Cohabiting Dissolution
Mean assets-debt					
Secured debt	$101,000	$106,000	$73,000	$57,000	$43,000
Unsecured debt	$12,000	$12,000	$11,000	$9,300	$11,000
Liquid assets	$114,000	$122,000	$51,000	$40,000	$29,000
Illiquid assets	$268,000	$282,000	$175,000	$138,000	$107,000
Median assets-debt					
Secured debt	$63,000	$70,000	$20,000	$0	$0
Unsecured debt	$1,700	$1,800	$1,900	$600	$1,400
Liquid assets	$20,000	$24,000	$3,800	$1,700	$1,000
Illiquid assets	$180,000	$191,000	$100,000	$4,400	$17,000
Mean monthly income	$7,300	$7,500	$5,800	$5,500	$4,900
Mean age	44	45	41	39	37
Relationship type (percent)					
Cohabiting	7	—	—	84	16
Married	93	97	3	—	—
Employed (percent)					
Female	37	36	44	44	45
Male	63	64	56	56	55
Households with children (percent)	55	56	60	40	40
Race-ethnicity (percent)					
Non-Hispanic black	7	7	10	11	12
Latino	13	12	16	18	13
Non-Hispanic other race	6	6	5	4	4
Non-Hispanic white	74	75	68	67	71
Education (percent)					
Less than high school	10	9	13	16	14
High school	25	24	29	30	32
Some college	33	33	37	36	38
Four year degree or more	32	34	21	18	16
Number of relationships	76,092	62,242	5,218	6,313	2,319
Relationship-months	1,738,432	1,550,577	63,009	103,539	21,307

Source: Authors' compilation based on SIPP data.
Note: Statistics weighted using national sampling weights. Monetary values reported in 2013 dollars.

each of the asset and debt measures for inclusion in the regression models, so that our coefficients represent how a standard deviation change in assets or debts influences relationship stability.

Race and Ethnicity

The SIPP asks directly about the race and ethnic origin of participants. We use the race and ethnicity of the reference person as our measure. We maintain four categories: *non-Hispanic white*, *non-Hispanic black*, *Hispanic*, and *non-Hispanic other race*. Table 1 shows the proportion of the sample in each racial-ethnic category as well as the share of each group who experience a marital separation (given that they were married) or a cohabiting union dissolution (given that they were in a cohabiting union). Table A2 shows differences in mean and median wealth and debt accumulation among racial-ethnic groups.

Education
The SIPP asks about years of education completed for the reference person, which we recode into a four-category measure: *less than high school* (fewer than twelve years of school), *high school* (twelve years of school), *some college* (thirteen to fifteen years of school), and *four-year degree or higher* (sixteen years of school or more). Table 1 shows the proportion of household heads with each level of education, as well as the percentages from each educational category of those who experience a marital separation or a cohabiting union dissolution.

Macroeconomic Conditions
We measure macroeconomic conditions in two ways. First we include a measure of *state-level unemployment*. We use monthly unemployment rates from the Bureau of Labor Statistics' (BLS) Local Area Unemployment Statistics series at the state level. These unemployment data were merged with the SIPP data by month-year and the reference person's geographic location.[5] Paul Amato and Brett Beattie (2011) find that unemployment tends to have the strongest effect on divorce when considering unemployment rates within the year or with a year lag. However, unemployment rates rose fairly quickly during the Great Recession's fallout; thus, following Harknett and Schneider (2012), who analyze a similar period, we separate the unemployment rates into quartiles and lag the quartiles by three months. As a second measure of the macroeconomic conditions, we include a measure of *national-level recession* using the U.S. Business Cycle Expansions and Contractions data from the National Bureau of Economic Research. Our period of analysis includes the 2001 recession, which lasted from March 2001 until November 2001, as well as the Great Recession, which lasted from December 2007 until June 2009. We merge these data with our SIPP sample by month-year.

Additional Time-Varying Controls
Total monthly family income is measured in each month by calculating the sum of the SIPP-generated total person income measures for the reference person and his or her spouse or partner. *Age* is included as the reference person's age in years. We include a dummy variable indicating whether the reference person has *children* living in the household. We also include dummy variables for *employment* that indicates whether the male partner is employed and whether the female partner is employed. In some analyses, we include a dummy variable indicator for whether the couple experienced an income shock, measured as having experienced a reduction in income in the previous month from the month before. We also include a measure of material hardship in some analyses. For this measure, we used a SIPP topical module question asked once in the 1996, 2001, and 2004 panels and twice in the 2008 panel,[6] which asks respondents whether they had difficulty meeting any of their essential household expenses, such as mortgage or rent payment, utilities bills, or medical expenses at any time in the past twelve months. We created a dummy variable for whether respondents experienced hardship and applied that variable to the past twelve months of observations for each respondent.

Method
Our analyses are based on event history models of time to union dissolution. We use Cox

---

5. For the 1996 and 2001 panels, the SIPP combines two sets of states. Those living in North Dakota and South Dakota were coded identically, as were those living in Vermont and Maine. We averaged the unemployment data for these sets of states and applied the average to respondents living in these areas.

6. The financial hardship question was asked in the following waves: wave 8 for the 1996 panel, wave 8 for the 2001 panel, wave 5 for the 2004 panel, and waves 6 and 9 for the 2008 panel.

proportional hazards models to estimate the risk of failure, or dissolution, as a function of wealth, debt, and other family characteristics. Respondents who enter the survey period already in a marriage or cohabiting relationship are immediately in the risk set. Respondents who enter unions later during a SIPP panel enter the risk set the first time the union is reported in the survey. We measure time as months since union entry (or since the survey began for those already in a union), and participants are censored at the end of the survey period. We allow respondents to contribute multiple dissolutions and adjust for multiple relationships with robust standard errors. Thus, our unit of analysis is the relationship-month rather than the person-month.[7]

Equation 1 specifies the following proportional hazards model:

$$h_n(t) = h_0(t) \exp(\beta_1 X_n) \quad (1)$$

where $h_0(t)$ represents the baseline hazard rate at time t and X_n represents the vector of independent variables. Because we conduct a monthly survival analysis, but our key asset and debt independent variables are measured only every twelve months in the topical modules, we forward-fill the asset and debt values between topical modules. For example, if a couple responds to the topical module in wave 3, and again in wave 9, we fill in the wave 3 values for waves 4 through 8. This assumes that asset and debt values do not change between waves, but it is better than the alternative of linear interpolation, which is problematic if couples end their unions between waves of the topical modules.

We conduct three main sets of survival analyses. The first estimates the effects of total net worth, as well as detailed measures of secured and unsecured debt and liquid and illiquid assets on relationship stability. We then add interaction terms to the model to test whether the associations between wealth and union dissolution differ for married and cohabiting couples. We also test whether they differ for older or younger cohorts. Finally, we examine whether the effects of wealth and debt on relationship stability show a nonlinearity, entering separate dummy variables for quartiles of the wealth and debt distributions.

In a second set, we explore the symbolic and material meanings of wealth for relationship stability. Following Schneider (2011), we proxy the symbolic value of wealth, meaning that assets serve as a signal to others that a couple has reached the marriage bar and, thus, when marriage is appropriate, by testing whether simply holding any assets or debts affects relationship stability. We do so by including dummy variables for whether a couple holds each type of asset or debt. We then test whether joint ownership of the home is associated with relationship stability, relative to just the male partner owning the home, just the female partner owning the home, or no homeownership. We also examine the material role of wealth by considering whether having assets reduces the effect of an income shock on relationship stability, and whether self-reported financial hardships explain the associations between debt and relationship stability.

In a final set of analyses, we examine whether wealth contributes to population-level inequalities in relationship stability by race-ethnicity or macroeconomic condition. Specifically, we measure the baseline differences in relationship stability by race-ethnicity and then add in a standard set of economic controls typically used by family researchers, which includes household income, education, and employment. We then test whether adding our asset and debt measures to the model explains any more of the racial-ethnic differences in relationship stability, net of the standard set of economic controls.

Finally, we add our macroeconomic variables of state-level unemployment and national recession to the models. We test whether the associations between wealth and relationship stability vary by macroeconomic context, and whether these effects vary for married and cohabiting couples.

---

7. To address censoring, we perform our analyses using two subsamples, which have relationship duration information, and thus, for these analyses, time is measured since the start of the relationship for everyone in the subsamples.

RESULTS

The median couple in our sample has a net worth of $115,000, a figure that varies considerably between married and cohabiting couples and by race-ethnicity. The median married couple had about $68,000 in secured debt, $1,800 in unsecured debt, and $23,000 in liquid assets and $189,000 in illiquid assets. The median cohabiting couple, by contrast, had no secured debt, $700 in unsecured debt, $1,500 in liquid assets, and $24,000 in illiquid assets. These socioeconomic differences are also reflected in the divergent monthly household incomes and educational distributions for the two groups. Consistent with prior research, we also observe stark wealth inequalities between white and black couples, with Latino and other race couples falling in between (see table A2).

Assets, Debts, and Relationship Stability

Table 2 presents results from a Cox proportional hazards model of union dissolution. Model 1 includes family-level net worth (total assets minus total debts) and our full set of controls. A standard deviation increase in the value of a couple's net worth decreases the risk of union dissolution by 31 percent ($exp(-0.377)-1$), controlling for other factors such as income, education, race, and employment. Model 2, which also adjusts for controls, tests whether components of net worth are differentially associated with relationship stability. We find that although a standard deviation increase in secured debt decreases the risk of dissolution by 12 percent, unsecured debt is not significantly associated the hazard rate. This is contrary to our predictions that secured debt would not affect short-term relationship stability and that unsecured debt would increase the hazard of dissolution. Liquid and illiquid assets are both associated with relationship stability as predicted, decreasing the risk of dissolution by 49 percent and 17 percent, respectively.[8]

In supplemental analyses, we examine whether assets and debts have nonlinear effects on relationship stability. To test for nonlinearity, we include asset and debt measures as quartile dummy variables rather than as continuous measures. The lowest quartile of each asset and debt measure is the reference category. We find evidence of relatively linear effects of asset holdings and secured debts on relationship stability, and the magnitude of the association increases monotonically as we move up the quartiles of the distribution (table A4). We do, however, find an interesting nonlinear association for unsecured debt, that only large amounts of unsecured debt have a significant negative influence on relationship stability. Those in the fourth quartile of unsecured debt (those holding the most unsecured debt) have an 8 percent higher risk of dissolution than those in the first quartile (those holding the least).[9]

Variation by Relationship Type and Age Cohort
Table 3 shows results from a set of models in which we explore how associations between wealth and relationship stability vary by relationship type and age cohort. First, we interacted the relationship-type dummy variable with each asset and debt measure (see table 3, relationship type). Models 1, 2, and 3 show that the associations of unsecured debt, secured

---

8. We reestimated models 1 and 2 above on two subsamples to ensure that our results were not driven by the left censoring in our full sample. Table A3 shows results that count time since the start of marriage for the subsample of respondents who completed the marital history topical module. It also presents results for the subsample of respondents, married or cohabiting, who entered a relationship during the survey period, for whom we observe the beginning of the relationship during a SIPP panel. The results for these subsamples do not differ substantively from the full sample results.

9. We also separated the value of a couple's mortgage and home value from these values, given that home equity makes up the largest share of most Americans' investment portfolios and their mortgages are the greatest contribution to their levels of debt (Wolff, this issue; Killewald and Bryan, this issue). We found that the asset-debt associations described are not simply a house effect: they hold for assets and secured debts other than homes as well. We also test whether being underwater on a mortgage—owing more than the house is worth—affects relationship stability, possibly by increasing the costs of dissolution. However, we do not find significant effects.

Table 2. Associations of Wealth and Debt with Risk of Romantic Relationship Dissolution

	Model 1	Model 2
Net worth (SD)	-0.377***	
	(0.0499)	
Detailed asset and debt amounts (SD)		
Secured debt		-0.129***
		(0.0266)
Unsecured debt		0.00728
		(0.00502)
Liquid assets		-0.668***
		(0.178)
Illiquid assets		-0.192***
		(0.0358)
Income (SD)	-0.0888***	-0.0121
	(0.0219)	(0.0213)
Male partner employed (0 = unemployed)	-0.550***	-0.527***
	(0.0346)	(0.0344)
Female partner employed (0 = unemployed)	-0.0361	-0.0292
	(0.0293)	(0.0292)
Race-ethnicity (0 = non-Hispanic white)		
Non-Hispanic black	0.312***	0.258***
	(0.0421)	(0.0424)
Hispanic	-0.131**	-0.154***
	(0.0467)	(0.0466)
Non-Hispanic other race	0.129*	0.108
	(0.0574)	(0.0576)
Education (0 = Less than high school)		
High school diploma or GED	-0.105*	-0.0764
	(0.0459)	(0.0458)
Some college	-0.151**	-0.0914*
	(0.0461)	(0.0463)
Four year degree or more	-0.578***	-0.452***
	(0.0541)	(0.0548)
Age	-0.0455***	-0.0424***
	(0.00142)	(0.00149)
Children in household (0 = no children)	-0.441***	-0.399***
	(0.0296)	(0.0299)
Cohabiting relationship (0 = married)	0.882***	0.850***
	(0.0762)	(0.0758)
Observations	1,738,432	1,738,432

Source: Authors' compilation based on SIPP data.
Note: Estimated using Cox proportional hazards models. Robust standard errors in parentheses. SD = standard deviation.
*$p < 0.05$, **$p < 0.01$, ***$p < 0.001$

Table 3. Associations of Wealth and Debt with Risk of Romantic Relationship Dissolution by Relationship Type and Cohort

Relationship Type	Model 1	Model 2	Model 3	Model 4
Secured debt	-0.133***	-0.129***	-0.129***	-0.129***
	(0.0267)	(0.0266)	(0.0266)	(0.0266)
Unsecured debt	0.00734	0.00696	0.00729	0.00727
	(0.00500)	(0.00521)	(0.00502)	(0.00504)
Liquid assets	-0.666***	-0.668***	-0.665***	-0.662***
	(0.178)	(0.178)	(0.178)	(0.178)
Illiquid assets	-0.193***	-0.192***	-0.192***	-0.199***
	(0.0358)	(0.0358)	(0.0358)	(0.0364)
Cohabiting relationship (0 = married)	0.945***	0.850***	0.808***	0.971***
	(0.0892)	(0.0769)	(0.135)	(0.0904)
Interactions				
Cohabit * secured	0.233			
	(0.119)			
Cohabit * unsecured		0.128		
		(0.171)		
Cohabit * liquid			-0.544	
			(1.362)	
Cohabit * illiquid				0.284**
				(0.100)
Age Cohorts	Model 5	Model 6	Model 7	Model 8
Secured debt	-0.221***	-0.129***	-0.138***	-0.128***
	(0.0358)	(0.0265)	(0.0263)	(0.0280)
Unsecured debt	0.00672	0.00807	0.00727	0.00720
	(0.00501)	(0.0291)	(0.00498)	(0.00494)
Liquid assets	-0.695***	-0.670***	0.121	-0.671***
	(0.180)	(0.179)	(0.283)	(0.190)
Illiquid assets	-0.195***	-0.192***	-0.185***	-0.198**
	(0.0354)	(0.0358)	(0.0350)	(0.0591)
40–64 cohort (ref = 18–39 years)	0.221***	0.231***	0.181***	0.232***
	(0.0497)	(0.0494)	(0.0507)	(0.0501)
Interactions				
40–64 cohort * secured	0.169***			
	(0.0420)			
40–64 cohort * unsecured		-0.000967		
		(0.0294)		
40–64 cohort * liquid			-1.065***	
			(0.305)	
40–64 cohort * illiquid				-0.00718
				(0.0599)

Source: Author's compilation based on SIPP data.
Note: Estimated using Cox proportional hazards models. N = 1,738,432. Robust standard errors in parentheses. Controls (income, employment, race, education, age, children, relationship type) in models, coefficients not shown. Asset and debt amounts measured in standard deviation units.
*$p < 0.05$, **$p < 0.01$, ***$p < 0.001$

debt, and liquid assets with the risk of relationship dissolution do not differ significantly for married versus cohabitating couples. Model 4, however, shows that illiquid assets significantly increase the risk of dissolution for cohabitating couples. We caution that this may be due to small numbers of cohabitating couples with illiquid assets. We therefore cannot reject the null hypothesis that assets and debts function similarly for married and cohabiting couples.

Table 3 also shows whether the associations between wealth and relationship stability differ for older and younger age cohorts. Our results here are largely consistent with predictions from a life-cycle model of savings and debt. A one standard deviation increase in the amount of secured debt decreases the risk of dissolution by 20 percent for younger cohorts, but only by 7 percent for older cohorts. Thus, secured debt is less protective of relationship stability for older couples than for younger couples. Unsecured debt has little association with stability for any age group. Model 7 shows that liquid assets have an increased protective effect among older couples. That is, a standard deviation increase in liquid assets among older couples decreases the risk of dissolution by 61 percent ($exp(-0.121-1.065)$); for younger couples, liquid assets are not significantly associated with relationship stability. The association between illiquid assets and relationship stability does not differ for older and younger cohorts.

Symbolic and Material Meanings of Wealth

Scholars have argued that wealth matters for relationships because of what it symbolizes, apart from its economic value (Schneider 2011; Zelizer 1997; Cherlin 2004). Ownership of assets, such as a home or a car, independent of their value, can be a symbolic marker of success and status; researchers have found that they matter for entry into marriage (Schneider 2011; Edin and Kefalas 2005). We build on this line of research by testing whether holding any asset or debt (in contrast to assessing the effect of amounts) is associated with relationship stability. The results indicate that simply having some assets and debts, versus none, is significantly associated with the risk of dissolution, controlling for other factors (see table A5).

The sole versus joint ownership of assets may also be symbolically significant, in that couples who hold their assets—homes, cars, bank accounts—jointly report greater commitment to their relationships and higher levels of relationship satisfaction, which may be the result of greater trust and support. The results indicate that sole homeownership, whether the owner is the woman or the man in the relationship, increases the risk of dissolution by about 60 percent over not owning (see table A5).[10] In contrast to the effect of sole ownership, jointly owning the home decreases the hazard rate by 49 percent over not owning. We therefore find strong support for the symbolic value of asset and debt holdings.

Wealth has potentially important material value for couples as well. They can liquidate asset holdings or draw on interest to provide extra income. Wealth is an obvious buffer against unexpected financial insecurities. To examine the material meaning of wealth for relationship stability, we ask whether the effect of income shocks on relationship stability was weaker for couples with greater asset holdings. We tested this by including an indicator for whether the couple experienced an income shock in the prior month, measured as a negative income change from the month before, and interacting this measure with liquid and illiquid assets (see table A6). A negative income shock increases the risk of dissolution, and liquid assets reduce it, though the coefficient does not reach conventional levels of statistical significance. Illiquid assets do not alter the effect of an income shock in any substantively or statistically significant way.

We also examine the possibility that debts are either markers of financial hardship or directly create financial hardship via the cost associated with debt repayment and other fees (see table A6). Consistent with prior re-

---

10. About 2 percent of our sample lives in a household in which the female partner is the sole owner of the house. About 2 percent live in a household in which the male partner is the sole owner.

search, we find that experiences of financial hardship increase the risk of relationship dissolution significantly. We also find that the financial hardship measure explains 29 percent of the association between large amounts of unsecured debt and relationship stability.[11]

Wealth and Racial Inequality in Relationships

Researchers have found that socioeconomic differences, measured by income, education, and employment, explain part of the relationship stability gap, but much remains unexplained. We examine whether assets and debts explain part of the black-white gap in relationship stability. Model 1 in table 4 includes only race-ethnicity dummy variables and controls for age, children, and relationship type. This first model shows that black couples are 53 percent more likely to end their relationships than white couples. Model 2 adds in the economic measures that previous research has found decrease this gap: income, employment, and education. Indeed, in this model, the likelihood of dissolution for black couples falls to 41 percent more than for whites, leaving a significant portion of the gap unexplained. Model 3 adds our measures for assets and debts. As these results show, the likelihood of dissolution for black couples is now 29 percent higher than for whites. This suggests that assets and debts reduce the black-white relationship stability gap by about 45 percent, which is about as much as the standard set of economic controls explained. In other words, assets and debts explain a substantial portion of the black-white gap in relationship stability, rivaling that of other standard socioeconomic measures.

We find no significant differences between the relationship stability of white and Latino couples when adjusting only for age, children, and relationship type. However, in model 2, where income, employment, and education are adjusted, Latino couples actually face an 11 percent lower risk of dissolution than white couples. Latinos are 16 percent less likely than whites to end their unions in model 3 when adding in assets and debts.

Macroeconomic Conditions and Relationship Stability

The theoretical predictions for how macroeconomic conditions shape divorce are mixed: some theories suggest that adverse conditions would reduce marital stability, and others that adverse conditions would actually promote marital stability by making it more costly to divorce. The predictions for cohabitation are more clear, however, suggesting that cohabitations would be more stable in times of macroeconomic hardship.

In this final set of results, we consider the effects of macroeconomic conditions on relationship stability and examine whether they differ for marriages and cohabitations. Models 1 and 2 in table 5 show that macroeconomic conditions do not attenuate the relationship between assets, debts, and relationship stability as we expected they might.

Model 2 of table 5 shows that couples living in states where unemployment levels are in the second are not at significantly more risk of dissolving their unions than those in states at just the first quartile (lowest unemployment). However, those in states in the third and fourth (highest unemployment) quartile face a 7 and 26 percent higher risk of union dissolution relative to those with the lowest unemployment. National-level recession increases the risk of dissolution by 54 percent. Model 2 adds the wealth and debt measures to the models. These measures do not appear to mediate the association between state-level unemployment and relationship dissolution.

Model 3 interacts the cohabitation dummy variable with the fourth quartile of unemployment dummy variable. The results indicate important differences in macroeconomic effects for married versus cohabiting couples—married couples face an increased hazard rate in poor macroeconomic conditions while cohab-

---

11. The models in the second panel of table A6 are estimated on a subset of observations because respondents' answers to the financial hardship question applied to only twelve months of the three- to four-year survey period, thus many observations could not be used for this analysis.

Table 4. Racial-Ethnic Differences in Relationship Stability

	Model 1	Model 2	Model 3
Race-Ethnicity (0 = non-Hispanic white)			
Non-Hispanic black	0.424***	0.341***	0.255***
	(0.0420)	(0.0420)	(0.0422)
Hispanic	0.0507	−0.119**	−0.168***
	(0.0435)	(0.0465)	(0.0464)
Non-Hispanic other race	0.0961*	0.138**	0.0970*
	(0.0575)	(0.0574)	(0.0576)
Secured debt			−0.135***
			(0.0263)
Unsecured debt			0.0141*
			(0.00501)
Liquid assets			−0.301***
			(0.0518)
Illiquid assets			−0.219***
			(0.0370)
Income		−0.129***	−0.00122
		(0.0216)	(0.0202)
Male partner employed (0 = unemployed)	−0.686***	−0.545***	−0.510***
	(0.0325)	(0.0346)	(0.0344)
Female partner employed (0 = unemployed)	−0.116***	−0.0233	−0.0208
	(0.0284)	(0.0293)	(0.0292)
Education (0 = less than high school)			
High school diploma or GED		−0.117**	−0.0835*
		(0.0460)	(0.0458)
Some college		−0.171***	−0.107**
		(0.0461)	(0.0461)
Four-year degree or more		−0.619***	−0.466***
		(0.0538)	(0.0539)
Age	−0.0501***	−0.0483***	−0.0424***
	(0.00134)	(0.00136)	(0.00145)
Children in household (0 = no children)	−0.427***	−0.441***	−0.394***
	(0.0293)	(0.0296)	(0.0299)
Cohabiting relationship (0 = married)	0.950***	0.888***	0.833***
	(0.0764)	(0.0765)	(0.0761)
Observations	1,738,432	1,738,432	1,738,432

Source: Authors' compilation based on SIPP data.
Note: Estimated using Cox proportional hazards models. Robust standard errors in parentheses. Asset and income variables measured in standard deviation units.
*$p < 0.05$, **$p < 0.01$, ***$p < 0.001$

iting couples actually face a decreased risk. That is, comparing two cohabiting couples, the couple living in a state with the highest quartile of unemployment rather than a state in the lowest quartile of unemployment is 16 percent less likely to break up ($exp(0.247–0.417)$). This provides support for the hypothesis that cohabiting relationships are more stable during tough macroeconomic times, and that marriages are less stable.

Table 5. Associations of Macroeconomic Conditions with Risk of Romantic Relationship Dissolution

	Model 1	Model 2	Model 3
Secured debt	−0.129***	−0.133***	−0.133***
	(0.0266)	(0.0262)	(0.0262)
Unsecured debt	0.00728	0.00696	0.00703
	(0.00502)	(0.00551)	(0.00547)
Liquid assets	−0.668***	−0.681***	−0.682***
	(0.178)	(0.180)	(0.180)
Illiquid assets	−0.192***	−0.186***	−0.186***
	(0.0358)	(0.0353)	(0.0353)
National recession (0 = no recession)		0.432***	0.433***
		(0.114)	(0.114)
Quartiles of state unemployment (0 = first quartile)			
Second quartile		0.0607	0.0604
		(0.0378)	(0.0378)
Third quartile		0.0745*	0.0743*
		(0.0379)	(0.0379)
Fourth quartile		0.233***	0.247***
		(0.0379)	(0.0382)
Cohabiting relationship (0 = married)	0.850***	0.835***	0.955***
	(0.0758)	(0.0763)	(0.0857)
Cohabit * fourth quartile of unemployment			−0.417*
			(0.169)
Observations	1,738,432	1,738,432	1,738,432

Source: Authors' compilation based on SIPP data.
Note: Estimated using Cox proportional hazards models. Robust standard errors in parentheses. Controls including income, employment, race, education, age, and children are in all models. Asset and income variables measured in standard deviation units.
*$p < 0.05$, **$p < 0.01$, ***$p < 0.001$

DISCUSSION

Our analysis provides a nuanced portrait of how wealth is related to the stability of family relationships and explores how this association varies across types of debt and types of unions. We find that both liquid and illiquid assets are associated with the stability of marital relationships. Consistent with Schneider (2011), we find evidence that these associations reflected both the material as well as the symbolic values of wealth for relationships. Evidence also suggests that liquid assets buffered against the adverse consequences of transitory shocks to income. The protective effect of liquid assets was particularly pronounced for older age cohorts, consistent with a life-cycle theory of savings. Holding any kind of asset is associated with relationship stability, consistent with an interpretation that assets hold symbolic meaning, independent of their actual amount. The joint ownership of assets also appears to have symbolic value for relationships, given that joint ownership of a home is associated with relationship stability relative to renting, but sole ownership by either partner is less stable than not owning a house.

Associations between debt and relationship stability are more mixed. Large amounts of unsecured debt are associated with a reduction in marital stability, in part because these couples reported greater financial hardship. Unsecured debt may therefore either create financial hardship directly or be a marker for it. Secured debts are associated with an increase in marital stability, however. Secured debts, like mortgages, are investments made to boost long-term well-being, which may explain why they are associated with an increase rather than a decrease in stability. This may also explain why secured debt is a stronger predictor of relationship stability for younger couples than for older couples. Another possibility for the differences in the strength of the association between secured debt and dissolution for older and younger couples may be that investment or willingness to take on secured debt is a stronger signal of maturity in younger couples; older couples may have other signals to rely on (Brüderl and Kalter 2001).[12] However, if unsecured debt worked solely as a signaling mechanism, illiquid assets would differ between older and younger cohorts, which we do not find.

Although theory suggests that wealth and debt shape union stability differently for married and unmarried couples, we find little evidence for this in our analysis. If marriage is protective because of its legal and institutionalized commitment mechanisms, married couples might be more likely to stay together in the face of adverse wealth conditions. If, however, couples hold marriage in high esteem, as the marriage bar theory suggests, married couples might be more likely to break up in the face of asset or debt adversity than cohabiting couples. Contrary to both of these theories, we find no significant differences between married and cohabiting couples in terms of how wealth and debt shaped the stability of their romantic unions. Several possible reasons clarify this null finding. First, it could be that both theories are at work and cancel each other out. Second, the relatively few cohabiting unions in our analysis and large standard errors around our interaction terms mean that we cannot rule out potentially meaningful differences among these two types of unions.

Consistent with prior research, we find substantial racial differences in relationship stability: black couples were 53 percent more likely to end their relationships than whites were. The conventional socioeconomic measures of income, employment, and education explained a portion of this black-white gap in relationship stability. When we include these measures in the models, the increased risk of dissolution for blacks relative to whites drops by 23 percent to 41 percent. When we add measures of wealth and debt to the models, they explain a significant additional portion of the gap: the greater relative likelihood of dissolution for blacks drops to 29 percent, a further reduction of about 29 percent. Prior research finds that wealth measures explained about 30 percent of the black-white marriage gap in marriage entry (Schneider 2011); here we find that wealth also explains a significant portion of the black-white gap in the stability of relationships after they form. This reduction may occur because wealth has a similar use value within couples of any race-ethnicity, buffering hardships or smoothing consumption. However, wealth may not serve the same symbolic value within relationships of all races and ethnicities because different racial-ethnic groups do not have the same access to assets (Brimmer 1988). For example, black Americans have more difficulty getting a mortgage or getting the same type of mortgage as white Americans (Rugh and Massey 2010). Examining the effect of different types of assets on the racial gap in relationship stability is an important area for future research. Our results suggest that the black-white wealth divide may have lasting consequences for the intergenerational reproduction of inequality via its effects on family instability, independent of other measures of socioeconomic status.

Finally, we examine the role of macroeconomic conditions on the stability of family relationships. We find that high levels of state unemployment (in the top quartile) were associated with an increased risk of dissolution, relative to periods of low unemployment. We also examine whether these associations differ for cohabiting unions and predict that cohabiting unions may be more stable during hard times because cohabitation allows for pooling limited resources. We find support for this theory in that cohabiters' risk of dissolution is significantly lower in states with high unemployment than in states with low unemployment.

Our analysis has several limitations that readers should keep in mind when interpret-

---

12. We thank a reviewer for pointing this out.

ing the findings. First, our use of the SIPP data precludes our ability to look at longer-term trajectories of marital instability and wealth accumulation over the entire life course, as each SIPP panel lasts only three to four years. Second, our analysis has focused on wealth as a key predictor of relationship stability, but relationship instability is also an important potential cause of declining assets or growing indebtedness; indeed, divorce is one of the key antecedents of bankruptcy (Sullivan, Warren, and Westbrook 1999). Isolating the causal effect of relationship instability on changes in wealth is tricky: a host of unobserved factors could cause both relationship instability and financial hardship (Fisher and Lyons 2006). This is clearly an important question for future research to disentangle because it can help provide more precise estimates of the role of family instability in producing wealth inequality (see Killewald and Bryan, this issue).

Taken together, our results highlight the important yet understudied role of wealth on the stability of family relationships. Much of the research has focused on how wealth explains gaps in marriage entry; here, we find that wealth plays an important role in shaping marital stability as well. Debt and assets are significantly associated with the stability of both marital and cohabiting relationships. The importance of debt and assets remains net of the standard set of socioeconomic controls of education, employment, and income, and the magnitude of wealth effects is often comparable to the magnitude of these measures. Furthermore, assets and debts appear to have not only material value for relationships, buffering against income shocks and either creating or ameliorating financial hardships, but also symbolic value. Ownership of assets in and of themselves can be a marker of status, and joint ownership can signal relationship commitment. Because family instability has adverse consequences for children (McLanahan, Tach, and Schneider 2013), our results suggest that family instability may be one important mechanism through which the intergenerational transmission of wealth inequality operates. As a result, policy interventions that reduce wealth inequality may also reduce inequalities in children's exposure to family instability.

Table A1. Content and Variable Names of SIPP Assets and Debt Survey Questions

Measures	SIPP Variable Contents	SIPP Variable Name
Unsecured debt	Credit card or store debt with partner	ealjdab or taljdab
	Credit card or store debt owed by reference person	ealidab or talidab
	Loans owed with partner	ealjdal or taljdal
	Loans owed by reference person	ealidal or talidal
	Other debt owed with partner	ealjdao or taljdao
	Other owed by reference person	ealidao or talidao
Secured debt	Debt on jointly held stocks or mutual funds	esmjmav or tsmjmav
	Debt on reference person's stocks or mutual funds	esmimav or tsmimav
	Debt on mobile home or lot	tmhpr
	Principle owed on mortgage	tmor1pr (more than one owner possible, applied proportionally)
	Principle owed on rental properties owned with partner	trjpri (half value applied to both partners)
	Principle reference person owes on rental properties	tripri
	Auto loans	tcarval1, tcarval2, tcarval3 (applied proportionally to owners)
	Business debt	tvbde1, tvbde2 (applied proportionally to owners)
Liquid assets	Equity in investments	eoaeq (not asked in 2004 or 2008)
	Amount in joint interest earning account	tiajta
	Amount in reference person interest earning account	tiaita
	Amount in joint checking account	taljcha
	Amount in reference person checking account	talicha
	Amount in joint bonds/US securities	timja
	Amount in reference person bonds/US securities	timia
	Value of joint stocks or mutual funds	esmjv or tsmjv
	Value of reference person stocks or mutual funds	esmiv or tsmiv
	Face value of U.S. savings bonds	talsbv
	Market value of IRA account(s)	talrb
	Market value of KEOGH account(s)	talkb
	Market value of 401K	taltb
Illiquid assets	Value of house	tpropval (applied proportionally)
	Value of mobile home	tmhval
	Value of other real estate	tothreva (applied proportionally)
	Value of car(s)	carval1, carval2, carval3 (applied proportionally)
	Value of rental property jointly held not with partner	trtsha
	Value of rental property jointly held with partner	trjmv
	Value of rental property held by reference person	trimv
	Amount owed for sale business/property	ealowa or talowa
	Principle *owed* on mortgage	tmip
	Principle *owed* on mortgage jointly held	tmjp
	Business equity	tvbva1, tvbva2

Source: Authors' compilation from SIPP codebooks.
Note: Some variable names change between panels.

Table A2. Economic Characteristics by Race-Ethnicity, 1996–2013

	Non-Hispanic White	Non-Hispanic Black	Hispanic-Latino	Non-Hispanic Other Race
Secured debt				
Have (percent)	73	57	50	62
Mean (if have)	$149,000	$125,000	$143,000	$189,000
Median (if have)	$118,000	$95,000	$111,000	$155,000
Unsecured debt				
Have (percent)	66	63	53	56
Mean (if have)	$19,000	$17,000	$14,000	$19,000
Median (if have)	$7,000	$7,000	$5,000	$7,000
Liquid assets				
Have (percent)	91	75	65	86
Mean (if have)	$152,000	$52,000	$38,000	$107,000
Median (if have)	$44,000	$11,000	$5,000	$27,000
Illiquid assets				
Have (percent)	99	92	91	95
Mean (if have)	$300,000	$172,000	$173,000	$307,000
Median (if have)	$205,000	$111,000	$94,000	$203,000
N	1,325,775	129,946	183,205	99,506

Source: Authors' compilation based on SIPP data.
Note: Statistics weighted using national sampling weights. Values reported in 2013 dollars. Race is the race of the household reference person.

Table A3. Robustness Analyses: Without Left Censoring

	Marital History Subsample		New Relationship Subsample	
	Model 1	Model 2	Model 3	Model 4
Net worth	−0.299***		−0.243	
	(0.0446)		(0.144)	
Secured debt		−0.0841**		−0.0765
		(0.0272)		(0.0584)
Unsecured debt		0.00542		−0.112
		(0.00575)		(0.0801)
Liquid assets		−0.349*		−0.496
		(0.166)		(0.277)
Illiquid assets		−0.110***		0.0206
		(0.0332)		(0.0635)
Income	−0.0256	0.0108	−0.140**	−0.116*
	(0.0219)	(0.0222)	(0.0491)	(0.0548)
Male employed (0 = unemployed)	−0.603***	−0.590***	−0.228**	−0.221**
	(0.0412)	(0.0412)	(0.0742)	(0.0758)
Female employed (0 = unemployed)	−0.0583	−0.0499	−0.128*	−0.123
	(0.0348)	(0.0347)	(0.0644)	(0.0655)
Race-ethnicity (0 = non-Hispanic white)				
Non-Hispanic black	0.206***	0.179***	0.181*	0.168
	(0.0518)	(0.0522)	(0.0885)	(0.0870)
Hispanic	−0.0894	−0.0999	−0.170	−0.181
	(0.0540)	(0.0540)	(0.0970)	(0.0978)
Non-Hispanic other race	0.0839	0.0760	0.0951	0.0854
	(0.0676)	(0.0678)	(0.118)	(0.118)
Education (0 = less than high school)				
High school diploma or GED	−0.128*	−0.112*	−0.154	−0.146
	(0.0547)	(0.0547)	(0.0961)	(0.0967)
Some college	−0.223***	−0.189***	−0.267**	−0.245*
	(0.0548)	(0.0551)	(0.0950)	(0.0965)
Four-year degree or more	−0.696***	−0.627***	−0.551***	−0.495***
	(0.0636)	(0.0649)	(0.113)	(0.119)
Age	−0.0124***	−0.0115***	−0.00633*	−0.00614*
	(0.00207)	(0.00210)	(0.00285)	(0.00295)
Children (0 = no children)	−0.0921*	−0.0777*	−0.0409	−0.0408
	(0.0378)	(0.0379)	(0.0624)	(0.0622)
Cohabiting (0 = married)			0.249*	0.246*
			(0.107)	(0.105)
Observations	1,547,889	1,547,889	85,758	85,758

Source: Authors' compilation based on SIPP data.
Note: Estimated using Cox proportional hazards models. These analyses are limited to one failure per subject. Robust standard errors in parentheses. Asset and income variables measured in standard deviation units.
*$p < 0.05$, **$p < 0.01$, ***$p < 0.001$

Table A4. Predicted Nonlinear Associations of Wealth and Debt on Risk of Union Dissolution

	Model 1	Model 2
Secured debt (ref = first quartile)		
Fourth quartile	−0.135***	−0.136***
	(0.0377)	(0.0377)
Mortgage (sd)	−0.0331	−0.0196
	(0.0243)	(0.0262)
Unsecured debt (ref = first quartile)		
Second quartile	0.00619	0.00580
	(0.0542)	(0.0542)
Third quartile	0.0252	0.0248
	(0.0344)	(0.0344)
Fourth quartile	0.0736*	0.0735*
	(0.0341)	(0.0341)
Liquid assets (ref = first quartile)		
Second quartile	−0.139***	−0.139***
	(0.0358)	(0.0359)
Third quartile	−0.371***	−0.372***
	(0.0425)	(0.0425)
Fourth quartile	−0.484***	−0.484***
	(0.0529)	(0.0529)
Illiquid assets (ref = first quartile)		
Second quartile	−0.265***	−0.265***
	(0.0376)	(0.0376)
Third quartile	−0.327***	−0.326***
	(0.0396)	(0.0396)
Fourth quartile	−0.340***	−0.339***
	(0.0467)	(0.0467)
Home equity (sd)	−0.238***	−0.248***
	(0.0306)	(0.0319)
Mortgage circumstance		
Underwater		−0.0949
		(0.0676)
Observations	1,738,432	1,738,432

Source: Authors' compilation based on SIPP data.
Note: Estimated using Cox proportional hazards models. Robust standard errors in parentheses. SD = standard deviation. Controls for income, employment, race, education, age, children, relationship type included in all models. Respondents' holdings of secured debts, less the value of the mortgage, did not fall into the 2nd or 3rd quartiles and therefore are omitted. This reflects the fact that, expect for mortgage debt, most people do not have much other secured debt, expect for those who own businesses, who then tend to hold large amounts of other secured debt. Underwater is a dummy variable indicating whether respondent owes more on mortgage than the current value of the house.
*$p < 0.05$, **$p < 0.01$, ***$p < 0.001$

Table A5. Associations of Joint and Sole Wealth and Debt Ownership with Risk of Romantic Relationship Dissolution

	Model 1	Model 2	Model 3
Has secured debt (0 = does not have)	−0.390***	−0.140***	−0.140***
	(0.0298)	(0.0342)	(0.0342)
Has unsecured debt (0 = does not have)	0.0853**	0.0803**	0.0801**
	(0.0289)	(0.0289)	(0.0289)
Has liquid assets (0 = does not have)	−0.261***	−0.210***	−0.210***
	(0.0365)	(0.0360)	(0.0360)
Has illiquid assets (0 = does not have)	−0.377***	−0.328***	−0.328***
	(0.0514)	(0.0511)	(0.0511)
Joint versus sole homeownership (0 = do not own)			
One partner owns home		0.468***	
		(0.0484)	
Partners jointly own home		−0.674***	−0.674***
		(0.0384)	(0.0384)
Male partner solely owns home			0.425***
			(0.0630)
Female partner solely owns home			0.509***
			(0.0611)
Observations	1,738,432	1,738,432	1,738,432

Source: Authors' compilation based on SIPP data.
Note: Estimated using Cox proportional hazards models. Robust standard errors in parentheses. Controls for income, employment, race, education, age, children, relationship type included in all models.
*$p < 0.05$, **$p < 0.01$, ***$p < 0.001$

Table A6. Associations of Financial Insecurity with Risk of Romantic Relationship Dissolution

Financial Insecurity	Model 1	Model 2	Model 3
Secured debt	-0.129***	-0.129***	-0.128***
	(0.0266)	(0.0266)	(0.0266)
Unsecured debt	0.00718	0.00714	0.00715
	(0.00503)	(0.00504)	(0.00504)
Liquid assets	-0.672***	-0.857**	-0.671***
	(0.178)	(0.168)	(0.178)
Illiquid assets	-0.193***	-0.193***	-0.210***
	(0.0358)	(0.0356)	(0.0404)
Income	-0.00770	-0.00622	-0.00711
	(0.0211)	(0.0208)	(0.0210)
Income shock (0 = no shock)	0.138***	0.163***	0.149***
	(0.0301)	(0.0324)	(0.0315)
Interactions			
Income shock * liquid assets		0.583	
		(0.317)	
Income shock * illiquid assets			0.0586
			(0.0539)
Observations	1,738,432	1,738,432	1,738,432

Financial Hardship	Model 4	Model 5
Secured debt		
Fourth quartile (ref = first quartile)	-0.0366	-0.0464
	(0.0757)	(0.0753)
Mortgage (SD)	-0.103	-0.114*
	(0.0584)	(0.0578)
Unsecured debt (ref = first quartile)		
Second quartile	-0.00282	-0.0158
	(0.118)	(0.117)
Third quartile	0.115	0.0722
	(0.0724)	(0.0726)
Fourth quartile	0.189**	0.135
	(0.0729)	(0.0732)
Financial hardship (0 = no hardship)		0.679***
		(0.0670)
Observations	446,379	446,379

Source: Authors' compilation based on SIPP data.
Note: Estimated using Cox proportional hazards models. Robust standard errors in parentheses. SD = standard deviation. Controls for income, employment, race, education, age, children, relationship type included in all models. Respondents' holdings of secured debts, less the value of the mortgage, did not fall into the 2nd or 3rd quartiles and therefore are omitted. This reflects the fact that, expect for mortgage debt, most people do not have much other secured debt, expect for those who own businesses, who then tend to hold large amounts of other secured debt. Models 4 and 5 have liquid and illiquid assets as quartile variables in the models. Asset and income variables measured in standard deviation units.
*$p < 0.05$, **$p < 0.01$, ***$p < 0.001$

REFERENCES

Addo, Fenaba R., and Sharon Sassler. 2010. "Financial Arrangements and Relationship Quality in Low-Income Couples." *Family Relations* 59(4): 408–23.

Amato, Paul R., and Brett Beattie. 2011. "Does the Unemployment Rate Affect the Divorce Rate? An Analysis of State Data 1960–2005." *Social Science Research* 40(3): 705–15.

Amato, Paul R., and Stacy J. Rogers. 1997. "A Longitudinal Study of Marital Problems and Subsequent Divorce." *Journal of Marriage and Family* 59(3): 612–24. doi: 10.2307/353949.

Arkes, Jeremy, and Yu-Chu Shen. 2014. "For Better or for Worse, but How About a Recession?" *Contemporary Economic Policy* 32(2): 275–87. doi: 10.1111/coep.12029.

Armour, Philip, Richard V. Burkhauser, and Jeff Larrimore. 2014. "Levels and Trends in US Income and Its Distribution: A Crosswalk from Market Income Towards a Comprehensive Haig-Simons Income Approach." *Southern Economic Journal* 81(2): 271–93.

Axinn, William G., and Arland Thornton. 2000. "The Transformation in the Meaning of Marriage." In *The Ties That Bind: Perspectives on Marriage and Cohabitation*, edited by Linda J. Waite. New York: Aldine de Gruyter.

Bitler, Marianne, and Hilary Hoynes. 2015. "Living Arrangements, Doubling Up, and the Great Recession: Was This Time Different?" *American Economic Review* 105(5): 166–70.

Bricker, Jesse, Alice Henriques, Jacob Krimmel, and John Sabelhaus. 2015. "Measuring Income and Wealth at the Top Using Administrative and Survey Data." *FEDS* working paper no. 2015-30. Washington: Board of Governors of the Federal Reserve System.

Brimmer, Andrew. 1988. "Income, Wealth, and Investment Behavior in the Black Community." *American Economic Review* 78(2): 151–55.

Brown, Meta, Andrew Haughwout, Donghoon Lee, and Wilbert van der Klaauw. 2010. "The Financial Crisis at the Kitchen Table: Trends in Household Debt and Credit." *FRB of New York Staff Report* no. 480. New York: Federal Reserve Board. Accessed May 4, 2016. https://www.newyorkfed.org/medialibrary/media/research/staff_reports/sr480.pdf.

Brüderl, Josef, and Frank Kalter. 2001. "The Dissolution of Marriages: The Role of Information and Marital-Specific Capital." *Journal of Mathematical Sociology* 25(4): 404–21.

Bucks, Brian K., Arthur B. Kennickell, and Kevin B. Moore. 2006. "Recent Changes in U.S. Family Finances: Evidence from the 2001 and 2004 Survey of Consumer Finances." *Federal Reserve Bulletin* 92(March): A1–38.

Bumpass, Larry, and Hsien-Hen Lu. "Trends in Cohabitation and Implications for Children S Family Contexts in the United States." *Population Studies* 54 (1): 29–41. doi: 10.1080/713779060.

Cherlin, Andrew J. 2004. "The Deinstitutionalization of American Marriage." *Journal of Marriage and Family* 66(4): 848–61. doi: 10.1111/j.0022-2445.2004.00058.x.

Cherlin, Andrew, Erin Cumberworth, S. Philip Morgan, and Christopher Wimer. 2013. "The Effects of the Great Recession on Family Structure and Fertility." *Annals of the American Academy of Political and Social Science* 650(1): 214–31. doi: 10.1177/0002716213500643.

Chowdhury, Abdur. 2013. "'Til Recession Do Us Part: Booms, Busts, and Divorce in the United States." *Applied Economics Letters* 20(3): 255–61. doi: 10.1080/13504851.2012.689104.

Cohen, Philip N. 2014. "Recession and Divorce in the United States, 2008–2011." *Population Research and Policy Review* 33(5): 615–28. doi: 10.1007/s11113-014-9323-z.

Conger, Rand D., Katherine J. Conger, and Monica J. Martin. 2010. "Socioeconomic Status, Family Processes, and Individual Development." *Journal of Marriage and Family* 72(3): 685–704. doi: 10.1111/j.1741-3737.2010.00725.x.

Conger, Rand D., and Glen H. Elder Jr. 1994. *Families in Troubled Times: Adapting to Change in Rural America. Social Institutions and Social Change*. New York: Aldine de Gruyter.

Conger, Rand D., Glen H. Elder Jr., Frederick O. Lorenz, Katherine J. Conger, Ronald L. Simons, Les B. Whitbeck, Shirley Huck, and Janet N. Melby. 1990. "Linking Economic Hardship to Marital Quality and Instability." *Journal of Marriage and Family* 52(3): 643–56. doi: 10.2307/352931.

Conley, Dalton. 1999. *Being Black, Living in the Red: Race, Wealth, and Social Policy in America*. Berkeley: University of California Press.

Czajka, John L., Jonathan E. Jacobson, and Scott Cody. 2003. *Survey Estimates of Wealth: A Comparative Analysis and Review of the Survey of Income and Program Participation*. Washington,

D.C.: Social Security Administration. Accessed May 4, 2016. https://www.ssa.gov/policy/docs/contractreports/SurveyEstimatesWealth.pdf.

Dew, Jeffrey. 2007. "Two Sides of the Same Coin? The Differing Roles of Assets and Consumer Debt in Marriage." *Journal of Family and Economic Issues* 28(1): 89–104. doi: 10.1007/s10834-006-9051-6.

———. 2011. "The Association Between Consumer Debt and the Likelihood of Divorce." *Journal of Family and Economic Issues* 32(4): 554–65. doi: 10.1007/s10834-011-9274-z.

Dew, Jeffrey, and Joseph Price. 2011. "Beyond Employment and Income: The Association Between Young Adults' Finances and Marital Timing." *Journal of Family and Economic Issues* 32(3): 424–36. doi: 10.1007/s10834-010-9214-3.

Drentea, Patricia. 2000. "Age, Debt and Anxiety." *Journal of Health and Social Behavior* 41(4): 437–50. doi: 10.2307/2676296.

Edin, Kathryn, and Maria Kefalas. 2005. *Promises I Can Keep: Why Poor Women Put Motherhood Before Marriage.* Berkeley: University of California Press.

Ellwood, David T., and Christopher Jencks. 2004. "The Uneven Spread of Single-Parent Families: What Do We Know? Where Do We Look for Answers?" In *Social Inequality*, edited by Kathryn Neckerman. New York: Russell Sage Foundation.

Fisher, Jonathan, David Johnson, Jonathan P. Latner, Timothy Smeeding, and Jeffrey Thompson. 2016. "Inequality and Mobility Using Income, Consumption, and Wealth for the Same Individuals." *RSF: The Russell Sage Foundation Journal of the Social Sciences* 2(6). doi: 10.7758/RSF.2016.2.6.03.

Fisher, Jonathan D., and Angela C. Lyons. 2006. "Till Debt Do Us Part: A Model of Divorce and Personal Bankruptcy." *Review of Economics of the Household* 4(1): 35–52.

Gibson-Davis, Christina M. 2009. "Money, Marriage, and Children: Testing the Financial Expectations and Family Formation Theory." *Journal of Marriage and Family* 71(1): 146–60. doi: 10.1111/j.1741-3737.2008.00586.x.

Gibson-Davis, Christina M., Kathryn Edin, and Sara McLanahan. 2005. "High Hopes but Even Higher Expectations: The Retreat from Marriage Among Low-Income Couples." *Journal of Marriage and Family* 67(5): 1301–12. doi: 10.1111/j.1741-3737.2005.00218.x.

Gudmunson, Clinton G., Ivan F. Beutler, Craig L. Israelsen, J. Kelly McCoy, and E. Jeffrey Hill. 2007. "Linking Financial Strain to Marital Instability: Examining the Roles of Emotional Distress and Marital Interaction." *Journal of Family and Economic Issues* 28(3): 357–76. doi: 10.1007/s10834-007-9074-7.

Harknett, Kristen S., and Daniel J. Schneider. 2012. "Is a Bad Economy Good for Marriage?: The Relationship Between Macroeconomic Conditions and Marital Stability from 1998-2009." NPC working paper no. 12-06. Washington, D.C.: National Poverty Center. Accessed May 4, 2016. http://npc.umich.edu/publications/u/2012-06%20NPC%20Working%20Paper.pdf.

Hellerstein, Judith K., and Melinda Sandler Morrill. 2011. "Booms, Busts, and Divorce." *The B.E. Journal of Economic Analysis & Policy* 11(1). doi: 10.2202/1935-1682.2914.

Hurst, Erik, Ming Ching Luoh, Frank P. Stafford, and William G. Gale. 1998. "The Wealth Dynamics of American Families, 1984-94." *Brookings Papers on Economic Activity* 29(1): 267–337. doi: 10.2307/2534673.

Keister, Lisa A. 2000. *Wealth in America: Trends in Wealth Inequality.* Cambridge: Cambridge University Press.

Kennedy, Sheela, and Larry Bumpass. 2008. "Cohabitation and Children's Living Arrangements: New Estimates from the United States." *Demographic Research* 19(47): 1663–92. Accessed May 4, 2016. http://www.demographic-research.org/Volumes/Vol19/47/19-47.pdf.

Kenney, Catharine T. 2004. "Cohabiting Couples, Filing Jointly? Resource Pooling and U.S. Poverty Policies." *Family Relations* 53: 237–47.

Killewald, Alexandra, and Brielle Bryan. 2016. "Does Your Home Make You Wealthy?" *RSF: The Russell Sage Foundation Journal of the Social Sciences* 2(6). doi: 10.7758/RSF.2016.2.6.06.

Lamont, Michèle, and Virág Molnár. 2002. "The Study of Boundaries in the Social Sciences." *Annual Review of Sociology* 28(January): 167–95. Accessed May 4, 2016. http://www.jstor.org/stable/3069239.

Lloyd, Kim M., and Scott J. South. 1996. "Contextual Influences on Young Men's Transition to First Marriage." *Social Forces* 74(3): 1097–19. doi: 10.1093/sf/74.3.1097.

Lundberg, Shelly and Robert A. Pollak. 2013. "Cohabitation and the Uneven Retreat from Marriage in the US, 1950–2010." *NBER* working paper no. 19413. Cambridge, Mass.: National Bureau of Economic Research.

McLanahan, Sara A. 2004. "Diverging Destinies: How Children Are Faring Under the Second Demographic Transition." *Demography* 41(4): 607–27. doi: 10.1353/dem.2004.0033.

McLanahan, Sara A., and Christine Percheski. 2008. "Family Structure and the Reproduction of Inequalities." *Annual Review of Sociology* 34(1): 257–76. doi: 10.1146/annurev.soc.34.040507.134549.

McLanahan, Sara, Laura Tach, and Daniel Schneider. 2013. "The Causal Effects of Father Absence." *Annual Review of Sociology* 39: 399–427.

Modestino, Alicia Sasser, and Julia Dennett. 2013. "Are American Homeowners Locked into Their Houses? The Impact of Housing Market Conditions on State-to-State Migration." *Regional Science and Urban Economics* 43(2): 322–37. doi: 10.1016/j.regsciurbeco.2012.08.002.

Modigliani, Franco, and Richard Brumberg. 1954. "Utility Analysis and the Consumption Function: An Interpretation of Cross-Section Data." Reprinted in *The Collected Papers of Franco Modigliani*, vol. 6, edited by Francisco Franco, 2005. Cambridge, Mass.: MIT Press.

Mykyta, Laryssa, and Suzanne Macartney. 2011. "The Effects of Recession on Household Composition: 'Doubling Up' and Economic Well-Being." *Social, Economic, and Household Statistics Division* working paper no. 2011-04. Washington: U.S. Census Bureau.

Oliver, Melvin L., and Thomas M. Shapiro. 1995. *Black Wealth, White Wealth: A New Perspective on Racial Inequality*. New York: Taylor & Francis.

Oppenheimer, Valerie Kincade, Matthijs Kalmijn, and Nelson Lim. 1997. "Men's Career Development and Marriage Timing during a Period of Rising Inequality." *Demography* 34(3): 311–30. doi: 10.2307/3038286.

Pfeffer, Fabian T., Sheldon Danziger, and Robert F. Schoeni. 2013. "Wealth Disparities Before and After the Great Recession." *The Annals of the American Academy of Political and Social Science* 650(1): 98–123. doi: 10.1177/0002716213497452.

Pfeffer, Fabian T., and Robert F. Schoeni. 2016. "How Wealth Inequality Shapes Our Future." *RSF: The Russell Sage Foundation Journal of the Social Sciences* 2(6). doi: 10.7758/RSF.2016.2.6.01.

Piketty, Thomas. 2014. *Capital in the Twenty-First Century*. Boston, Mass.: Harvard University Press.

Rauscher, Emily. 2016. "Passing It On: Parent-to-Adult Child Financial Transfers for School and Socioeconomic Attainment." *RSF: The Russell Sage Foundation Journal of the Social Sciences* 2(6). doi: 10.7758/RSF.2016.2.6.09.

Rugh, Jacob S., and Douglas S. Massey. 2010. "Racial Segregation and the American Foreclosure Crisis." *American Sociological Review* 75(5): 629–51.

Saez, Emmanuel. 2009. "Striking It Richer: The Evolution of Top Incomes in the United States (Update with 2007 Estimates)." Berkeley, Calif.: Institute for Research on Labor and Employment. Accessed May 4, 2016. http://escholarship.org/uc/item/8dp1f91x.

Saez, Emmanuel, and Gabriel Zucman. 2014. "Wealth Inequality in the United States since 1913: Evidence from Capitalized Income Tax Data." *NBER* working paper no. 20625. Cambridge, Mass.: National Bureau of Economic Research. Accessed May 4, 2016. http://www.nber.org/papers/w20625.

Sassler, Sharon. 2004. "The Process of Entering into Cohabiting Unions." *Journal of Marriage and Family* 66(2): 491–505. doi: 10.1111/j.1741-3737.2004.00033.x.

Schaller, Jessamyn. 2012. "For Richer, If Not for Poorer? Marriage and Divorce over the Business Cycle." *Journal of Population Economics* 26(3): 1007–33. doi: 10.1007/s00148-012-0413-0.

Schneider, Daniel J. 2011. "Wealth and the Marital Divide." *American Journal of Sociology* 117(2): 627–67. doi: 10.1086/661594.

Sherraden, Michael. 1991. *Assets and the Poor: A New American Welfare Policy*. New York: M.E. Sharpe.

South, Scott J. 1985. "Economic Conditions and the Divorce Rate: A Time-Series Analysis of the Postwar United States." *Journal of Marriage and Family* 47(1): 31–41. doi: 10.2307/352066.

Sullivan, Teresa A., Elizabeth Warren, and Jay Lawrence Westbrook. 1999. *As We Forgive Our Debtors: Bankruptcy and Consumer Credit in America*. Washington, D.C.: Beard Books.

Tach, Laura, and Kathryn Edin. 2013. "The Compositional and Institutional Sources of Union Dissolution for Married and Unmarried Parents in the United States." *Demography* 50(5): 1789–818. doi: 10.1007/s13524-013-0203-7.

Tach, Laura, Ronald Mincy, and Kathryn Edin. 2010. "Parenting as a 'Package Deal': Relationships, Fertility, and Nonresident Father Involvement Among Unmarried Parents." *Demography* 47(1): 181–204. doi: 10.1353/dem.0.0096.

Thornton, Arland, and Linda Young-DeMarco. 2001. "Four Decades of Trends in Attitudes Toward Family Issues in the United States: The 1960s Through the 1990s." *Journal of Marriage and Family* 63(4): 1009–37. doi: 10.1111/j.1741-3737.2001.01009.x.

Treas, Judith. 1993. "Money in the Bank: Transaction Costs and the Economic Organization of Marriage." *American Sociological Review* 58(5): 723–34.

Veblen, Thorstein. 1973. *The Theory of the Leisure Class: An Economic Study of Institutions*. Boston, Mass.: Houghton Mifflin Harcourt.

Ventura, Stephanie J., and Christine A. Bachrach. 2000. "Nonmarital Childbearing in the United States, 1940–99." *National Vital Statistics Reports* 48(16). http://eric.ed.gov/?id=ED446210.

Westat. 2001. *Survey of Income and Program Participation Users' Guide: Supplement to the Technical Documentation*, third edition. Washington: U.S. Census Bureau. Available at: https://www2.census.gov/programs-surveys/sipp/guidance/SIPP_USERS_Guide_Third_Edition_2001.pdf (accessed August 5, 2016).

Western, Bruce, Deirdre Bloome, Benjamin Sosnaud, and Laura Tach. 2012. "Economic Insecurity and Social Stratification." *Annual Review of Sociology* 38: 341–59.

Wolff, Edward N. 1995. "The Rich Get Increasingly Richer: Latest Data on Household Wealth During the 1980s." In *Research in Politics and Society*, edited by Richard E. Ratcliff, Melvin L. Oliver, and Thomas M. Shapiro. Greenwich, Conn.: JAI Press.

———. 2016. "Household Wealth Trends in the United States, 1962 to 2013: What Happened over the Great Recession?" *RSF: The Russell Sage Foundation Journal of the Social Sciences* 2(6). doi: 10.7758/RSF.2016.2.6.02.

Yadama, Gautam N., and Michael Sherraden. 1996. "Effects of Assets on Attitudes and Behaviors: Advance Test of a Social Policy Proposal." *Social Work Research* 20(1): 3–11. doi: 10.1093/swr/20.1.3.

Zelizer, Viviana A. 1997. *The Social Meaning of Money: Pin Money, Paychecks, Poor Relief, and Other Currencies*. Princeton, N.J.: Princeton University Press.

PART IV
Essay

Wealth and Secular Stagnation: The Role of Industrial Organization and Intellectual Property Rights

HERMAN MARK SCHWARTZ

Changes in firm strategy and structure partially explain the sources and consequences of rising wealth inequality in America. Combining use of state-created monopolies around intellectual property rights (IPRs) for profitability and firm-level strategies to transform their industrial organization by pushing physical capital and noncore labor outside the boundaries of the firm leads to rising levels of wealth and income inequality among firms as well as individuals. Income inequality among firms in turn reduces growth in productive investment and thus in aggregate demand. Slower growth reflexively deters firms from new investment, aggravating the shortfall in aggregate demand. Decreased protection for IPRs and increased protection for subcontracted workers would help increase aggregate demand and thus push growth back to its prior level, as well as reducing wealth and income inequality among individuals.

Keywords: inequality, industrial organization, intellectual property, profits

What explains rising economic inequality, particularly wealth inequality? What is the connection between rising economic-wealth inequality and secular stagnation? The other analyses in this special issue answer these questions using econometric techniques to tease out how specific individual or household characteristics such as, for example, marital status, incarceration, or geographic location contribute to wealth outcomes, or they present a series of snapshots for the distribution of wealth and consumption. These analyses are valuable, providing targets for narrow policy interventions and information for future studies. By contrast, this article looks at firms and the macroeconomy to complement the essentially microeconomic studies in this volume.

Firms are the ultimate source of income and wealth. They provide most of the net productive investment that generates the growth that validates wealth, which, after all, is simply a claim on future profits and production. Unless it is inherited, individual wealth has to come from somewhere in the economy. The faster economic growth is, the more likely it is that rising employment and income drive rising individual and household wealth for the broader population. By contrast, as Edward Wolff shows elsewhere in this issue, macroeconomic instability and stagnant growth after 2007 contributed to falling wealth outside of a narrow slice of U.S. households.

Analyses linking rising household inequality to macroeconomic stagnation posit a rela-

Herman Mark Schwartz is professor in the Department of Politics at the University of Virginia.

The author would like to thank John Echeverri-Gent, Lindsay Flynn, Ronen Palan, Bent Sofus Tranøy, and the anonymous reviewers for comment and criticism. Earlier versions presented at the Russell Sage Foundation, the University of North Carolina, Harvard University, the University of Virginia Batten School of Public Policy, and Yale-National University of Singapore also benefited from audience comments and questions. Responsibility remains with the author, however. Direct correspondence to: Herman Mark Schwartz at schwartz@virginia.edu, Politics Department, University of Virginia, PO Box 400787, Charlottesville VA 22904.

tively simple mechanism. Higher-income individuals have a lower marginal propensity to consume (Stockhammer 2015). This lower propensity to consume plausibly reduces aggregate demand, slowing growth. But this answer is self-evidently incomplete. First, as noted, it explains neither where household income comes from nor why income inequality has been rising. Second, it ignores other important parts of aggregate demand, and thus why higher savings do not produce higher investment. Conventionally, gross domestic product (GDP) is the sum of C + G + I + (X − M), that is, consumption, government spending on goods and services, investment and net exports. The change or delta (Δ) in GDP is the sum of the various changes in each of these four components. Consumer spending unquestionably constitutes the bulk of demand in the U.S. economy, ranging from 65 to 70 percent of GDP in any given year in the past four decades. But the other 30 to 35 percent is hardly residual. Indeed, given the inevitable decline in household income during a recession, the whole point of countercyclic fiscal policy is to boost both C and G by replacing lost C with automatic government transfers as well as creating positive ΔG via infrastructure or other nontransfer spending; the point of monetary policy is to boost investment (to create positive ΔI) to compensate for declining investment.

When John Maynard Keynes wrote in 1936, the vast majority of households lived from paycheck to paycheck, so it was obvious that household consumption was a secondary factor in the formation of new income. This is less true today, given the availability of credit and the modicum of assets the average household owns (see Wolff, this issue). Still, recent survey data suggest that about 60 percent of U.S. households have less than $1,000 in liquid savings and that one-third of those households do not have a bank savings account. For most households, then, credit is a buffer against falling income rather than a net increase. In the other 40 percent of households, most credit is mortgage credit, but conventionally new housing construction is categorized as a fixed investment. Consequently, investment and government spending still dominate because they constitute the majority of net new spending, and it is this delta that matters for growth.

To the extent that we live in a world of rising household income inequality (Piketty and Saez 2006), it could be argued that the lower marginal propensity to consume at the top of the income pyramid could generate additional savings that then flows into some sort of investment. Yet investment growth is both unusually weak and at historically low levels as a share of GDP (U.S. Bureau of Economic Analysis [BEA] 2014, table 1.1.6). This raises an interesting question: why does the extra saving by higher income households not translate into growth promoting investment? The annual increase in U.S. private fixed nonresidential investment after 2001 has been substantially slower than the prior decade, aside from the rebound year of 2012. Moreover, the absolute level of investment is also flat. Obviously, the housing bubble has something to do with that: real gross residential fixed investment in 2014 still only approximated the absolute level of spending in 1993. But corporate investment has also been tepid. As of December 2015, the absolute level of gross private fixed investment net of residential construction was only 12 percent above its 2007 level in real terms, net investment (which matters more) was 12 percent below the 2008 peak, and both were below trend (BEA 2009, table 5.2.6). The investment slowdown points us in the direction of corporate strategy and structure because corporations are what translate household savings into productive investment.

Government spending growth is just as tepid as corporate investment growth. Absolute U.S. government spending at all levels is roughly at the same level as in 2005 in real terms, having (understandably) fallen from its peak during the Obama stimulus period from 2010 to 2011. With respect to ΔG, total government spending on consumption and investment in 2015 was at roughly the same absolute level as in 2006, although GDP had grown 12 percent in real terms; federal spending absolutely was at 2007 levels, and state and local government spending was absolutely only a bit above the 2000 level (BEA 2014, tables 1.1.2, 1.16, and 3.9.6). As with the tepid investment response to historically low interest rates, government fiscal restraint has an important corporate component. The post-2008 crisis years have seen concerted political pressure from largely conservative parties to restrain government deficits.[1] To the extent that revenue growth is weak, so is spending growth. Tax cuts obviously constrain revenues. But corporate tax avoidance schemes that allocate profits to entities in tax havens also constrain revenue (Zucman 2015). As of 2015, the five hundred largest U.S. firms held $2.1 trillion offshore, avoiding an estimated $620 billion tax liability (McIntyre, Phillips, and Baxandall 2015). By way of comparison, the 2010–2011 Obama economic stimulus package amounted to $831 billion, suggesting that a stimulus-worth of untapped revenue sits idle; alternately, this $630 billion equals 20 percent of total government consumption and investment spending in 2015. Put differently, these offshore holdings were five times nonresidential fixed investment in 2014, suggesting that simply spending them down over the next decade might boost net investment by 50 percent each year over that decade.

This article thus looks to inequality in corporate income (profit) and wealth (market capitalization) for a major source of rising inequality in household income and wealth, and thence slower growth. Secondarily—because profits must be earned before they can be sequestered in tax havens—it looks at the limits to fiscal policy created by firms' use of tax havens. Put simply, rising income (profit) and wealth inequality among *firms* is what drives much of both rising individual income and wealth inequality and much of the tepid investment response to the greatest monetary stimulus in U.S. history.

Changes in U.S. firms' strategy and structure drive interfirm inequality. Firms' strategies for profitability increasingly depend on legally constituted monopolies, particularly but not exclusively the patent and copyright system, and from intangible assets and regulatory monopolies more generally. Firms possessing intellectual property rights (IPRs) can use them to extract monopoly rents from other firms and consumers, producing interfirm inequality of profits. Firms' structure has also changed in response to financial market pressure to maximize shareholder value—that is, return on assets. This pressure forces or induces firms to pursue industrial organization strategies that shift labor and physical assets outside the legal boundaries of the firm, producing individual-level inequality and weakening the rate of growth of consumption. Shifting physical assets outside the firm means that firms with strong IPR positions accumulate monopoly rents but have no incentive to invest back in the real economy, weakening investment growth. Evidence is increasing that firms with higher profits also pay higher wages (Song et al. 2015; Barth et al. 2014), so shifting labor outside firms with strong IPRs or other monopoly positions and into firms with no ability to extract rents contributes to rising household income inequality by polarizing the wage structure. On one side are firms in highly competitive markets whose profitability depends on depressing wages; on the other side are firms accruing monopoly rents and sharing part of those rents with their increasingly smaller slice of the total workforce.

Interfirm inequality dampens investment; interpersonal inequality dampens demand; these contribute to secular stagnation. In turn, slow growth intensifies pressure on politicians to pursue self-defeating strategies of fiscal austerity, weakening growth of government spending. Although these processes do not explain everything about modern inequality or slower growth, they do suggest that a significant part of that inequality and stagnation is neither inevitable nor irremediable. Because rising inequality stems from the combination of state-constituted monopolies and changes in industrial organization, public policy can address at least part of the problem of rising wealth and income inequality.

SECULAR STAGNATION?

Growth in the U.S. economy slowed markedly in the 2000s. Real GDP and real per capita GDP respectively increased by roughly 37 percent and 24 percent in the 1970s, 1980s, and 1990s (yes, even the often lamented 1970s). But these

---

1. Conservative parties account for the majority of cabinet years in the rich OECD countries after 2008.

growth rates halved after 2000. U.S. growth rates remained among the highest for the twenty-two rich OECD countries,[2] which saw an even greater slowdown in aggregate GDP, though less of one in per capita GDP growth. Worse, from 2009 to 2015, of a total of 154 possible country-years for these twenty-two countries, only eight years had no output gap, and the OECD as a whole has had a persistent output gap of about 2.4 percent of GDP (OECD 2015a). Is this slowdown and the past decade in particular a case of secular stagnation? Strictly speaking, secular stagnation arises from insufficient aggregate demand. Arguments positing a supply side basis for slow growth are not, strictly speaking, secular stagnation arguments. Although I offer an argument based on aggregate demand, the supply-side arguments for slow growth need to be taken seriously and accommodated in an argument that stresses demand-side factors. Focusing on the wealth and income distribution effects of IPRs allows us to combine important supply- and demand-side factors.

Robert Gordon (2012, 2014) argues that the United States and other rich OECD economies have exhausted the stock of truly revolutionary supply-side technologies. Flush toilets matter more than flash telephones in the sense that new technology yields diminishing returns in productivity in comparison with the once-only technological breakthroughs of the century from 1850 to 1950. This explains the productivity and thus growth slowdown that began in the 1970s. In addition, slower population growth also slows aggregate GDP growth, though its effects on productivity are less obvious. Dismissing optimists such as Paul Markillie (2012), Erik Brynjolfsson and Andrew McAfee (2014), and Michael Rüßmann and colleagues (2015), Gordon suggests that the natural rate of productivity growth will revert to its historic level of about 0.25 to 0.33 percent per year over the rest of the century.

Gordon's argument comports with Joseph Schumpeter's (1939, 1942) about the importance of clusters of radical innovation for igniting growth. Schumpeter argues that without a cluster of radical innovations, growth settles into a "circular economy" pattern in which profits cover depreciation and managerial salaries for owners, but per capita growth is nugatory.[3] Schumpeter's circular flow economy is Gordon's economy. For Schumpeter, rapid growth requires bold entrepreneurs, and entrepreneurs require the prospect of monopoly rents to propel them into action. Indeed, unlike most neoclassical economists, Schumpeter explicitly praises monopoly:

> A system—any system, economic or other—that at *every* given point of time fully utilizes its possibilities to the best advantage may yet in the long run be inferior to a system that does so at *no* given point of time, because the latter's failure to do so may be a condition for the level of speed of long-run performance. (1942, 83)

The possibility of radical innovations in product and process creates the possibility for quasi-monopoly rents for firms at the technology frontier; the prospect of rents catalyzes credit creation to bring those technologies to market.[4] But without rents, radically new technologies will not come into the market. Schumpeter expects these rents to dissipate over time, throwing the economy back into a circular flow state. Yet, if Gordon is right, then we currently see Schumpeterian rents without (significant) innovation or growth. If Schumpeter is right, then Gordon is mistaken about the growth and investment implications of the new technologies identified by the optimists he dismisses. To rephrase Solow about this paradox, why does the current round of technological innovation show up in profitability but not the productivity statistics, and why is there an ap-

---

2. The countries are the United States, Canada, Japan, Korea, Britain, Ireland, France, Germany, Italy, Austria, Spain, Portugal, Switzerland, Netherlands, Belgium, Denmark, Finland, Norway, Sweden, Luxembourg, Australia, and New Zealand.

3. Schumpeter's circular flow economy thus differs from the Ricardian stationary economy in its assumption that some incremental innovation occurs.

4. Serial entrepreneur (PayPal, Palantir) Peter Thiel (2014) recently popularized this argument in *Zero to One*.

parent disconnect between innovation, rents, and investment levels? Keynes suggests some demand-side answers to these questions.

The shortest possible version of Keynes's *General Theory* is that the economy possesses multiple stable equilibrium states rather than one optimal state posited by neoclassical economics (1936, see in particular chapter 16). At one extreme is a high-investment, high-wage, high-demand equilibrium that generates high profits, high employment, and high growth. The other extreme is a low-investment, low-wage, low-demand equilibrium that generates low profits, low employment, and low growth, rather like Schumpeter's circular economy. Keynes divided demand up into two components. D1 connoted household consumption (C in modern GDP accounting), which, as noted, Keynes assumed was relatively stable given households' lack of access to credit or savings and also because of the stickiness of wages. D2 connoted demand for investment goods (I in modern GDP accounting), which both suffered from volatility and, when rising, provided for a powerful increase in demand through its multiplier effects. Keynes anticipated the later division of demand into C + G + I, given that his solution for weak C + I was an increase in government spending, G.

The essential mechanism maintaining Keynes's lower equilibrium is not so much feeble entrepreneurs—though fear does deter investment—but rather rational responses to slow or slowing growth. Firms facing weak demand would not invest, for fear of creating overcapacity and decreased profits. Instead, whatever profits they generated would simply accumulate in banks as firms used profits to retire debt (Koo 2011). (Today they park profits overseas instead.) This reduction in D2 or I would create a self-sustaining slack economy in which low demand deterred new net investment, and in which low new net investment in turn assured continued low demand. In this economy savings pile up, producing low interest rates, but low interest rates fail to induce new investment given weak demand and investor fear. This is the essence of the liquidity trap. Keynes puts this issue succinctly, answering the question of why the lower marginal propensity to consume on the part of the rich, or for our purposes the lower marginal propensity to invest on the part of rich firms, does not automatically result in more savings and more investment:

> Those who think [that savings automatically get productively invested] are deceived, nevertheless, by an optical illusion, which makes two essentially different activities appear to be the same. They are fallaciously supposing that there is a nexus which unites decisions to abstain from present consumption [saving] with decisions to provide for future consumption [productive investment]; whereas the motives which determine the latter are not linked in any simple way with the motives which determine the former. (1936, 21)

Although an individual act of saving seemingly increases the potential pool for investment, that saving—in the absence of an automatic mechanism producing investment—subtracts from demand, leading to a decrease in someone else's income and thus diminishing the total pool of savings available for investment. Declining investment produces declining savings, as the data show (see Wolff, this issue). Keynes saw the central economic problem as assuring that investment grew, and equally importantly grew consistently, in order to maximize employment. Schumpeter (1942) argued that the state should get out of the way of heroic entrepreneurs sparking a new round of growth through innovation; Keynes argued that the state had to inject demand into the economy, encouraging risk averse firms to invest rather than pile up cash. This visibly increased demand would calm Keynes's timorous entrepreneurs and induce matching private investment. The strong multiplier effects of state-sponsored investment would provide the new goods and services needed to absorb the initial injection of money and thus prevent inflation. They would also generate the income needed to supply savings for this new investment. State-sponsored investment thus had public goods aspects (as indeed does all productive investment and credit creation).

As with Peter Thiel's and Robert Gordon's updating of Schumpeter, Keynes's arguments also have modern carriers, as in Lawrence

Summers's (2014) revival of Alvin Hansen's (1939) secular stagnation arguments. Summers's analysis, however, largely concentrates on low nominal interest rates as an indicator of excess savings. Like Keynes, Summers sees the zero-bound as an impediment to policy-making because monetary authorities cannot push nominal rates below the zero-bound (2014, 29).

Schumpeter's and Keynes's analyses seem somewhat at odds on the current situation. On the one hand, low interest rates should crowd investment into highly promising technologies. Indeed this seems to be the case with Silicon Valley's "unicorns"—software-based firms with private or public equity market valuations over $1 billion that promise to capture enormous monopoly rents (such as Uber, Flipkart, Delivery Hero). Moreover, contra Keynes, profits appear to be at secular highs. According to the McKinsey Global Institute, global firms' net income after taxes and interest payments rose by a factor of five from 1980 to 2013, and tripled before taxes and interest (Dobbs et al. 2015).[5] The share of profits in global GDP also rose from 7.6 percent to 9.8 percent from 1980 to 2013; for U.S. firms, profits after tax rose from an average of 4.2 percent of gross domestic income in the 1980s to 6.1 percent in the decade to 2014 (Dobbs et al. 2015; FRED n.d.).

On the other hand, despite high profitability and extremely low interest rates, ever more cash seems to be piling up in ever fewer firms' hands without generating much Schumpeterian investment. Low interest rates have facilitated increased U.S. corporate borrowing, but this debt is not used for real investment. Instead, U.S. firms have poured more money into stock buybacks and dividends than into fixed investment. Joshua Mason reports that each additional dollar of corporate earnings or borrowing yielded only 10 cents of investment in the 2000s, versus 30 to 40 cents the 1960s (2015, 19). In principle, money returned to households via share buybacks could be channeled into investment by other firms. In practice, given the massive inequality in household equity ownership, much of the money returned to individual households flows into passive investments and nonproductive "assets" that are actually positional goods of one sort or another. Eventually this money ends up as the $2.5 trillion in excess reserves banks have parked at U.S. Federal Reserve banks. This is the modern version of Keynes's liquidity trap.

Corporate wealth is very unequally distributed. At the beginning of 2014, the world's 1,200 largest nonfinancial firms collectively held about $3.5 trillion in cash or cash equivalents. Firms with more than $2 billion held 85 percent of this cash, and the top 10 percent of firms held a bit more than 50 percent (Burn-Murdoch and Bennetzen 2014; see also Pinkowitz, Stulz, and Williamson 2012). Among these firms, U.S. firms—the majority of the top 10 percent—held 50 percent of all cash, and Apple alone accounted for 5 percent of global cash and thus 10 percent of U.S. firms' cash. As the next section shows, this pattern of inequality in corporate cash holdings is connected to differential control over intellectual property or access to rents because these cash holdings are retained profits qua rents. The combination of unequally distributed cash holdings and the passive investment of those holdings is the material manifestation of the liquidity trap.

INTERFIRM PROFIT AND WEALTH INEQUALITY

Why do firms have such large cash hoards, and which firms? Why is monetary policy ineffective in motivating use of those hoards? This section examines the distribution of profits and cash holdings among global publicly listed firms to show why Schumpeter's rents pool in Keynes's liquidity trap. Juan Sánchez and Emircan Yurdagul report that U.S. corporate cash holdings were at historically high levels relative to the size of the economy in 2013, amounting to a full $5 trillion for all publicly held U.S. firms, as opposed to just those within the global 1200, and $1.6 trillion for U.S. nonfinancial firms (2013, 5; see figure 1). Moreover, the rate of cash accumulation accelerated from roughly 7 percent per year, 1980 to 1995, to 10 percent, 1995 to 2010. The rate of growth was

---

5. McKinsey authors analyzed all global firms with annual revenues over $200 million, a bit more than twenty-eight thousand in total (Dobbs et al. 2015).

Figure 1. U.S. Corporate Cash Holdings

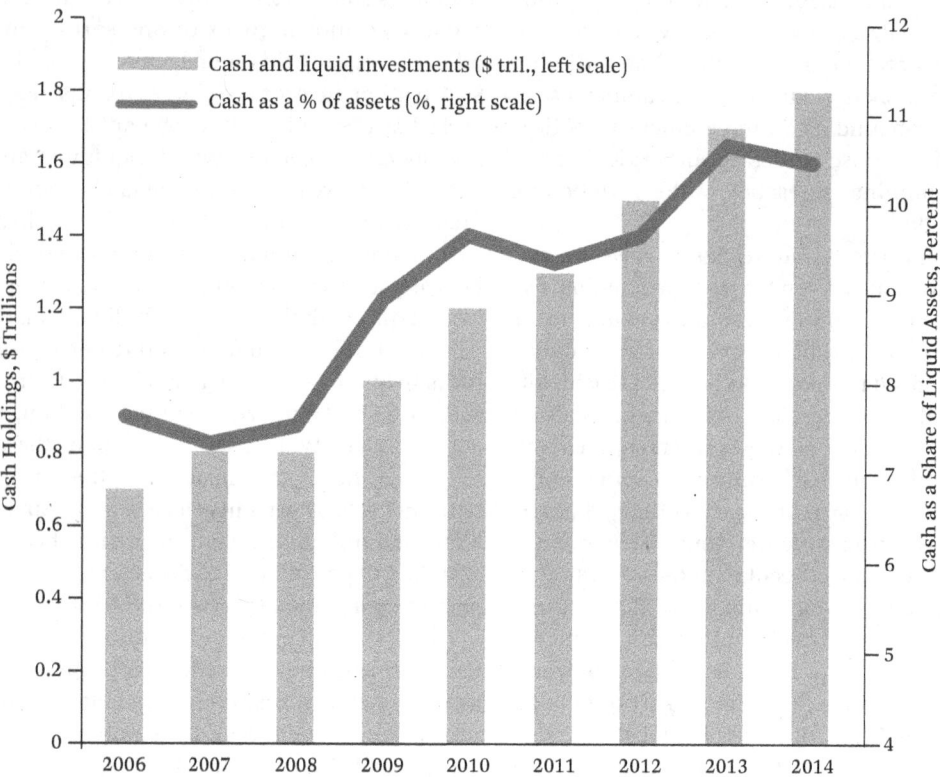

Source: Author's compilation based on Mergent Online (2015) data.

even faster at the end of the second period. The net result is that the ratio of corporate cash holdings to GDP rose from about 6.5 percent to about 14.5 percent from 1990 to 2014.

This cash is distributed quite unequally. Of the roughly $1.8 trillion in domestic cash U.S. firms held at the end of 2014, the top four firms accounted for 21 percent and the top twenty-five firms (the corporate 1 percent) for almost 50 percent (Monga 2015). This inequality necessarily reflects differences in the underlying profitability of firms, because cash holdings necessarily arise from profits, which in turn create differences in market capitalization.[6]

Using a different dataset than Sánchez and Yurdagul (2013), Jason Furman and Peter Orszag report that the variance in nonfinancial corporate return to investment has increased significantly over the past thirty years, confirming rising inequality in profitability (2015, 9–10).

This inequality can be seen by constructing Gini indices for the two thousand publicly listed firms in the Forbes Global 2000 (FG2k) and for the 5,267 publicly listed nonfinancial firms in the Osiris database that had operating revenues exceeding $1 billion in 2014 (Forbes 2015; Bureau Van Dijk 2015).[7] The FG2k firms

---

6. Firms could increase their cash holdings by borrowing and then holding cash, but aside from this being economically irrational when it is above the level needed to finance ongoing operations, the net debt to equity ratio for the nonfinancial U.S. S&P 500 has fallen by two-thirds over the past twenty years (Compustat).

7. Not all firms in the Forbes Global 2000 have positive profits. Given that the Gini index does not work well with negative numbers, I opted to simply truncate the data series for each year of the Global 2000 at the Nth firm before firms had negative profits. Alternately, I could have simply bottom coded all firms making losses as 0. This latter technique is the one that the Luxembourg Income Study uses when dealing with negative household

account for roughly one-third of all corporate profits in any given year. The annual Gini index for profits among the FG2k firms over the 2006 to 2015 period averaged 0.649; the Gini for total profits by all U.S. firms in the FG2k 2006 to 2015 was higher at 0.744. The Gini for sales and assets was 0.59 each. Stripping out financial firms and utilities, the FG2k Ginis remain largely the same. Gini indices for profits by the nonfinancial firms in the Osiris dataset show a similar pattern. To eliminate noise, I aggregated profits into five-year periods beginning in 1990 and ending in 2014. The average Gini over this much larger set is unsurprisingly higher than for the FG2k, at 0.792, because it includes a much longer tail of low or no profit firms, even after truncating firms with losses. Truncating the Osiris data at two thousand firms over the same period as the FG2k generates a similar Gini at 0.639, even though the Osiris set excludes financial firms. This pattern of inequality holds across sectors in the Osiris data.

This high level of inequality in firms' profitability translates into inequality in their wealth—market capitalization—and consequent to that inequality in the wealth and income of the people employed by those firms. The average Gini for market capitalization among the FG2k firms was 0.607. These Ginis are considerably higher than the corresponding indices for individual or household inequality in a wide range of countries (table 1).

The unequal distribution of global profits is replicated inside national economies. Table 2 compares the eight largest sectors inside the United States, Germany, and Japan in terms of their share of total profits, and thus firms' ability to accumulate corporate wealth in the form of both retained earnings and market capitalization, for firms from those countries and in the FG2k list. This comparison is crude, given that firms inside the same nominal category do not necessarily have the same degree of IPR heaviness, as the subsequent discussion of firms based on the Osiris data shows. It is based on profits as a percentage of sales, a slightly unusual indicator, a choice I justify later. But it still provides an interesting snap-

Table 1. Corporate Profit Inequality and Household Income Inequality

Forbes Global 2000 firms, average 2006 to 2015	0.649
Osiris top 2000, 2005 to 2014	0.639
Osiris 5267 average 1990 to 2014	0.792
Select countries, household income inequality 2013	
South Africa	0.650
Brazil	0.532
United States	0.411
United Kingdom	0.380
Germany	0.306
Denmark	0.269
Norway	0.268
Sweden	0.240

Source: Author's calculations from Forbes Global 2000 data, Osiris database, and OECD-iLibrary.org (Bureau van Dijk 2015; Forbes 2015; OECD 2016).

shot of sectoral dominance in the three largest market economies, and the degree to which profits are above average in those sectors. For example, both the centrality of automobile manufacturing in Germany, and its mediocre profitability (despite Porsche's outlandish 2008 financial coup squeezing VW shares) are evident. Automobile firms in both Japan and Germany make returns that exceed both their U.S. auto counterparts and their own national averages, but which nonetheless are lower than the economy-wide average for the United States. Likewise, four of the eight largest sectors by profit volume in the United States arguably are IPR firms. But aside from Japanese pharmaceutical firms—whose prices are tightly regulated by the Japanese state and who are notoriously bad at innovation—the IPR sectors everywhere all have ratios of profit to sales well above their national averages.

The distribution of U.S. corporate cash holdings suggests that IPRs explain these differences in profitability. This distribution is both unequal and favors firms controlling significant IPRs. Table 3 displays the ten largest

---

incomes. However, the former technique lowers the final Gini coefficient and thus provides a more conservative estimate of inequality among firms. Thanks to Lindsay Flynn and Annie Rorem for discussions about this issue.

Table 2. Eight Largest Sectors in Forbes Global 2000

United States	Share of Total Profits for U.S. FG2k Firms	Profit as Percentage of Sales	Japan	Share of Total Profits for Japanese FG2k Firms	Profit as Percentage of Sales	Germany	Share of Total Profits for German FG2k Firms	Profit as Percentage of Sales
Oil and gas operations	12.46	8.0	Auto and truck manufacturers	14.31	3.7	Auto and truck manufacturers	25.72	5.0
Banks - major	7.74	5.1	Banks - major	13.93	3.4	Insurance - diversified	12.42	2.8
Pharmaceuticals	4.93	8.9	Trading companies	8.85	3.4	Diversified chemicals	11.74	6.0
Conglomerates	4.28	8.2	Telecommunication services	7.20	5.4	Utilities - electric	11.30	4.0
Software and programming	3.69	21.4	Pharmaceuticals	4.00	5.3	Conglomerates	6.61	4.9
Computer hardware	3.36	10.4	Auto and truck parts	3.85	3.3	Banks - major	6.04	1.7
Utilities - electric	3.25	6.5	Transportation - rail	3.60	4.3	Software and programming	3.66	17.7
Computer services	3.15	15.3	Iron and steel	3.59	4.4	Pharmaceuticals	2.64	16.2
These sectors as % of total economy	42.9			59.3			80.1	
Average for economy		5.9			2.8			3.4

Source: Author's calculation from Forbes Global 2000 data for indicated years.

Table 3. Top Ten U.S. Firms by Cash Holdings at December 2014

Company	$ Billions
Apple[a]	178.0
Microsoft[a]	90.2
Google[a]	64.4
Pfizer[b]	53.6
Cisco Systems[a]	53.0
Oracle[a]	44.7
Johnson & Johnson[b]	33.1
QUALCOMM[a]	31.6
Medtronic[b]	31.1
Merck & Co.[b]	29.2
Total	608.9
Total as a percentage of $1.78T holdings by 2000 firms	33.8

Source: Author's compilation based on Mergent Online (2015) data.
[a]tech industries
[b]pharmaceuticals

firms in terms of offshore cash holdings. These firms collectively hold about one-third of the total cash held by the two thousand largest U.S. firms. The predominance of tech and pharmaceutical firms in this list is obvious. Indeed, as table 2 might suggest, only two U.S. oil firms and two banks break the top twenty. By contrast, the two largest automobile firms in the world, VW and Toyota, collectively employing about 930,000 people and generating nearly $0.5 trillion in annual revenue, together held only about $60 billion in cash in 2014, about the same as Google, with sixty thousand employees and $66 billion in revenue.

We would expect large sectors, such as autos in Germany or Japan, to capture a large share of profit simply because they account for a large share of economic activity. The question is whether those profits are disproportionate to the size of the sector. This is the first reason I use net profit as a share of operating revenues as an indicator. Although there is no reason to expect profit as a percentage of sales to equalize over time, profit relative to operating revenue is a reasonable indicator of the degree to which a firm captures value from the value chain of which it is part. This is a reasonable indication of the degree to which monopoly power is successfully exercised.

To operationalize this, I selected the three hundred largest firms in the Osiris dataset by cumulative net profit over four five-year periods starting in 1995. These firms account for roughly 60 percent of the net profit of the five thousand plus firms in the dataset for any given period. Because we are concerned with the delta in investment and in government revenues, these firms matter as they are both big and control the bulk of profits. At the same time, the choice of a global rather than U.S. dataset is a conservative option, given the predominance of U.S. firms in many IPR sectors. I aggregate the net profit and operating revenues for these firms by NACE sector in five-year periods beginning in 1990.[8] Aggregating data to the sector level is also a conservative choice. I then calculated the average ratio of tangible fixed assets to intangible fixed assets for the same periods for a given sector. Table 4 presents the results of a simple correlation of the share of net profit in operating revenues against the ratio of intangible fixed assets to tangible fixed assets. Despite the enormous positive "China" shock to profits for oil and materials based firms in the 2000s, it shows a steadily increasing correlation from 1995 to 2014. Though none of these rise to the level of statistical significance, the last period is close at $p = 0.106$. Figure 2 presents the data for the twenty largest sectors visually, the size of the bubble being proportional to the sector share of total profit. The three outliers to the northwest are real estate, pipelines, and coal mining. The last two benefited from China's outsized demands for energy, and the first from the housing bubble. Stripping them out would make the correlation statistically significant at $p = 0.05$.

The second reason to use the ratio of net profit to operating revenue as an indicator of market power relates to changes in industrial organization that affect the distribution of income to individuals. IPR firms have a dispro-

---

8. NACE (nomenclature statistique des activités économiques dans la communauté européenne) is the standard industrial classification scheme for the European Union (see Eurostat 2008).

Table 4. Net Profit to Operating Revenues

	1995–1999		2000–2004		2005–2009		2010–2014	
	All Twenty Sectors	Excluding Outliers	All Twenty Sectors	Excluding Outliers	All Twenty Sectors	Excluding Outliers	All Twenty Sectors	Excluding Outliers
Correlation	0.1436	0.3544	0.1519	0.2224	0.2509	0.587	0.3625	0.8313
p-value	0.5457	0.1365	0.5227	0.36	0.2861	0.0104	0.1162	0.0000
N	20	19	20	19	20	18	20	17

Source: Author's calculation from Osiris data (Bureau van Dijk 2015).

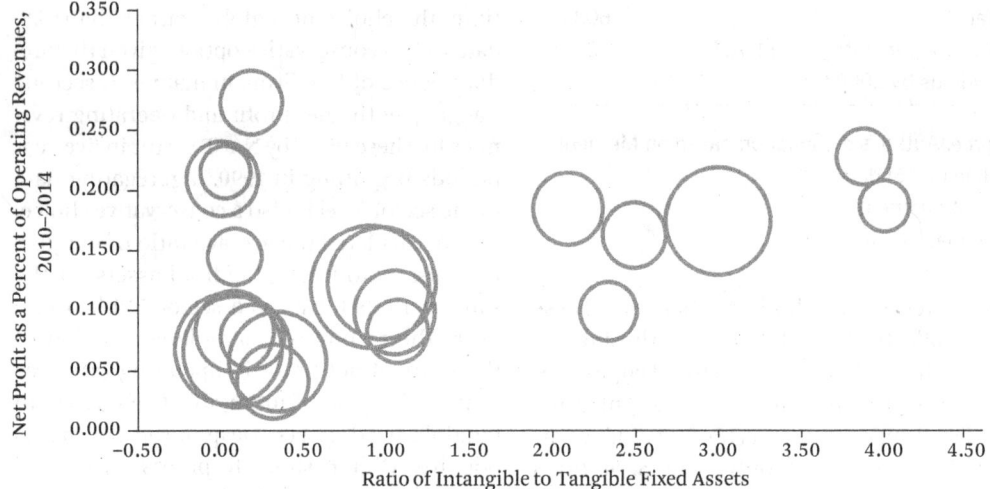

Figure 2. Net Profit Versus Fixed Assets, Top Twenty Sectors by Profit, 2010–2014

Source: Author's compilation based on Osiris data (Bureau van Dijk 2015).
Note: Circles are proportional to share of profits for top three hundred firms.

portionately large share of profits relative to operating revenue or sales, and have disproportionately large cash holdings. An unequal distribution of profit among firms is nothing new, as the Osiris data show. The Gini for corporate profits was as skewed in the 1990s as it is today. Also, the giant mass production firms that dominated the economy of the 1950s and 1960s probably captured outsized profits via oligopolistic competition. Yet the economy had strong growth, a relatively equal distribution of income, and smaller pools of retained earnings compared with today because the form of industrial organization redistributed those profits not only widely within the firm but also across firms with much larger headcounts than today.

To understand what changed, we have to look at how IPR firms generate profit and how the predominant form of industrial organization has evolved over the past four decades. Put simply, the nature of IPRs as monopolies allows the profits that these monopolies generate to accrue in firms with a lower propensity to invest, allows those firms to shrink their labor footprint to the smallest possible size (which concentrates wage income), and allows those firms to shift profits to low tax venues with greater ease than the industrial behemoths of the 1960s could. The following sections discuss the sources of monopoly power and changes in industrial organization, that is, the new combination of strategy and structure.

Strategy: IPRs, Monopoly Profits, and Industrial Inequality

Mid-twentieth-century firms' profitability depended on their control over physical capital and the efficient management of that physical capital. The biggest and most profitable firms were those controlling large fixed investments (Piore and Sabel 1984). These firms did most of their production in-house, and their employee base incorporated a huge range of ancillary services supporting production (Lazonick 2009). Think: the old GE or GM. GM's employee headcount in 1960 was roughly six hundred thousand, and it did (inter alia) its own accounting, cleaning, and catering. It produced 70 percent of its value in-house, and designed and built most of its machinery. The nearest equivalent today would be Samsung, a diversified industrial giant, which draws some inputs from its *chaebol* family members while exploiting Korean small and medium-sized enterprises. In the 1960s, tangible assets such as plant and equipment constituted 80 percent of the stock market capitalization of the S&P500 (OceanTomo). Stock market capitalization is the equivalent of a firm's wealth and a reasonable approximation of its power (Weber 1978, 93, 108, 638; Nitzan 1998).

Today, firms' profitability largely depends on their control over intangible assets, which largely means IPRs such as patents, copyright, and trademark. The biggest firms in terms of market capitalization and profitability are those controlling the most valuable patent and IPR portfolios. In a significant change in industrial organization, these firms largely subcontract everything not related to the direct production of their IPRs, shrinking their employee base to the absolute minimum. This subcontracting includes the physical production of goods. Think: Apple. Apple's employee headcount is about ninety thousand, but sixty thousand of these are contract workers in its retail stores. Apple subcontracts virtually all of its physical production to firms such as Foxconn (Hon Hai Precision) that use cheap Chinese labor. Apple makes nothing physical itself, aside from a few highly specialized servers. By 2005, intangible assets constituted 80 percent of the market capitalization of the S&P500.

IPRs give their owner a legal monopoly. Inequality among firms arises from the increasing density of IPRs in a handful of firms. Paul Samuelson (1954), Elinor Ostrom (2010) and James Buchanan (1965) define goods using the two binary characteristics of excludability (essentially, can I legally prevent someone from consuming a good?) and rivalry-subtractability in consumption (does my consumption of a good subtract from what you can consume of that good?). This defines four types of goods: private goods, public goods, common pool goods, and club goods.

In Ostrom's (2010) terms, information wants to be a public good, that is, one that is nonrival (nonsubtractable) in consumption and nonexcludable and thus "free" (but see Doctorow 2014). In the extreme case, a digital copy of a piece of music using a standard coding format can be distributed to anyone with a device that can play that codec. Production costs for digitized music are essentially the studio rental fee. Given very low costs of production for the first digital version, the average cost of production is minimal and the marginal cost of reproduction is virtually zero (some electricity is consumed downloading and playing the file). Digitized music is close to being a pure public good—nonexcludable, nonsubtractable. How can actors producing music be profitable in this environment? In the absence of profits, why would they produce public goods in the first place?

Profits can only arise if the state creates and enforces excludability via IPRs. IPRs transform public goods into club goods by creating excludability (Buchanan 1965) and create a possible incentive for production. In this process, the state creates and enforces both the quantity and quality of excludability and thus determines the potential profitability of any given club good. Thus the music industry has directed major lobbying efforts toward creating, enforcing, and extending the Digital Millennium Copyright Act (DCMA) of 1998 as well as toward doubling the copyright period through the Copyright Extension Act of 1998. The DMCA makes it illegal to thwart copyright protection methods using software or hardware. According to the Center for Responsive Politics, the Recording Industry of America Association (RIAA) spent roughly $90 million lobbying over the decade of the 2000s and an additional $50 million in litigation against alleged pirates.[9] All this lobbying was directed at steadily expanding the scope and effectiveness

---

9. See the Center for Responsive Politics, http://www.opensecrets.org (accessed May 23, 2016).

of restraints on copying of digitized information and thus making it possible to monetize digitized music. The quality of these property rights (their duration, exceptions, or mandates for licensing) matters as much as the quantity (the simple fact of a patent or copyright). Politically defined IPRs determine a significant part of the profitability of a club good and thus the equity market capitalization of the firms producing club goods.

In the worlds of legal and economic theory, IPRs are not a problem. Theoretically, these monopolies expire and are subject to competition through innovation.[10] Practically, though, the link between stock market capitalization and cash flow built on existing monopolies prevents this. Firms' market capitalization is based on current and expected cash flow. Firms with monopolies have a large expected cash flow and thus a large market capitalization relative to their asset base. This market capitalization allows them to preempt competition by using their monopoly profits and stock to buy up potential competitors. Consider the iconic information economy firm Google. Google has bought Motorola Mobility (cell phones), Nest (in-home data collection), Waze (mapping and traffic info), AdMob (cell phone advertising), YouTube (ad delivery channel), and more. As a strategic matter, each of these purchases protects part of Google's franchise (indeed the business press often uses exactly this language to explain the whys and wherefores of these acquisitions). This is why 85 percent of U.S. firms with a return on capital over 25 percent in 2003 were still enjoying that level of return in 2013 (Furman and Orszag 2015, 11), and why IPR intensive firms held the bulk of corporate cash in 2014.

The IPR phenomenon is not limited to nominally high-tech firms, and in any case, some firms that manufacture high-tech goods, such as Flextronics, do so with low margins. Rather, the distinguishing features here are the adoption of a profit strategy in which state-granted monopolies generate corresponding monopoly rents, and of an industrial organization structure that shrinks the employee headcount. This combination extends all the way from iconic tech firms, such as Apple, to decidedly low-tech but not old-fashioned firms, such as McDonald's, which control brands. Between the two are hotel brands, branded beverage producers, pharmaceuticals, suppliers of branded business services, producers of branded consumer goods, finance, and firms controlling various regulated reticulation networks.

Monopoly rents and profits accruing to IPRs would not matter if the industrial structure in turn distributed those profits to a broad base of workers, or ploughed them back as investment, or saw them captured as tax revenue. To return to the beginning of the article, these profits would then expand some component of C + G + I, leading to growth. The intangibility of IPRs allows firms to pursue strategies that reduce the flow of profit back into consumption, investment, and taxes. Put simply, that IPRs are intangible allows firms to shift the legal ownership of profit into global tax havens in an exaggerated version of the transfer pricing that multinational firms used to use as a tax avoidance strategy. On the industrial organization side, that IPRs can be used to capture monopoly profits from a value chain, and the intangibility of IPRs, allows firms to push physical capital assets and noncore labor outside the legal boundaries of the firm, creating wage inequality. As with tax avoidance strategies, this structure maximizes the return on (now reduced) assets, garnering rewards from financial markets focused on shareholder value. Finally, IPR firms do not need to invest much to expand production because production is contracted out. This produces a situation in which IPR firms retain profits without investing them, and firms that could be doing investment with high multiplier effects both lack the profits to make that investment and correctly fear overcapacity in an era of slow growth.

Tax Avoidance Strategies

The connection between IPRs and tax avoidance—and thence weaker government revenue

---

10. Economists traditionally argue that these monopolies are necessary to provide incentives for innovation (for arguments about the weak links between patents and innovation, see Boldrin and Levine 2008; Boyle 2008; Baker 2008).

and spending—is the simplest to limn. Unlike factories, intellectual property rights can be housed anywhere without affecting the final cost of production. The corporate entity that owns these IPRs can be relocated by a parent seeking to avoid taxation. Apple and Coca-Cola provide the best examples of tax avoidance (for general arguments, see Palan, Murphy, and Chavagneux 2013; Altschuler, Shay, and Toder 2015; and Gravelle 2015). Apple is essentially only a producer of intellectual property (IP). It produces only a handful of highly specialized servers internally. Its product is fully intangible: the iOS and the physical design of its products. The intangibility of both of these allows Apple to shift legal ownership of the rights to 40 percent of the revenues generated by that IP to a shell corporation, Apple Sales International. Apple Sales International had no employees until 2013 and is located in Ireland. It is technically the entity that contracts with, for example, Hon Hai for the production of Apple products and licenses Apple's various operating systems to Hon Hai for installation on those products. Those products are physically produced in China and shipped directly to Apple distributors worldwide. Apple Sales International literally does nothing beyond appending its name to various contracts. It collects massive amounts of revenue from every transaction, however. It attracts no legal tax liability because Apple deliberately structured it in ways that would prevent it from being legally domiciled in either the United States or Ireland for tax purposes (U.S. Senate 2013).

Coca-Cola operates a similar tax avoidance strategy. The formula for Coca-Cola is held by an Irish shell company controlled by Coca-Cola. It is then licensed back to Coke U.S., which produces the physical, flavored syrup that is shipped to franchised bottlers in the United States. These franchisees have slightly more control over their operations than franchised fast food chains in that they can vary how they use their machinery. The result, though, is much the same: the IPR-based profit component of the value chain is segregated legally into a stand-alone firm (and within that firm to a stand-alone daughter firm in a tax haven) to maximize shareholder value and return on assets for that firm. Coca-Cola actually tried to bring production in-house in the 2000s, only to return to its franchising strategy by the end of the decade. This kind of tax evasion and avoidance could not be done as easily if firms were physically producing goods in facilities that were integrated with IP production. Most tax authorities use a substantial presence test that would attach taxation to the value created in that factory, as data generated by Eric Toder (2011) show. Non-IPR multinational firms can and do use transfer pricing to shift revenue into more tax-friendly jurisdictions. But the need for physical proximity to markets or for skilled labor limits the degree of freedom they have in locating production in tax-friendly jurisdictions.

These tax avoidance strategies limit the state's ability to use the welfare state to ameliorate income disparities or to increase government spending to revive the economy. The ratio of after-tax profit to before-tax profit in the United States was roughly 66 percent in the 1980 to 2000 period but rose by 10 percentage points to roughly 76 percent in the 2001 to 2014 period (FRED n.d.). This is a shift of 3.3 percent of GDP—roughly the typical federal budget deficit—from tax revenues to corporate profits. To the extent that these tax avoidance strategies work best for IPR-rich firms, they also produce some of the inequality of corporate profits and cash holdings noted earlier. The implied tax liability on the $2.1 trillion of unrepatriated profits held offshore by the five hundred largest U.S. firms as of early 2015 equates to an estimated $620 billion (McIntyre, Phillips, and Baxandall 2015). In effect, a second 2010–2011 Obama economic stimulus package worth of untapped revenue sits idle, reducing G, if these funds were spent at once. But these holdings are the product of years of accumulation. Even using a flow measure, the annual amounts are nontrivial: the Congressional Joint Committee on Taxation (Gravelle 2015, 20–21) estimates revenue losses at $85 billion for 2014, which is also the rough midpoint of Gabriel Zucman's (2015) estimated range of $55 billion to $133 billion for 2013. On a flow basis, $85 billion equals 27 percent of 2014 corporate tax revenues and 17 percent of the 2014 U.S. federal budget deficit.

Structure: Industrial Organization and Income Inequality

Firms with IPRs have also benefited from a change in industrial organization driven by the spread of the shareholder value model since the 1980s. As Alfred Chandler notes, strategy determines (industrial) structure (1990). The shareholder value strategy emphasizes reducing the footprint of labor and physical assets inside a company (Lazonick 2009). Put simply, if what matters to financial markets is return on assets, then dividing a large numerator (monopoly profits) over a small denominator (the costs of labor and physical assets) produces the biggest financial market bang for the buck. Not coincidentally, this approach also allows management to reward itself lavishly as a firm's market capitalization rises. Financial markets thus press firms to contract out physical-asset-heavy production and contract in or out labor-intensive services when those things are not a core activity for the firm. Both processes concentrate income. Sociologists have long noted that firms tend to harmonize wages inside the firm, a finding confirmed by a recent study of the tax returns of 6 percent of all U.S. employees (Song et al. 2015). Janitors directly employed by highly profitable firms are better paid than janitors working for low-profit firms contracted in by higher profit firms. Concentrated profits and wealth among a few firms lead to concentrated income among people because firms pay out their earnings to a relatively small pool of employees and shareholders. By contrast, firms with large fixed physical asset bases are vulnerable to cyclic downturns, concentrating losses on their owners and workers. Skills-based technical change, an effect complementary to the one described here, accounts for at most one-quarter of rising income inequality (Michaels, Natraj, and Van Reenen 2014).

Studies have shown that rising wage inequality stems from differences in firms' productivity and profitability. Put simply, the richer firms controlling IPRs pay their (core) workers better, and their management more extravagantly, than firms with a tangible asset profile (Barth et al. 2014). Ja Song and his colleagues used a random sample of 6 percent of all IRS form W2 data and covering 100 percent of U.S. firms (2015, 3).[11] Their sample set allowed them to avoid top-coding, imputation, and measurement error because it drew on actual wage payments made by employers. They report that "virtually all of the rise in earnings dispersion [in the United States from 1978 to 2012] between workers is accounted for by increasing dispersion in average wages paid by the employers of these individuals." The better-paying firms were the ones with higher productivity and thus higher profits. Song and colleagues calculate that individuals in the top 1 percent of income earners typically worked in firms paying about double the average wage (2015).[12] Furman and Orszag similarly calculate that about two-thirds of the increase in the income share of the top 1 percent by income in the United States is attributable to increased wages (2015, 3). The dispersion of earnings between firms is consistent with the earlier argument about industrial organization.

As David Weil argues, over the past two decades firms have limited their legal liabilities by shifting noncore labor outside the firm and then contracting that labor back in (2014; see also Autor 2003, 2014; Katz and Krueger 2016). Contracted labor includes not only unskilled labor intensive tasks like janitorial services, but also what might otherwise appear to be core tasks, such as semiskilled assembly line labor. Thus even core automobile assemblers now have substantial numbers of temporary workers on their assembly lines. Weil (2014) shows that the share of workers in some form of contingent or subcontracted employment ranges from one-sixth of the U.S. workforce on a narrow definition (Katz and Krueger 2016), to

---

11. IRS Form W2 is the employer's report of wages and benefits paid to a specific individual in a given tax year. This information is transmitted to both the individual (to accurately prepare a tax filing) and the tax authorities (to prevent misreporting and underreporting).

12. Lawrence Mishel (2015) has criticized some of the Song and colleagues (2015) findings on the basis that there has been no increasing dispersion of wages between top employees and average employees in general, but he does not dispute the finding of interfirm dispersion, which is mostly what concerns us.

as much as one-third if employees at fast food and other franchises are included.

Rather than internalizing an occupationally diverse workforce inside the legal boundaries of the firm, U.S. firms now tend to externalize noncore activities as well as direct production. Functionally, this takes the form of sending labor-intensive, loosely coupled work to low-wage zones inside the United States and, perhaps more commonly, developing Asia. Legally, this takes the form of pushing workers out of the firm and then bringing them back in as employees of different firms providing some service to the core firm. It can even take the form of hiring in direct production workers from labor contractors. This outsourcing (and off-shoring) creates firms with more internally homogeneous work forces while creating more interfirm heterogeneity. It also concentrates revenues on the relatively small number of direct employees remaining in the core firms holding IPRs. This structure allows those IPR-holding firms to avoid sharing rents inside the firm with what would otherwise be a more heterogeneous and larger labor force (Abraham and Taylor 1996). A wide range of firms have adopted this structure, but it is most easily accomplished by IPR-heavy firms.

By contrast, the prevailing form of industrial organization fifty years ago tended to equalize wages and produce intrafirm rent sharing. GM and other firms largely designed their product in-house, operated factories to build components and final products, and hired their own cleaners, security, and so on. Indeed, GM reputedly produced 70 percent of its value internally. They of course patented (trademarked) their intellectual property. But their more limited rents from IPR were distributed to the entire workforce because either unions' or firm's desires for internal labor peace tended to compress wages (Swenson 1989). Equally, these firms' oligopoly rents were redistributed both internally (as in France, Germany, and the United States) and often across the entire economy (as in Sweden and Australia), in response to union pressure. The result was slightly underpaid skilled workers, significantly overpaid unskilled workers (because they had access to health and pension benefits), less variance across firms, and thus less income inequality overall. The closest firms to this older model today would be Samsung or Intel, which still retain substantial manufacturing capacity in-house and have high labor headcounts. This older form of internal cross-subsidization tempered income inequality.

Today, labor-light strategies now extend even into the heart of the old physical economy. Led by Toyota and Honda, who in their formative years only produced 20 percent and 30 percent of the value of a car in-house respectively, and who made generous use of contract labor, Japanese carmakers in the United States (and Japan) increasingly staff their assembly lines with contract workers (see, for example, Weisman 2014; Farmer 2015). Contract workers account for about half the line workers at Subaru's Japanese factories. They account for about 30 percent of labor in Toyota's Canadian factories and 20 percent in its U.S. factories. Nissan's factory in Tennessee may have as many as 60 percent of line positions filled by so-called perma-temps. The U.S. auto manufacturers negotiated a similar two-tier workforce with the United Automobile Workers union during the 2008–2010 crisis, though this arrangement is now unraveling.

At the other end of the spectrum, the high-tech world is full of firms that simply do design and then contract out actual physical production to tangible-asset-heavy manufacturers, and the low-tech world of firms controlling brands similarly works on brand management without doing the actual production of services. Apple, as noted, produces virtually no physical objects. But firms such as ARM (cell phone processor chips), Qualcomm (cellphone switching software and chip design), or Nvidia (graphics processors) operate on similar lines, relying on specialist, physical capital-intensive silicon foundries to build their chips. These foundries are major capital investments, semiconductor fabs typically costing between $1 and $5 billion. Samsung's largest fab cost $10 billion, for example. Finally, the labor-intensive assembly steps are done by specialist assemblers, such as Hon Hai Precision, Flextronics, or Pegatron, using low-wage labor in Asia or Eastern Europe.

This tripartite industrial architecture—high

profit human capital-intensive design firms controlling IPRs, moderately profitable but cyclically vulnerable physical capital-intensive production firms, and low-profit labor-intensive assembly or service delivery firms—is replicated over the entire IPR sector regardless of the technology involved. Thus, in the low-tech hotel and hospitality sector, the typical format is a firm that controls the brand name, a variety of real estate investment trusts (REITs) or real estate firms that own the actual buildings, and disposable labor contractors supplying cleaning and front desk staff. For example, the British hotel giant InterContinental owns only eight physical properties, but licenses its brand to (sometimes quite large) firms operating the rest of the almost five thousand hotels bearing its name. Hilton Hotels similarly only owns about 4 percent of the roughly 4,100 properties operating under its collection of brand names. Firms such as LaborReady and Adecco's Hospitality Staffing Solutions provide labor to hotel operators on demand. Airbnb carries this to an extreme, owning no physical assets whatsoever. In the retail sector, Weil (2014) reports that WalMart's warehouses—something you might imagine to be a core operation for a gigantic retail firm—are actually operated and supplied by the specialist logistics firm Schneider, which then contracts labor from manpower firms like Premier Warehousing Ventures.

Finally, the entire franchise economy also has this structure. In a typical fast-food franchise, the franchisor will supply machinery (built by a different physical-asset-heavy firm), menus, branding, and detailed instructions on food preparation and presentation. Many also supply some start-up capital for franchisees in the form of loans. (McDonald's also usually buys the real estate on which the franchisee's restaurant sits and then rents that to the franchisee.) Franchisors also typically dictate prices to franchisees. The franchisor thus controls virtually all aspects of the operation of the restaurant, and generates profit from everything that goes into the restaurant. The only cost the franchisee typically controls is staffing and wages. The income dynamics here are easy to understand. Franchisees have every incentive to depress wages and hyperexploit their workers to maximize their own profit, and franchisors are able to extract maximum revenue from their tied franchisee clients.

Table 5 presents this three-tier industrial structure via comparisons of employee head count, profits, and profit per employee for some of the firms involved in production of the iPhone, using average revenues, profits and employee headcounts for the 2010–2014 period to even out some of the effects of the recession. The firms chosen are the two producers of the most expensive physical components, the major assemblers, and the largest suppliers of intellectual property. From the typical $630 sale price of an iPhone6, Apple collects $367 in gross revenue (and $319 in net revenue), Samsung collects $65 for the processor and memory, Toshiba collects $37 for the display, Qualcomm collects $15 for the WLAN and cellular software, and Foxconn collects $15 for assembly, according to the technology research firm iSuppli (see also Kraemer, Linden, and Dedrick 2011). Qualcomm's outsized returns in table 5 reflect royalties on the core software connecting handsets to the cellular network; Qualcomm collects money on virtually every handset sold globally, not just Apple products.

It could be argued that the end of internal cross-subsidization present in this new three-tier structure simply reflects a deeper and more efficient division of labor enabled by new information technologies that allow for better monitoring of performance across firm boundaries. But this argument actually supports the points cited. If this deeper division of labor is more efficient, why has growth faltered rather than revived as four decades of change in industrial organization removed damaging internal cross-subsidies? Moreover, our main point is precisely that the removal of internal cross-subsidies concentrates income into lower-headcount firms that capture monopoly rents via IPRs. Finally, better monitoring of performance and in particular labor performance across firm boundaries suggests that brand owners and franchisors are de facto the employer of those workers. Their de jure distance obviates the need to share part of the rent with those workers. So arguments about a technologically enabled division of labor simply "avert their eyes" from the macroeconomic

Table 5. Representative Firms Involved in Production of Apple iPhones, 2010-2014

	IPR (human capital) intensive		Fixed physical asset intensive		Labor intensive	
	Apple	Qualcomm	Samsung	Toshiba	Hon Hai	Pegatron
Makes what?	Design, iOS	WIFI & signal processor software	CPU & DRAM	NAND, touchscreen	Physical assembly	Physical assembly
Labor head count	70,540	25,520	270,000	203,502	898,500	131,625
Gross profit / worker	$833	$515	$236	$113	$12	$14
Net profit / worker	$449	$223	$71	$4	$4	$2
Fixed physical assets / worker	$185	$10	$229	$47	$13	$17
Net profit / fixed assets	243%	2167%	31%	9%	28%	11%
Net profit / sales	23.1%	29.5%	11.1%	1.1%	2.6%	0.9%

Source: Author's compilation based on Osiris data (Bureau van Dijk 2015).
Note: Gross and net profit is US$ 1,000s; fixed assets per worker is US$ 1,000s.

consequences of that new form of industrial organization, and the way in which that form of organization is rooted in legal rather than functional realities.

Investment, IPRS, and Slow Growth

Finally, this new three-tier industrial organization also inhibits net new investment two ways. The human-capital intensive IPR-based firms that accumulate the most profits have the least incentive or need to invest them productively to expand production. The physical-capital intensive firms that need increased investment to expand production face macro- and microeconomic disincentives to invest.

Human capital-intensive firms based on IPRs have no incentive or need to recycle profits as significant new productive investments. They do need to recycle profit to develop new products and improve old ones, and indeed a major strategy for these firms is the creation of rapid emotional or functional obsolescence, as with Apple's series of iPhones. But this requires relatively little spending in comparison with firms making physical products. Expanding the output of software, screenable media, or even many pharmaceuticals does not require massive investment in a new plant. Most pharmaceutical plants run at about one-third of capacity in comparison with automobile factories (McKinsey Global Institute 2012, 54), and producing an additional unit of a program or MP3 file costs nothing. Developing new drugs does entail large fixed up-front costs, but the pharmaceutical industry spent more on mergers and acquisitions than on new drug development over the past eighteen years, suggesting that profits are not being invested in new productive capacity. In either case, most of the cost of new investment for IPR firms is hiring additional workers. Even if this adds to employment, the multiplier effects are weak. These workers are largely concentrated in a few locations, and the additional wages flow into competition over positional goods and especially real estate.

The incentive to invest more is also weak. First, intangible assets do not physically depreciate via production, so to spend money replacing them is pointless. Equally, expanding output does not require more machinery or plants. In contrast to the old physical economy, this reduces gross investment and possibly net investment. Second, by definition, a monopoly prevents competitive entry and thus weakens the pressure to invest in more productive capacity. IPR firms use their thicket of patent and copyright to deter entry (Bessen, Meurer, and Ford 2011). Wendy Schacht reports that patents significantly raise the costs incurred by non–patent holders wishing to use the idea or invent around the patent by an estimated 40 percent for pharmaceuticals, 30 percent for major new chemical products, 25 percent for typical chemical goods, and roughly 7 percent to 15 percent for electronics (2006, 5–6). The rational business strategy is to milk the revenue stream from an IPR as long as possible, making the occasional incremental investment to ward off potential competitors. Finally, the clearest evidence that the major IPR-based firms abjure new investment is the piles of cash noted earlier. If they needed to spend it, they would be doing so.

By contrast, physical-capital intensive firms do need to replace physically depreciating equipment, and should need to expand plants to meet rising demand. Yet these firms also invest less than they might. Why? First, in general they have been historically reluctant to risk creating excess capacity. One reason for the robust investment growth of the postwar era was the reassuring stability of demand growth, which allowed for easy planning and validation of new investment. In today's slow growth environment, the normal productivity creep of 2 to 3 percent is often enough to handle increased demand in the rich economies. Second, one of the major reasons for adopting new ITC technologies and automation is that doing so permits less-costly replacement of depreciating capital and faster turnover of new capital. From a profitability standpoint, this helps lower the denominator in the return on assets equation. But it does not increase aggregate demand to the degree that building older, dumber facilities did in the past. Although faster utilization of capital implies more demand at some point in the future, individual firms both live in the present and cannot count on this demand.

The clearest evidence of the degree to which physical-capital intensive firms have more difficulty accumulating investment funds is to contrast two best-in-class firms. Toyota's $35 billion cash reserve was built up over the four decades in which it was the benchmark for the automobile industry. Apple's $178 billion cash reserve accumulated in less than a decade, a pace roughly sixteen times faster.

The argument here is not that the three-tier industrial structure prevents all investment. The main point is that it reduces *new net* investment and thus slows growth. Slower growth in turn inhibits net new investment, much as John Maynard Keynes argued eighty years ago.

POLICY IMPLICATIONS

A recent OECD study reports that the two point increase in the Gini index in the nineteen rich OECD countries, 1985 to 2005, shaved 4.7 percentage points off cumulative growth, 1990 to 2010 (2015b). That translates to $2 trillion in lost GDP per year in the OECD. This article argues that part of this rising inequality and slower growth can be attributed to the combined effects of changes in corporate strategy and structure. A minority of firms with strong IPRs is able to extract large rents from the economy, and the shift to a three-tier industrial structure prevents the redistribution of those rents into the broader economy. The concentration of large profits into fewer firms and hands increases income inequality. The lower marginal propensity of high-income firms to invest and high-income individuals to consume reduces growth in aggregate demand. This macroeconomic focus helps us understand the limits on purely individual strategies of wealth accumulation analyzed in the other papers in this issue, given that most U.S. wealth is largely corporate debt and equities whose long-term values are tied to U.S. and global growth rates.

What policy responses are possible? The most obvious are to use tax policy to redistribute income to the bottom 80 percent so that postmarket incomes are more equal; to modify patent protection so that premarket incomes are not as unequal among firms and people; to change the relationship between lead firms and their subcontractors and franchisees so that lead firms bear some responsibility for labor conditions and wages in firms technically outside their legal boundaries but functionally inside given the degree of control that lead firms exercise; to thoroughly squash tax havens so that income accruing to intangibles cannot be domiciled in some mysterious space free of taxation; and to aggressively use antitrust policy to prevent incumbents from preemptively buying up potential or existing rivals.

The central policy should aim to weaken monopoly power in the dynamic markets generating growth. Changes in tax policy and welfare spending aimed at individuals help remedy the *postmarket* distribution of income. But to the extent that wealth inequality arises from industrial organization and IPRs then policy interventions also need to change the *premarket* inequality of income among firms. For example, patent and copyright duration could be shortened and the hurdle for patent approval increased to reduce firms' ability to use a thicket of patents to deter competitive entry by other firms. Federal government prizes could replace patents as an incentive toward discovery, such as the robotics challenges of the Defense Advanced Research Projects Agency (Baker 2008).

These policies work with the market to reduce corporate concentration of income, and by doing so should speed up growth, which has positive consequences for employment. Slowing or reversing the concentration of corporate income helps reduce individual income inequality in the short and long term. In *Alice Corp vs CLS Bank International*, the Supreme Court has taken one step by imposing stricter criteria for issuing a patent. It remains to be seen, however, whether the U.S. Patent and Trademark Office follows through. Currently, it is moving only hesitantly toward new processes and standards while it awaits political signals from the administration or a clearer set of guidelines from the courts (interview with the author).

With respect to the new three-tier industrial structure, labor law should make lead employers legally joint employers with their franchisees and labor subcontractors. As with patents, this process has begun. In a recent decision

(*Browning-Ferris*), the National Labor Relations Board ruled that two entities are joint employers "if they share or codetermine those matters governing the essential terms and conditions of employment" which includes "hiring, firing, discipline, supervision, and direction," as well as "wages and hours," "the number of workers to be supplied, controlling scheduling, seniority, and overtime, and assigning work and determining the manner and method of work performance." The NLRB said that even if this coordination was not done "directly and immediately," it was enough if control "affects the means or manner of employees' work and terms of employment, either directly or through an intermediary." This test is still a fairly strict one but again only a first step toward reform. The U.S. business community is already mobilizing to reverse the decision. As with the make-up of the Supreme Court, much rests on the outcome of the 2016 election because a new president will have the opportunity to appoint successors to the wave of board members appointed by President Obama in 2013.

Finally, the recent disclosures of widespread individual tax avoidance in the Panama Papers (Mossack Fonseca scandal) and the obviousness of corporate tax avoidance through corporate inversions have led the Obama administration to rewrite regulations to deter inversions, to use antitrust investigations to deter consolidation, and to open a conversation on tax havens.

Secular stagnation and wealth inequality are not the outcome of blind technological or demographic forces over which we have no control. Wealth inequality starts with firms. Wealth inequality results in part—perhaps a large part—from the current structure of property rights, which creates monopoly profits and larger market capitalization for a select group of firms. Those profits create firm-level inequality in profits that in turn creates individual income inequality. This concentration is partly responsible for secular stagnation, given the low marginal propensity of rich firms to invest and the lower marginal propensity of rich households to consume. The quantity and quality of IPRs are political outcomes and thus can be changed in ways that increase aggregate demand. Doing so would benefit both the economy as an abstract entity, which would make economists happier, and people, which would make them happier.

REFERENCES

Abraham, Katherine G., and Susan K. Taylor. 1996. "Firms' Use of Outside Contractors: Theory and Evidence." *Journal of Labor Economics* 14(3): 394–424.

Altshuler, Rosanne, Stephen Shay, and Eric Toder 2015. "Lessons the United States Can Learn from Other Countries' Territorial Systems for Taxing Income of Multinational Corporations." Washington, D.C.: Urban Institute and Brookings Institution Tax Policy Center.

Autor, David H. 2003. "Outsourcing at Will: The Contribution of Unjust Dismissal Doctrine to the Growth of Employment Outsourcing." *Journal of Labor Economics* 21(1): 1–42.

———. 2014. "Polanyi's Paradox and the Shape of Employment Growth." NBER working paper no. 20485. Cambridge, Mass.: National Bureau of Economic Research.

Baker, Dean. 2008. "Financing Drug Research: What Are the Issues?" *Industry Studies* working paper no. 2008-06. Pittsburgh, Pa.: University of Pittsburgh.

Barth, Erling, Alex Bryson, James C. Davis, and Richard Freeman 2014. "It's Where You Work: Increases in Earnings Dispersion Across Establishments and Individuals in the U.S." NBER working paper no. 20447. Cambridge, Mass.: National Bureau of Economic Research.

Bessen, James E., Michael J. Meurer, and Jennifer L. Ford 2011. "The Private and Social Costs of Patent Trolls." *Law and Economics* research paper no. 11-45. Boston, Mass.: Boston University.

Boldrin, Michele, and David K. Levine. 2008. *Against Intellectual Monopoly*. Cambridge: Cambridge University Press.

Boyle, James. 2008. *The Public Domain: Enclosing the Commons of the Mind*. New Haven, Conn.: Yale University Press.

Brynjolfsson, Erik, and Andrew McAfee. 2014. *The Second Machine Age: Work, Progress, and Prosperity in a Time of Brilliant Technologies*. New York: W. W. Norton.

Buchanan, James M. 1965. "An Economic Theory of Clubs." *Economica* 32(125): 1–14.

Bureau Van Dijk. 2015. "Osiris: Information on Listed Companies, Global." Accessed October 18, 2015.

http://www.bvdinfo.com/en-us/our-products/company-information/international-products/osiris.

Burn-Murdoch, John, and Magnus Bennetzen. 2014. "Where Are the World's Corporate Cash Reserves?" *Financial Times*, January 21, 2014. Accessed May 23, 2016. http://www.ft.com/intl/cms/s/0/4892f01c-82bf-11e3-9d7e-00144feab7de.html#axzz49bykGlrg.

Chandler, Alfred D. 1990. *Strategy and Structure: Chapters in the History of the Industrial Enterprise*. Cambridge, Mass.: MIT Press.

Dobbs, Richard, Tim Koller, Sree Ramaswamy, Jonathan Woetzel, James Manyika, Rohit Krishnan, and Nicolo Andreula. 2015. *Playing to Win: The New Global Competition for Corporate Profits*. New York: McKinsey Global Institute.

Doctorow, Cory. 2014. *Information Doesn't Want to Be Free: Laws for the Internet Age*. San Francisco: McSweeney's.

Eurostat. 2008. *NACE Rev. 1: Statistical Classification of Economic Activities in the European Community*. Luxembourg: European Commission.

Farmer, Blake. 2015. "Nissan Is Growing Like Crazy in Tennessee, and Most New Hires Are Long-Term Temps." *Nashville Public Radio*, February 4, 2015. Accessed May 23, 2016. http://nashvillepublicradio.org/post/nissan-growing-crazy-tennessee-and-most-new-hires-are-long-term-temps.

Forbes. 2015. "The World's Biggest Public Companies: China Takes Lead on 2015 Global 2000." Accessed May 23, 2016. http://www.forbes.com/global2000.

FRED. n.d. Federal Reserve Economic Database. Federal Reserve Bank of St. Louis. Accessed May 23, 2016. https://research.stlouisfed.org/fred2.

Furman, Jason, and Peter Orszag. 2015. "A Firm-Level Perspective on the Role of Rents in the Rise in Inequality." Presentation at "A Just Society" Centennial Event in Honor of Joseph Stiglitz, Columbia University. New York City (October 16, 2015). Accessed May 23, 2016. https://www.whitehouse.gov/sites/default/files/page/files/20151016_firm_level_perspective_on_role_of_rents_in_inequality.pdf.

Gordon, Robert J. 2012. "Is U.S. Economic Growth Over? Faltering Innovation Confronts the Six Headwinds." *NBER* working paper no. w18315. Cambridge, Mass.: National Bureau of Economic Research.

———. 2014. "The Demise of U.S. Economic Growth: Restatement, Rebuttal, and Reflections." *NBER* working paper no. w19895. Cambridge, Mass.: National Bureau of Economic Research.

Gravelle, Jane G. 2015. "Tax Havens: International tax Avoidance and Evasion." *CRS* report no. RL40623. Washington: Congressional Research Service.

Hansen, Alvin E. 1939. "Economic Progress and Declining Population Growth." *American Economic Review* 29(1): 1–15.

Katz, Lawrence F., and Alan B. Krueger. 2016. "The Rise and Nature of Alternative Work Arrangements in the United States, 1995–2015." Unpublished paper, Harvard University, Cambridge, Mass.

Keynes, John Maynard. 1936. *The General Theory of Employment, Interest and Money*. London: Palgrave Macmillan.

Koo, Richard C. 2011. *The Holy Grail of Macroeconomics: Lessons from Japan's Great Recession*. New York: John Wiley & Sons.

Kraemer, Kenneth L., Greg Linden, and Jason Dedrick. 2011. "Who Captures Value in the Apple iPad and iPhone?" *PCIC* working paper. Irvine: University of California.

Lazonick, William. 2009. "The New Economy Business Model and the Crisis of U.S. Capitalism." *Capitalism and Society* 4(2): art. 4.

Markillie, Paul. 2012. "A Third Industrial Revolution: Special Report on Manufacturing and Innovation." *Economist*, April 12, 2012.

Mason, Joshua William. 2015. "Disgorge the Cash: The Disconnect Between Corporate Borrowing and Investment." New York: Roosevelt Institute. Accessed May 23, 2016. http://rooseveltinstitute.org/wp-content/uploads/2015/09/Disgorge-the-Cash.pdf.

McIntyre, Robert, Richard Phillips, and Phineas Baxandall. 2015. *Offshore Shell Games 2015: The Use of Offshore Tax Havens by Fortune 500 Companies*. Washington, D.C.: Citizens for Tax Justice.

McKinsey Global Institute. 2012. *Manufacturing the Future: The Next Era of Global Growth and Innovation*. New York: McKinsey Global Institute.

Mergent Online. 2015. Accessed August 30, 2015. http://www.mergentonline.com/basicsearch.php.

Michaels, Guy, Ashwini Natraj, and John Van Reenen. 2014. "Has ICT Polarized Skill Demand? Evidence from Eleven Countries over Twenty-

Five Years." *Review of Economics and Statistics* 96(1): 60–77.

Mishel, Lawrence. 2015. "New Research Does Not Provide any Reason to Doubt that CEO Pay Fueled Top 1% Income Growth." *Economic Policy Institute Working Economics Blog*. June 2, 2015. Accessed June 2, 2015. http://www.epi.org/blog/new-research-does-not-provide-any-reason-to-doubt-that-ceo-pay-fueled-top-1-income-growth/.

Monga, Vipal. 2015. "Record Cash Hoard Concentrated Among a Few Companies." *Wall Street Journal*, June 11, 2015. Accessed May 23, 2016. http://blogs.wsj.com/cfo/2015/06/11/record-cash-hoard-concentrated-among-few-companies/.

Nitzan, Jonathan. 1998. "Differential Accumulation: Towards a New Political Economy of Capital." *Review of International Political Economy* 5(2): 169–216.

OECD. 2015a. *Economic Outlook 2015-2*. Paris: OECD Publishing.

———. 2015b. *In It Together: Why Less Inequality Benefits All*. Paris: OECD Publishing.

———. 2016. "OECD on-line database." Accessed August 10, 2015. http://www.OECD-iLibrary.org.

Ostrom, Elinor. 2010. "Beyond Markets and States: Polycentric Governance of Complex Economic Systems." *American Economic Review* 100(3): 641–72.

Palan, Ronen, Richard Murphy, and Christian Chavagneux. 2013. *Tax Havens: How Globalization Really Works*. Ithaca, N.Y.: Cornell University Press.

Piketty, Thomas, and Emmanuel Saez. 2006. "The Evolution of Top Incomes: A Historical and International Perspective." *NBER* working paper no. w11955. Cambridge, Mass.: National Bureau of Economic Research.

Pinkowitz, Lee, René M. Stulz, and Rohan Williamson. 2012. "Multinationals and the High Cash Holdings Puzzle." *NBER* working paper no. w18120. Cambridge, Mass.: National Bureau of Economic Research.

Piore, Michael, and Charles Sabel. 1984. *Second Industrial Divide: Possibilities for Prosperity*. New York: Basic Books.

Rüßmann, Michael, Markus. Lorenz, Philipp Gerbert, Manuela Waldner, Jan Justus, Pascal Engel, and Michael Harnisch. 2015. *Industry 4.0: The Future of Productivity and Growth in Manufacturing Industries*. Boston, Mass.: Boston Consulting Group.

Samuelson, Paul A. 1954. "The Pure Theory of Public Expenditure." *Review of Economics and Statistics* 36(4): 387–89.

Sánchez, Juan M., and Emircan Yurdagul. 2013. "Why Are Corporations Holding So Much Cash?" *Regional Economist*. St. Louis: Federal Reserve Bank. Accessed May 23, 2016. https://www.stlouisfed.org/Publications/Regional-Economist/January-2013/Why-Are-Corporations-Holding-So-Much-Cash.

Schacht, Wendy H. 2006. "Patent Reform: Issues in the Biomedical and Software Industries." *CRS* report no. RL33367. Washington: Congressional Research Service Accessed May 23, 2016. https://www.fas.org/sgp/crs/misc/RL33367.pdf.

Schumpeter, Joseph A. 1939. *Business Cycles: A Theoretical, Historical, and Statistical Analysis of the Capitalist Process*. New York: McGraw-Hill.

———. 1942. *Capitalism, Socialism, and Democracy*. New York: Harper and Brothers Publishers.

Song, Ja, David J. Price, Fatih Guvenen, and Nicholas Bloom. 2015. "Firming Up Inequality." *LSE Centre for Economic Performance* working paper no. 1354. London: London School of Economics. Accessed May 23, 2016. http://cep.lse.ac.uk/pubs/download/dp1354.pdf.

Stockhammer, Engelbert. 2015. "Rising Inequality as a Cause of the Present Crisis." *Cambridge Journal of Economics* 39(3): 935–58.

Summers, Lawrence. 2014. "Reflections on the 'New Secular Stagnation Hypothesis.'" In *Secular Stagnation: Facts, Causes, and Cures*, edited by Richard Baldwin and Coen Teulings. London: Center for Economic Policy Research-CEPR.

Swenson, Peter. 1989. *Fair Shares: Unions, Pay, and Politics in Sweden and West Germany*. Ithaca, N.Y.: Cornell University Press.

Thiel, Peter. 2014. *Zero to One: Notes on Startups, or How to Build the Future*. New York: Crown Business.

Toder, Eric. 2011. "Which Industries Pay Corporate Income Taxes?" Washington, D.C.: Urban Institute and Brookings Institution Tax Policy Center.

U.S. Bureau of Economic Analysis (BEA). 2009. "Selected NIPA Tables: Saving and Investment." Washington: U.S. Department of Commerce. Accessed December 21, 2015. https://www.bea.gov/scb/pdf/2009/09%20September/nipa5_0909.pdf.

———. 2014. "Selected NIPA Tables: Real Gross Domestic Product, Chained Dollars." Washington: U.S. Department of Commerce. Accessed December 21, 2015. http://bea.gov/national/pdf/dpga.pdf.

U.S. Senate. Permanent Subcommittee on Investigations. 2013. "Offshore Profit Shifting and the U.S. Tax Code—Part 2 (Apple Inc.)." Statements of Carl Levin (D-MI) and John McCain (R-AZ). Washington: Government Printing Office. Accessed May 23, 2016. http://www.hsgac.senate.gov/subcommittees/investigations/hearings/offshore-profit-shifting-and-the-us-tax-code_-part-2.

Weber, Max. 1978. *Economy and Society*. Edited by Gunther Roth and Claus Wittich. Berkeley: University of California Press.

Weil, David. 2014. *The Fissured Workplace: Why Work Became So Bad for So Many and What Can Be Done to Improve It*. Cambridge, Mass.: Harvard University Press.

Weisman, Jonathan. 2014. "Permanent Job Proves an Elusive Dream." *Washington Post*, October 11, 2014. Accessed May 23, 2016. http://www.washingtonpost.com/wp-dyn/articles/A22773-2004Oct10.html.

Wolff, Edward N. 2016. "Household Wealth Trends in the United States, 1962 to 2013: What Happened over the Great Recession?" *RSF: The Russell Sage Foundation Journal of the Social Sciences* 2(6). doi: 10.7758/RSF.2016.2.6.02.

Zucman, Gabriel. 2015. *The Hidden Wealth of Nations: The Scourge of Tax Havens*. Chicago: University of Chicago Press.